Shelter

Lyme Regis: visitors' buoys in the summer, exposed to southwest.

River Exe: sheltered in the river. Visitors' buoys and anchorages. Sandbanks at the entrance. Strong currents.

Teignmouth: sheltered in the harbour. Visitors' pontoon. Sandbanks at the entrance.

Torquay: all weather. Marina and town pontoons. Berthing in the centre of the town.

Brixham: all weather. Marina and visitors' pontoons.

River Dart: all weather. Marinas, visitors' buoys and pontoons.

Salcombe: sheltered in the river. Visitors' buoys. Sand bar at the entrance.

River Yealm: sheltered in the river. Visitors' buoys. Sand bar at the entrance.

Plymouth Sound: all weather. Several marinas. Numerous anchorages and buoys.

Looe: drying harbour wall.

Fowey: all weather. Visitors' pontoons and buoys.

Mevagissey: harbour wall and visitor buoy. Exposed to the east.

Falmouth: all weather. Several marina. Numerous anchorages and buoys.

Helford River: sheltered in the river. Visitors' buoys. Exposed to the east.

Porthleven: drying harbour wall. Exposed to the southwest.

Penzance: locked harbour, visitor space. Waiting buoys outside.

Newlyn: all weather. Transitory pontoon space for visitors.

Isles of Scilly: numerous anchorages. Visitors' buoys at St Mary's and New Grimsby Sound. Exposed at each location depending on conditions.

LYME BAY
Lyme Regis
River Exe
River Teign
Torquay
Brixham
River Dart
Salcombe

WEST DEVON
Bigbury Bay
River Avon
River Erme
River Yealm
Plymouth
River Tamar
River Lynher

EAST CORNWALL
Looe
Polperro
Fowey
St Austell Bay
Mevagissey
Falmouth
River Helford

MOUNTS BAY
Mullion Cove
Porthleven
St Michael's Mount
Penzance
Newlyn

Fuel

Exmouth, Torquay, Brixham, River Dart, Salcombe, Plymouth, Looe, Fowey, Falmouth, Penzance, Newlyn, St Mary's.

Lifts

At least 30 tons at Darthaven Marina, Dartside Quay, Plymouth and Falmouth.

Drying pads at Brixham, River Dart and Plymouth.

Chandleries and repairs

Extensive chandleries in Brixham, Kingswear (River Dart), Plymouth, Fowey, Falmouth and Newlyn. Small chandleries in Exmouth, Teignmouth, Torquay and Looe.

Yards and winter storage in the River Dart, Plymouth and Falmouth. Local engineers at every harbour or nearby.

ISLES OF SCILLY
St Mary's
St Agnes
Grimsby Sounds
Bryher
Tresco
St Martin's

Published by
Imray Laurie Norie & Wilson Ltd
Wych House, St Ives
Cambridgeshire PE27 5BT England
Tel +44 (0)1480 462114
Fax +44 (0)1480 496109
Email ilnw@imray.com
www.imray.com

1st edition 2011

© Carlos Rojas and Susan Kemp-Wheeler 2011
Carlos Rojas and Susan Kemp-Wheeler have asserted their right to be identified as the
authors of this work in accordance with the Copyright, Designs and Patents Act 1988.

© Plans Imray Laurie Norie & Wilson Ltd 2011
© Town plans Ordnance Survey - Crown Copyright and Database 2011
© Aerial photographs Patrick Roach and Imray Laurie Norie & Wilson Ltd 2011
© Photographs Susan Kemp-Wheeler and Carlos Rojas 2011

© Crown copyright

The plans and tidal information have been reproduced with the permission of the
Hydrographic Office of the United Kingdom (Licence No. HO151/951101/01) and the
Controller of Her Britannic Majesty's Stationery Office.

ISBN 978 184623 202 2

British Library Cataloguing in Publication Data.
A catalogue record for this book is available from the British Library.

PLANS

The plans in this guide are not to be used for navigation. They are designed to support the
text and should at all times be used with navigational charts.

CAUTION

While every care has been taken to ensure accuracy, neither the Publishers nor the Authors
will hold themselves responsible for errors, omissions or alterations in this publication. They
will at all times be grateful to receive information which leads to the improvement of the
work. Please forward any suggestions or corrections to the publishers at the above address.

CORRECTIONAL SUPPLEMENTS

This book will be amended at intervals by the issue of correctional supplements. These will
be published on our website www.imray.com and may be downloaded free of charge.

Printed in Croatia by Zrinski

THE WEST COUNTRY

Lyme Bay to the Isles of Scilly

Carlos Rojas
&
Susan Kemp-Wheeler

Imray Laurie Norie & Wilson

Contents

Acknowledgements

This book could not have been written without the help of many people. Special thanks go to Susan's family who live in the West Country: Peter, Yvonne, Matthew, Katie, David and Joy Wheeler in Falmouth, and John and Marion Wheeler in Sidmouth, all of whom shared information and gave us hospitality. Jennie and Cliff Coath provided a cream tea to photograph and eat! Harold and Elizabeth Lloyd shared their knowledge of Dartmouth and the Royal Navy.

Professor Gary Nichols explained some geology and Neil Garrick-Maidment shared his knowledge of seahorses. Viv Canning told us about her family in Topsham and Lizzy at Crystal Moon gave us an ammonite to photograph. The Patent Office were hugely helpful in tracking down drawings and thanks goes to The Very Revd Dr Christopher Hardwick, Dean of Truro, and to Rector Nick McKinnel, from the Minster Church of St Andrew's, Plymouth, for permission to print our photographs of their stained glass windows. Steve Trewhella supplied a photograph of a spiny seahorse and Janet Baxter took the photo of the bottlenose dolphin and calf. Alasdair Moore of Tresco Abbey provided a picture of New Grimsby Sound and The British Museum photographed the Cookworthy Mug for us and gave us permission for it to be reproduced. David Walker took us into Brixham fish market very early one morning and explained the auctioning process. The aerial photographs are by Patrick Roach. Neil Penman, of South West Marine Training, spent some time sailing with us. We thank him for sharing his extensive knowledge about the West Country and his skills as a yachtsman.

Finally a big thank you goes to the Imray team and especially to Willie Wilson for his support, and Alison Wilson, Elinor Cole and Jill Coleman for being such conscientious editors.

Our grateful thanks, not just to those we have mentioned but also to numerous others who have made recommendations and given us information that we have passed on.

About the authors

Carlos and Susan have extensive knowledge of the West Country. It is where Susan grew up and where many of her family still live. In 2008 they moved their sailing boat to the area and have greatly enjoyed exploring the southern coast of Devon and Cornwall and the Isles of Scilly.

They hope you find *The West Country* a useful book and welcome your comments and suggestions for improvement.

Gig practice, Isles of Scilly

Introduction

We are delighted to share with you our experience of the West Country. Although this book is primarily a pilot book, designed for the sailor, it is also intended to be a guide to much enjoyment ashore. Some readers will already know the area well but there have been many recent developments. The shoreline has been given World Heritage Status, Living Coasts has opened at the harbour in Torquay, the Royal William Victualling Yard welcomes visitors for the first time in nearly two-hundred years, seahorses can been seen at the National Marine Aquarium and have been found along the coast. For those who have never sailed in the West Country, a huge treat is in store. To all who make the journey: Bon voyage!

The countryside and wildlife

Specifying which parts of the West Country lie in an Area of Outstanding Natural Beauty or are Sites of Special Scientific Interest can be tiresome because it needs to be written time and time again. There are tourists, and during August especially the rivers and marinas can feel rather crowded, but even so this is a very special place to be. For time away from your vessel, the 613-mile South West Coast Path is easily accessed and there are undemanding walks between Looe and Polperro, Brixham and Dartmouth and through the Undercliff from Lyme Regis to Axmouth. Some estuaries are still fringed with forests of ancient oak and Frenchman's Creek on the Helford remains 'still and soundless', as described by Daphne du Maurier in her eponymous novel. In this part of England there are many rare and protected wildflowers. The spotted catsear, bloody cranesbill and hairy greenweed inhabit the Lizard. The white rock rose, pyramidal orchids and viper's bugloss can be seen at the Berry Head National Nature Reserve, a short walk from Brixham marina. If formal gardens are more to your liking then you will be spoilt for choice in Cornwall. Stopping in Mevagissey would give you easy access to The Lost Gardens of Heligan and Lamorran House can be reached on foot from St Mawes. From the King Harry ferry pontoon in the Fal it is possible to walk to Trelissick, a 500-acre park with formal gardens created in 1937. Trelowarren, Trebah and Glendurgan, are horticultural musts within easy access of a mooring in the Helford River. Tresco Abbey Gardens on the Isles of Scilly has plants from over 80 countries and is often dubbed 'Kew with the roof off'.

Those preferring to remain on board may find that nature comes to them as the West Country is visited by 17 species of whales, dolphins and porpoises, including long-finned pilot whales, minke and killer whales (orcas). It is not even that unusual to come across a basking shark. These are the second largest fish in the world and can grow up to 12m, which is as long as a London bus. Their huge mass is sustained by tiny zooplankton, which they filter from seawater at a rate of up to 2,000 cubic metres per hour, the capacity of an olympic swimming pool! Occasionally there is a leatherback turtle to be seen but this is a rare treat

as, although it is the most widespread reptile on earth, their numbers have decreased so much they are now critically endangered. Our native seals are commonly seen on the Isles of Scilly and there is a small population in Lyme Bay. Sighting is only guaranteed, however, if you visit the Seal Sanctuary at Gweek.

For those who are prepared to get into the water there are many treats including two British species of seahorse. The short-snouted *Hippocampus hippocampus* lives in open sand while the spiny *Hippocampus guttulatus* lives amongst seagrass (which is damaged by inconsiderate anchoring). The Salcombe estuary is a good place to find seahorses and is also home to a very rare fan mussel that can grow to over 1ft in diameter. Recognised dive sites on the Isles of Scilly number over 150. Numerous species of sponge have settled around the islands and seventy-four species of algae have been recorded, together with fan and sunset corals, dead man's fingers and jewel anemones. In July 2008 the largest edible crab on record was found in Lyme Bay. It weighed 17lbs and was 12 inches across which is one inch wider than the record holder displayed in the Museum National Histoire Naturelle in Paris.

The twitchers on board will have plenty to do. The Western Rocks and Annet on the Isles of Scilly have breeding colonies of lesser black-backed gulls and storm petrels and the Berry Head National Nature Reserve, near Brixham, has the largest colony of guillemots in England. There is a hide and videocam and also excellent facilities for observing the great horseshoe bats that live in the caves below.

Slapton Ley National Nature Reserve teems with house martins, sand martins, swallows and swifts when they return from migration and this is the place to see and hear the secretive reed warbler and the great crested grebe. In summer, Cetti's warbler is often seen skulking in the reeds. The five-hundred acre Dawlish Warren Nature Reserve attracts sea and wading birds in their thousands, including curlews, redshanks, greenshanks, dunlins and oystercatchers together with the little egret, a recent colonist from France. Out on the water you can expect to see guillemots, fulmars, shags, kittiwakes, razorbills, herring and black-backed gulls, storm-petrels, long-tailed and pomarine skua and the sooty and Balearic shearwater.

Finally, it would be splendid to see a chough. A relative of the jackdaw, this large bird with blue-black plumage and a distinctive curved red bill was reintroduced to Cornwall in 2001 after a 30-year absence. It appears on Cornwall's coat of arms.

Geology and pre-history

Those with an interest in geology will be in their element sailing along the West Country shoreline as the cliffs expose 180 million years of geological history from the Triassic to the Cretaceous period. Designated a World Heritage Site in 2001, the Jurassic

The fishing fleet at Beer

coast, stretching from Orcombe Point near Exmouth to the Old Harry's Rocks near Swanage, is also a great place to look for fossils. On the beach at Lyme Regis amateur archaeologist Mary Anning found the first ichthyosaur in 1814 and the first flying reptile, a dimorphodon, in 1828. Today there are expert-led fossil hunts along Monmouth Beach, east of the Cobb, where ammonites are exposed at low tide. The fossils in Kent's Cavern, about a mile from the harbour at Torquay, include animals that were living in the West Country 500,000 years ago. There are the remains of ancestral cave bears, cave lions, sabre-toothed cats, mammoths and woolly rhinos. With low sea levels, early humans, bipedal hominids, moved out from Africa and eventually crossed land that brought them to Britain. Plants grew abundantly in the West Country and there were even hippopotamuses roaming around. At very low tides fossilised tree trunks can be seen on the beach at Torbay. These are the remains of a submerged forest that once extended to France.

The oldest European fossil from modern man, homo sapiens, is a 31,000 year old teenager's jawbone with teeth that was found in 1925 in Kent's Cavern, where it is on display. Scattered tribes existed by hunting and gathering until about 4,000 BC, when Neolithic peoples, arriving from mainland Europe, began to cultivate the land and farm livestock. Flint arrowheads and some chambered tombs exist from this period but there are far more archaeological remains from the Bronze Age that followed and many can be seen on the Isles of Scilly. The 'Old Man of Gugh' is a menhir, or monumental stone, that is thought to have been standing for about 3,500 years. At Green Bay on Bryher the boundary of a Bronze Age field, a reave, is still marked by a line of large seaweed-covered boulders disappearing into the water and there are foundations of Bronze Age round houses nearby. The Giant's Tomb on St Mary's is an excellent example of an entrance grave that exists only here and in West Cornwall.

By about 500BC the Celts were established and making tools and weapons out of Iron. Little remains from the Iron Age though Halangy Down Ancient Settlement, on the Isles of Scilly, has a good example of a courtyard house.

The Romans and the Normans

Recorded history begins with the Romans, who occupied Isca Dumnoniorum, the name they gave to Exeter. Axmouth was the most important harbour in the West Country and goods were carried along the Fosse Way, a first-century Roman road built between Exeter and Lincoln. The caves a mile inland from Beer were quarried for limestone and today an informative tour takes the visitor 200ft below ground. Stone from here has been used since Roman times and more recently in the construction of Westminster Abbey, Windsor Castle and the Tower of London.

The Romans left the Celts, west of Exeter, much to their own devices and Cornwall was not fully assimilated into England until a spirited resistance against the Saxons failed in 926. The Saxons and Celts then came together to repel the Danes, who occupied Exeter for a short while until it was taken in 1066 by William the Conqueror, who established a Norman kingdom throughout the land. Exeter cathedral has two magnificent Norman towers and, on a smaller scale, the church in Axmouth has impressive Norman origins. With care it is possible to sail up the Dart to Totness where there is a remarkably intact Norman castle built to a motte-and-bailey design. In Cornwall, manor houses were taken by the Normans to form the basis of an earldom held by William's half-brother Robert of Mortain, who was probably the first person to bear the title Earl of Cornwall. In 1337 these lands were granted to Edward III's son, the Black Prince, and have since belonged to the eldest son of the English sovereign, who acts as Duke of Cornwall.

The wool trade, mining and fishing

Devon was producing a significant amount of cloth by the 12th century as its fertile inland pastures were ideal for sheep. The cloth was exported to mainland Europe from Totnes, Dartmouth and Exeter. Trade from Exeter was impeded when both the Countess of Devon, Isabella de Fortibus, and Hugh de Courtenay, Earl of Devon, built weirs across the River Exe in the 13th century to power mills on their estates thereby blocking the Exe to ocean-going vessels. Goods had to be transported to the quay at Totnes until merchants built the Exeter Canal in 1563. The canal was extended in 1701 and again in 1827. Today, a night or two spent within Turf Lock is a memorable experience and small ferries enable easy access to Exeter Quay and the city beyond.

Further west, where minerals had been extracted since prehistoric times, mining had taken off by the 12th century and Cornwall was the biggest supplier of tin in Europe. The miners themselves were so important that in 1198 Henry II enshrined their rights in law, long before written legal codes existed elsewhere, and miners were beholden only to the local Stannary Courts. The Cornish Stannary Parliament last assembled in Truro in 1752 but stannary law has never been abolished and Cornish nationalists still claim the right to veto British legislation! By 1862 the West Country had 340 mines employing 50,000 people, but within 40 years huge surface deposits of tin discovered abroad sent the industry into decline. In July 2006 the Cornish and West Devon mining landscape was awarded World Heritage Status. There are the remains of engine houses, beam engines, mines, foundries, fuse works, industrial harbours

Dinner

and tramways to be seen. The Royal Cornwall Museum in Truro traces the history of mining in the West Country and has an internationally important collection of minerals.

In the Middle Ages, fishing was the most important industry after the wool trade and mining. Huge quantities of sardines and pilchards provided food, light and income. For about 4 months of the year men known as huers would look out to sea from a high vantage point and alert the fishermen to passing shoals. The derelict remains of a huer's hut can be seen on Burgh Island near to the 14th-century Pilchard Inn and the term 'hue and cry' has passed into the language (*hue* is old French for shout). Beer, Polperro, Mevagissey and Brixham are all fishing towns that have retained their medieval layout.

It was in Brixham that trawling with weighted nets was invented and by the 1850s the town had the largest fleet of sailing smacks anywhere in England. Some have been lovingly restored. *Pilgram*, built in 1895, and *Vigilance*, built in 1926, are often to be seen out on the water.

Protests and the Cornish language

Having been used to self-governance, the Cornish tried to rebel against dictates that arrived from London. 15,000 Cornish men went to London to protest against taxes imposed on them by the Tudor state in 1497 but were easily defeated and their leaders executed. Resentment continued and a second revolt, defeated in a battle at Clyst St Mary near Topsham, occurred in 1549 against the Act of Uniformity, which insisted on the Book of Common Prayer and simplified English service instead of the Latin Mass. This was especially galling to the Cornish who, at the time, were non-English speaking. The last monoglot Cornish speaker is thought to have been Chesten Marchant who died at Gwithian in 1676. In 1777 the last native speaker, Dorothy Pentreath, died at Mousehole and it was a dead language until the early 1900s when renewed interested in Cornish heritage lead to a revival. Whilst there is still disagreement as to whether it should be called Kernewek, Kernowek or Curoack a standard written form has been prepared by the Cornish Language Partnership in association with scholars from around the world. The County Council is now asking that Cornish be recognised by the EU as an official regional or minority language like Welsh or Gaelic. Hopefully this will lead to some European funding for teaching the language to schoolchildren. Today, Cornish is spoken fluently by only about 300 adults.

Cornwall's Coat of Arms has a bearded fisherman, a tin miner, a chough resting its claws on a Ducal Coronet, and a shield enclosed by waves. The golden roundels, or 'bezants', are of unknown origin. Properly referred to as a 'full achievement', it was registered in 1939.

Maritime matters

Under threat of war from Spain and France defences were built along the southwest coast during the 16th century. Pendennis Castle and its twin opposite straddle the entrance to the Fal and both can be visited. The carvings on the castle at St Mawes are considered better than on any other fortification built by Henry VIII. Pendennis Castle was the setting for an historic siege during the English civil war and today medieval jousts take place periodically. The Star Castle on St Mary's, built in 1593, is now a hotel.

Drake, Raleigh and Grenville were all born in the West Country, which grew in importance as trade with the Atlantic took off and maritime prowess not only defended the realm but also extended it. Plymouth became an important port and it was here, in 1580, that Drake returned to a hero's welcome having circumnavigated the world. He subsequently became mayor of Plymouth and an MP, sitting on the committee that granted Raleigh a licence to establish a colony in Virginia, although this was unsuccessful. When the great Spanish Armada were seen off Plymouth Hoe, legend has it that Drake calmly finished a game of bowls before taking to the sea to bring about a marvellous defeat. In truth there were a number of separate battles and the outcome was not a success for either side. Drake's role in English history should not be underestimated, however. His jointly financed acts of piracy set a new pattern and provided investors with the funds to establish the East India Company that extended Britain's territory throughout the world.

Plymouth harbour was the departure point for the the Pilgrim Fathers aboard the *Mayflower* in 1620, as well as for Captain Cook and Charles Darwin on their great expeditions. In 1691 King William III founded The Royal Naval Dockyard, a site that grew from 5 to 330 acres. It was renamed 'Devonport' in 1824. Today there are guided tours, which may include stepping aboard a nuclear submarine. The magnificent Georgian buildings jutting out into the River Tamar served as the Royal Navy victualling yard until decommissioned in 1992. The buildings are now full of luxury apartments. There is also a bar, with restaurants expected, and the Ministry of Defence has plans for a visitor centre.

It was in Brixham that William of Orange landed in 1688 and a statue marks the spot. He declared 'The liberties of England and the protestant religion I will maintain' and, marching unopposed to London, became King William III while the catholic King James II went into exile.

Porcelain, tourism and the arts

In the mid 1740s William Cookworthy from Kingsbridge discovered kaolin, or china clay as it is known, at Tregonning Hill in Cornwall and become the first European to produce porcelain. His Plymouth China Works were very successful but the patent was eventually sold to Josiah Wedgwood. By 1858 forty-two mining companies were producing 65,000 tons of china clay in Cornwall every year. Pits and tips had changed the Cornish landscape forever. Today china clay is Cornwall's largest industry. Charlestown still looks much like an 18th-century working port and just inland the China Clay Country Park Mining and Heritage Centre is hugely informative.

The West Country began to establish itself as a holiday destination when the Napoleonic wars (1802-15) prevented the fashionable Grand Tour of Europe. Mass tourism followed once the railway was extended to Exeter in 1840 and into Cornwall in 1859. There were objections, such as those from the Vicar of Torre who argued that two hotels in Torquay would be detrimental to the town's moral health, but in general the West Country community set about catering for tourists with alacrity. Teignmouth constructed a two-mile long pier in 1860 and used it to segregate male and female bathers. Looe made bathing machines available from about 1800. Pulled into the water by horses, women could emerge shielded from public view thereby enjoying the advantages of the sea whilst maintaining decorum.

At the end of the 19th century Cornwall became fashionable as a place to paint. United in their desire to capture the real lives of the local fishing and farming community, the artists worked 'en plein air' and became known as the Newlyn School. *A Fish Sale on a Cornish Beach* painted by Stanhope Forbes in 1885 brought the group international recognition.

Writers have made the West Country their home too. John Fowles lived much of his adult life in Lyme Regis

Pretty cottages

Friendly locals

and the Cobb will be associated forever with the film version of his iconic book *The French Lieutenant's Woman*. Daphne du Maurier lived for many years in Cornwall where she was a member of the Cornish nationalist party, Mebyon Kernow. Although often criticized as intellectually lightweight, the glamour and romanticism of her early novels provided much-needed escape from the horrors of two world wars and she was a first rate storyteller as her novels set in the West Country, such as *Jamaica Inn, Frenchman's Creek* and *My Cousin Rachel*, attest. Agatha Christie grew up in Torquay. Known as the 'Queen of Crime', sales of her books have exceeded four billion. The popularity of Hercule Poirot was such that when she eventually killed him off his obituary appeared in *The New York Times*, the only fictional character ever to have done so. Her holiday home abuts the Dart and is open to the public. Aficionados can visit the places where some of her characters met a sticky end. She gained her impressive knowledge of poisons while working in a Torquay pharmacy.

WWII and recent developments

Many children were evacuated from London to the West Country during the second world war as it was considered relatively safe. However Exeter and Plymouth were substantially destroyed, Plymouth because of the dockyards and Exeter because of its cultural and historic interest, the so-called Baedeker raids which targeted cities that appeared in the Baedeker guidebooks. Slapton Sands was used for Exercise Tiger, in which thousands of US servicemen rehearsed for the D-Day landings. A surprise attack by

German E-boats in April 1944 killed 639 servicemen and at Torcross there is a memorial erected by the US Government alongside a Sherman tank that was recovered from the sea in 1984. The road, hard and slipway at Tolverne, River Fal, were constructed to enable 27,000 American troops to leave for the beaches of Normandy. Brixham was a major fuelling depot and also has the remains of a giant slipway. Brixham's emergency coastal defence battery is the best-preserved and most important site of its kind in the UK. It has Scheduled Monument status and there is a small museum nearby.

While sailing in the West Country it would be a shame not to enjoy some recent developments. The Eden Project houses over a million plants in a 160-year-old exhausted china clay quarry. Huge biomes, looking like giant golf balls, create rainforest and other environments from around the world. Even the soil has been custom-made with the help of academics from the University of Reading. The scale is breathtaking. The Tower of London can easily fit inside and many plants are so large that they have to be pruned by abseilers. Tate St Ives opened in 1993 and is well worth a visit, as is the Penlee Gallery in Penzance for its collection of art from the Newlyn School. The National Maritime Museum in Falmouth opened in 2003 and houses an internationally acclaimed collection of small boats in an architecturally impressive building. The National Marine Aquarium in Plymouth has over 400 species in 50 different habitats ranging from West Country coast to coral reefs. It is home to our national collection of seahorses.

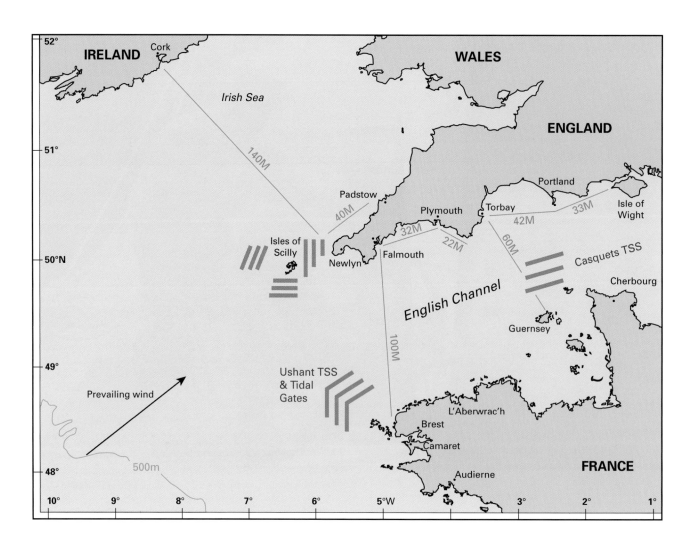

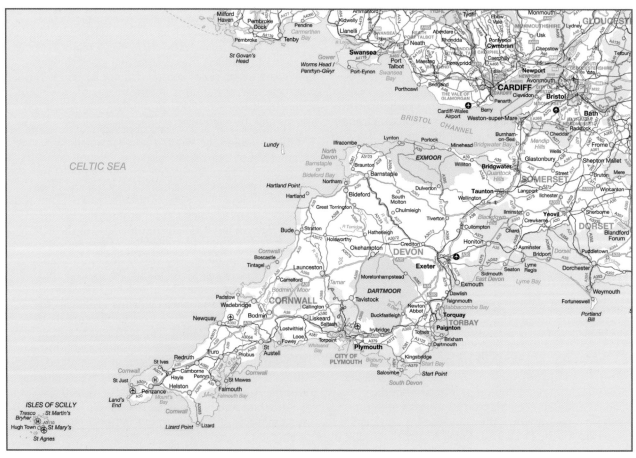

Information for the yachtsman

With the exception of the Isles of Scilly, West Country sailing is not difficult. There are relatively short distances to cover, offshore hazards are well marked and there are extensive lights should it be necessary to arrive at night. Many visitors enjoy tucking into the crab and lobster but beware of the pots! They are numerous and some are poorly marked.

Going west with the prevailing southwesterly wind against a strong tidal stream can be uncomfortable and, of course, the very significant tidal gates at Portland, Start Point, The Lizard and Land's End need to be factored in!

The south coast divides into four cruising areas, separated by major headlands. Lyme Bay is a long stretch with no significant harbours west of Portland so from the east a common passage is directly to Torbay or Dartmouth. Further west Plymouth and Falmouth are all weather harbours with pretty destinations near by. Mount's Bay on the western edge of Cornwall is small and rather remote and 28 miles away from Land's End are the glorious and temperate Isles of Scilly.

The north coast of Cornwall is not covered in this book but information can be found in Peter Cumberlidge's book *Bristol Channel & Severn Cruising Guide*, published by Imray.

When to go

There is less rain, fewer gales and more sunshine along the coast of the West Country in spring and summer than in autumn and winter. In summer the gulf stream maintains coastal temperatures above average for the country, an effect that gets stronger the further south and west you go. In the Isles of Scilly cut flowers are grown all year round. Atlantic swell can be significant in the winter but diminishes in late spring.

If you take into account the weather, the temperature, Atlantic swell and daylight hours then May to September is the best time to sail in the West Country. However, the shoulder period, April and October, can also be pleasant.

Coming from the east

Tidal streams in the channel are a very important consideration when coming from the east. There are also significant headlands where the tidal stream is stronger, and where races and overfalls are a regular feature.

The traffic separation zone between Land's End and the Isles of Scilly is for north/south bound shipping. There is less traffic than along the English Channel but it is nevertherless significant. Always cross the lanes on a 90° heading.

Distances from the Needles are (italics indicate distances to the entrance):

Location	Distance	Distance cum	Hours 5knots
Needles	0	0	0
South of Anvil Point (Poole, Swanage)	16M	16M	5.2
South of Portland Bill	17M	33M	6.6
- Dartmouth	43M	76M	15.2
South of Start Point	50M	83M	16.4
- Plymouth	22M	105M	21
- Falmouth	54M	137M	27.4
South of The Lizard	62M	145M	29
- Penzance	19M	164M	32.8
Runnel Stone south of Land's End	20M	165M	33
Scilly	23M	188M	37.6

It is important to plan for several very significant factors:

- Tidal races off Portland and The Lizard. Keep 5M south of these headlands to clear very confused seas.

- Races and overfalls in the Isles of Scilly, in addition to rotary tidal streams.

- Tidal flow around Portland and the Lizard. Fighting a foul tide wastes considerable time and reduces options available for unplanned events, as well as being demoralising.

If coming from the Solent it is best to leave the Needles when the tide just begins to be favourable (Portsmouth HW -1h). This provides a fair tide all the way to Portland, and additional speed passing south of Portland, just before the tide begins to turn (Plymouth HW -1h). Alternatively head for Swanage Bay to await a fair tide (greatly preferable to fighting against 3 knots at springs off Portland Bill).

After Portland the passage to Dartmouth will always involve a period against the tide, but the strength of the current is considerably less.

From Start Point to The Lizard is 62M (12 hours), so careful timing ensures a fair tide past both headlands.

Finally, the passage to Scilly from The Lizard is 43M (nearly 9 hours). From Runnel Stone the best time to start the crossing is from HW Dover -2h to +1h (southwest to west direction). The tide is across the

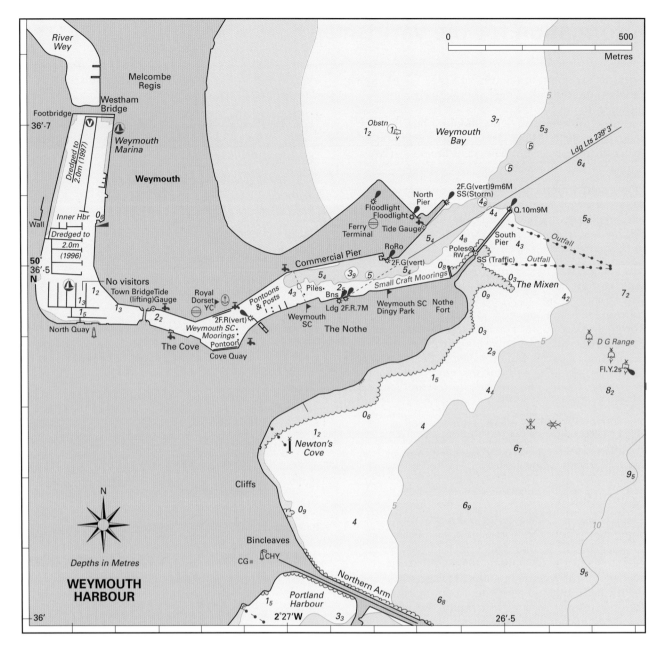

passage most of the way so heading is an important factor. Tidal streams near Scilly are strong and it is recommended that a first approach is made through the main east entrance to St Mary's Road, south of St Mary's Island. At certain states of tide, overfalls can develop in the northeast and northwest.

Portland Race

The Portland Race develops as a result of two tidal streams running south on each side of the headland. The effect lasts for 10 hours:

- From HW Plymouth +0500 (HW Portland +0400, HW Dover -0040)
- to HW Plymouth +0200 (HW Portland +0100, HW Dover +0340).

The race can be avoided by remaining 5M south of the Bill.

An inshore passage also avoids the race but should be attempted only in daylight, with offshore winds and in calm conditions, and never in strong wind against

tide. The passage involves hugging the coast from 2-3M north of the Bill and then sailing south during a three hour window of fair tide. The Admiralty tidal stream atlases are detailed and strongly recommended.

The Lizard

Significant races and overfalls develop off The Lizard, which can be avoided be remaining 5M south. A passage exists close to shore but is never free of confused seas.

Land's End

There are very dangerous reefs and rocks off Land's End, and tides close to shore are strong and unpredictable. In adverse winds or bad weather stay well south of Runnel Stone Q(6)+LFl.15s, and west of Carn Base Q(9)15s and Longships Fl(2)WR.10s.

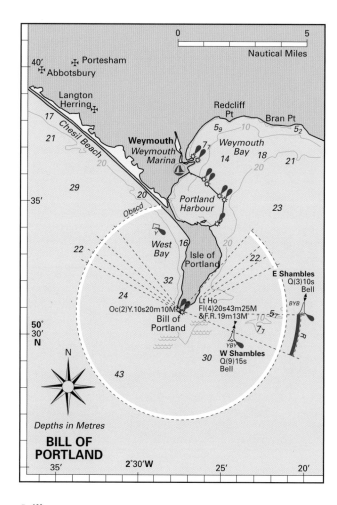

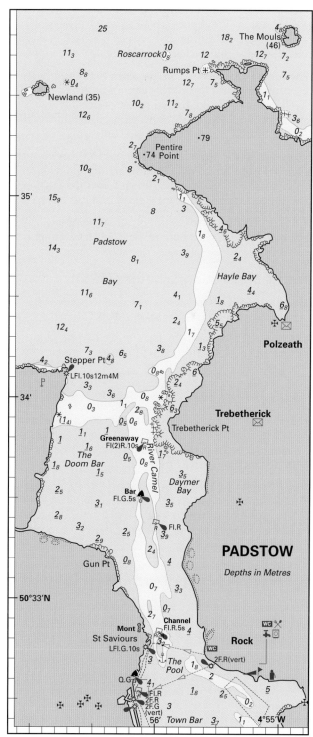

arrive at the Isles of Scilly or starting to round Land's End with plenty of daylight ahead.

For the Isles of Scilly try to arrive on the north side with a fair tide that allows St Mary's Sound to be approached between HW Plymouth +2h and -6h.

If your destination is Newlyn, a fair tide from Runnel Stone begins at HW Dover +5h. If aiming for Helford or Falmouth, the 20M stretch between the Runnel Stone and The Lizard has a fair tide from HW Dover +0500 to HW Dover -0300 (5 hours).

There is a traffic separation zone between Cornwall and the Isles of Scilly which should be crossed on a heading of 90°.

Scilly

The tidal streams around the Isles of Scilly rotate. The general directions are:

- West from HW Plymouth +5h to -6h
- North from HW Plymouth -5h to -4h
- Northeast from HW Plymouth -3h to -1h
- East at HW Plymouth
- South/southeast from HW Plymouth +1h to +2h
- Southwest/west from HW Plymouth +3h to -6h.

Significant overfalls develop south, northwest and northeast of the islands as follows:

- South: at all times except HW Plymouth -4h and HW +2h
- Northwest (approach to Old and New Grimsby Sounds): HW Plymouth -4h to -3h and HW +1h.
- Northeast (Eastern Isles and approach to Crow's Sound): HW Plymouth -4h to -1h, HW Plymouth +1h to +3h.

Coming from Ireland

The passage from Cork to the Isles of Scilly or Land's End is 140M, or 28 hours at 5 knots. Tide is not a strong consideration until close to the English coast as it is largely across the passage heading. Given just over one day of travel to cross the Celtic Sea, it is advisable to set off in the very early morning so as to

Coming from north Cornwall

A passage to Mounts Bay or Falmouth from North Cornwall requires very careful planning to negotiate the complexities of the tidal stream around Land's End. Detailed tidal atlases show a stream close to shore between St Ives and Land's End which runs counter to the main stream and can be used in good weather. Aim to reach the Runnel Stone with a fair tide for the 8M to Newlyn (from HW Dover +5h) or maximum fair tide for 20M to clear the Lizard (from HW Dover +3h).

Coming from France

The distance between the West Country and France or the Channel Islands depends on the point of departure and target destination. Guernsey to Dartmouth is only 60M but it is 120M between Brest and the Isles of Scilly. This is the difference between a long 12h day and a passage that includes a night at sea.

The prevailing southwesterlies mean that conditions are often favourable, but this cannot be relied upon. Swell in the English Channel is not of oceanic size, but a mixture of comfortable and confused sea during the passage is likely depending on tide and wind.

There are traffic separation schemes (TSS) between the Channel Islands and mainland England, and around Ushant (Isle d'Ouessant) off Brest. Cross the lanes on a 90° heading and maintain a good lookout.

You are certain to cross shipping at some point, whether in the TSS or not, as the English Channel is a very busy commercial route.

Traffic Separation Schemes (TSS)

There are several traffic separation schemes which may be crossed on passage to the West Country:

- Casquets TSS: between 10M northwest of Alderney and 20M southeast of Start Point in a north/northeast-west/southwest direction. There is plenty of room between the TSS and Alderney for the safe passage of yachts.

- Ushant TSS: northwest of Ushant (Isle d'Ousessant) in a northeast-southwest direction. The east-going lane begins 25M off the island. The inshore traffic zone reaches up to 8M northwest.

- Off Land's End TSS: between the Isles of Scilly and Land's End in a north-south direction. There are inshore traffic zones east which have dangers within them (Car Base and Longships east, Seven Stones west).

- South of Scilly TSS: south of the Isles of Scilly in a east-west direction, 5M off the Western Isles and Bishop's Rock. The inshore traffic zone between the TSS and the islands is subject to tidal races and overfalls and should be avoided except in calm conditions and at the right state of tide.

- West of Scilly TSS: west of the Isles of Scilly in a north-south direction, 5M off the islands. The inshore traffic zone between the TSS and the islands is subject to tidal races, and overfalls closer to the islands, and should be avoided except in calm

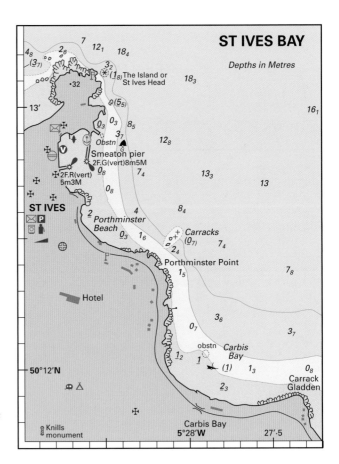

conditions and at the right state of tide. There are dangers towards the east (Bishop Rock, Crim Rocks).

Emergencies

The West Country is covered by excellent rescue services and assistance. If possible always raise an alarm through DSC, as this conveys your position accurately and is the preferred system for rescue coordination.

- HM Coastguard monitor VHF Channel 16 and DSC Channel 70 H24 (Falmouth also monitors DSC on MF 2182kHz), in addition to broadcasting Maritime Safety Information every 4 hours. There are Maritime Rescue Coordination Centres at Portland, Brixham and Falmouth.

  Portland Coastguard ☎ 01305 760439
  MMSI 002320012
  Brixham Coastguard ☎ 01803 882704
  MMSI 002320013
  Falmouth Coastguard ☎ 01326 317575
  MMSI 002320014

- The RNLI, a charity, provides 24-hour lifeboat rescue services up to 100M offshore. Their main sea-going lifeboats are at Exmouth, Brixham, Salcombe, Plymouth, Fowey, Penlee, Padstow and St Ives. Smaller stations are at: Lyme Regis, Teignmouth, River Dart, Plymouth, Looe, Falmouth, The Lizard, Penlee, Sennen Cove, St Mary's, St Ives, St Agnes, Newquay and Padstow.

- HM Coastguard Search and Rescue helicopters are based at Lee-on-Solent and Portland.

- The National Coastwatch Institution keeps a visual watch out to sea. The West Country is well served by this excellent voluntary service, with stations at:

Tor Bay ☎ 01803 411145
Bass Point (Lizard) ☎ 01326 290212
Charlestown ☎ 01726 817068
Exmouth ☎ 01395 222492
Froward Point (Kingswear) ☎ 07976 505649
Gwennap Head (St Levan) ☎ 01736 871351
Nare Point (Lizard) ☎ 01326 231113
Penzance ☎ 01736 367063
Polruan ☎ 01726 870291
Portland Bill ☎ 01305 860178
Portscatho ☎ 01872 580180
Prawle Point (Salcombe) ☎ 01548 511259
Rame Head (Plymouth) ☎ 01752 823706
Teignmouth ☎ 01626 772377
Boscastle ☎ 01840 250965
Cape Cornwall ☎ 01736 787890
St Agnes ☎ 01736 787890
St Ives ☎ 01736 799398
Stepper Point ☎ 07810 898041

Chandleries & repairs

Every harbour authority has contact with mechanics and electricians, and a good knowledge of chandleries and hardware stores, so it should always be possible to get repairs, spares and advice when required.

Brixham, Plymouth, Falmouth and Newlyn have the most extensively stocked chandleries and can get unusual equipment couriered in when required. There is a lot to be said for taking along digital photographs of objects that cannot be removed.

The services of divers can be arranged by discussion with marina staff.

Tides and Currents

Tides in the West Country are strong and the height of water is often crucial. Many attractive destinations have shallow depths and there can be sandbars to clear such as at the entrance to Salcombe. The range is not less than 2m at neaps but is 5m or more at springs. There are numerous tidal prediction methods, ranging from tide tables in the Almanacs and tide books, to online web services, software for computers and recently mobile phone applications, including our own Tides Planner for the iPhone. The ultimate source of all tidal information in the UK is the Hydrographic Office, which is based in Taunton.

Tides are subject to the influence of the weather which can be very significant. Pressure increases or decreases the height of the water by 1cm for every mbar. Predictions are reduced to a pressure of 1013mbar. Wind, by 'pushing' water, can also change tidal height. Given the tidal ranges in the West Country, these factors are not usually critical but they should be taken into account if operating at the margins, such as when mud-skipping or getting to a pontoon or wall with low charted depth.

Tidals streams should be considered when navigating river entrances and during passages at sea. At the Lizard, Land's End, and around the Isles of Scilly

the sea can be very disturbed and dangerous. On the ebb, water leaving the Exe, Teign, Salcombe, Avon, Hamoaze and Fal can flow very fast.

For all tide calculations Britain is on UT (GMT) and daylight saving/summer time is in place from the end of March to the end of October. The Almanac and other tide tables are generally written in UT so one hour needs to be added during daylight saving. This also applies to the Admiralty's online EasyTide. Computer packages generally take care of local time automatically.

Weather

The Gulf Stream and prevailing southwesterly winds dominate the weather in the West Country. It is often unsettled but the Azores high, when it extends sufficiently towards the northeast, can bring settled periods of sunshine in spring and summer. Sea temperatures are the warmest in the country and have the smallest range. In West Cornwall and the Isles of Scilly the annual average temperature of the sea and of the land is 12°C. Generally the West Country is warmest in July and August with an average maximum temperature of 19°C.

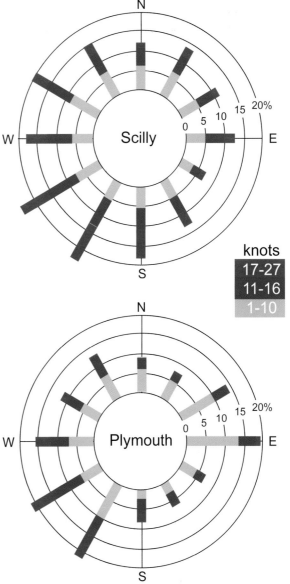

Wind roses , based on Met Office public data

Rainfall, influenced by the temperature of the sea, Atlantic low-pressure systems and the altitude of the land, is highest in the autumn and lowest in the spring. It is often fine at the coast when there is rain inland; the coast receives half the amount of rain that falls on the tors of Dartmoor.

The sea temperature is warmest in late summer and autumn. This creates greater humidity and it rains more in August than in July, and more in the autumn than in the spring when the sea is cold. Rain, often substantial in the autumn, is associated with significant Atlantic lows.

Fog and low-lying sea mist is not uncommon in the summer, especially around the Isles of Scilly. Close to shore, be aware of ferries and small fishing boats that continue to operate.

Winds are stronger around the West Country coast than anywhere else in the country except Scotland, as the Atlantic weather systems are met full on. The Isles of Scilly have about 24 days with gales each year, while Plymouth has 16.

Some river moorings and marinas can be surprisingly lively when you are hoping for a quiet night. The Bight in Salcombe, for example, can be very uncomfortable with a southerly wind against tide. Falmouth Town Marina is unpleasant in a strong easterly, which also makes it very difficult to leave!

The Appendix gives information about obtaining weather forecasts. Many marinas also provide information, usually from websites. Maritime Safety Information (MSI), obtainable through Navtex, gives offshore weather information. Synoptic charts enable predictions to be made up to 5 days ahead.

Swell

Ocean swell generated by significant weather systems, sometimes deep in the Atlantic, can build up especially in the west. Some anchorages also become untenable when local wind creates swell. Some marinas are more exposed to swell than others (Brixham in easterlies, Falmouth in east/northeasterlies).

Entrances that are susceptible to significant swell are highlighted in the text. If swell moves fuel around it can lessen the range under engine and stir up sediment, which can block filters.

Firing Range, Naval Exercise Area

Daily firing and naval exercises (Sunfacts and Gunfacts) are included in the Maritime Safety Information (MSI) radio broadcasts by HM Coastguard.

There are frequent exercises involving warships and submarines in the area south of Plymouth. Naval vessels have responsibility for safety but it is best to avoid the area.

Gunnery practice takes place to seaward of Dodman Point and Gribbin Head once or twice a week during the day. Details can be obtained (in addition to radio MSI brodcasts) from the Flag Officer Sea Training ☎ 01752 557550 or from FOST OPS on VHF 74. Warships fire from 2.5-9M SEE of Gribbin Head to an area 3.7M SE of Dodman Point marked by three yellow buoys (see Admiralty Chart 1267):
A Fl.Y.10s 50°08´.53N 4°46´.37W
B Fl.Y.5s 50°10´.31N 04°45´.00W
C Fl.Y.2s 50°10´.41N 04°47´.51M

The Marines have a firing range east of Straight Point near Exmouth. The seaward area is marked by three yellow buoys.

Mud and rock-hopping

There are many picturesque destinations in shallow or drying areas, including some of the best sections of rivers. A rising tide is the mindful skipper's safety net, should the ground be touched. In addition, fin keel boats may benefit from legs to maintain stability.

Dangers are well marked but careful navigation is recommended, especially near the coast and around the Isles of Scilly.

Fishing

There are numerous fishing boats operating in the West Country, including:

- Boats in groups searching for and tracking shoals of fish with sonar
- Leisure fishermen in small, fast boats
- Boats towing or guarding nets in small channels
- Pairs of boats with nets between them (indicated by a flashing light)
- Boats creating a circle with their net to catch sardines or mackerel.

The main fishing harbours are Brixham and Newlyn with smaller fleets at Lyme Regis, River Exe, Teignmouth, Dartmouth, Plymouth, Looe and Falmouth.

Fishing pots are numerous in depths up to 150m. Some have pick-up buoys with floating lines trailing. Many of the markers are submerged at high water when there is a strong tidal stream.

Fish farms

In comparison to Spain and France there are few fish farms. However, a pilot project has begun in Lyme bay, where Offshore Shellfish intend to site the largest offshore mussel farm in Europe. Over 15 square kilometres of seabed is to be leased from the Crown Estate with the intention of producing 10,000 tonnes of mussels each year for the export market.

Where there are oyster farms anchorage is prohibited. These areas are well marked in the charts, for example at the upper reaches of the River Helford.

Shipping

Plymouth and Falmouth have a substantial amount of shipping, but the number of large vessels is small when, for example, compared to the Solent.

The English Channel is very busy at all times and a good watch should be maintained.

Fuel and refuelling

There are many refuelling stations along the coast (see detailed sections of the book, and the inside cover).

'Red' diesel, with its significant tax reduction, is no longer available for leisure craft.

Berthing and anchoring

All marinas operate pontoons for berthing alongside. In addition there are swinging moorings and some fore-aft moorings administered by marinas, sailing clubs and harbour authorities.

Marina facilities are generally maintained to a high standard. They always include toilets and showers and some also have laundry facilities.

Anchorage is not permitted in areas used by the Royal Navy and where shellfish are farmed. There are further areas where a voluntary code is in place to protect marine environments important to wildlife, such as eel grass.

The use of a tripping line is advisable if entering an anchorage in the dark because of possible ground tackle associated with buoys. Fishing areas can appear unused yet have ground tackle present.

Swimming areas near to beaches are enclosed by buoys in the summer. These can reduce the degree of protection seen from the chart as boats are required to anchor further offshore.

Yacht and Sailing Clubs

There are numerous yacht and sailing clubs in the West Country. They generally have good facilities and welcome visitors. Members of clubs with reciprocal arrangements have free entry but generally fees are modest. Several clubs have restaurants and bars and some can also provide berthing in swinging moorings or pontoons.

Holding tanks & heads

- No discharge in port is permitted.

- Up to 4 miles from shore discharge after treatment is permitted (but no solids or discolouration of the water).

- From 4-12 miles discharge is acceptable if crumbled and disinfected.

- More than 12 miles offshore any discharge is permitted.

Laying up

The following places are recommended:

Lyme Bay: Dartside Quay and Darthaven Marina.

Plymouth: Plymouth Yacht Haven Marina and Mayflower Marina.

Falmouth: Mylor Yacht Harbour and Falmouth Yacht Marina.

Water

A hose-pipe with a variety of end fittings is needed. Water from marinas is clean and drinkable, but bottled water is universally available.

Electricity

The marinas have modern electrical systems with power breakers and clean earth. Most connections are 16A. It is worth carrying a 16A/32A adapter for occasional use.

Cooking Fuel

Camping gaz is available from chandleries and nearby camping sites, many of which will deliver to a marina. Marina staff will know who to contact.

Provisions

Provisioning is straightforward, as there are many shops and 'express' supermarkets within easy reach of marinas. The Co-operative, Tesco and Sainsbury's all operate in the West Country. Small independent stores often sell local produce. Some shops are exceptional, such as Country Cheeses which has branches in Topsham and Totnes. Fish and shellfish are a real treat.

Radio services

Safety

HM Coastguard monitor VHF Channel 16 and DSC Channel 70 H24 (Falmouth also monitors DSC on MF 2182kHz), in addition to broadcasting Maritime Safety Information every 4 hours. There are Maritime Rescue Coordination Centres at Portland, (Portland to Topsham in the River Exe), Brixham (Topsham to Dodman Point) and Falmouth (Dodman Point to Cape Cornwall).

If possible always raise an alarm through DSC, as this conveys your position accurately and is the preferred system for rescue coordination.

Weather

Maritime Safety Information (MSI) is broadcast by HM Coastguard, national and local radio.

BBC Radio 4: LW 198kHz FM 92.4-94.6MHz

- 0048 LT: shipping, inshore waters, coastal station reports

- 0520 LT: shipping, inshore waters, coastal station reports

- 1201 LT (LW only): shipping

- 1754 LT: shipping.

Navtex: coverage up to 270M around the coast, on 490kHz (UK inshore forecast in English, foreign forecast in national languages) and 518kHz (forecast in English). Niton Navtex broacasts in UT:

- 518kHz at 0040, 0440, 0840, 1240, 1640, 2040
  490kHz at 0120, 0520, 0920, 1320, 1720, 2120

Brixham and Falmouth Coastguard VHF call on channel 16 announcing MSI will be broadcast on channel 10, 23, 73, 84 or 86.

Brixham and Falmouth Coastguard VHF 10,23,73,84,86

UT	Shipping	Inshore	Wind warnings	Outlook
0110		√	√	√
0410		√	√	
0710	√	√	√	√
1010		√	√	
1310		√	√	√
1610		√	√	
1910	√	√	√	√
2210		√	√	

Portland Coastguard VHF: call on channel 16 announcing MSI will be broadcast on channel 10, 23, 73, 84 or 86.

Portland Coastguard VHF 10,23,73,84,86

UT	Shipping	Inshore	Wind warnings	Outlook
0130		√	√	√
0430		√	√	
0730	√	√	√	√
1030		√	√	
1330		√	√	√
1630		√	√	
1930	√	√	√	√
2230		√	√	

Harbour Radio Stations

Generally VHF 80. Details in port boxes within the book.

Formalities

The following documents (originals and copies) will be required on board:

- Certificate of registry, or Small Ships Registry documents.
- Insurance valid for the cruising area, including adequate third-party cover.
- Evidence that VAT has been paid on the boat (such as a VAT receipt or a Bill of Sale on older boats).
- Ship's radio licence and radio operator's licence.
- Ship's log, itinerary and crew list.

If arriving from another EU country you do not need to fly flag Q, complete any paperwork or contact Customs unless you have non-EU nationals, or animals, on board, or goods to declare. In these circumstances you must call the Customs Yachtline on ① 0845 723 1110.

If arriving from a non-EU country you must fly flag Q within 12M of the coast and complete form C1331. On arrival contact the Customs Yachtline on ① 0845 723 1110.

Information for the tourist

Transport

See www.travelinesw.com for information online about public transport in the West Country.

Airports

Exeter airport has both domestic and international flights. Plymouth airport has domestic flights and flights to Ireland and the Channel Islands. Newquay airport has domestic flights only. From Penzance helicopters fly to the Isles of Scilly.

Train

There are extensive rail connections throughout the West Country with high speed trains from Penzance, Plymouth and Exeter to Bristol, London and beyond.

Branch lines reach many of the smaller towns.

For online information and ticket booking see www.firstgreatwestern.co.uk or www.thetrainline.com.

Bus

There are numerous buses and coaches throughout the West Country. National Express, First and Stagecoach are available for longer journeys. Bus stations are shown on town maps.

Taxis

Taxis and mini-cabs are numerous. Most have metres or will agree a fare ahead of travel.

Car hire

All major car hire companies operate in the West County. Details are given with town information. Many require online reservation.

Health

The West Country is covered by the National Health Service. Marina staff will have information about how to find a medical practitioner or hospital with Accident and Emergency facilities. Details and phone numbers are given for the majority of locations covered in the book.

European citizens should hold an EC Health Card, which has replaced the E111. The NHS will generally provide treatment, particularly in an emergency, without any administrative check.

Pharmacies

All the main towns have pharmacies.

Emergencies

999 is the telephone number that gives access to police, fire and ambulance.

Money and security

Cash dispensing machines and branches of banks are numerous. The West Country is generally safe and friendly but, as always take care in large crowds where there may be pickpockets.

Opening hours

Shops are generally open from 0900 to 1730 and are closed on Sundays. However, this is changing and some shops now open on Sundays from 1000 to 1600. Some large supermarkets, for example Tescos, are open all day everyday apart from December 25th.

Since 2005 pubs and bars have been able to apply for a license to serve alcohol 24 hours a day. However, many continue to close at 2300.

Cafés generally serve food throughout the day but more formal restaurants are open for lunch from 1200 to 1500 and dinner from 1800 to 2300.

Communications

The market for land and mobile telephone is deregulated, so there are numerous providers of services for both. Reception for 3G is very wide, generally better with Vodafone and O2 who have the most extensive infrastructure. Along the coast 3G disappears when away from port as does voice in the more remote areas.

Post

There are post offices in every town, providing all the usual services including registered delivery. International courier services, such as UPS and DHL, cover the West Country. Seek information from marina offices.

Internet

Some marinas have Internet facilities for their customers to use. Broadband is universal so connection speeds are good. Internet cafés are widespread.

There are increasingly good deals for modem connection through USB-3G devices, including on a pay-as-you-go basis, and this can provide easy Internet connectivity independent of wi-fi that may be provided by the marina or local café. Smartphones also provide quick and easy access to the Internet.

Navigational reference

Time

The UK keeps Greenwich Mean Time (UT) which advances one hour in summer. Almanac and online marine resources from the Admiralty (e.g. EasyTide) give times in UT, so one hour needs to be added in the summer. Electronic products generally convert automatically to local time.

Chart datum

All depths given in this book are those above or below chart datum. This is the depth at which the sea level will not drop under normal circumstances, and is hence conservative for navigation. For British Admiralty and Imray it is the Lowest Astronomical Tide (LAT). Swell, atmospheric pressure and wind affect depth and should be taken into account, especially in situations with little margin.

Heights

British Admiralty charts are switching from a system of using Mean High Water Springs (MHWS) to a datum of Highest Astronomical Tide (HAT).

Horizontal chart datum

Positions derived from a GPS have to be referenced to some datum. This can normally be set by the user, but will usually default to the World Geodetic System 1984 (WGS 84). It is important to check this in the system you are using. Equally important, check that this is the same datum as used on the chart (either electronic or paper) to plot position.

Bearings

All bearing given are in degrees True. Use the charts to establish exact magnetic variation. In 2007 the variation was between 3°20′ and 3°45′ west, decreasing about 9′ annually.

Lights

The majority of the lights shown on the harbour and anchorage plans and within the text have abbreviated characteristics (not showing distance and height for easier reading). The exception to this is where particular attention is drawn to lights for navigation when transiting offshore.

Buoyage

The system used for buoyage in the West Country, as in all of Europe, is IALA region A.

Charts

Available charts are listed in the Appendix. Note that where reference to a particular chart is made in the text an electronic copy on a chart plotter is an acceptable alternative.

Passage, harbour and anchorage plans

The latitude and longitude given in the port boxes are solely to locate the chart, not the harbour or anchorage, and cannot be used for navigation. The plans themselves are for illustrative purposes only.

Blue demarcations are used to indicate shallows to avoid in rough weather. Red demarcations indicate unmarked isolated areas, generally more than 0.5M offshore, which are a danger in all circumstances.

Tidal Streams

Tidal Stream diagrams show rates in knots at neaps and springs. 05,11 indicates 0.5 knots at neaps and 1.1 knots at springs

Isles of Scilly

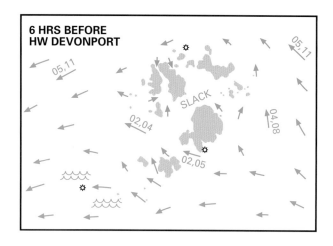

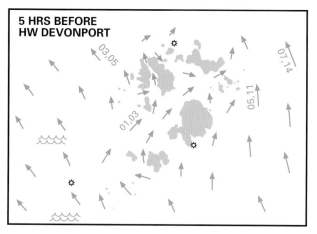

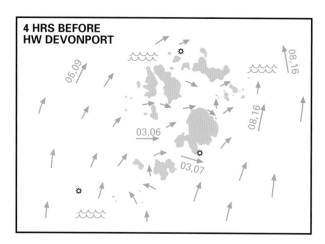

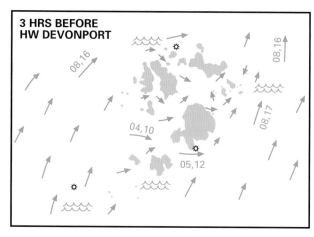

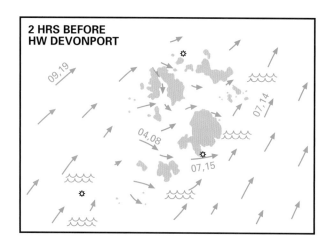

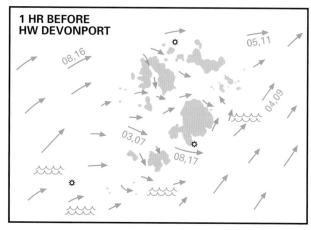

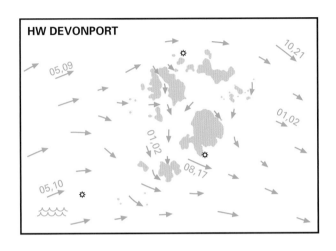

HW DEVONPORT

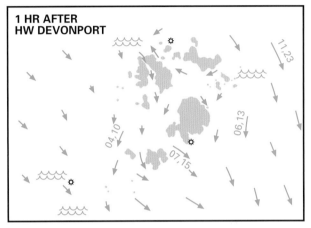

1 HR AFTER
HW DEVONPORT

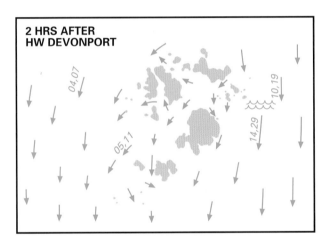

2 HRS AFTER
HW DEVONPORT

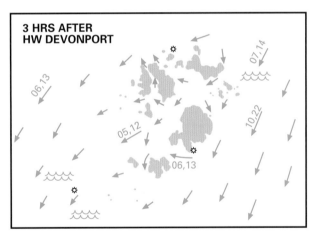

3 HRS AFTER
HW DEVONPORT

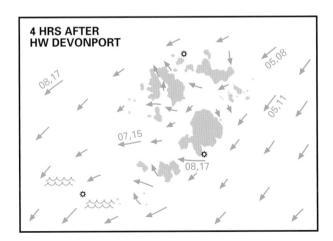

4 HRS AFTER
HW DEVONPORT

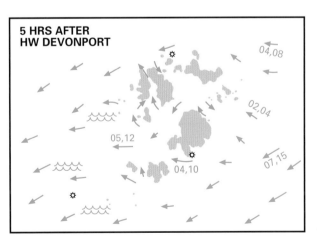

5 HRS AFTER
HW DEVONPORT

West English Channel

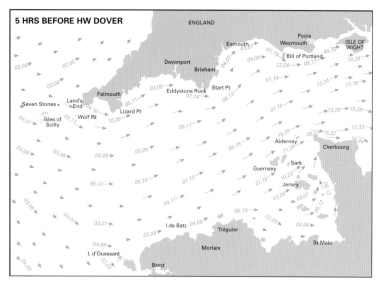

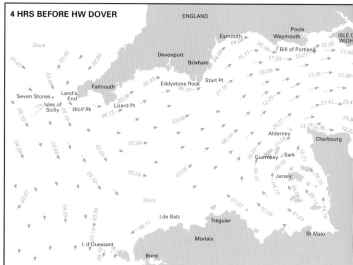

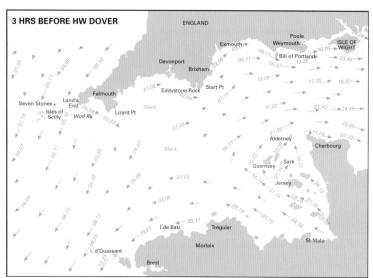

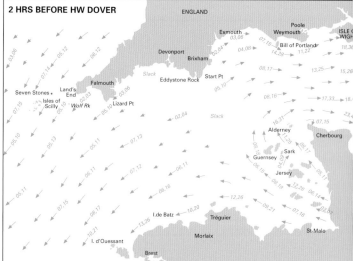

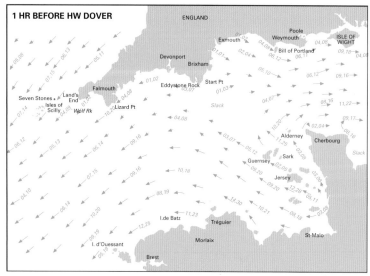

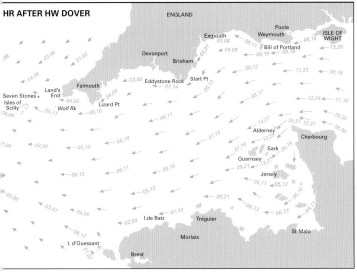

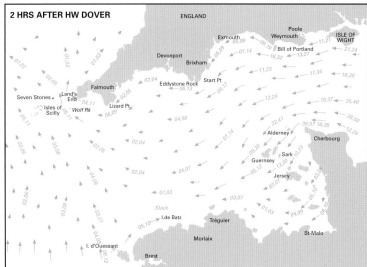

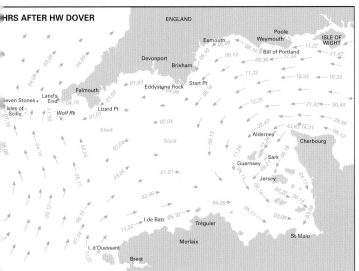

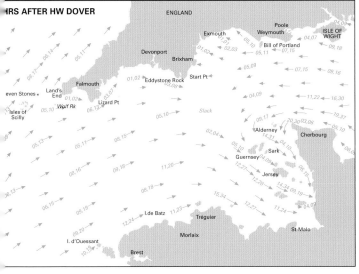

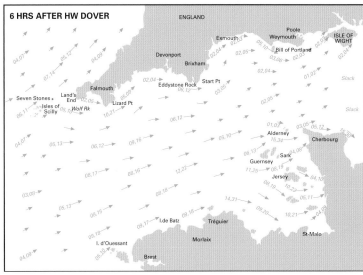

Portland Bill

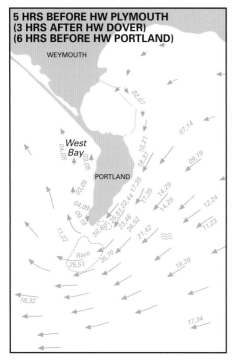

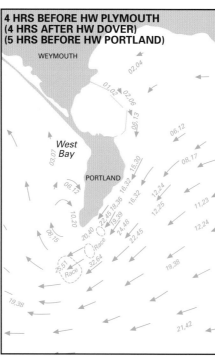

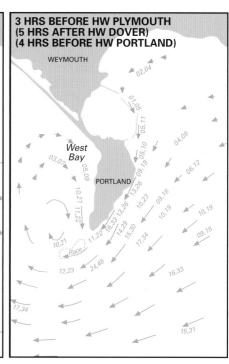

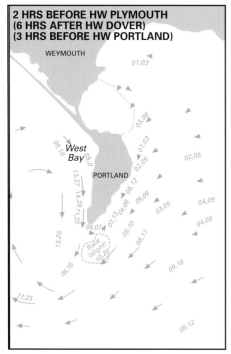

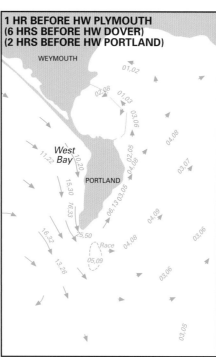

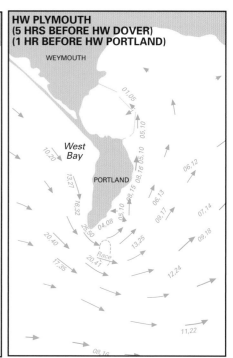

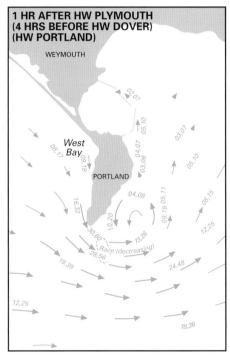

1 HR AFTER HW PLYMOUTH
(4 HRS BEFORE HW DOVER)
(HW PORTLAND)

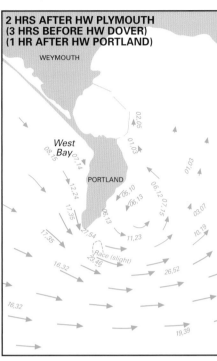

2 HRS AFTER HW PLYMOUTH
(3 HRS BEFORE HW DOVER)
(1 HR AFTER HW PORTLAND)

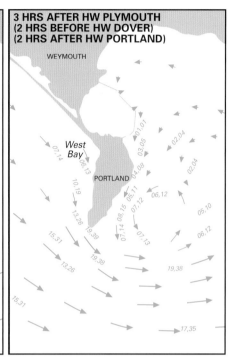

3 HRS AFTER HW PLYMOUTH
(2 HRS BEFORE HW DOVER)
(2 HRS AFTER HW PORTLAND)

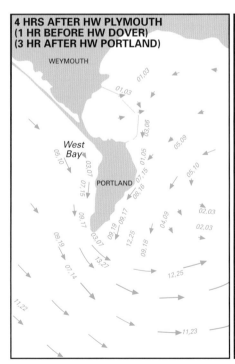

4 HRS AFTER HW PLYMOUTH
(1 HR BEFORE HW DOVER)
(3 HR AFTER HW PORTLAND)

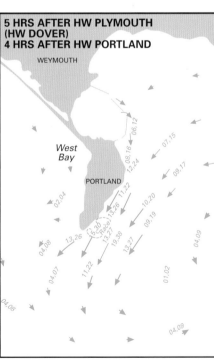

5 HRS AFTER HW PLYMOUTH
(HW DOVER)
4 HRS AFTER HW PORTLAND

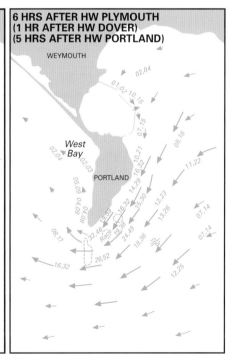

6 HRS AFTER HW PLYMOUTH
(1 HR AFTER HW DOVER)
(5 HRS AFTER HW PORTLAND)

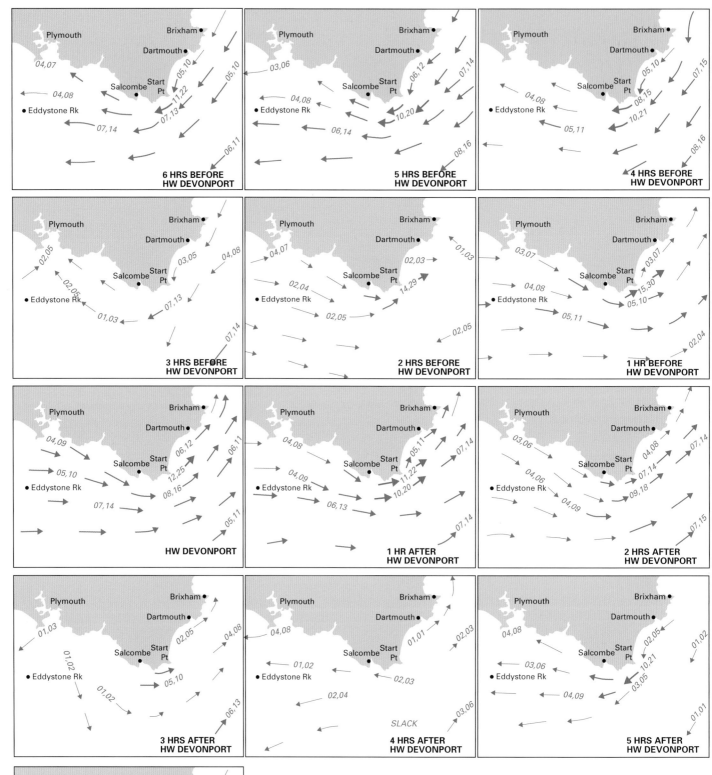

Start Point

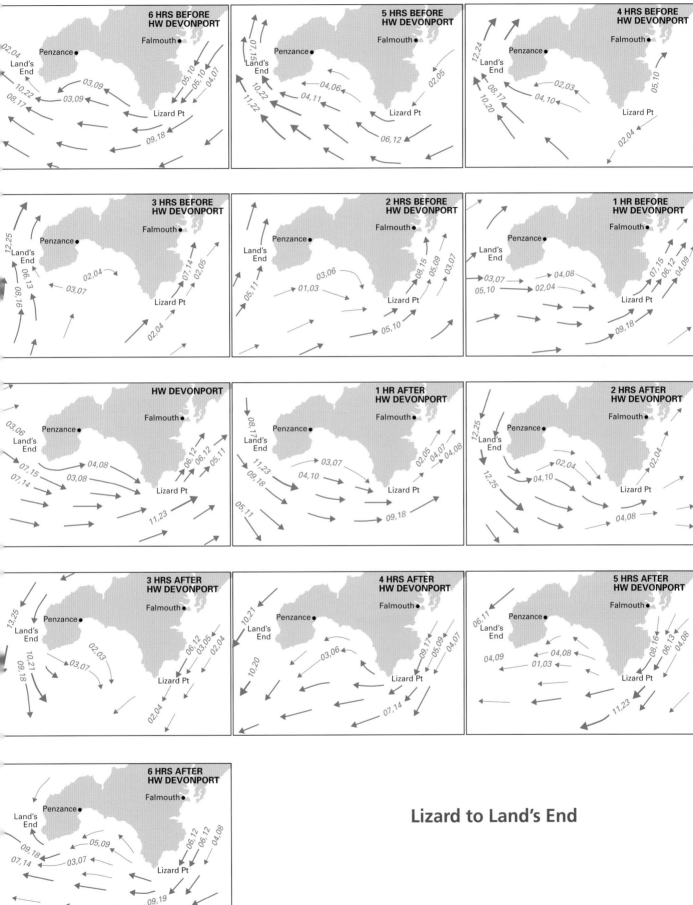

Lizard to Land's End

Lyme Bay

West Bay to Salcombe
Jurassic Coast, fishing harbours and rivers

Lyme Bay
West Bay to Salcombe

The sweep of land around Lyme Bay is exceptionally pretty and sailing here is immensely enjoyable. On the water there are often dolphins and harbour porpoises to be seen, and casting an eye ashore along the Jurassic coast (which runs from Exmouth to Swanage) 185 million years of geological history from the Mesozoic Era are laid bare. There are red sandstone sea stacks from the Triassic period at Ladram Bay, white chalk cliffs from the Cretaceous period at Beer Head and rocks full of fossils from the Jurassic period at Lyme Regis.

Some of the more difficult harbours and anchorages in the east are just a short taxi or bus ride away from places of interest. From West Bay you can get to Bridport, a pretty market town, where rope and net making began in the 13th century when both hemp and flax were found to thrive on nearby land. Originally meeting the needs of the Royal Navy, rope from Bridport was also used for the hangman's noose. Today the town provides nets for major football championships and for Wimbledon.

The Cobb at Lyme Regis, immortalized in the film of The *French Lieutenant's Woman*, is an iconic landmark. There is the excellent Philpot Museum to visit and guided fossil hunting trips along the shoreline. A seven-mile walk westwards takes you through the Undercliff, Britain's first nature reserve, with habitat of international importance.

From beach huts on the shingle at Beer you can tuck into a delicious crab sandwich, though also consider looking down on your craft at anchor from the beer garden of the Anchor Inn, a short walk uphill. One mile west of the village are the Beer Quarry Caves where an interesting guided tour takes visitors two hundred feet below ground. Quarried since Roman times, Beer stone has been used in numerous public buildings including Westminster Abbey, St Paul's Cathedral and the Tower of London.

Further west the River Exe looks especially tempting at high tide, though the vast expanse of water at its mouth is deceiving and care should be taken as the navigable channel changes amidst continually shifting sand and silt. The enormous mud bank known as Cockle Sand is a Site of Special Scientific Interest and an internationally important habitat for wading and migrating birds.

Exeter, Devon's county town, is six miles upstream and well worth a visit, though to get here by boat you need to go into the canal from Turf Lock and have enough clearance to make it under the M5 motorway. With care the river Exe is navigable to Topsham, a

The entrance to the River Dart

Dartmouth Castle

Golden Vanity, a historic Brixham trawler

Sailing in Salcombe

delightful small town with a big history. The Exe had silted up by the 14th century and goods, coming and going from Exeter, were transported 'by horse, cart or waggon' from Topsham until the canal was complete. The town is especially interesting architecturally as many of the houses have Dutch gables built by merchants trading with Holland. There is also an excellent museum and plenty of pubs and restaurants.

Tor Bay is a justifiably popular sailing destination and both Torquay and Brixham have excellent marinas. Interesting trips ashore from Torquay include a visit to Paignton Zoo Environmental Park, renowned for its conservation work and crocodile swamp! Living Coasts, a recent offshoot next to the harbour, has a fabulous collection of penguins, puffins and octopus. Access to Exeter by train from Torquay is very straightforward and the journey along the coast is magnificent.

Brixham marina is next to a busy fishing port. There is a pleasant and easy walk into the town and a slightly harder, but very rewarding, walk up to Berry Head National Nature Reserve. Check out the programme of ranger-guided walks as these include a visit to a guillemot colony, which swells to over a thousand birds during the breeding season, a look at some rare wildflowers and an evening watching greater horseshoe bats as they emerge to feed (electronic bat detectors provided). If you have children on board they might well enjoy Brixham's outdoor seawater swimming pool. With its old-fashioned changing rooms and tiered surround it feels as if time here has stood still.

The River Dart has an air of aloofness. It is less associated with the holiday crowd than with a community going about its business as usual. Devon crabs are landed in huge numbers, though discretely, and from its magnificent setting at the mouth of the river the Royal Naval College, Britannia, gets on with the job of training officers. Sailing in this pristine environment, set mainly within an Area of Outstanding Natural Beauty, lifts the soul! Easy trips ashore include a journey by steam train along the Dart valley to Paignton and, from a mooring at Dittisham, a visit to Greenway, the former holiday home of Agatha Christie. Now in the hands of the National Trust, there are warden-guided walks including one that leaves at 5.30am to hear the dawn chorus and ends with breakfast.

The Salcombe-Kingsbridge estuary is not considered an estuary at all by some as there is no river flowing into it and is therefore more of a ria. Designated a Marine Site of Special Scientific Interest in 1987, it has extensive eelgrass beds and if you snorkel this is a great place to look for our two native seahorse species. Great care should be taken to drop anchor only in designated areas. Salcombe itself is a busy tourist destination with many restaurants and bijou shops. It is especially crowded in August, with up to five boats abreast on the visitor buoys. If you like to be part of the crowd, the 'in-crowd' that is, then this is the place to be.

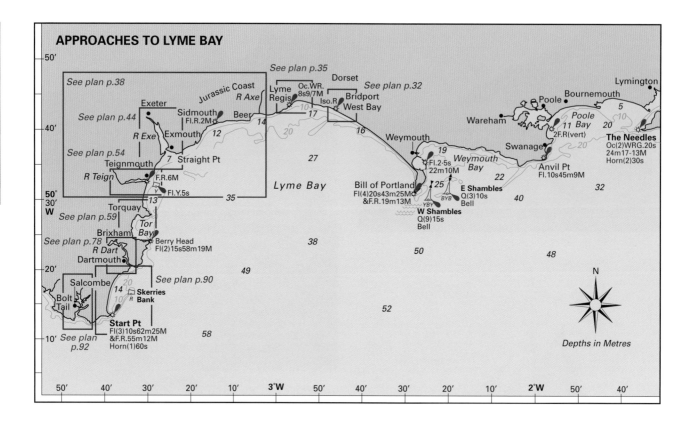

APPROACHES TO LYME BAY

Sailing from West Bay to Salcombe

Lyme Bay is a wide open area of sea between Portland Bill and Start Point. The tidal stream lessens within the bay but is considerable around the Bill, where dangerous races and overfalls reach 3-5M out to sea. Chesil Beach in the east is a natural bank of pebbles, unwelcoming to any boat, so West Bay, 18M from Portland Bill, should be the first port of call. West Bay now has a breakwater that shelters the harbour from southwesterlies but there is not enough depth to remain afloat other than in the pool of the inner harbour where there is little space. 6M further west, Lyme Regis' anchorage or visitors' buoys are a better bet for an overnight stay in calm conditions. The harbour wall can be used for short stops (time enough to have a brief visit to this historic town) though all other spaces are taken by local boats. Beer and Seaton, 7M west of Lyme Regis, can also be a good place to stop in calm weather. Beer is a delight, best attempted by dinghy when a temporary pontoon has been wheeled down to the water's edge as the pebble-beach is quite steep.

The River Exe, 14M from Beer and 36M from Portland Bill, is the first of the long tidal estuaries you met sailing west. Shelter is good in the river but the entrance is tricky due to a very strong tidal stream and ever-shifting sand and mud banks. Do not attempt this entrance in bad weather or a strong southerly wind against the ebb. The estuary is very pretty, especially upstream. There are anchorages and visitors' buoys, some excellent pubs and exceptional birdlife.

5M south of the Exe, Teignmouth and Shaldon abut the entrance of the River Teign. The entrance channel passes between shallow banks, not to be attempted in anything other than good conditions. There are visitors' pontoons at Teignmouth but the river is blocked by a road bridge so excursions upstream are only possible in small craft.

Further west there are delightful anchorages off Oddicombe beach and Hope Cove before Tor Bay opens out. 40M from Portland Bill, Tor Bay is the most popular destination in Lyme Bay. Facing east, thus sheltered from the prevailing southwest, the bay has long been used as an anchorage for large boats and, in centuries past, as a place to assemble the naval fleet. Today there are often cargo ships to be seen. Some are empty and waiting for business while others are packed to the gunnels with cargo of such little value that it is not (yet) worth offloading. The marinas of Torquay and Brixham are all-weather harbours. Brixham has a large fishing fleet, one of the largest in England, while Torquay and Paignton are favoured holiday destinations.

The River Dart is one of the highlights of any sailing trip to the West Country. It is picturesque and has plenty of space and facilities for the visitor. From Portland Bill it is 43M and from Tor Bay it is 8-10M. Dartmouth is home to Britannia Royal Naval College which can be visited on guided tours.

In Start Bay it is possible to anchor at the southern end of Slapton Sands, though even in calm weather the tide will line your vessel parallel to the coast and cause it to roll.

The Salcombe estuary beyond Start Point is idyllic, though often very busy with up to five boats sharing a buoy in August. The entrance has a sandbar. The fairway in front of Salcombe lies in a southwesterly

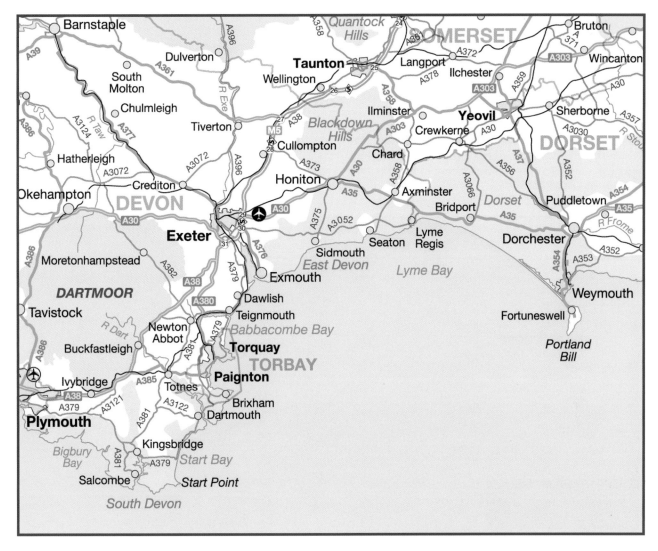

direction where wind is often funnelled. This can get quite uncomfortable in wind-over-tide.

Initial shelter

Torquay, Brixham and Dartmouth are all-weather harbours with good marinas and plenty of facilities.

Other ports and facilities

Lyme Regis has visitors' buoys outside in the summer and space for anchoring. The harbour dries and is full of local boats. Contact the harbourmaster for berthing against the quay.

There are visitors' buoys in the River Exe (The Bight and opposite Starcross), and a number of anchorages. Upstream it is possible to enter the Exeter Canal at Turf Lock and also to lie alongside the quay at Topsham (dries, very soft mud) or use one of the pontoons belonging to Trout's Yard (shallow). The entrance to the river should not be attempted in bad weather and tidal streams should be taken into account.

Teignmouth has visitors' pontoons, albeit often occupied by local boats. The entrance should not be attempted in bad weather.

Salcombe has visitor buoys and a pontoon, plus good anchorage upstream. The entrance has a sand bar.

Emergencies

The RNLI stations are at Weymouth, Lyme Regis, Exmouth, Teignmouth, Brixham, River Dart and Salcombe. The larger lifeboats are at Weymouth and Brixham.

The Maritime Safety Co-ordination Centre (MRCC) is based at Brixham and monitors Channel 16 and DSC Channel 70. Coast radio stations (Coastguard) are based at Portland and Brixham and transmit Maritime Safety Information (see appendix for timings). The harbours mentioned as initial shelter have significant medical facilities.

Provisioning

There are shops and pubs serving food within easy reach of the beach at Lyme Regis and Beer. Exmouth, Teignmouth, Torquay, Brixham, Dartmouth and Salcombe all have plenty of shops and supermarkets reasonably close to the harbours. There are pubs serving food near to the water upstream in the River Exe (Cockwood, Turf Lock, Totnes) and the River Dart (Dittisham).

Repairs and chandleries

There are boat lifts at Haldon Pier in Torquay and at Darthaven Marina and Dartside Quay in the River Dart.

Marinas will have access to mechanic, rigging and electronic expertise. There is a concentration of services in the River Dart at the Dartside Quay yard and Darthaven Marina. Brixham is also a good place to access services and the inner harbour has a drying pad. The most extensive chandlers are in Darthaven Marina and Brixham.

Fuel

- Exmouth harbour: entrance channel pontoon (diesel only)
- Torquay: South Pier (diesel and petrol)
- Brixham: marina pontoon (diesel only)
- River Dart: barge in the fairway (diesel and petrol), Dart Marina (diesel only)
- Salcombe: barge in the fairway (diesel and petrol).

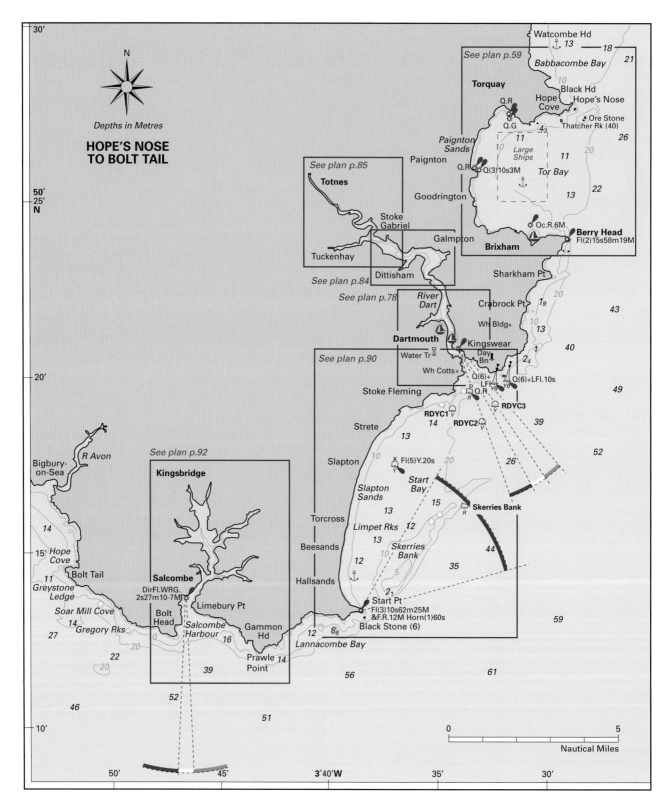

Transport

High-speed trains from London and Bristol stop at Exeter and Totnes. Some also stop at Newton Abbot.

The line from Exeter to Newton Abbot has stops at Dawlish Warren, Teignmouth and Newton Abbot, where a branch line connects to Torquay and Paignton.

Trains also run between Exeter, Honiton, Axminster and Crewkerne.

Buses are numerous and connect all the seaside towns.

Exeter airport has national and some international flights.

Passages

The distances from Portland Bill to destinations in Lyme Bay, assuming 5 knots, are:

- Berry Head 40M or 8 hours
- River Exe 36M or 7 hours
- Tor Bay 40M or 8 hours
- River Dart 43M or 9 hours
- Start Point 52M or nearly 11 hours.

The prevailing wind is from the southwest so these passages can often be a long beat.

Coming from the east the tide around Portland Bill must be negotiated with great care and good timing. In bad weather pass 10M south of the Bill and well clear of Shambles Bank to avoid the races, overfalls and confused seas that tidal streams create. The inner passage should only be attempted in daylight and good weather while keeping a keen lookout for pots which are set right in the passage. The main introduction to this book provides further details.

There are plenty of fishing boats working Lyme Bay, though in general there are few craft in comparison with, for example, the Solent. Fishing pots are abundant in anything up to 50m. Shipping is not intensive.

The beach at Beer

Dittisham ferry

Kingswear

⚓ West Bay Harbour (Bridport)

West Bay Harbour offers shelter from the prevailing southwest, either at the breakwater wall or inside the fishing harbour (with permission from the harbourmaster). Do not approach in strong southeasterly conditions, which create a treacherous swell in the entrance channel. Minimum depth is only 0.75m in the outer harbour, while the pool in the fishing harbour has 2m.

Bridport, just under a mile north, is a picturesque and historic small town with good facilities.

Approach & entrance

West Bay Harbour should NOT be approached in strong east/southeast conditions, when a strong swell builds up at the entrance and in the outer harbour.

Otherwise the approach is straightforward, in the white sector (331°-341°) of the harbour light F.WRG.

Berthing & facilities

The outer harbour can accommodate 10 yachts in depth of 0.75m, against piles spaced 3 metres apart. There are recessed ladders for access to the quay. A short pontoon near the launching ramp can be used by yachts. A significant swell builds up inside in east to southeast winds.

The old fishing inner harbour is guarded by a cill and has a tide gauge on the side. Inside there is a deep pool, providing at least 2m where fishing boats tie up, but with little space for manoeuvring. The

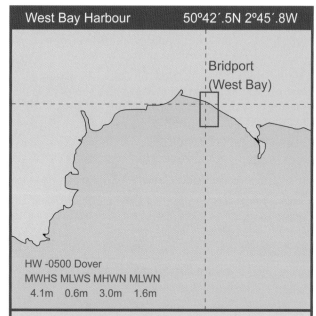

West Bay Harbour   50°42´.5N 2°45´.8W

Bridport (West Bay)

HW -0500 Dover

MWHS	MLWS	MHWN	MLWN
4.1m	0.6m	3.0m	1.6m

West Bay Harbour

- Approach: do no attempt in strong E/SE, otherwise straightforward in white sector of harbour light F.WRG (331°-341°)
- Entrance: dangerous in strong E/SE; cill at start of channel to inner harbour
- Shelter from SW, very exposed in SE conditions
- Outer harbour: 0.7m depth 10 berthing spaces along the wall, 2 at pontoon; piles every 3m
- ⚓ Inner harbour: space for 2 yachts along the wall, in pool with minimum depth of 2m (need harbourmaster permission)
- Harbourmaster: ☎ / Fax 01308 423222 VHF Channel: listen 16, working 11 (0800-1800 in the summer, 7 days a week)

harbourmaster will accommodate up to two yachts alongside the quay if there is room. The pool is created by water from the River Brit pouring in when the jetty sluice is opened. Be aware of the flow when manoeuvring.

Food & transport

There are many places to eat in West Bay. The Riverside Restaurant is exceptionally good for fish. They are aware of diminishing fish stocks and a sustainability log can be viewed in reception showing that 90% of their food is sourced locally. West Bay crab linguine is especially recommended! The West Bay Hotel also has excellent food and a good selection of locally brewed fine ales. Sladers Yard is well worth a visit for its gallery which sells contemporary British art, furniture and craft. Located in a beautiful stone warehouse, it has a licensed café and good organic food.

For provisions, Morrisons supermarket is about one mile away along West Bay Road. Bridport itself has all you would expect of a small town.

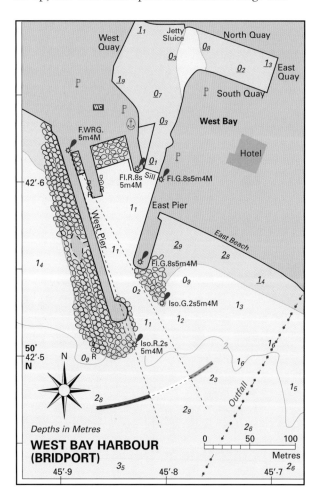

West Quay · 1_1 · Jetty Sluice · North Quay · 0_8 · 0_3 · 0_2 · 1_3 East Quay · 1_9 · P · 0_7 · P South Quay · WC · P · 0_3 · West Bay · Hotel · 0_1 · P · F.WRG. 5m4M · Fl.R.8s Sill 5m4M · Fl.G.8s5m4M · 1_1 · East Pier · West Pier · 1_1 · East Beach · 2_9 · 2_8 · 1_4 · Fl.G.8s5m4M · 0_9 · 1_4 · 0_2 · Iso.G.2s5m4M · 1_3 · 1_1 · 1_2 · 1_6 · Iso.R.2s 5m4M · 2 · 1_6 · 50° 42´.5 N · 0_9 · 2_3 · Outfall · 1_5 · 2_8 · 2_9 · 2_6

Depths in Metres

0   50   100
Metres

WEST BAY HARBOUR (BRIDPORT)

45´.9 · 3_5 · 45´.8 · 45´.7 · 2_6

Bridport

- X53 Jurassic Coast (Exeter-Seaton-Beer-Bridport-Lyme Regis and beyond)
  Bus no. 31 Axminster-Lyme Regis-Bridport-Dorchester-Weymouth
- Regular buses from West Bay to Bridport
- Trains from Axminster and Dorchester
- Dorset Vehicle Rentals, The Old Generating Yard, St Swithins Road, Bridport, DT6 5DW
  01308 458888 / 08000 515253
- Morrisons: West Bay Rd, between Bridport and West Bay
- Restaurants, pubs and cafés in Bridport town centre and in West Bay
- Tourist Information Centre, 47 South St 01308 424901
- Bridport Community Hospital, Hospital Lane, North Allington, Bridport DT6 5DR
  01308 422371

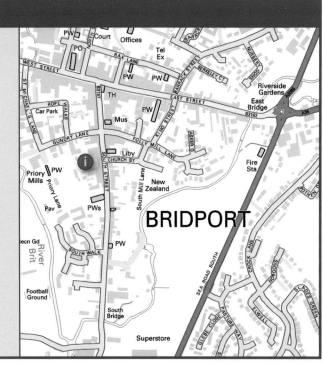

On Wednesdays and Saturdays there are street markets selling local produce and there is a Farmers Market on the second Saturday of each month.

There are regular buses to Bridport from West Bay, and from Bridport buses on to Yeovil and Dorchester. National Express run coaches along the South Coast, Dorchester to Lyme Regis. The nearest train station is at Dorchester.

Interest

West Bay Harbour has benefited from a major re-development, completed in 2005. The old pier has been replaced and there are now some swish sea-facing apartments. Fishing boats are still at work but the character of the harbour has changed, with lots of pleasure craft and divers using the launching ramp. West Bay is a popular destination for tourists on a sunny day.

A harbour was built here in the 13th century for the transport of rope, made locally and sold to the Royal Navy and to the hangman. The harbour diminished in importance once transport by train was possible, but then expanded with the fishing industry and changed its name from Bridport to West Bay.

Bridport town is two miles away. If you are interested in the history of rope making the museum in South Street is worth a visit. There are many listed buildings attesting to the town's wealthy past. The Bull Hotel, in East street, makes use of a 17th-century coaching

West Bay harbour

inn and is a relaxed place to hang out. The Literary and Scientific Institute, established in the 1860s to encourage 'the intellectual and moral improvement of all classes', is where Francis Newbury was educated. He later found fame in association with the architect Charles Rennie Mackintosh. It is hoped that the abandoned Grade II listed Georgian building will eventually become an arts centre. The Chantry in Lower South Street is the town's oldest building and served as a lighthouse when boats could navigate up the River Brit.

Dorchester has lots of good things to do. The Dinosaur Museum and Dorset County Museum are both excellent. The latter has a writers' gallery that includes a recreation of Thomas Hardy's study and some of the best Roman mosaics in the country. The Old Crown Court where the Tolpuddle Martyrs were sentenced in 1834 can also be visited.

West Bay outer harbour, piles for mooring and pontoon
Inner harbour on the right

West Bay inner harbour (dries) - deep pool on the right

⚓ Ⓥ Lyme Regis

The historic fishing harbour of Lyme Regis is protected by the Cobb, but is only for boats that can dry out. Outside the harbour there are visitors' buoys and an anchorage which is good in settled conditions.

Situated in the heart of the Jurassic coast, Lyme Regis is a very popular tourist destination. The Cobb gained iconic status when it was used as a setting for the film of *The French Lieutenant's Woman*, a novel by John Fowles. Many people arrive, hammer in hand, seeking fossils.

Lyme Regis Harbour

Approach & entrance

The approach to Lyme Regis is straightforward. Entrance to the inner harbour can be dangerous in strong easterlies or with any substantial swell.

- Keep at least 300m south of the Cobb to avoid shallows and rocks.

- Approach the harbour on a 284° bearing; at night remain in the white sector of the harbour wall Oc.WR.8s and transit with shoreside F.G.

- In daylight aim for the end of the Cobb extension (red beacon). Leave a good 50m to port.

Berthing & facilities

The fishing harbour is protected but dries, good for bilge keelers. It is ususally full but can accommodate up to 11m. Visitors can berth at the outer end of

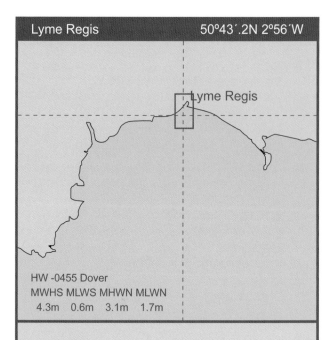

Lyme Regis   50°43´.2N 2°56´W

HW -0455 Dover
MWHS MLWS MHWN MLWN
4.3m   0.6m   3.1m   1.7m

Lyme Regis

- Approach straightforward
- Narrow entrance to harbour can be difficult; sheltered
- Ⓥ 5 visitors' buoys (orange) outside the fishing harbour 0.8m minimum (deep draught boats may ground in spring tides); can roll in swell
- Fishing harbour dries; visitors can dry in sand at Victoria Pier (dries 1.3m)
- Harbourmaster:
  ☎ 01297 442137 / 07870 240645
  VHF Channel: listen 16, working 14
- Lyme Regis Sailing Club: showers, bar
  ☎ 01297 442800 lymeregissailingclub.co.uk
- ⛽ Fuel: from nearby garage

Victoria Pier (dries to 1.3m) for short visits, or stay overnight by arrangement with the harbourmaster.

There is water at the Cobb. The sailing club in Victoria Pier has showers.

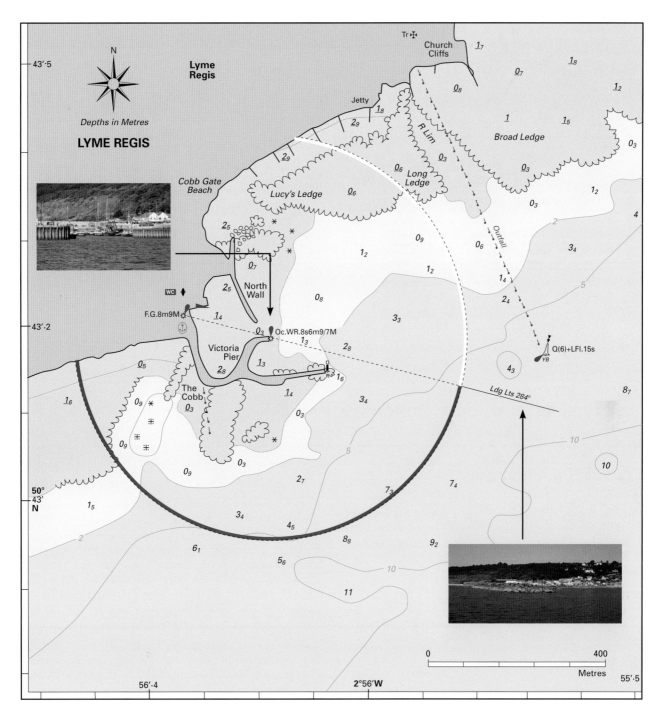

LYME REGIS

Depths in Metres

N

Lyme
Regis

43'·5

Church
Cliffs

Tr ✠

1₇

1₈

0₇

1₂

0₈

Broad Ledge

Jetty

1₈

1

1₅

0₃

2₉

R Lim

2₉

Cobb Gate
Beach

Lucy's Ledge

0₆

Long
Ledge

0₃

0₃

2

Long
Ledge

0₆

0₃

4

2₅

0₆

0₉

0₆

3₄

5

0₇

1₂

1₂

1₄

North
Wall

0₈

2₄

WC

2₅

3₃

F.G.8m9M

1₄

Q(6)+LFl.15s

Oc.WR.8s6m9/7M

0₃

YB

Victoria
Pier

1₃

2₈

4₃

8₇

1₃

1₆

0₅

2₈

1₄

3₄

Ldg Lts 284°

10

The Cobb

0₉

0₃

0₃

1₆

0₉

7₃

7₄

10

0₉

0₃

2₇

50°
43'
N

0₉

1₅

3₄

4₅

8₈

9₂

2

6₁

5₆

10

11

0 _____ 400

Metres

56'·4

2°56'W

55'·5

Lyme Regis from the sea

Lyme Regis

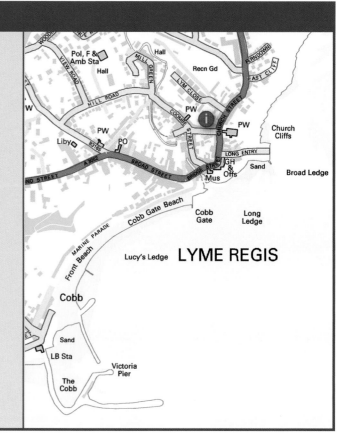

- X53 Jurassic Coast Bus (Exeter-Seaton-Beer-Bridport-Lyme Regis and beyond) Bus no. 31 Axminster-Lyme Regis-Bridport-Dorchester-Weymouth
- Trains from Axminster and Dorchester
- Practical Car & Van Rental, Marlborough Rd, Musbury, Axminster EX13 8AX ☎ 01297 553700
- The Co-operative, Broad Street, Lyme Regis DT7 3QF ☎ 01297 442082
- Tesco Superstore, Shand Park, West St, Axminster EX13 5NG ☎ 0845 6779019
- Restaurants: along Church Street and Broad Street; cafés on Marine Parade; pubs near the Cobb
- Tourist Information Centre: Church Street ☎ 01297 442138
- Bridport Community Hospital, Hospital Lane, North Allington, Bridport, Dorset DT6 5DR ☎ 01308 422371
- Axminster Hospital, Chard Street Axminster EX13 5DU ☎ 01297 630400

⚓ⓥ Buoys & Anchorages

ⓥ Five orange visitors' buoys are set outside the harbour during the summer, with a minimum depth of 0.8m. Vessels of deeper draught may ground during spring tides. The harbour wall offers some protection from the prevailing southwest but the buoys and anchorage are exposed.

Space between the south cardinal and the visitors' buoys is good for anchoring. However, the relative protection of the harbour is lost the further you move out. As with the buoys, swell may be an issue.

Food & transport

There are grocery and tourist shops along Church Street and Bridge Street and many pubs and restaurants cater for tourists. The Oyster and Fish House, owned by Mark Hix, serves fresh seafood simply prepared. Some of the tables have superb views over the Cobb while others reveal the drama of an open kitchen.

There is no train station but Lyme Regis is well served by buses that travel all along the Jurassic Coast from Weymouth (via Dorchester) to Exmouth.

Interest

Lyme Regis is a popular seaside town with a long and varied history. It is situated in the heart of the Jurassic Coast and many people come to search for the remains of ichthyosaurs, plesiosaurs and dimorphodon (see 'The Jurassic Coast' on page 42). While you can join geologist-led fossil hunting trips, your best chance of seeing such creatures from the past is a visit to the excellent Philpot Museum on the sea front. The building itself is an architectural gem, with a beautiful spiral staircase and rotunda.

A walk along the historic Cobb is not to be missed. There is a model of an early wooden version in the museum. These days the Cobb is associated with the film of *The French Lieutenant's Woman* (see 'Literary West Country' on page 37) starring Jeremy Irons and Meryl Streep. John Fowles lived in Lyme Regis for many years and Jane Austin, a frequent visitor, set her novels *Persuasion* and *Northanger Abbey* here.

A seven-mile walk along the Undercliff from Lyme Regis to Axmouth takes you through internationally important habitat, now managed by English Nature. If you prefer to walk just one way the return journey can be made by bus.

Lyme Regis flourished from 1500 to 1700 as a centre of trade with the Americas and southern Europe. In 1609 George Somers, Mayor of Lyme Regis and naval hero, sailed to Virginia to rescue the British colony established by Walter Raleigh. This led to the discovery of Bermuda, known officially as Somers Isles and a British colony ever since.

During the English Civil War, in 1685, the Duke of Monmouth landed in Lyme Regis. The town was besieged by loyalist forces and twenty-three rebels were executed. The genteel character of the town today comes from the 18th century when it became established as a tourist resort as a result of a new pastime: sea bathing. The elegant Georgian houses along the sea front and lining the steep roads inland come from the prosperity that followed.

For many people a good holiday includes a good holiday read. Popular writers associated with West Country sailing destinations include Agatha Christie, Daphne du Maurier and John Fowles, the first two having spawned literary festivals in Torquay and Fowey respectively.

The popularity of Hercule Poirot and Miss Marple has led to Agatha Christie (1890-1976) becoming known as the 'Queen of Crime'. Sales of her books exceed four billion, a number reputedly surpassed only by the Bible. She was born and raised in Torquay where she worked at the Town Hall as a nurse during the first world war. Two years later she transferred to the local pharmacy and it was here that she gained an impressive knowledge of poisons! In 1915 a diminutive Belgian refugee on a Torquay tram led to her inventing Poirot, the name Hercule being a pun on the detective's small stature. His popularity worldwide was such that when she eventually killed him off his obituary appeared in *The New York Times*, the only fictional character ever to have done so.

In 1990 the 'Agatha Christie mile' was established, a walk along the seafront in Torquay that takes in eleven locations associated with her. For example, the Imperial Hotel is the Majestic in *Peril at End House* and the setting for the last chapter of *Sleeping Murder*, Miss Marple's final mystery. Slightly further afield is Burgh Island, a holiday destination for Poirot in *Evil Under the Sun*. This is also the setting for Christie's most popular book: *And Then There Were None*. Ten people with blood on their hands are marooned on the Island as guests of Mr and Mrs U.N. Owen. Mirroring the poem *Ten Little Soldiers*, the book's original title, they are then murdered exactly as the poem foretells. The first is dispatched by an unsuspecting glug of cyanide: 'Ten little Soldier boys went out to dine; One choked his little self and then there were nine'. The second is murdered by an overdose of a sleeping draft: 'Nine little Soldier boys sat up very late; One overslept himself and then there were eight'. Eight more deaths follow in mysterious circumstances, but who is responsible?

Torre Abbey, situated on Torquay seafront, is worth a visit in its own right but also for the Agatha Christie garden. Here you will find many of the plants featured in her books, including prunus cultivars (from their stones comes cyanide) and *datura* whose hallucinogenic seedpods she used to induce madness. Real aficionados can guess the titles of four of her short stories from clues hidden in some of the beds.

Although Christie left Devon as a young woman, she continued to visit and in 1938 bought Greenway, her beloved holiday home. Both the house and gardens can now be visited as they are in the hands of the National Trust. Getting there involves a short, but steep, walk from the quay at Dittisham, on the River Dart.

Film buffs everywhere will associate the Cobb in Lyme Regis with Sarah, dressed in a sweeping black cape, looking forlornly out to sea in *The French Lieutenant's Woman*, John Fowles's iconic novel. The book, published in 1969, was an exciting new kind of writing, a Victorian romance with contemporary comment, layers of truth, fantasy and self-reflection, its multiple endings labelled 'postmodern playfulness'. Fowles had already begun the book when he moved from London to a remote farmhouse in Dorset in 1965. Finding total solitude 'a bit monotonous', he moved to Belmont House in the centre of Lyme Regis 3 years later and remained there until his death in 2005. Belmont House is now in the hands of the Landmark Trust and will hopefully open to the public before long.

Although Fowles published a number of novels, some critics think that he tried too hard to break new ground. *The Magus* became a 1960s cult classic, drawing comparisons with *The Tempest* and *The Odyssey*, but the film was considered an embarrassing failure. When Woody Allen was asked about his life he said he would do everything the same 'with the exception of seeing *The Magus*'.

Harold Pinter's screenplay of *The French Lieutenant's Woman* came out in 1981, staring Meryl Streep and Jeremy Irons, and was five-times Oscar-nominated. With it Fowles gained celebratory status but he remained a recluse. His booklet *A Short History of Lyme Regis* (1982) is still available. His papers reside at the University of Texas USA.

Daphne du Maurier (1907-89) was born in London but spent most of her life in Cornwall where she was a member of the Cornish nationalist party, Mebyon Kernow. She is generally considered a romantic novelist and her work is often criticized as intellectually lightweight, but the glamour and romanticism of her early novels provided much-needed escape from the horrors of two world wars, though her endings were rarely happy. Later, when writing was dominated by 'angry young men', her work was thought to belong to a bygone era but it remains hugely popular, even today. She is a first-rate storyteller and her ability to transport the reader to another place is exceptional. Who, for example, does not recognize the opening of *Rebecca*: 'Last night I dreamt I went to Manderley again'. Made into a film directed by Alfred Hitchcock, it won an Oscar for Best Picture in 1941. *Jamaica Inn*, *Frenchman's Creek* and *My Cousin Rachel* are also well known, both as books and films, and her terrifying short story *The Birds* has become a Hitchcock film classic.

Daphne du Maurier was one of five 'Women of Achievement' selected for a set of British stamps issued in August 1996.

Beer to River Teign

Beer to Teignmouth is one of the most stunning coastal regions in the UK. Part Heritage Coast, part Area of Outstanding Natural Beauty, its unique geological features were given World Heritage Status in 2001.

Numerous sailors just pass by, as stopping here is something of a challenge, but there are picture-

postcard villages to visit and a real sense of achievement if you get into Axmouth (small boats only) or negotiate the shallow estuaries of the Exe and Teign. A holiday would be made by anchoring at Beer and going ashore for a crab sandwich, and Topsham is a real treasure.

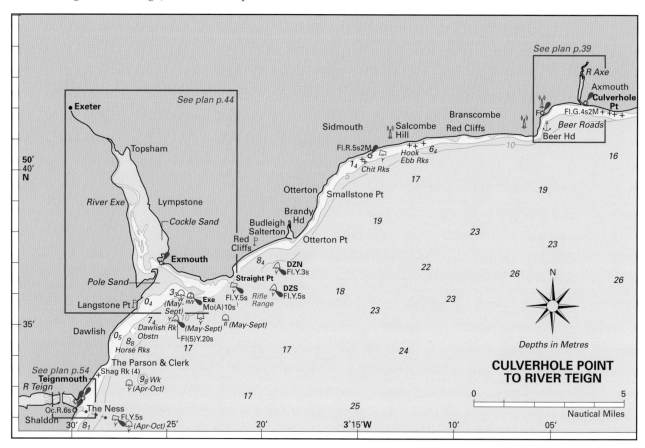

Axmouth harbour, looking towards the entrance
Sailing Club pontoons on the right, Harbourmaster berths on the left

Seaton shingle beach
Axmouth Harbour entrance on the right

Axmouth & Beer

Axmouth is a small drying harbour with a narrow entrance, only suitable for boats up to 8.5m LOA and 1.5m draught. The harbour (once inside) is very protected.

The anchorage at Beer is one of the most picturesque in Devon, with some protection afforded by Beer Head. Beer is a picture-perfect village, well worth the effort to get ashore.

⚓ Axmouth

The approach to Axmouth Harbour is straightforward but the very narrow entrance is not the easiest to identify. It is to the right of Seaton shingle beach and close to Haven Cliff.

- The entrance channel bar dries: approach only 0.5 hour either side of HW.

- The entrance is formed by two shingle spits that shift and are not marked, so local knowledge or a sounding is required. A yellow buoy outside can be used to wait while considering options.

- Aim for the Fl.G.4s beacon with green triangle topmark sited on the pier, starboard side.

- Immediately after the entrance the channel turns on a 90° dogleg to port. The tide may be strong (5 knots on spring ebb) and there may be swell, so you need sufficient way to steer the manoeuvre.

Berthing & facilities

Past the rigours of the entrance you will be in a very protected haven. The Sailing Club may be able to provide you with a berth, rafted up in one of the fore-aft moorings or on their new pontoon. Alternatively contact the harbourmaster for arrangements alongside the quay.

There are a number of workshops in the harbour that may be able to assist with repairs.

The Sailing Club has showers and a good bar with a view of the beach. The Harbour Inn in Axmouth, beyond the bridge, is welcoming and Seaton is only a short distance away for places to eat and provisions.

The narrow entrance to Axmouth Harbour

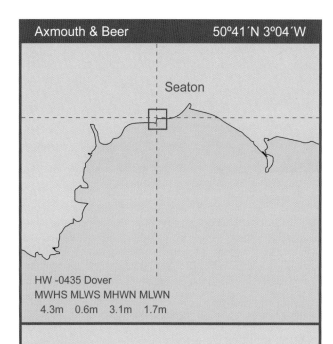

Axmouth & Beer · 50°41′N 3°04′W

Seaton

HW -0435 Dover

MWHS	MLWS	MHWN	MLWN
4.3m	0.6m	3.1m	1.7m

Axmouth

- Approach: difficult to distinguish, shingle spit
- Entrance: HW+/- 1, bar dries, channel not marked, narrow entrance, very STRONG TIDE
- Boats up to 8.5m LOA, 1.5m draught; harbour dries
- Axe Yacht Club: moorings, pontoon, bar, showers ☎ 01297 20043 info@axeyachtclub.co.uk www.axeyachtclub.co.uk
- Harbourmaster VHF06 ☎ 07939 044109

Beer

- Straightforward approach
- Exposed except in NW to N winds; subject to swell

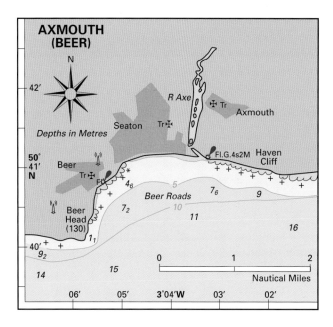

AXMOUTH (BEER)

N

42′

Depths in Metres

50° 41′ N

R Axe

Tr · Axmouth

Seaton · Tr

Tr

Beer

Tr

FC

Fl.G.4s2M · Haven Cliff

4₆

5

7₆

9

Beer Roads

7₂

10

11

16

Beer Head (130)

1₁

40′

9₂

14

15

0 · 1 · 2

Nautical Miles

06′ · 05′ · 3°04′W · 03′ · 02′

Beer

⚓ Beer

Beer is a delightful anchorage but should only be used in very calm conditions and winds from north to northwest. Beer cliff provides some shelter from the prevailing southwest but it is normally not enough to prevent swell, which can make anchoring unpleasant.

• From the east stay at least 200m from the Beer Head as rocks extend south to sea.

• From south or west proceed along the cliff, at least 50m away, to avoid rocks.

• Anchor in clean sand on the shelf 3-10m deep. Beware small boat moorings close to the beach.

The beach is steep and difficult to climb, though manageable in a dinghy in flat, calm conditions. Sometimes there is a temporary pontoon belonging to a company that rents self-drive motor boats. In any kind of swell it is probably best to aim for the western side of the beach or be prepared to emulate a landing we remember well for its final approach: hurried, ungraceful and ultimately very wet.

The Beer fishermen's tripper boats and wheeled pontoon

Food & transport

On the shingle beach there are a number of cafés providing all-day refreshments, including delicious sandwiches made from locally caught crab and a plentiful Beer Beach Breakfast. Deck chairs can be rented by the hour. The beach is EU recognised for safe bathing. A short but steep climb uphill takes you past a small shop selling fish landed on the beach, often including crab, scallops and lobster, and into the centre of the village, where there is a post office and various places to eat.

The grass terrace of the Anchor Inn is a very good place to have a meal while keeping an eye on your craft in the water. Cream teas are a speciality.

Beer & Axmouth Interest

Beer is one of the prettiest villages in East Devon. Many of the buildings are faced with flint, a hard glassy stone found in nearby chalk rock, though there are also the more typical west country cottages of cob and thatch. There is a stream running down to the sea and, in summer, masses of flowers in tubs and hanging baskets. It is situated in a former tree-filled valley and the name Beer is a corruption of the Old English word *bearu*, meaning small wood. Many people visit Beer with the intention of walking, as the dramatic

The Anchor Inn terrace

Axmouth, Seaton and Beer

🚌 Buses from Seaton to Axminster and Lyme Regis - Harbour Road, Harepath Road

🚋 Seaton Tramway to Colyton; nearest main station at Axminster

🏪 Co-operative, Seaton: between Fore Street and Harbour Road

🍴 Beer: several pubs/restaurants in Fore St

🍴 Seaton: Harbour Rd, Fore St

🍴 Axmouth: historic pubs

ℹ Seaton Tourist Information Centre, The Underfleet, Seaton, Devon EX12 2TB
☎ 01297 21660

⚓ Seaton Chandlery: roadside opposite harbour car park ☎ 01297 24774

✚ Seaton & District Community Hospital, Valley View Rd, Seaton, Devon EX12 2UU
☎ 01297 23901

Sir Walter Raleigh

Walter Raleigh was born around 1552 in East Budleigh, 2 miles inland from Budleigh Salterton. His family were persecuted for their protestant beliefs during the reign of catholic Mary I but he developed a strong relationship with her successor, Elizabeth I and, along with Francis Drake, played a colourful role in Elizabeth's tussles with Spain over land and treasure. His early years were spent in Ireland suppressing rebellions against the Crown, for which he was rewarded with 40,000 acres of land, though much of this fortune was subsequently lost. A favourite at court, he was knighted in 1585 and appointed Warden of the Stannaries (see 'The mining industry' on page 174). Raleigh made 3 attempts to establish a colony in Virginia, North America, but was unsuccessful, partly due to a lack of finance and partly due to neglect when he chose to rob Spanish merchant vessels of their treasure in preference to replenishing supplies. North Carolina was part of Virginia at the time and its capital, Raleigh, is named in his honour.

In 1594 Raleigh set sail for Manoa, the legendary Spanish city of gold. His book *The Discovery of Guiana* gives an exaggerated account and is

thought to have contributed to the legend of El Dorado. In 1596 he took part in the attack on Cádiz but a period ashore then saw him elected to Parliament and speaking on naval matters. In 1597 he represented Devon and Dorset and by 1601 he was also the MP for Cornwall!

At court Raleigh fell in and out of favour. He was first imprisoned for secretly marrying Bess Throckmorton, a Lady in Waiting to the Queen, and then again when sentenced to death for treason against James I. Eventually pardoned, he again set off in search of El Dorado but in the process attacked the Spanish outpost of Santo Tomé de Guayana. This led to an outraged Spanish ambassador demanding that the former sentence be reinstated and he was beheaded in 1618. Raleigh was one of the people to popularise tobacco smoking and a small tobacco box was found in his cell with the inscription *Comes meus fuit illo miserrimo tempo* (It was my companion at that most miserable time).

headlands either side of the village provide some of the most spectacular scenery in the whole of the 613M South West Coast Path. The town itself came to prominence in Roman times when the 2nd Augusta Legion settled where Exeter now is. Looking around for building materials they found a seam of fine limestone in Beer's massive chalk cliffs and established a quarry, which was worked continuously until the 1920s. Today it is open to the public, with tours lasting about an hour. Beer Stone Caves are a short, one-mile, walk from the village. Buildings that have used Beer stone in their construction, or ornament, include Westminster Abbey, the Tower of London, Windsor Castle, Hampton Court, Buckingham Palace and Exeter Cathedral.

The notorious smuggler Jack Rattenbury was a native of Beer. His book *Memoirs of a Smuggler* (1837) has been reprinted and is an excellent read.

Axmouth, a mile inland, was the most important harbour in the west of England from the Iron Age to the Middle Ages. Phoenician traders are known to have visited and in Roman times large cargo ships would carry goods to and from the Fosse Way, a first-century road that ran between Exeter and Lincoln via Axmouth. However, in the 14th century heavy storms caused part of Haven Cliff to collapse, partially blocking the estuary and leading to the development of a shingle bank. This in turn trapped silt coming downstream, which led to the establishment of salt marshes. John Leland described how, in the 17th century, 'Men of Seton' tried to divert the course of the river to re-establish their harbour but they soon admitted defeat and, instead, built a bank beside the marshes to reclaim land for pasture. The bank was later used for a branch railway. Today it is used by the Seaton Tramway (① 01297 20375), providing visitors with a delightful three-mile journey along the

Axe estuary to Colyton. Axmouth has an interesting Norman church containing Roman remains and some medieval frescos. There is a festival in the town, with illuminated floats, over August Bank Holiday. From the beach there is a delightful seven-mile walk along the coast to Lyme Regis through land known as The Undercliff (see 'The Jurassic Coast' on page 42). If you enjoy birdwatching then the Seaton Marshes Nature Reserve is a must. Today Axmouth harbour is small and dries. It is used primarily by small pleasure craft and fishing boats.

To the west of Beer is Branscombe. The cargo ship *Napoli* was run aground here in 2007 when damage to her hull put her in danger of breaking up mid-channel. Although there were alarming headlines an environmental disaster was averted. Engine and fuel oil was pumped off in an orderly fashion and few containers lost overboard. Debris and containers washed ashore led to some disgraceful looting, but most of the cargo remained submerged until salvaged along with the hull. Luckily there is no evidence now that it ever happened.

Seaton Tramway: travel in style

The Jurassic Coast

The fringe of land from clifftop to low-water mark that stretches from Orcombe Point, near Exmouth, to Old Harry Rocks, near Swanage, was designated a World Heritage Site in 2001. Looking ashore at the colour and strata of the cliffs provides a 'walk through time' spanning 180 million years of geological history.

Rocks seen in the headlands and sea stacks between Exmouth and Sidmouth were formed in the Triassic period 250-200 million years ago. The climate was similar to the Namib desert today and the land part of a super-continent called Pangaea. The rock is red because deserts contain little organic material and in its absence iron forms red oxides. In this period the first dinosaurs evolved, as did most of our four-legged animals, including frogs, turtles and crocodiles. Few fossils from that time exist but the remains of 10 species of reptile, amphibian and fish were found here.

The cliff face just beyond Sidmouth reveals what geologists call the 'Great Unconformity'. This refers to a clear division between rocks of differing periods. Here red rock from the Jurassic period is capped by yellow upper greensand and chalk formed 160 million years later.

Further east at Beer a quirk of geology has preserved white chalk cliffs formed when millions of microscopic algae died in the shallow sub-tropical seas and swamps of the Cretaceous period, 140-65 million years ago. Beer Quarry Caves a mile beyond the village provide an opportunity to go 200ft underground in an informative tour lasting about an hour. Stone was mined here from Roman times to the 1920s. Classed as 'freestone', because it could be cut or sawn in any direction, it was especially popular for the carving of statues and used in numerous public buildings including Westminster Abbey, the Tower of London and Windsor Castle. Many of the figures adorning the West front of Exeter Cathedral are carved in Beer Stone.

Geoneedle at the start of the Jurassic Coast Orcombe Point, Exmouth

The shoreline from Axmouth to Lyme Regis is known as The Undercliff and in 1959 it became one of Britain's first nature reserves, now managed by English Nature. The reserve was formed entirely from landslides, the most famous being on Christmas Eve 1839. Technically what happened was a blockslide involving a huge piece of land moving towards the sea and creating a small, natural harbour. Questions were raised in Parliament about it becoming a port for the Navy and its fame spread. Day trips were arranged by paddle steamer and prints and engravings made available. It was even the subject of a musical composition, the Landslide Quadrille. More landslides followed, however, and it disappeared as quickly as it was created. Today the South West Coast Path takes you on a 7-mile walk through internationally important habitat of open ground, woodland and dense scrub.

The cliffs either side of Lyme Regis come mostly from the Jurassic period, 200-140 million years ago. This is the best known of the geological periods represented along this stretch of coast and gives the site its name. In the Jurassic period sea levels rose and fell in a series of cycles but eventually the sea became shallower, creating an environment of islands rather like the Caribbean today. As forests grew, tropical swamp life flourished, making Lyme Regis an exceptionally good place for finding fossils. Local woman Mary Anning (1799-1847) is credited with many significant finds including the first ichthyosaur in 1814, the first complete plesiosaur in 1824 and the first flying reptile, a dimorphodon, in 1828. Her story is told in the town's Philpot Museum, where we also learn that fashionable Victorian ladies wore earrings of polished dinosaur droppings without knowing whence they came. Today expert-led fossil hunting expeditions start at the museum and amateur finds remain important. From 2002-7 an almost complete eight-foot skull of a plesiosaur was pieced together from 28 bones found mainly on the beach by local collectors. Monmouth Beach east of the Cobb has huge ammonites embedded in rocks that are exposed at low tide. Ammonites, dinosaurs and many marine reptiles became extinct at the end of the Cretaceous period, 65 million years ago.

Excellent guided fossil hunts take place along the shoreline in Lyme Regis; details from the Tourist Information Centre. *The Official Guide to the Jurassic Coast* is very informative and is sold throughout the West Country.

River Exe

The entrance to the River Exe is always a challenge as there are frequently changing sand banks and a tidal flow of up to 5 knots in front of Exmouth harbour. It should not be attempted in strong southeasterly conditions, particular on the ebb.

'Getting there' as opposed to 'being there' may well motivate many visitors who head upstream, but the pontoons at Turf Lock and the quay at Topsham are great destinations for those with a sense of adventure. Boats without height restrictions can reach as far as Exeter through the Canal.

Approach & entrance

The entrance to the Exe has a bar and a channel that changes regularly. Depth over the bar can be as low as 0.5m. One strategy is to approach on the flood, another at a time when the strength of tide at the entrance is minimal. An approach from HW-2 gives the comfort of a rising tide and a better view of the dangers but after Checkstone Ledge (No.10) the tide is likely to be very strong. More water means that the dangers are less obvious but there is less tide to worry about as long as the buoyage can be trusted. The authors' choice of HW-1 at the entrance seems to be a good compromise.

The main dangers near the channel (apart from running aground in the sand) are Maer Rocks, Conger Rocks and Checkstone Ledge.

Remember the buoys may not be where they are marked on your chart. These general guidelines apply:

- DO NOT approach in strong onshore winds, particularly against the ebb.

- Plan the approach on the basis of 0.5m charted depth. Keep a good watch on DEPTH at all times.

- Aim for the Exe safe water mark Mo(A)10s. This is a good location from which to get an initial view of the approach and spot the first buoys of the channel, which in 2010 formed a straight corridor.

- Follow the buoys up to R8 Q.R.

- From R8 Q.R the entrance transit 305° (lit Iso.2s+Q) may be followed, between steep-to Pole Sand and the shore. The sea wall post (front) and customs house post (back) are very difficult to spot during the day.

- The tide picks up strength from R8 Q.R and can be up to 5 knots. In front of Exmouth Quay there is often a lot of turbulence as the ebb gets around the corner from The Bight.

Navigation in the River Exe

At the right state of tide it is possible to reach Topsham, after which it dries. Beware: the tide flows fast on the ebb.

The channel is marked by buoys which tend to be more numerous in green than red. As always in a river it is best to keep to the outside of bends, where the water gouges a deeper channel. Do not be tempted to cut corners unless you fancy a few hours wedged in the mud. In the early part of the channel there are plenty of boats on moorings to help identify deep water.

- From R12 unlit before Exmouth Harbour entrance turn sharply southwest. You need to be determined, as this is at right angles to the tide that flows in a northwesterly direction.

River Exe entrance, Starcross and Lympstone in the distance

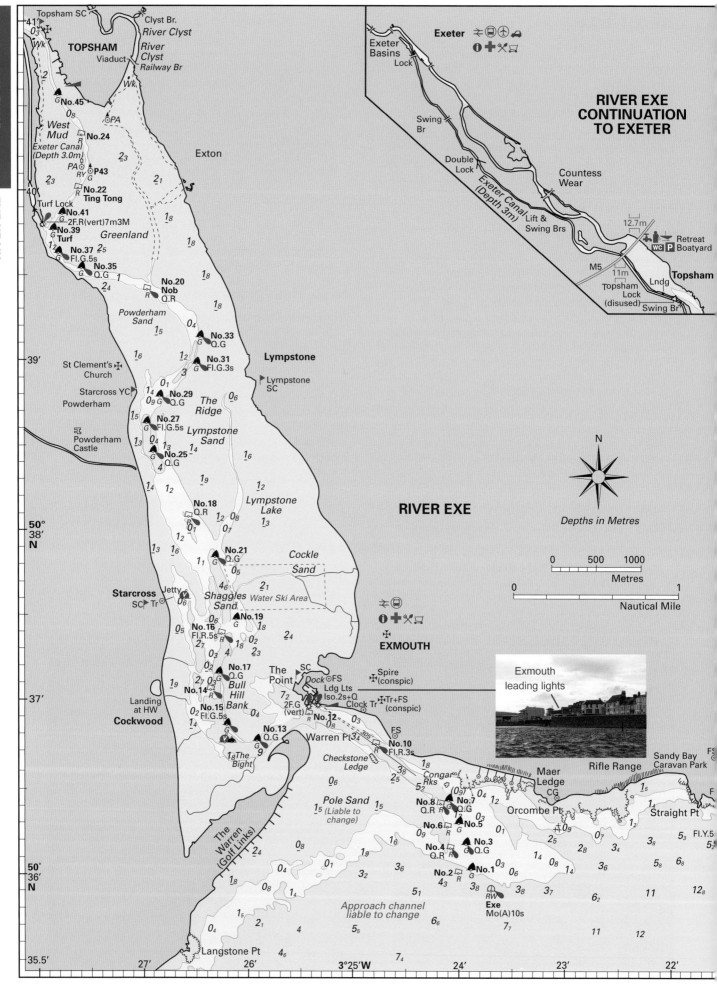

Topsham SC
Clyst Br.
River Clyst
TOPSHAM
Viaduct
River Clyst Railway Br

41'
O3
Wk
Wk
No.45
G
O8
West Mud
No.24
Exeter Canal (Depth 3.0m)
PA
RY G P43
40'
No.22
Ting Tong
Turf Lock
No.41
G 2.F.R(vert)7m3M
No.39
Turf
Greenland
No.37
No.35
G Fl.G.5s
G Q.G
No.20
Nob Q.R
R
Powderham Sand
No.33
G Q.G
No.31
Fl.G.3s
Lympstone
Lympstone SC

Exton

RIVER EXE CONTINUATION TO EXETER

Exeter
Exeter Basins Lock
Swing Br
Double Lock
Exeter Canal (Depth 3m)
Lift & Swing Brs
Countess Wear
12.7m
Retreat Boatyard
WC P
M5
11m
Topsham Lock (disused)
Topsham
Lndg
Swing Br

St Clement's Church
Starcross YC
Powderham
No.29
G Q.G
The Ridge
No.27
G Fl.G.5s
Lympstone Sand
No.25
G Q.G
Powderham Castle
No.18
Q.R
R
Lympstone Lake

N
Depths in Metres

0   500   1000
Metres
0   1
Nautical Mile

RIVER EXE

No.21
G Q.G
Cockle Sand
Water Ski Area
Starcross
SC Tr
Jetty V
Shaggles Sand
No.19
No.16
Fl.R.5s
R
No.17
Q.G
Bull Hill Bank
No.14
R
No.15
Fl.G.5s
G
Cockwood
No.13
V
Q.G
G 9
The Bight

EXMOUTH

Exmouth leading lights

The Point
SC
Dock FS
Ldg Lts
Iso.2s+Q
Clock Tr
2.F.G (vert)
R
No.12
Warren Pt
FS
No.10
R Fl.R.3s
Spire (conspic)
Tr+FS (conspic)

Checkstone Ledge
Congar Rks
Maer Ledge CG
Rifle Range
Sandy Bay Caravan Park
FS

No.8
Q.R R
No.7
G Q.G
Orcombe Pt
Straight Pt
Pole Sand (Liable to change)
No.6
R
No.5
G
No.4
Q.R R
No.3
G Q.G
No.2
R
No.1
G
Fl.Y.5
RW
Exe Mo(A)10s

The Warren (Golf Links)
Approach channel liable to change

Langstone Pt

50° 40' N
39'
50° 38' N
37'
50° 36' N
35.5'
27'   26'   3°25'W   24'   23'   22'

- After about 150m you should be in the flow that bends round to the north, The Bight. Follow the course marked to starboard by G13 Q.G and G15 Fl.G.5s, sailing between lines of boats on moorings. Yellow visitors' buoys are set in The Bight.

- After R14 (unlit) and G17 Q.G there are two choices. West of Starcross Sand you can find a mooring or anchor opposite Starcross (Starcross Brunel Tower conspicuous). To the east you continue up the river, heading for R16 Fl.R5s (Shaggles Sand) and G19 unlit, where there is an anchorage.

- Continue past the yellow buoys marking a Water Ski Area to port, then G21 Q.G and R18 Q.R, leaving boats on moorings to port. From here you should be able to see St Clement's Church on the western shore and Powderham Castle on the hill beyond it. Between G21 Q.G and G.25 Q.G is the first shallow patch you will cross (min depth 0.2m).

- Continue round G25 Q.G, G27 Fl.G.5s and G29 Q.G. The tide can be strong around this bend in the river. Starcross Yacht Club appears to port as you turn, past the church and opposite G29 G.Q. Across the water you will see Lympstone, a number of boats on drying moorings, a church and a small drying harbour.

- Turn further towards G31 Fl.G.3s and G33 Q.G keeping close to them on the starboard side of the channel. Cutting the corner here will ground you in Powderham Sand. Between G31 Fl.G.3s and R20 Q.R is the second shallow patch you will cross.

- After R20 Q.R you will begin to discern Turf Lock about 1M up river. To get there continue past G35 Q.G and G37 Fl.G.5s.

- Depth in the area south of Turf Lock is 0.9m and there is one visitors' buoy.

- Exeter Canal is deep (3m) but there is a height restriction of 11m at the motorway bridge. If you can get through, the swing bridge at Countess Wear opens to give a clear run to Exeter. If you intend to enter the canal you need to co-ordinate with the Exeter Canal Harbour Office for timings.

- From Turf Lock the channel is narrow and steep, outlined by buoys and markers of various shapes: G39 unlit, G41 unlit, R22 unlit, green post 43, R24 unlit and finally G45 unlit at Topsham. The channel is shallow with depths down to 0.1m.

- After Topsham the river dries.

Berthing & facilities

Options include visitiors' buoys, anchorages and a limited set of pontoons. Most buoys are administered by the Powderham Estate. There are pontoons at Exmouth Marina (small vessels), Turf Lock (3m) and Topsham (1m), and buoys at Starcross and various other places.

The quay at Topsham can be used; it dries with very soft mud. Space at the northern end is used by the pleasure trip boats and must be left clear during the day. The mud at the wall gently rises towards the

southern end, making that section unreachable by vessels over 1.5m in draught except during spring tides.

🕐 Exmouth Dock

The old dock was turned into a marina and residential complex in the early 1990s. All the pontoons are privately owned but it may be possible to find a berth if one of the owners is away. There is a minimum depth of 2m. Contact the dockmaster for berthing and/or opening the entrance bridge, on VHF 14 or ☎ 01395 269314.

The entrance to the marina is a relatively narrow channel, with a waiting pontoon to starboard. There is a convenient fuel pump at the pontoon.

The current in front of the entrance channel is very strong. DO NOT attempt except in slack tide.

There is a buoy marked ECC Visitors in the pool north of the entrance, among numerous local boat moorings. This buoy can be used temporarily while waiting to enter Exmouth Dock.

⚓ The Bight

Several yellow visitors' buoys marked 'visitors' are set among other moorings in The Bight. They are administered by the Exeter River Harbour Authority (VHF12).

Exmouth Dock harbour

Exmouth entrance: pontoon and fuel to starboard

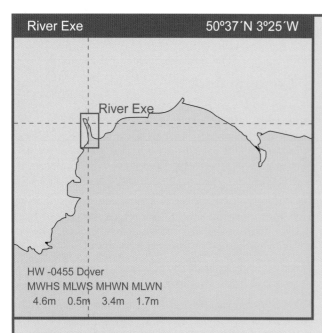

River Exe   50°37′N 3°25′W

River Exe

HW -0455 Dover

MWHS	MLWS	MHWN	MLWN
4.6m	0.5m	3.4m	1.7m

River entrance

- Approach: shallow, beware Pole Sands and Conger and Maer rock dangers; best HW-1
- DO NOT attempt in strong onshore winds against the ebb

Exmouth Dock

- Narrow entrance, only in slack water; bridge
- Visitors if berth empty
- Dockmaster VHF14 ☏ 01395 269314
- 2m minimum depth
- Fuel in the entrance channel pontoon
- Various services in the dock
- Exmouth water taxi in season VHF 37

The Bight

- Mooring buoys (yellow marked Visitors)
- Exeter River Harbour Authority VHF12

Starcross

- Mooring buoys, arrange through Starcross Garage ☏ 01626 890225/07855 450269 or Star Cross Fishing and Cruising Club ☏ 01626 891996
- Starcross Garage in jerry cans
- Showers at club

Starcross Yacht Club (Powderham)

- Showers
- ☏ 01626 890470 during race days
- http://www.starcrossyc.org.uk/

Turf Lock (Exeter Canal)

- Pontoons at the lock, canal 3m depth
- One visitors' buoy in river 0.9m
- Entrance at HW (0700-1600): arrange ahead
- Exeter Canal Office ☏ 01392 274306

Topsham

- Quay wall berths in very soft mud
- 4 visitors' moorings in hammerhead pontoons 1m MLWS/2m MLWN: firm shingle south end Trout's Boatyard ☏ 01392 873044
- Showers and toilets
- Fuel from Retreat Boatyard at HW
- Various services in the boatyard

The Atmospheric Railway

In 1843 Isambard Kingdom Brunel was appointed chief engineer to the South Devon Railway Company and became responsible for extending the line from Exeter St David's to Plymouth and beyond. Having been impressed with 'atmospheric propulsion' that he had seen in Dublin and Croydon Brunel persuaded shareholders to adopt a system whereby the carriages would be pushed along by air compressed in a series of pumping stations along the route. Brunel thought this method would be more environmentally friendly and result in a quieter, smoother journey than by conventional steam engine. He thought it would be better able to cope with the steep gradients beyond Newton Abbot and that it would be cheaper both to build and to run.

Despite being good in theory, there were numerous practical problems right from the start and locals were soon referring to the project as the 'atmospheric caper'. Leather flaps used to seal the air pipes were kept supple with tallow which made them irresistible to rats, the pumping engines were designed for pipes that were thirteen inch, not fifteen as installed on the rails, and freezing winter weather caused valves to seize up and pipes to crack. Eight pumping stations, about three miles apart, worked to a timetable but there was no way of communicating delays so coal was wasted maintaining pressure. Leakage meant that three times more power was required than predicted and it soon became evident that the 'air-powered vacuum service' was more expensive to run than conventional locomotives and less reliable. There were even occasions when third-class passengers were made to get out and push! Soon the world's longest atmospheric railway was abandoned, having run from just February until September 1848.

The only physical reminder left is the pumping station at Starcross, a striking landmark built in the Italianate style that was popular at the time. It is now used by the Starcross Fishing Club.

Buoys and anchorage at the entrance to the River Exe

⚓ G19 buoy

On the right of Starcross Sand, south of and around G19 buoy, there is an anchorage in 2m. Holding is good in sand. This is a convenient place, near to Exmouth, though uncomfortable in strong winds against the ebb.

ⓥ Starcross

Between Starcross Sands and Starcross, having taken the left hand lane from G15 there is a whole line of moorings before the ferry jetty. To arrange a mooring call Starcross garage (☎ 01626 890225 or mobile ☎07855 450269) or the Starcross Fishing and Cruising Club (☎ 01626 891996). The garage can provide fuel in jerry cans.

At Starcross it is no longer possible to land on the Ferry Jetty, convenient though it was. The company will welcome you for journeys to and from Exmouth on their ferry, but it locks access to the pontoon to stop people fishing from there. To land with a dinghy aim for an underpass below the railway line.

Immediately south of the ferry jetty the underpass leads to the sailing club/train station car park. The Starcross Fishing and Cruising Club conveniently maintain a layer of pebbles on top of the mud alongside the pier. A short distance further south another underpass below the railway line takes you into the drying Cockwood (pronounced 'Cockood') harbour, where two pubs will reward your endeavour.

Lympstone

There is an unmarked channel (dries) towards Lympstone, the beginning of which may work as an anchorage in 0.5m mud. There is a very small drying harbour and a number of drying moorings outside, all mud. Lympstone is a very pretty village with two good pubs, but be sure of your timings: dragging a dinghy a long way through mud is no fun at all.

ⓥ Starcross Yacht Club (Powderham)

Starcross Yatch Club has a stunning setting with St Clement's Church and Powderham castle behind. You can dry out in front of the club among the buoys at Powderham Sands. The club is very active and one of the oldest in Britain. They have showers available and on race days can be contacted on ☎ 01626 890470.

Starcross Yacht Club behind G27 buoy

ⓥ Turf Lock (Exeter Canal)

Turf Lock is the entrance to Exeter Canal, a 3m deep channel which runs all the way to Exeter through what is now a natural conservation area. Unfortunately it is not possible to reach Exeter Quay unless you can clear the 11m height restriction under the M5 motorway.

ⓥ Outside the lock there is one yellow visitors' buoy in 0.9m. You can check if it is empty by phoning Turf Ferry (☎ 07778 370582), which provides a service between the lock and Topsham. The buoy is administered by the Exeter Canal Office (☎ 01392 274306), with whom you should arrange entry and exit through the lock. The lock is operated only when high water falls within working hours, 0700-1600. The canal staff will go out of their way to make entrance and exit easy and pleasurable.

Starcross Brunel tower, private jetty and landing, with underpass to car park

- The canal lock opens near high water. Exeter Council staff come to operate the lock, but only if a vessel is scheduled for entry/exit.

- Communication is by hand signals, but its opening is obvious - keep an eye on the lock door. If in doubt call the office who can alert their staff.

- Slightly deeper water is towards the steps/bank on the river side. Towards the lock door you should be aiming to align with the lock direction, at around 20° from the initial line of approach. Turn gently towards starboard on entrance. You may touch the mud, most likely continuing to plough through. Giving yourself some margin by arriving on a rising tide is always helpful.

Inside the lock there is a wide area for turning and pontoons, also managed by Exeter Canal Authority, which can accommodate about 10 boats. There is space at Topsham Lock (disused), where turning is possible, and the Exeter Canal Basin. Check with the office or staff before venturing up.

Turf Lock Hotel is a good place for a drink or a meal and is very popular with walkers and cyclists. In the summer there are barbecues in the garden, which is huge. The trip from Turf Lock to Exeter Basin in a dinghy takes you through some wonderful countryside and is a great adventure, albeit 5M so be sure of fuel.

Entering the Exeter Canal at Turf Lock

Why it's worth the effort

The reason Turf Lock only opens at HW

Turf Lock, Exeter Canal and Topsham

⚓ Topsham

Topsham is the last practical navigable destination in the River Exe, which dries above this point. The Quay has a good wall to berth against, your boat sinking into the mud as it dries. As there is not always room available check ahead with Turf Ferry or Trout's Boatyard, who will be happy to advise. The northern side of the quay is used by the pleasure trip boats and must be left clear during the day. The mud at the wall gently rises towards the southern end, making that section unreachable by vessels over 1.5m in draught except during spring tides.

The outer side of pontoons owned by Trout's Boatyard (☎ 01392 873044) is available for visitors, in 1m MLWS/2m MWLN. The Retreat Boatyard (☎ 01392 874720) has fuel (diesel alongside at HW) and gas. Trout's Boatyard has showers and toilets.

- 🚌 Bus station: Royal Avenue EX8 1EN
  ☎ 01395 272395
  Frequent service to Topsham and Exeter
  (including Exeter Airport and Train
  Station)

- ⇄ Branch line to Lympstone, Topsham and
  Exeter and from Exeter onto Starcross,
  Dawlish Warren and Teignmouth

- 🚗 Practical Car Hire, 4 Bakery Mews,
  Withycombe Village Road,
  Exmouth EX8 3AT ☎ 01392 25403

  Exeter: all main companies

- 🛒 Co-operative (☎ 01395 27895) and
  Somerfield, Magnolia Walk, Exmouth
  EX8 1HB (near the dock)

  Tesco Superstore, Salterton Rd,
  Exmouth EX8 2NP ☎ 0845 6779265

  Co-operative, 15 Fore St, Topsham EX3
  0HF ☎ 01392 873048

  Londis Stores, The Strand, Starcross
  EX6 8PR ☎ 01626 890237

- 🍴 Restaurants, pubs and cafés Exmouth Town
  Centre and Topsham

  Pubs at Turf Lock and Double Lock (Exeter
  Canal) and Cockwood

- ℹ Tourist Information Centre, Alexandra Terrace,
  Exmouth EX8 1BD ☎ 01395 222299

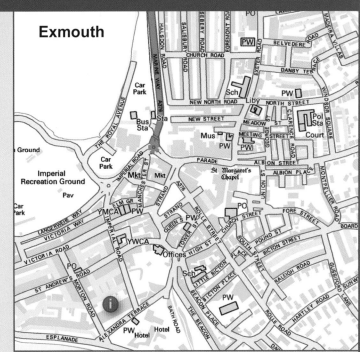

Exmouth

- ⚓ Peter Dixon Chandlery, Pilot Wharf, Victoria
  Road, Exmouth EX8 1XA ☎ 01395 273248

- ✚ Exmouth Hospital, Claremont Grove, Exmouth
  EX8 2JN ☎ 01395 279684

  Exeter: several major hospitals

Food & transport

Exmouth is a large town in walking distance of the harbour. Topsham is much smaller but has the basics along with a branch of County Cheeses, an especially good cheese shop in Ticklemore Street. Starcross has just one convenience store.

Noteworthy places to eat include The Abode, Michael Cane's restaurant situated by the Cathedral in Exeter (reservations required, ☎ 01392 223638) and Les Saveurs (☎ 01395 269459), a new fish restaurant in Exmouth. In Topsham there are a number of excellent wine bars and bistros including *La Petite Maison*, an

Alongside Topsham quay, at high and low water

Anglo-French restaurant housed in an historic curved and bow-windowed building. Many pubs also serve good food. Bridge Inn, Topsham, is full of character and has a good selection of local ales. The Anchor Inn at Cockwood serves mussels from the River Exe cooked in 27 different ways, including curried and in a Caribbean broth with pineapple and Malibu! At Turf Lock and Double Lock, along the Exeter canal, there is a popular pub that serves food.

Transport is abundant, with buses and an excellent branch line train service. There are small ferries between Topsham and Turf Lock and between Turf Lock and Exeter Quay.

Interest

There is no shortage of things to do and places to visit on both sides of the River Exe and nearby coast. A geoneedle on Orcombe Point cliffs, Exmouth, marks the start of the World Heritage Jurassic Coast (see 'The Jurassic Coast' on page 42) and here you can join the South West Coast Path. Exmouth has seen a lot of recent development around the quay. Inland is a quirky 16-sided house called A la Ronde. Built in the 18th century by two spinster cousins, it houses their collections from a grand tour of Europe and has an impressive gallery of shells. Now managed by the National Trust, it is open to visitors between April and October.

Further East is Budleigh Salterton, an old-fashioned seaside town with promenade and sea huts. A splendid walk takes you from the eastern end of the beach along the River Otter to Otterton, 1.5M away. Otterton is a quintessential Devon village with longhouses of cob and thatch and a stream trickling through. The Mill (℡ 01395 568521) is now an arts and crafts centre with a good café-restaurant. On designated days it is possible to watch wholemeal flour being stone-ground in the traditional way using water power from the River Otter.

Topsham is a delightful destination. There are good places to eat, nice boutiques and a huge antique centre for the shoppers on board, and no less than ten pubs. Although these days visited by just a small number of pleasure craft, it was once one of the busiest ports in England. From here coal was imported from Wales and woollen cloth exported to Holland, the bell-shaped gabled ends of houses by the quay revealing a Dutch influence. For over five hundred years Topsham was also important for shipbuilding and two families, the Holmans and the Davys, dominated. John Holman owned a fleet of ships and became a pioneer of maritime insurance. His daughter Dorothy (1888-1983) established the Topsham museum, which is a delight. Local maritime history is told in a spacious sail loft while other rooms display her furniture and artefacts in a typical 17th-century merchant's house. Her diaries make an amusing read. Attracted to a shop assistant when taking some furs to be altered, she writes 'I hope he isn't vulgar, as you would expect a shop assistant to be. I should hate to have a feeling for anyone vulgar'. Dorothy's brother Leigh

There are still salmon, bass, mullet, flatfish, eel and whitebait in the River Exe, although no longer in any great numbers. The largest salmon caught in the estuary was 61lb 4oz according to the records in Topsham Museum. Enterprising fishermen still set out long nets across the river channels near Turf Lock and Topsham during the summer months hoping for a valuable catch.

The one that got away

was married to Vivien Leigh for a short period and, although she never lived in Topsham, the museum has a room dedicated to her and displays the nightdress she wore in *Gone with the Wind*. The museum is run entirely by volunteers and it is their delicious cakes that are served in the garden.

A day trip to Exeter is recommended (see 'Exeter' on page 52) though it has not been possible to sail to Exeter along the River Exe for hundreds of years. The Countess of Devon, Isabella de Fortibus, built a weir across part of the river in the 13th century to power the mills on her estate. Although the tide reached the city until 1312, navigation was completely ruined by Hugh de Courtenay, Earl of Devon. Being 'offended and incensed by the city' and with 'wrathful humour (that) could not be pacified' he set about his 'mischievous purpose' of building weirs and blocking the river with timber and gravel. Having built a quay at Topsham, four miles from Exeter, he then became the recipient of tolls for all shipping to and fro, though he was eventually executed for treason. Powderham Castle, his family home near Starcross, is open to the public.

Exeter city traders wanting to restore access to the sea built a canal parallel to the Exe in 1563. The first stretch (1.75M, 16ft wide, 3ft deep) constructed by John Trew was navigable for vessels up to 16 tons. By 1677 more of the river had silted up so it was extended to Topsham and in 1701 deepened to permit ocean-going ships. A further extension built in 1827

reached Turf Lock and was large enough for vessels of 400 tons. The canal's importance declined with the wool industry and the rise of the railway. Esso and the Water Board continued to use it for many years but commercial operations ceased altogether in 1997. Passing through pristine natural landscape, the canal and towpath are now popular for walking, cycling and canoeing. There are ferries between Topsham and Turf Lock, Turf Lock and Double Lock, and Double Lock and Exeter Quay. Turf Lock and Double Lock both have popular pubs that serve food.

The train journey from Exeter to Newton Abbot via Dawlish and Teignmouth is spectacular and well worth taking if you have time to spare. Initially running along the western side of the Exe estuary, the track continues along the coast within a few feet of the sea. In stormy weather onshore winds blow spray over the carriages and there are times when the line becomes dangerous and is suspended for a day or so, which always leads to calls for a more reliable inland route. This controversial line owes its existence to Isambard Kingdom Brunel (see 'The Atmospheric Railway' on page 46).

The five-hundred acre Warren Nature Reserve, which includes the estuary of the River Exe, is a Site of Special Scientific Interest. It attracts some unusual sea and wading birds in their thousands. Dawlish Warren has an excellent beach for swimming and a challenging 18-hole golf course.

Exeter

Devon's county town Exeter makes for an enjoyable day ashore. Although the city was heavily bombed during the second world war, much of its medieval heritage remains. There are also plenty of shopping opportunities.

Top of the list of sights is the cathedral, begun in Norman times but most revered for its decorated Gothic architecture. Innovations such as pointed arches, ribbed vaulting and flying buttresses take the strain of supporting the building, leaving a graceful, spacious interior lit by enormous tracery windows. At 350ft the cathedral has the longest unbroken stretch of Gothic vaulting anywhere in the world. To prevent neck strain, mirrored trolleys reflect the decorated bosses which include depictions of the murder of Thomas Becket and the soul's struggle with 'the flyshe, the world and the devil'. Be sure not to miss the Minstrels Gallery which is superb. Built about 1360, it shows twelve angels 'playing on instruments of musick', including the clarion, cittern, bagpipe, rebec, sackbut, syrinx, regals, psaltery, shawm, gittern, timbrel and cymbals.

The astronomical clock built in 1484 predates Copernicus's discovery that the earth is not the centre of the universe and both the sun and moon are shown orbiting the earth. At 23 metres high the Bishop's throne is the largest piece of ecclesiastical furniture in Britain. The East window contains some superb medieval stained glass and the misericords, dating from 1260 and possibly the oldest in the country, show a crocodile swallowing its prey and a very early depiction of an elephant. The cathedral's refectory provides good food in a wonderful setting.

Free walking tours of the city depart from outside the Abode restaurant next to the cathedral. They last 90 minutes and no booking is required (Red Coat Guided Tours ☎ 01392 265203). With time and money to spare, lunch at the Michelin-starred Abode would be memorable.

Exeter's underground passages are well worth a visit as long as you don't suffer from claustrophobia. Dating from the 14th century, they were built to maintain the pipes that brought fresh drinking water into the city from nearby springs. They have been recently renovated so the visit is rather sanitised (hard hats but no rats) though fascinating as animated guides give a thirty-minute history of the city which includes information about the Civil War and the outbreak of cholera.

Exeter's 14th-century Guildhall should not be missed. It is said to be England's oldest municipal building still in regular use. Open to the public most days, it has an impressive Renaissance portico, panelled chamber and collar-and-brace timber roof. Nearby Magdalen Road is full of specialist food shops and boutiques.

The historic quayside is now a place for recreation amidst restored industrial architecture including warehouses dating from 1835. Bikes and canoes can be rented and there are pubs and cafés for alfresco dining. The Quay House Visitor Centre has a free audio visual display of the city's history. Nearby is the customs house, which was built in 1681 (free summer 30-minute, guided tours on Sundays). The Royal Albert Memorial Museum, housed in a wonderful Victorian building, is currently closed for renovation.

Exeter

◉ Bus station: Paris Street

X53 Jurassic Coast Bus (Exeter-Seaton-Beer-Bridport-Lyme Regis and beyond)

⇌ Train station: Exeter St David's, Bonhay Road, Exeter EX4 4NT - main line to Penzance, Bristol and London - branch line to Topsham, Lympstone, Exmouth and to Starcross and Dawlish Warren

🚗 Hertz ☎0870 850 7196, National ☎01392 250 858, Thrifty ☎01392 207 207 at Marsh Barton Trading Estate, Exeter EX2 8QU

✗ Restaurants, pubs and cafés: High St, Queen St, South St and at Exeter Quay

❶ Tourist Information Centre: Paris Street, Exeter EX10 1JJ ☎ 01392 265 700

✚ Royal Devon & Exeter Hospital, Barrack Road, Exeter EX2 5DW ☎01392 411 611

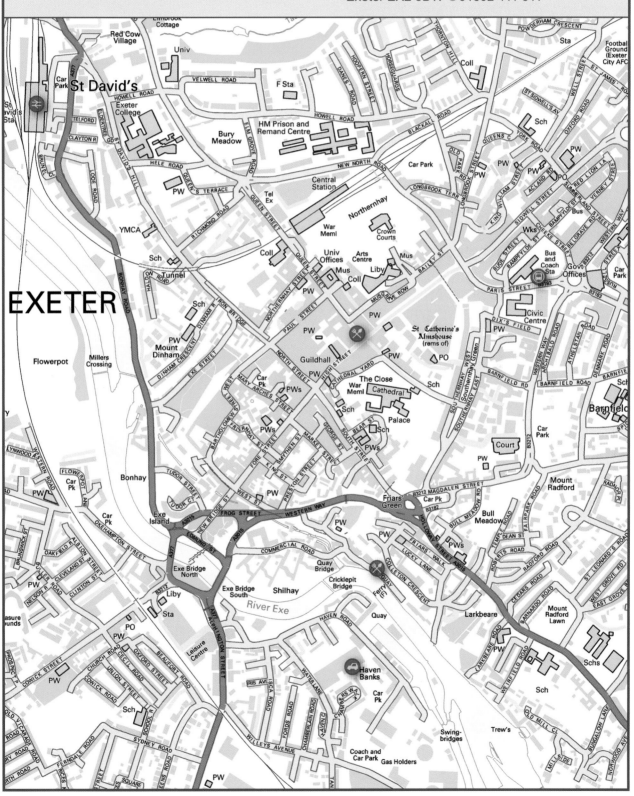

River Teign

The estuary of the River Teign provides shelter between the River Exe and Tor Bay, albeit requiring the sailor to negotiate frequently changing sandbanks at the entrance. Once inside there are visitors' pontoons but travel upstream is limited by a road bridge and shallow water.

Teignmouth to the north is a mixed bag. There is a pier and esplanade and some grand Victorian buildings looking out to sea, but the town also has some industry and a slightly rough side. Shaldon opposite has olde worlde charm and is altogether more genteel.

ⓥ Teignmouth

Approach & entrance

The entrance to the River Teign can be DANGEROUS in heavy weather. The East Pole Sand bar and The Point change frequently, so the wise course of action without abundant local knowledge is to time the entrance for good weather and high water.

There are 2 or 3 marker buoys used for pilotage set in the approach but they are moved frequently and do not necessarily mark the channel.

- Approach keeping a clearance of at least 0.5M from the coast until you are due east of the river entrance. You can use the beach huts at The Point on the northern side and training wall light

Oc.R.6s on the southern side as approximate markers to help place yourself. The beachside houses at Shaldon will appear in between.

- Coming from the south you can use the F.R lights on 334° to ensure you are well away from the Ness rocks; stay to the east of this transit.

- The channel is marked by charted buoys (all lit). An additional set of unlit uncharted red buoys are set between the first charted red Fl.R.2s and the training wall beacon Oc.R.6s. Deeper water in the channel is towards the port side during the approach. Mimimum charted depth in the channel is 0.3m, but the banks on either side dry to between 0.5m and 2m.

- From a position to the east of the first channel buoys you can approach on a 265° course. There is a helpful transit between the training wall beacon and two white strips on the rock behind.

- Near the training wall beacon turn northwest, aiming to stay in the deeper water on the outside bend of the river entrance. Depth increases rapidly in a pool around the turn.

- Past The Point you have buoys Fl.R.2s, Fl.G.2s, Fl.R.2s in sequence marking the deep channel.

Visitors' pontoons are on the right beyond the second Fl.R.2s buoy.

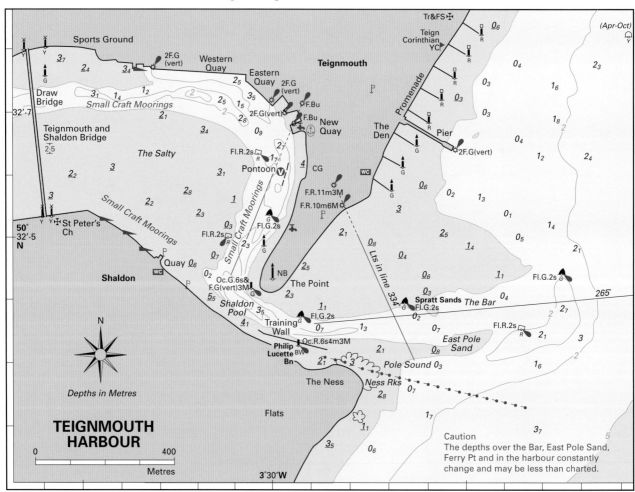

Visitors' pontoons in Teignmouth

The ferry at Shaldon

The River Teign approach

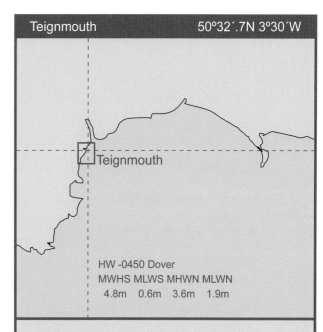

Teignmouth 50°32´.7N 3°30´W

HW -0450 Dover
MWHS MLWS MHWN MLWN
4.8m 0.6m 3.6m 1.9m

Teignmouth

- Approach: shallow, beware East Pole Sand; best HW
- DO NOT attempt in strong onshore winds or any significant swell
- Ⓥ Visitors' berths at harbourmaster pontoons; 2m minimum depth
- Harbourmaster
  ☎ 01626 773165 / 07796 178456 VHF12
  http://www.teignmouthharbour.com/
- Water from a tap on the shore

Teignmouth

🚌 Bus to Exeter and Torquay

🚆 Trains to Dawlish, Starcross, Exeter and Plymouth

🏪 Co-operative, 8 Bank St, Teignmouth TQ14 8AL ☎ 01626 772657

Londis, 11 Fore St, Shaldon TQ14 0DZ ☎ 01626 873426

🍴 Restaurants, pubs and cafés in Teignmouth and Shaldon

ℹ Tourist Information Centre, The Den, Sea Front, Teignmouth TQ14 8BE ☎ 01626 215666

⚓ Chandlers: Brigantine Chandlery & Clothing Store, The Quay, Strand, Shaldon TQ14 0DL ☎ 01626 872400

C2 Marine, La Jolla, Dunmore Drive, Shaldon TQ14 0BJ ☎ 01626 873692

✚ Teignmouth Hospital, Mill Lane, Teignmouth TQ14 9BQ ☎ 01626 772161

Teignmouth

Berthing & facilities

Visitors may use pontoons at Teignmouth, which are administered by the harbourmaster. They are often occupied by local boats and a tidal eddy forms around them. They are not connected to the shore so a dinghy is required for landing on the beach at Teignmouth or Shaldon, which is straightforward.

Food & transport

Teignmouth is a small town with a full range of shops including several supermarkets. The Owl and the Pussycat restaurant (☎ 01626 775321), in pedestrianised Teign Street, sources all its ingredients locally. It serves an excellent brunch and a traditional Sunday lunch.

Some fast cross-country trains stop at Teignmouth and go on to Exeter, London, Truro etc. Buses go to from Teignmouth (Regent Street and Wellington Street) to Exeter, Dawlish, Newton Abbot and Torquay.

Shaldon has a variety of village shops, including a chemist, a convenience store and greengrocers. There are tea shops and a number of pubs that serve food. The Clifford Arms is noted for real ale and for jazz (☎ 01626 872311). The Ferry Boat Inn (☎ 01626 872340) has an upstairs restaurant with gorgeous views of the Teign Estuary. Ode, a delightful restaurant housed in a 3 story Georgian town house, sources its ingredients locally and is recommended (☎ 01626 873977). A ferry between Shaldon and Teignmouth saves a walk across the bridge (☎ 07760 240927).

Interest

Teignmouth became a fashionable seaside resort in the late Georgian and early Victorian period and much of its architecture dates from this time. Old Teignmouth had been preoccupied with salt production, rope walks and fishing before they turned to cater for the leisured classes who arrived on a new form of transport: the locomotive. An esplanade was constructed, nearly two miles long, and when a pier was built in 1860 it was used to segregate male and female bathers. Today the esplanade and pier team with day trippers while the rest of the town gets on with business as usual. The quay is still active, used by large ships to transport clay. In the past granite from Dartmoor was shipped from here to London where it was used to build the British Museum and London Bridge.

The museum in French Street, Teignmouth, is worth a visit. There is information about the Atmospheric Railway (see 'The Atmospheric Railway' on page 54) and about Donald Crowhurst's participation in the 1968 Sunday Times Golden Globe single-handed, non-stop race around the world. Crowhurst entered the race to get publicity for the Navicator, a radio detection finder that he had invented and put into production. The business was failing, he was heavily in debt, and he somehow deluded himself into thinking that he would win the Golden Globe and thereby stave off financial ruin. His boat, the *Teignmouth Electron*, was untested and unprepared and Crowhusrt himself had only the experience of a weekend sailor. Early on he began to radio false position reports, which he might have got away with had the misfortunes of his fellow competitors not meant that he would probably finish first. With humiliation and financial ruin on the horizon he disappeared, having probably committed suicide in the Caribbean. The race was won by Robin Knox-Johnson who donated his winnings to the Crowhurst family.

Other former residents of Teignmouth include John Keats, who in 1818 wrote part of *Endymion* at Keats House, and Charles Babbage, the early 19th-century mathematician and engineer credited with inventing the computer.

Shaldon has olde worlde charm and is one of the most picturesque villages in Devon. On Wednesdays (May to September) some of the villagers dress in Georgian costume in celebration of 1785 Day. There are stalls selling local produce and, after 7pm, a Punch and Judy show. Shaldon Wildlife Park (☎ 01626 872234), set in an acre of woodland garden, is home to several species of endangered animal. This is the place to come if, as the brochure says, you are 'mad about meerkats, in love with lemurs or potty about parrots'. The town hosts a water carnival on the first Saturday of August.

Teignmouth beach

There has been a foot-ferry crossing between Teignmouth and Shaldon since the 13th century. The black and white design on the gunwales of today's ferry emulates the Elizabethan galleon. The ferry has remained unchanged for about three hundred years, except for modernisation in 1909 when the oars were replaced with a motor.

Teignmouth Victorian Pier and beach huts

Sand eels

The fishermen below are catching sand eels just off Teignmouth.

Sand eels are the 'new whitebait'. They are served in many fish restaurants and are easy to prepare on board as follows:

With a sharp knife chop their heads off and draw your finger along the body to remove the innards.

Wash and pat dry, then coat with flour and shallow fry until crispy.

Serve with fresh bread and a squeeze of lemon. Delicious!

Tor Bay

Tor Bay offers shelter from the prevailing southwest and for centuries has served as an anchorage for large ships. Also known as the English Riviera, the bay is a very popular holiday destination. Torquay provides easy access to Living Coasts, a splendid offshoot of Paignton Zoo and from Brixham it is just a short walk to the Berry Head National Nature Reserve. Brixham still has a large fishing fleet and in 2011 a new fishing harbour was opened by Princess Anne.

For the sailor Tor Bay offers shelter in all weathers and at all states of tide. There are two main marinas

and several sheltered anchorages. In southwesterlies the wind funnels through the valleys and particularly across the marina at Brixham, but swell only builds up when the wind blows hard from the east. Shelter is always secure but, as with any sea-exposed harbours, some extra precaution maybe required.

North of Tor Bay, Hope Cove, Anstey's Cove and Babbacombe Bay are delightful anchorages. The cliffs offer protection from the southwest, even in gales.

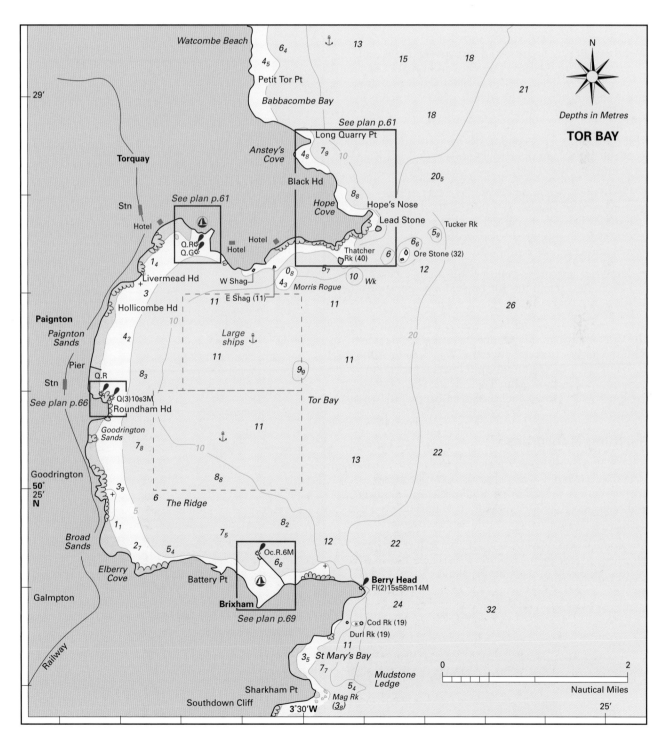

🕐 Torquay

Torquay is an all-weather harbour almost entirely dedicated to leisure craft. In addition to the extensive facilities of the MDL marina, the new pontoons (2008) installed by Tor Bay Council add a significant amount of berthing space, particularly for visitors.

Torquay is the largest town in the English Riviera. It still has Victorian elegance but there are also less endearing modern buildings. There is plenty to do in walking distance of the harbour.

Approach & entrance

The approach to Torquay Harbour is straightforward in all weather, with care needed only in a southeasterly gale. The harbour is well lit.

From the north:

• Choose your route coming into Tor Bay, either to the east of Ore Stone island or between the island and the shore. Beware: there are no lit marks on Ore Stone or Thatcher Rock islands. It is possible to sail quite close to the islands which are steep-to.

From any direction once inside Tor Bay:

• Ensure you keep a good 0.5M from the north shore of the bay to avoid the rock dangers (Morris Rogue 0.8m).

• Leave the green buoy Q.G (May-Sept) to the southwest of Haldon Pier to starboard. Enter the harbour between Haldon Pier Q.G and Princess Pier Q.R. Beware: there is obscured traffic including large ferries behind the harbour walls.

• The MDL marina is to port (2F.R lights on each hammerhead) and the Tor Bay Council pontoons to starboard.

Entrance to the inner harbour is over a hydraulic cill and under a bridge. The bridge opens by arrangement with the harbour office between HW+/-3, in daytime hours. During these times the cill lowers, providing a minimum depth of 2.2m. The entrance lights show three red when closed and two green over white when open.

Berthing & facilities

The MDL marina has no dedicated space for visitors so can be used only when berth-holders are away; arrange this on arrival or try booking ahead. Showers and other facilities are excellent. The marina has a car park, which is convenient but rather expensive.

The council pontoons have space for visitors on the the seaward side facing Haldon Pier. There is also a visitors' pontoon in the inner harbour.

Hope Cove and Anstey's Cove

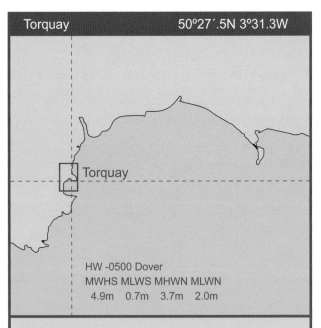

Torquay   50°27´.5N 3°31.3W

Torquay

HW -0500 Dover
MWHS MLWS MHWN MLWN
4.9m   0.7m   3.7m   2.0m

Torquay

• Approach and entrance straightfoward
• Sheltered harbour, anchorages exposed in easterlies
⚓ Fuel end of South Pier, pontoon on south side ☎ 01803 294509 / 07786 370324 VHF M Riviera Fuel
⚓ Boat lifting crane at Haldon Pier ☎ 01803 296570 Tor Bay Seaways
🔧 Mechanic electrician through marina or harbourmaster

Marina

• No dedicated visitors' berths, arrangements with marina office for empty spaces; space for large boats
• 1.3m minimum depth
• ☎ 01803 200210 Fax 01803 200225
• VHF80
• torquaymarina@mdlmarinas.co.uk
• Water and electricity at the pontoons
• Showers, laundry

Council Pontoons

• Visitors' pontoons in space between Haldon Pier and marina seaward outer pontoon
• Visitors' pontoon in inner harbour (access times HW+/-3 cill and bridge)
• ☎ 01803 292429
• VHF14
• Water, electricity at the pontoons
• www.tor-bay-harbour.co.uk

Royal Tor Bay Yacht Club

☎ 01803 292006; restaurant and showers

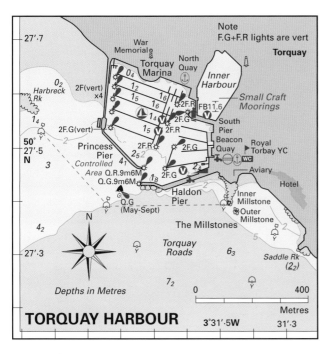

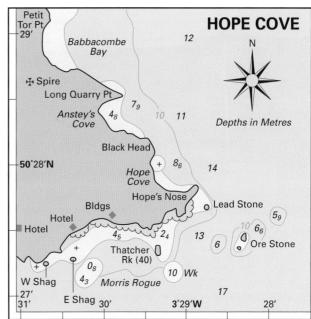

⚓ Anchorages

There are a number of very picturesque anchorages near Torquay, with good cover in westerly conditions. All become uncomfortable with wind from the east and in any trailing swell.

⚓ Watcombe Beach

A very small and beautiful cove, with enough space to swing for one boat.

⚓ Oddicombe Beach

A good wide shelf with depths between 5 and 10m, sand bottom. Two buoys are available for customers of the Cary Arms (☎ 01803 327110), a boutique hotel opened in 2009. Anchor on the southern side (on the north side an uncharted rock dries 0.3m, 0.5 cable east of the café). A funicular, opened in 1926, descends 240ft to the beach.

Pier on south side of Oddicombe beach

Torquay harbour

Anstey's Cove

Thatched cottages at Cockington

⚓ Anstey's Cove

This small cove is cosy and offers much better protection than Oddicombe Beach. It's about 200m wide, has a depth of 5m and a sandy bottom. Uncharted rocks close to the shore. Following a cliff fall there is no access from the shore.

⚓ Hope Cove

More open and bigger than Anstey's Cove but equally delightful. The cliffs are also steep-to but you need to be careful with the ledge on the north side. The bottom is sand with depths between 5 and 10m.

Enjoying the peace at Hope Cove

The Torquay Pavillion

⚓ Off Torquay harbour

Anchor to the west of Princess Pier or southeast of Haldon Pier in depths of at least 3m.

Food & transport

Torquay is a large town with plenty of places to eat and victual. The high street is in walking distance of the harbour. The Elephant (Beacon Terrace. ☎ 01803 200044) overlooking the harbour offers fine dining (one Michelin star) and has a brasserie. Bianco's is a

Victorian houses in Torquay

Torre Abbey gardens

Torre Abbey

good, family run Italian restaurant and their new fish bistro, Number 7, has had good reviews.

The train station is in Rathmore Road, near the sea front to the west of the municipal gardens. It is served by a branch line from Newton Abbot.

There are plenty of bus stops along Tor Bay Road and Rathmore Road. Long distance coaches leave from the coach station in Lymington Road at the top of the town.

There is a ferry service across Tor Bay to Brixham. A high speed catamaran ran for a while but has been discontinued.

Interest

Torquay is a specially good destination if you are looking for time away from your craft as there are interesting things to do in walking distance of the marina. Torre Abbey, the oldest building in the town, was founded in 1196 as a monastery for the Premonstratensian order of Canons, known as White Canons, who followed a strict routine of silence and prayer. The monastery was the richest of its kind by the 15th century, earning £1.8 million a year. This wealth was used to build Torquay's first real harbour and found the nearby market town of Newton Abbot, where Canons sold produce from their extensive lands. The Abbey's medieval barn, built to store taxes paid to the abbey in the form of grain, became known as the Spanish Barn during the Armada in 1588. Sir Francis Drake accepted the surrender of the stricken *Nuestra Señora del Rosario* of the Armada (a lucky break as it was carrying some very senior officers such as Admiral Don Pedro de Valdés, and one third of the fleet's money). Three hundred and ninety seven of her prisoners were held in the (Spanish) barn for a fortnight. After the monasteries were dissolved in 1536 the abbey became home to the Cary family until

Torquay Harbour, Council pontoons in foreground

The funicular at Oddicombe beach

1930 when it was bought by the local authority for £40,000 for use as an art gallery. Pre-Raphaelite art of national standing is on display today, including Holman Hunt's *The Children's Holiday*, Edward Burne-Jones' cartoons and William Blake's sketches for the *Book of Job*. A £6-million restoration project was completed in July 2008. The abbey consists of two Grade I and four Grade II listed buildings and has Scheduled Ancient Monument status.

After all that culture you might like to visit Living Coasts on Beacon Quay, whose large nets are easily spotted up hill from the harbour. This seaside extension to Paignton Zoo is first rate. Designed as a marine aviary, the project focuses on the coastline, locally, nationally and globally. All the animals have been bred in captivity or are rescued birds that would not have survived in the wild. There are auks, terns, penguins, guillemots, puffins, wading estuary birds, sea ducks, seals and facts galore: guillemots lay pyriform (pear-shaped) eggs so if they are disturbed they roll around in a circle rather than falling off the cliff ledge; gentoo penguins reduce their heart rate from 80 to 20 beats per minute when they dive. There's plenty for children to do and the waterside café has stunning views across the bay. A joint saver ticket would enable you to visit Paignton Zoo Environmental Park as well, a short bus or taxi ride away. Renowned for its conservation work and

Tern and penguins at Living Coasts

crocodile swamp, the zoo has over three thousand animals and makes a good day out.

Kent's Cavern, an easy one-mile walk from the harbour, is interesting for its calcite deposits which include flowstone, shark's fin, straws, helictites, stalactites and stalacmites and for the remains of animals that were living in the West Country 500,000 years ago. The fossils include those from ancestral cave bears, cave lions, sabre-toothed cats, mammoths and woolly rhinos and, remarkably, a 31,000 year old teenager's jawbone with teeth, which is the oldest fossil of modern man ever found in Europe.

Over the years Torquay has attracted many famous writers, including Rudyard Kipling, Oscar Wilde, Arthur Conan Doyle and Charles Darwin, but it is Agatha Christie, the 'Queen of Crime', who is most associated with the town. Although she was born and grew up here she spent most of her adult life in London, but not before a diminutive Belgian refugee on a Torquay tram led to the invention of Poirot. You can take a one-mile walk along the seafront to see eleven locations with which she is associated. Torquay Museum (529 Babbacombe Road ☎ 01803 293975) has some of her memorabilia, though much of it has been moved to Greenway, her holiday home on the River Dart (see 'Literary West Country' on page 37). Torre Abbey now has a garden of plants that are featured in her books, including *prunus* cultivars, (from which comes cyanide) and *datura*, whose hallucinogenic seedpods she used to induce madness.

Torquay has been a holiday destination ever since the early 19th century when the Napoleonic wars prevented people holidaying in France. In 1815 Napoleon himself was a prisoner aboard *HMS Bellerophon* in Tor Bay while a decision was made about his future. It is said that when he first saw the bay he cried out *'Quel bon pays!'*

In 1821 the town was still small with a population of less than two thousand but massive growth associated with the holiday industry was on its way. In 1822 a second hotel was opened though objections were raised by the Vicar of Torre who believed that "Two hotels in the town would be detrimental to its moral health". Its mild climate made it especially attractive to 'health tourists' and two thousand hotel bedrooms were available by 1850. In 1864 the Western Morning News described Torquay as "the most opulent, the handsomest and the most fashionable watering place in the British Isles". It continued to develop under the guidance of William Kitson (1800-1883), a man credited with good decisions regarding the provision of water, sewers and street lighting. Many of the town's grand buildings remain. The beautiful stone arches of the Bath Saloons, built in 1857, have been incorporated into Living Coasts.

One nearby village that resisted all development is Cockington. It is picture-postcard attractive and would make an enjoyable visit inland.

If time allows, a visit to Exeter is thoroughly recommended. The journey there along the coast by train is magnificent.

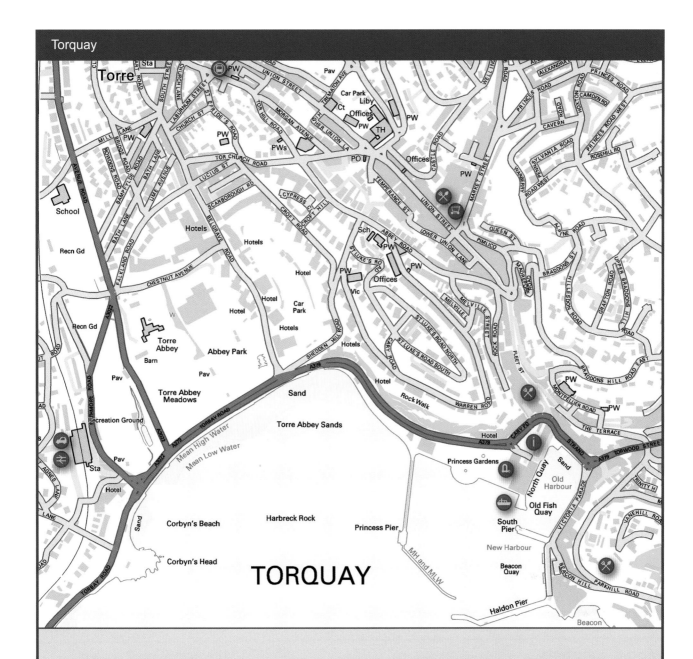

⊕ Bus station, Lymington Road TQ1 4BD
   ☎ 01803 329531

⇌ Train station, Rathmore Road, Torquay TQ2 6NU

Branch line to Newton Abbot and Paignton

⛴ Paignton Pleasure Cruises and *Western Lady*

🚗 Thrifty, Railway Station, Rathmore Road, Torquay TQ2 6NT ☎ 01803 294786

United Rental, 6 Woodlands Close, Old Woods Trading Estate, Torquay TQ2 7BD
☎ 01803 612622

Practical Car & Van Rental,
141 St. Marychurch Rd, Torquay TQ1 3HW
☎ 01803 323323

🛒 Marks & Spencer, Union Square Shopping Centre, Torquay TQ1 3UT

Somerfield, Union St, Torquay TQ1 3UT

Tesco Metro, 25-26 Fleet St, Torquay TQ1 1DB

✕ Restaurants, pubs and cafés: Union Street, The Strand, seafront and harbour

❶ Tourist Information Centre, Vaughan Parade, Torquay TQ2 5JG ☎ 01803 297428

⚓ Torquay Chandlers, The Pavilion, Vaughan Rd, Torquay TQ2 5EQ ☎ 01803 211854

Some services and chandlery at the quay, north side

✚ Torbay Hospital, Lawes Bridge, Newton Rd, Torquay TQ2 7AA ☎ 01803 614567

⚓ Paignton

Paignton is a popular holiday resort with an excellent beach.

There is a drying harbour with a wall that can be used by visitors. Anchorage is good outside the harbour.

Approach & entrance

The approach to Paignton is straightforward. The harbour is on the northern side of Roundham Head and dries. Red cliffs are visible a long way off.

- Approach the area north of the harbour from the northeast, maintaining a distance from the reef that extends to sea. A cardinal Q(3)10s marks the eastern edge of the reef.

- From any direction maintain a distance of a least 150m to the shore to ensure clearance from drying and underwater rocks.

- Swimming areas, Torquay to Berry Head, are marked by yellow buoys and must be avoided.

- The harbour entrance (marked by a light Q.R.) is opposite to convention: keep to port side.

Berthing & facilities

Paignton harbour dries 1.8m. Visitors to 8m may berth alongside the eastern wall of the harbour (space very tight) or the use the three drying buoys outside, both in sand.

⚓ Anchorages

Anchor in 4-6m north of the harbour opposite Paignton Sands (sandy bottom). Keep away from the swimming areas.

South of Roundham Head anchorage is good opposite Goodrington Sands in 3-8m (sandy bottom). Do not approach the shore as there is a rocky outlet, extending out from the centre about 300m.

Food & transport

Paignton is a holiday town with many places to eat and drink in walking distance of the harbour. There are also supermarkets close by.

There are bus links to all local towns. Tor Bay buses use Paignton as an interchange, but journey time is often slow so a taxi may be preferable. A branch-line train goes to Torquay, but for enjoyment rather than expediency nothing beats travelling by steam (see below).

Interest

Paignton is a popular tourist destination. The sandy beach is half a mile long, with safe bathing and pedalos for hire. The 780ft pier, constructed in 1879, was once a stopping place for paddle steamers that travelled between Torquay and Brixham. The pier-head and associated buildings were destroyed by fire in 1919 and in 1940 the pier was sectioned because of concerns about a German invasion. Although it was reconnected once the war ended, the pier was neglected until 1980 when it underwent major

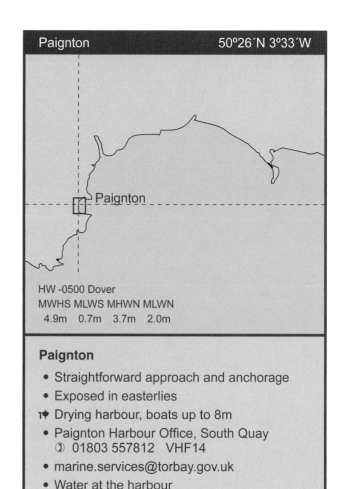

Paignton	50°26′N 3°33′W

HW -0500 Dover

MWHS	MLWS	MHWN	MLWN
4.9m	0.7m	3.7m	2.0m

Paignton

- Straightforward approach and anchorage
- Exposed in easterlies
- ⚓ Drying harbour, boats up to 8m
- Paignton Harbour Office, South Quay
  ☎ 01803 557812   VHF14
- marine.services@torbay.gov.uk
- Water at the harbour

redevelopment. Today it is one very long amusement arcade where you can buy home-made fudge, though most people will be tucking in to doughnuts, burgers and chips.

Paignton Zoo Environmental Park is a short distance away. You can plan your day around various talks given by the keepers and have a nice lunch in the Island restaurant. The zoo is committed to conservation and seventy of its two hundred and fifty exotic species are classed as endangered. A new crocodile swamp is especially impressive. A winding path enables you to see the crocodiles above and below the water and there are snakes and giant

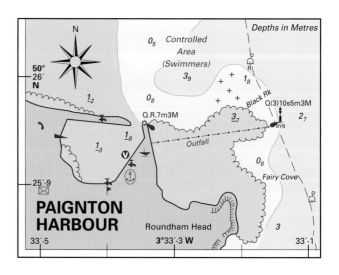

PAIGNTON HARBOUR

Paignton harbour

waterlilies, all observed to the sound of a tropical thunderstorm.

Oldway Mansion, half a mile from Paignton town centre, is well worth a visit (01803 20796). This grand grade II listed building used to belong to Isaac Merritt Singer, founder of the Singer Sewing Machine Company. It is now owned by Tor Bay Borough Council and is partly used for offices. Modelled on the Palace of Versailles it contains more than one hundred rooms which include a miniature hall of mirrors, a grand staircase and gallery, a ballroom and some magnificent painted ceilings. Lebrun painted *The Crowning of Josephine by Napoleon* for the staircase, but sadly only a replica is on display because the Council sold the original, which now hangs in the Palace of Versailles in France. Surrounding the mansion are seventeen acres of land with an Italian style grotto, caves, topiary, waterfall and maze. Buses from Paignton pass the entrance but you will need to ask the driver to stop.

The Paignton and Dartmouth Steam Railway (① 01803 555872) takes you back to yesteryear. The seven mile journey from Paignton to Kingswear in carriages pulled by Great Western locomotives follows the spectacular Tor Bay coast before disappearing into the wooded Dart valley. Whilst it may not be the most comfortable way to travel, the countryside is simply glorious.

Paignton

- Station Square, Paignton TG4 5EF
  Buses to Teignmouth, Shaldon, Torquay, Brixham and Totnes
- Train station: Station Square, Paignton TQ4 5EF
  Branch line train to Torquay
  Paignton to Dartmouth Steam Train
- United Rental, Paignton Railway Station, Paignton TQ4 5EF ① 01803 520494
  Sixt Rent A Car, Paignton Railway Station, Paignton TQ4 5EF ① 08701 567567
- Tourist trips round the bay and to Dartmouth from the harbour north side
- Co-operative, Crossways Shopping Centre, Hyde Road, Paignton TQ4 5BL
  ① 01803 558788
  Tesco, 2 Victoria Street, Paignton TQ4 5DL
  ① 0845 6779535
- Restaurants, pubs and cafés throughout the town
- Paignton Hospital, Church Street, Paignton TQ3 3AG ① 01803 547425 (minor injuries only)

🕐 Brixham

Brixham sits at the southern end of Tor Bay, protected by a 0.5M long breakwater that makes its harbour an all-weather destination.

Although there are plenty of tourists the town is associated primarily with fishing. Today the fleet is small in comparison to years gone by, but in terms of the value of the catch landed Brixham is the most important fishing port in England and Wales. Colourful fishermen's cottages cascade down the hillside and numerous cafés and restaurants line a picturesque inner harbour containing a full size replica of the *Golden Hind*. A paved promenade connects the MDL marina with the town. As there is only a tiny beach the promenade is usually lined with children dangling hooks with bacon attached over the seawall in an attempt to catch crabs.

Approach & entrance

The approach to Brixham is straightforward in all weathers, though strong winds can funnel through the valley from the southwest. There are no immediate dangers other than shellfish pots.

- From any direction head for the breakwater white lighthouse Oc.R.15s. Aim to leave it to port with a wide berth as beam trawlers that are obscured may suddenly emerge. Once in the fairway of the harbour keep to starboard which is marked by Fl.G and Fl.R buoys. The approach is in the white sector of light DirIso.WRG.5s. A large number of moorings are arranged on grids on both sides of the fairway.

- The channel on the east side of the harbour, next to the breakwater wall, is used by the lifeboat.

Berthing & facilities

Brixham has a number of options for visitors. Berthing is comfortable in most conditions except northerly when swell reaches into the harbour.

The MDL marina in the east of the harbour usually has space for visitors, though most of their pontoons are allocated to permanent berth holders. It is best to call ahead in the height of the summer. There are two pontoons extending from the quay. The MDL events pontoon is on the east side and has water and electricity.

The harbourmaster's pontoon (also know as the Heritage Pontoon) is on the west side, towards the inner harbour. Some of the restored Brixham trawlers may be berthed here though there is usually space for visitors. You many need to raft up. There is a water tap on the shore but no electricity.

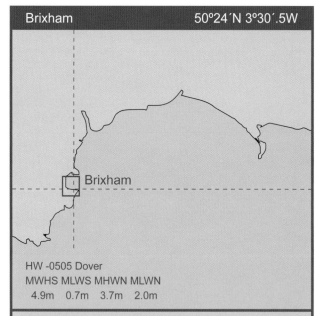

Brixham   50°24´N 3°30´.5W

Brixham

HW -0505 Dover

MWHS	MLWS	MHWN	MLWN
4.9m	0.7m	3.7m	2.0m

Brixham

- Approach: straightforward in all conditions
- Entrance: beware of beam trawlers appearing from behind the breakwater

Harbourmaster

- Alongside berthing on town pontoon
- Water at the quay, electricity at the pontoon
- 2m minimum depth
- ☎ 01803 853321 / 851854 VHF14
- Drying space in inner harbour wall

Brixham Yacht Club

- ☎ 01803 853332
- Pontoons may be used by visitors
- Bar, restaurant and showers

Brixham Marina

- Events pontoon next to town pontoon dedicated to visitors (no electricity)
- Visitors welcome in spaces in MDL marina: check with the office
- ☎ 01803 882929 VHF 80
- Water and electricity at the pontoons
- ⛽ Fuel immediately to starboard in the marina entrance
- 🔧 Numerous local services through marina
- Showers, laundry

Entrance to Brixham Marina on the left, visitors' pontoons and trawlers at fishing harbour on the right

Brixham harbour , moorings and marina

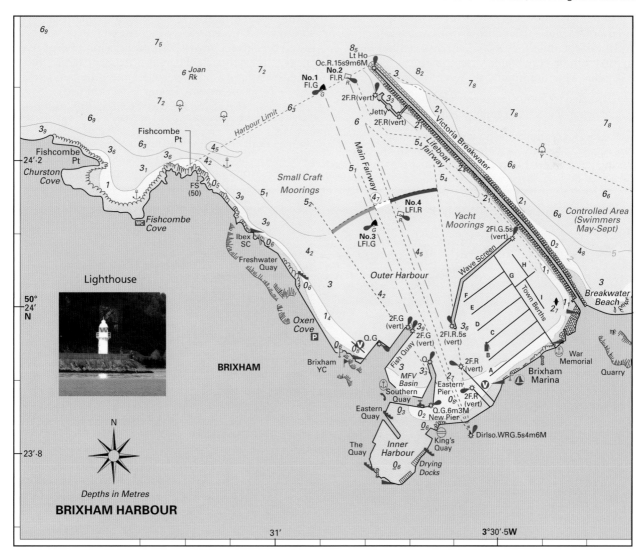

BRIXHAM HARBOUR

Depths in Metres

The *Golden Hind* replica in Brixham Harbour

Brixham Yacht Club's pontoons welcome visitors April to September but if a northerly swell has built up they can be very bouncy. Depth is 1.5m. The club has a bar, a restaurant and showers for visitors.

Harbourmaster moorings on either side of the entrance fairway can accommodate boats to 12m.

The fishermen's inner harbour dries and visitors are not accepted on any of its moorings. There are two drying pads where boats can dry against the quay; one involves resting on concrete, the other on hard sand. Harbourmaster permission is required.

⚓ Anchorages

Anchorage is not permitted within the harbour but there is plenty of space immediately northwest of the moorings. As the ground is foul in places a trip line is recommended. The anchorage becomes very uncomfortable if a swell has built up in north to northeasterlies.

Immediately to the northwest of the harbour, Fishcombe Cove is a delightfully peaceful anchorage offering good shelter in south to west conditions.

South of Berry Head, St Mary's Bay and the beach above Scabbacombe Head are settled-weather only anchorages. There are dangers (Mag Rock, Druids Mare and others) that cover at high water close to the beaches. Only approach with detailed charts or good local knowledge at hand.

Food & transport

There are many places to eat near the waterfront. Restaurants and fish and chip shops serve some of the freshest fish you will ever find as much of it will have been bought that day from the wholesale fish market a few yards away. The town has two small supermarkets, a butchers, a bakers and greengrocers selling local produce. The Brixham Deli, at the bottom of Fore Street, is excellent and serves very good breakfasts. Buses leave from behind Fore Street, near to the car park. There is a frequent service to Kingswear and Paington, where there are connections on to Totnes, Torquay, Exeter etc. Local taxis serve the marina (Brixham Taxis 01803 853000) and there is a taxi rank in town by the buses.

Ferries make frequent journeys across the Bay to Torquay. The *Western Lady* is run by locals and operates from 9am to 5pm in the summer.

Pyramidal orchid

Viper's bugloss

Berry Head lighthouse

Just behind the marina is a multi-storey car park where cars can be left long-term. Permits can be obtained from the marina office to save feeding the meter. The Breakwater car park by the marina is very convenient but ticket inspectors are ever-present, with fines likely for overstaying. The Breakwater Café nearby has wonderful views across the bay and serves delicious ice cream.

Interest

The first few houses that were built in Brixham were part of a farming community inland but by the time of The Domesday Book a fishing port had been established. Both parts of the town are now one but locals still joke about 'Cow Town' and 'Fish Town'. It was local men who pioneered trawling with weighted nets as a method of fishing and by the 1850s Brixham had the largest fleet of sailing smacks in England. Deep-sea fishing continued to grow and by 1900 almost 300 trawlers were based here. The modern fleet of about 100 trawlers and day boats is tiny by comparison but Brixham is still the most important fishing port in England and Wales when the value of the catch is considered. In 2008 £4 million was accounted for by scallops alone (see 'Brixham scallops' on page 75).

Brixham fishing harbour is now in the process of a major redevelopment, jointly financed by the EU and the local council. A new jetty has created 4,500 square metres of additional space for landing and processing. New legal requirements mean that white fish and black fish, such as the ink-carrying cuttlefish, have to be processed separately, but without development this was not possible. Currently the public have no access to the harbour area and all fish is sold at wholesale auctions from 6-8am. When the new building is complete it is expected to have a viewing platform, a fishmongers, restaurant and cookery school.

Brixham inner harbour

The annual trawler race

Fish auction early in the morning at Brixham

Although motor-powered trawlers now do the fishing you are likely to see some of Brixham's red-sailed fishing smacks out on the water and at the Heritage Pontoon in the harbour. The lovingly restored *Pilgram*, built in 1895, is the oldest of the fleet, while *Vigilance* (1926) is the last sailing smack to have been built here at Upham's Shipyard. Day trips or tours aboard these old vessels can be arranged and the Heritage Regatta in May is a delight. Those liking a faster spectacle should watch the annual trawler race in June when modern fishing boats race under engine power before a major celebration throughout the town.

Brixham's inner harbour has a full sized replica of the *Golden Hind*, the surprisingly small vessel in which Francis Drake circumnavigated the world and on which he was knighted by Elizabeth I (see 'Drake he was a Devon man' on page 125). Aboard you can see an extremely cramped surgeon's and carpenter's cabin and the captain's quarters.

The old fish market abutting the inner harbour is no longer used to process fish but is often a scene of lively entertainment. On summer evenings it is the venue for the Orpheus male voice choir and for the Brixham town band. Local artists and craft stalls are a feature on most summer days. The statue nearby is of William of Orange who landed here in 1688 and declared 'The liberties of England and the protestant religion I will maintain'. Marching unopposed from

Brixham to London, he became King William III while the catholic King James II went into exile.

A short walk uphill from the harbour takes you to the site of Brixham's second world war emergency coastal defence battery. It is the best-preserved and most important site of its kind in the UK and has Scheduled Monument status. A small museum has recently opened on the site.

The Brixham Heritage Museum is worth a visit. It is housed in the old police station and one of the cells has a scene of a man arrested for assaulting a policeman while drunk on cider, apparently a common problem in the early 1900s. There are displays about the fishing industry and the town's history, together with some very unsavoury facts: soldiers stationed at Berry Head barracks between 1794 and 1815 were given clean bedclothes only once every 3 months. Talks and lectures take place throughout the year.

The daily catch

East of the town is a giant slipway constructed during the second world war when Brixham was a major fuelling depot. From here troops and vehicles embarked for the D-Day landings. The breakwater was created in 1866 after a ferocious storm led to 40 ships being driven on to the rocks with the loss of 100 lives. The kilometre-long structure you see today was completed in 1916. Nearby is the shore base of the Tor Bay lifeboat.

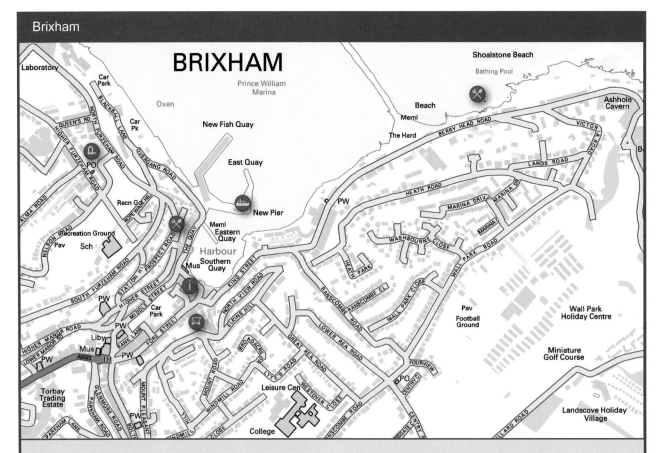

BRIXHAM

- Buses from Middle St to Paignton and Torquay
- Ferries to Torquay: *Western Lady* from the fishermens' quay
- Car hire: nearest at Paignton
- Co-operative and Tesco Express, Fore Street
- Restaurants, pubs and cafés: many abutting the harbour
- Tourist Information Centre, The Old Fish Market, The Quay, Brixham TQ5 8AW
  ☎ 01803 211211

- Bayside Marine Ltd, Furzeham Garage, Higher Furzeham Road, Brixham TQ5 8QP
  ☎ 01803 856771 - gas & chandlery delivery
  Gundry Marine, 4 The Quay, Brixham TQ5 8AW ☎ 01803 856 115

- Brixham Hospital, Greenswood Road, Brixham TQ5 9HW ☎ 01803 881399

Further west is the fantastic outdoor seawater Shoalstone Bathing Pool with tiered surround and pool-side changing booths. Everyday a huge valve is opened to let in fresh seawater but in stormy weather no valve is required! The pool began life in 1896 when walls were built around a particularly large rock pool. Redeveloped in 1926, it has hardly changed since and is free.

An excellent walk takes you from the harbour to Berry Head. Along the way, the Berry Head Hotel has an excellent terrace on which to have a drink while surveying the bay. Built as a military hospital during the Napoleonic Wars, it was once home to the Vicar of All Saints Church, the Revd Henry Francis Lyte, best known for writing the hymn *Abide with Me*.

Berry Head National Nature Reserve, a thirty-minute walk uphill from the marina, should not be missed. Dominated by two forts from the Napoleonic War era, spectacular limestone cliffs support both rare and protected wild flowers, such as the white rock rose,

pyramidal orchid and viper's bugloss, and the largest guillemot colony in England. Recent development has improved the visitor centre and there is an excellent café. The birds can be observed from a hide and videocam and there are excellent ranger-guided walks including one to see great horseshoe bats which live in the caves below. The lighthouse here is both the highest and the smallest in Great Britain. It is visible from more than 20M, thanks to 200ft of cliff, but is a dwarf at only 6ft from the ground. The South West Coast Path runs through the reserve. Kingswear is 8M away. The journey back can be made by bus or taxi.

Brixham scallops

Brixham scallops are commonly found on the menu of top-notch restaurants but the British have only recently come to appreciate this delicacy. Before the mid 1970s they were most likely to be used as bait and it was only with the development of overseas markets that they began to be caught in any great number. One hundred and thirty British vessels were fishing for scallops by 1978 and, although the number of boats has greatly diminished, about £4 million pounds' worth of scallops were landed in Brixham in 2008, a quarter of the harbour's catch in financial terms. Scallops are favoured by fishermen because they are sold for a premium, are not covered by quotas and are found just a few miles off the coast.

The growth in scallop fishing has led to conflict with environmentalists because scallops are caught with nets attached to heavy steel beams that are dragged along the seabed destroying everything in their path. The underwater forest of flora and fauna making up Lyme Bay has been especially at risk because this 30-mile-long reef system, lying 15–30 metres underwater, is prime scallop fishing ground. Surveys showing parts of the reef reduced to rubble led to a gentleman's agreement that the fishermen should avoid two areas particularly important for the protected pink sea fan, a pretty salmon-pink coral with delicate needles that can live up to 100 years, the Ross and sunset cup corals, sea sponges and brittle stars, a type of starfish. However, Natural England claimed that the bay was continuing to be 'raped and pillaged' and in July 2008 60 square miles of Lyme Bay, just less than 10%, was closed to scallop dredging and bottom trawling. Other types of fishing, including scuba diving for scallops, are unaffected. Eating only those scallops that have been dive-caught is best for our marine environment.

Once mature, scallops have few natural predators and can live for up to 20 years. When submerged and feeding they open their shell about 20 degrees allowing a mantle, hanging down like a curtain, to filter the water for nutrients. Water taken in around the shell edge and expelled near to the hinge by rapid contractions of the large white abductor muscle results in a form of jet propulsion. A number of bright eye spots allow it to detect changes in light intensity, offering some warning of predators and fishing gear.

Scallops are found in shallow water and at depths of up to 100m. They live on a variety of bottom substrates including rock, stone and mud. If the bottom is soft enough they will excavate a small crater and cover themselves with silt or gravel for camouflage. Scallops grow by adding bands, called striae, to their shell margin. As growth ceases in the winter the pattern changes so the age of a scallop can be estimated in a similar way to dating trees.

To shuck a scallop hold the shell flat side up. Insert a knife into one of the small openings either side of the hinge and pry the shells apart a little. To sever

the abductor muscle direct the tip of your knife to the shell's margin and sweep around the underside. They are most delicious in the autumn.

Scallops are hermaphrodites, so the crescent-shaped coral contains both male (pink, orange or red) and female (creamy white) parts, both of which can be eaten. Although they can reproduce alone cross-fertilization usually occurs.

To cook: Heat some butter in a frying pan until the milk solids turn a light nut-brown. Sear the white flesh for 1-2 minutes each side. Add the corals just before the end, together with a splash of white wine or calvados. Serve with steamed green beans, cherry tomatoes wilted in a pan, and walnut bread. A delicious and simple meal to prepare on board!

River Dart

The steep-sided Dart estuary is actually a ria, formed when sea levels rose and flooded the original river valley at the end of the last Ice Age. The water that flows here begins as a trickle high up on Dartmoor. At its mouth it is deep enough for naval ships to drop anchor in sight of the Britannia Royal Naval College situated on the hillside above Dartmouth. The town has been a thriving port since the 14th century and its links with the navy date back to 1863. Kingswear on the opposite bank is home to the Dart Valley Light Railway steam train which puffs its way to Paignton through idyllic countryside.

Dartmouth and Kingswear castles sit opposite one another at the mouth of the estuary. They were built at the end of the 15th century when a chain slung between them could be raised in defence. Dartmouth castle, the larger of the two, was the first in England to be constructed specifically to withstand artillery though this was never put to the test, leaving a well preserved building that is worth a visit. The towns are connected by two ferries, known as the upper and lower, both of which take cars.

Upstream is the pretty village of Dittisham, then Stoke Gabriel and little else besides woodland and pasture until the Elizabethan market town of Totnes, about 9.5M from the river mouth. Sailing all the way requires that you keep your wits about you and choose a suitable state of tide.

Most of the River Dart estuary and surrounding land is owned by the Duchy of Cornwall and a new 25-year lease was agreed in 2008.

Approach & entrance

The approach and entrance to the River Dart are straightforward in all but very strong southeast to south conditions. Swell in those circumstances can build up to the lower ferry and the water can be rough, particularly on the ebb. Dangers at the entrance include Mew Stone and Castle Ledge to starboard and Combe Point to port, but the entrance can be approached in any weather.

From the east:

- Keep well south of the two south cardinals that mark Mew Stone, in order to clear East Blackstone which is not marked. During the day and in good conditions it is perfectly possible to pass between East Blackstone and the shore, but beware of Nimble Rock 1m (north on the transit line East Blackstone-Start Point lighthouse).

- Once past the Mew Stone south cardinals VQ(6)+LFl.10s and Q(6)+LFl.15s aim for Castle Ledge Fl.G.5s. Do not be tempted to cut the corner as there are a number of dangers west of Mew Stone (the Verticals dry 1.8m, West Rock dries 0.3m, Bears Tail dries 0.6m) and a ledge from the shore to the green buoy (with 1.8m depth at Castle Rock).

- Past Castle Ledge Fl.G.5s remain in the white sector of the entrance light Iso.WRG.3s.

From the west:

- Keep a distance of at least 500m from the shore to avoid rock dangers near Coombe Point (Coombe Rocks dry 3.7m, Homestone 0.9m). A good strategy is to stay east of the 35° transit between Homestone Q.R and Castle Ledge Fl.G.5s.

- Leave the red can buoy Homestone Q.R to port.

- Continue towards Castle Ledge Fl.G.5s until you are in the white sector of entrance light Iso. WRG.3s.

Entrance to the River Dart

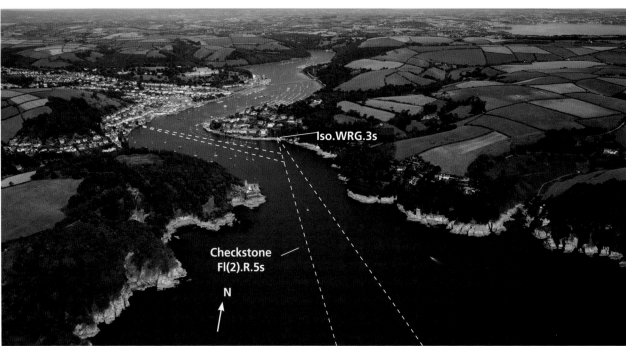

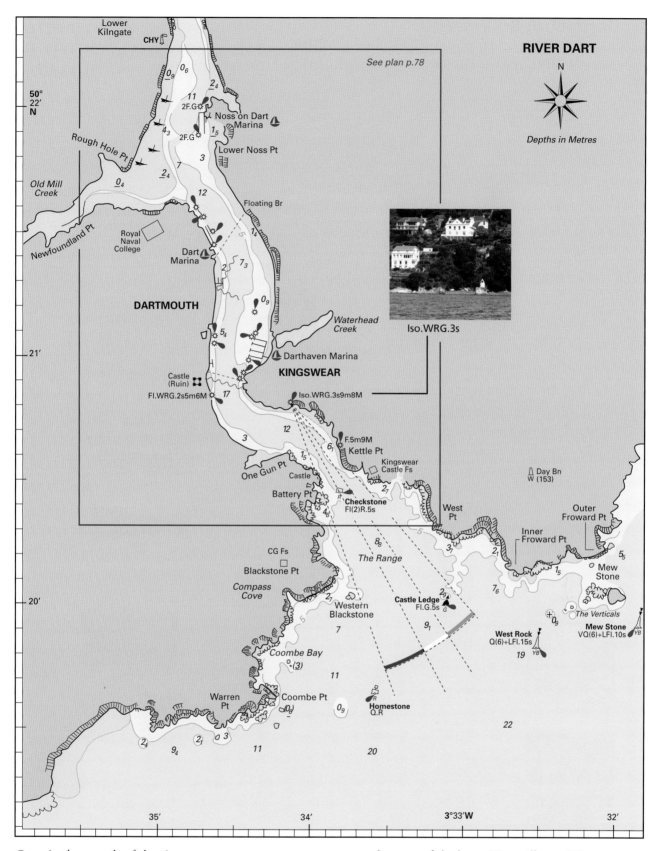

RIVER DART

N

Depths in Metres

See plan p.78

Lower Kilngate

CHY

0₉ 0₆

2₄

11
2F.G

Noss on Dart Marina

2F.G 1₅

Lower Noss Pt

Rough Hole Pt

4₃

3

7

2₄

Old Mill Creek

0₄

Newfoundland Pt

12

Floating Br

Royal Naval College

1₄

Dart Marina

7₃

2

DARTMOUTH

0₉

5₄

Waterhead Creek

Iso.WRG.3s

Darthaven Marina

Castle (Ruin)
Fl.WRG.2s5m6M

17

KINGSWEAR

Iso.WRG.3s9m8M

3

12

F.5m9M

6₁ Kettle Pt

1₅

Kingswear Castle Fs

Day Bn
W (153)

One Gun Pt

Castle

Battery Pt

4₆

Checkstone
Fl(2)R.5s

2₇

West Pt

Inner Froward Pt

Outer Froward Pt

5₅

3₇

2₁

Mew Stone

1₅

7₆

CG Fs

Blackstone Pt

8₈

The Range

Compass Cove

Western Blackstone

7

5

Castle Ledge
Fl.G.5s

2₉

9₁

3₇

0₉

The Verticals

Mew Stone
VQ(6)+LFl.10s
YB

West Rock
Q(6)+LFl.15s
YB

19

Coombe Bay

(3)

11

Warren Pt

Coombe Pt

0₈

0₉

Homestone
Q.R

22

2₄

2₁ 0₃

9₄

11

20

50°
22'
N

21'

20'

35'   34'   3°33'W   32'

Once in the mouth of the river entrance:

- Ensure you are in the white sector of entrance light Iso.WRG.3s on a course of 330° before you pass Castle Ledge Fl.G.5s. Rock danger Western Blackstone is close to the shore on the west side.

- Pass red can Checkstone Fl(2)R.5s on your port side. The Checkstone rock 0.3m is immediately to the west of the buoy. You will pass Kingswear Castle to Starboard and Dartmouth Castle to port.

- After 0.3M turn on a course of 295° in the white sector of Bayard's Cove light Fl.WRG.2s. Behind will be the beam of light F.5 from the Kingswear side. 100m from Bayard's Cove light the river opens to the north. Proceed in the main channel; your only concern will be the many moorings either side.

⚓ Dartmouth & Kingswear

Dartmouth and Kingswear offer the most sheltered harbour in Lyme Bay, protected by the river valley and a dogleg entrance that diminishes swell. There are numerous berthing and anchorage opportunities even in the busy summer season.

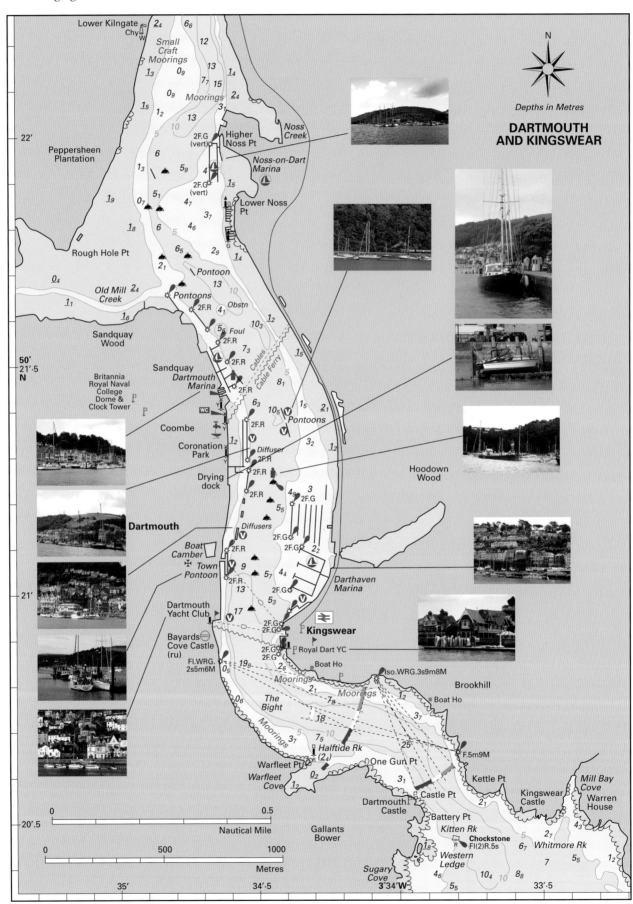

DARTMOUTH AND KINGSWEAR

Depths in Metres

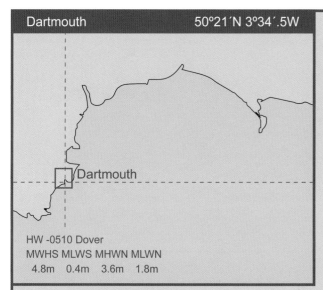

Dartmouth   50°21′N 3°34′.5W

Dartmouth

HW -0510 Dover
MWHS MLWS MHWN MLWN
4.8m   0.4m   3.6m   1.8m

Dartmouth & Kingswear

- Approach: straightforward, no dangers
- Entrance: straightforward except in very strong southeast to south on the ebb

Royal Dart Yacht Club

- Pontoon, showers and restaurant
  ☎ 01803 752496

Dartmouth Yacht Club

- Pontoon, showers and restaurant
  ☎ 01803 832305   max 9m LOA

DHNA

- Visitors' pontoons just before inner harbour - outside may be used overnight (after 1700); cul-de-sac inside
- 3 visitors' pontoons beyond inner harbour
- 1.3m minimum depth inside, 7m outside
- Scrubbing grid
- ☎01803 832337 VHF11
- info@dartharbour.org
- Water on the quayside
- Free council showers at the park toilet block

Darthaven Marina

- Visitors' spaces
- ☎ 01803 752545   VHF80
- Water and electricity at the pontoons
- Showers, laundry
- darthaven@darthaven.co.uk
- Large chandlery
- 35-ton travel hoist
- Marina workshop and engineering services

- Fuel barge on east side of main channel; VHF06 ☎ 07801 798861 / 01548 843838 Easter-30 Sep 0830-1700.
  1 Oct - Easter 0830-1700, closed Sat/Sun
- Water taxi VHF69, Puffin Water Taxis VHF08 07787 504007

Dart Marina

- Visitors by arrangement only
- ☎ 01803 833351 VHF80
- Water and electricity at the pontoons
- Showers, laundry

Noss Marina

- Visitors by arrangement only
- ☎ 07920 425451 / 425452   VHF80
- Water and electricity at the pontoons
- Showers, laundry

Dittisham

- Mooring buoys, min depth 2m up to 15m LOA

Dartside Quay (Galmpton)

- Dry berthing, very sheltered
- Galmpton Creek: access high water
- ☎ 01803 845445 VHF80
- Water and electricity
- 65-ton travel hoist
- Extensive services at the yard

Dartmouth is a picturesque town full of character. There are many restaurants and tourist shops but no mass tourism. Old buildings cling to the hillside, tier above tier, joined by almost vertical cobbled steps and the redbrick Britannia Royal Naval College looks down triumphantly from its magnificent hilltop setting. Across the water, Kingswear is primarily residential.

Approach & entrance

Once you have passed through the bight at the entrance you are in the wide well-lit stream of the river. Navigation is straightforward if you stay mid-stream, while either side you may need to manoeuvre among the many moorings and, in the season, anchored boats.

Always give priority and plenty of space to the tug-and-float Lower Ferry, which needs to manoeuvre in difficult tides. Upstream the Upper Ferry is chain operated and crosses frequently.

Berthing & facilities

There are many options for visitors and you will always find space, though in the middle of summer you may need to raft up. The river is controlled by the Dart Harbour and Navigation Authority (DHNA, 'Dart Nav' on VHF11) who manage moorings, refuse and embankments as well as specifying local rules.

At the entrance, the Royal Dart Yacht Club Kingswear accepts visitors on its summer pontoon (max 9m LOA). Visitors are welcome to use their showers and restaurant.

Opposite, the Dartmouth Yacht Club has a pontoon (seasonal) with 3 spaces for visitors' boats. Showers available.

A short way upstream are the first of the Dart Harbour and Navigation Authority (DHNA 'Dart Nav' VHF11) visitors' pontoons, the only ones linked to the shore. The outside pontoon can be used overnight between 1700 and 0900, when the pleasure boats stop. The space inside the pontoon, a cul-de-sac, is always available for visitors, with space for three boats alongside and another three rafted up.

On the Kingswear side you may anchor in the space between the large ship moorings and Darthaven Marina. This is a popular spot but holding is not completely reliable. You should not leave your boat unattended as space is at a premium and the tide strong. During the Regatta people go to extreme lengths to fit in and all kinds of spectacles ensue as the boats begin to swing.

Darthaven Marina at Kingswear accepts visitors and has good showers. Boats can be lifted from the quay by a 35T travel hoist and there is dry berthing space in the car park, although this is at a premium and priority is given to berth holders. The marina has engineering services and the most extensively stocked chandlery in the area.

Back on the Dartmouth side a further DHNA pontoon is available for visitors. On the shore, next to the steps in front of a block of flats, you can dry out on piles (spaced 1m apart at the bottom) or in mud slightly further upstream. At high tide the wall just north of the tourist rental boat pontoons (rings for lines) is a good berthing spot for a short stop. There are excellent free council showers in the toilet block on the edge of the park.

The fuel barge is stationed on the east side of the main channel. Overnight berthing against it is not permitted. The pontoons and trots to the east side of the fuel barge are allocated moorings, with a long waiting list.

The main DHNA visitor pontoons are located after the tourist berthing area. On the Dartmouth side

Dart entrance, Dartmouth, Dart Marina, views of Kingswear, Upper Ferry, Lower Ferry

you may berth only on the outside of the pontoon, up to 10 spaces alongside and a maximum of two boats rafted per space. On the Kingswear side you may berth either side: two pontoons, three spaces alongside and two boats rafted maximum. From both sides you need to use your dinghy or call the water taxi to get ashore.

Dart Marina occupies the space immediately beyond the Upper Ferry (chain ferry). Facilities ashore are good but space for visitors is very limited.

The MBNA buoys on the west side after Dartmouth Marina are controlled by the navy. Members of Britannia Society or RNSA may use them but must call ahead to arrange.

Noss-on-Dart Marina is located 0.5M beyond the Upper Ferry on the east side of the river. Space here is also at a premium, with even resident berth-holders rafted up in pairs.

A large marina is planned at Noss Creek but there are problems to surmount including contamination from previous engineering works and the protection of seahorses found nearby.

Anchoring is possible just beyond the Upper Ferry (east side) and just below Anchor Stone before Dittisham (between the channel and Parson's Mud).

Further upstream Dartside Quay, at Galmpton Creek, is a dedicated dry berthing yard, with a chandlery and extensive boat engineering services. Access is through a dedicated quay that is served by a 65T travel hoist. The creek dries so lift outs need to be around high water.

Food & transport

Dartmouth is a good place to victual as there are bakeries, delis and greengrocers as well as a small supermarket and an M&S Simply Food. While you are here it would be a shame not to try some local cheeses, such as Elmhurst and Rustic made on the Sharpham Estate and Ticklemore from slightly further upstream. The Sharpham Estate also produces award-winning wine. If you venture up the Dart you can anchor nearby and visit their Vineyard Café for lunch (April-Sept: booking required ☎ 01803 732178).

The Seahorse restaurant on Dartmouth Embankment is owned by Mitch Tonks and is highly recommended (☎ 01803 835147). For a more relaxed supper try his new venture nearby, The Rockfish. Here there are paper tablecloths stating 'tomorrow's fish is still in the sea' and although you get to use swish linen napkins the food (predominantly seafood and chips) is served in a cardboard box. Alf Rescos in Lower

Scenes from Dartmouth

Street serves all day breakfasts and has a fantastic atmosphere. St Barnabas church is now the impressive setting for a good Italian restaurant, The Dartmouth Apprentice. It is run by the charity Training for Life and profits are used to train local people wishing to enter the hospitality trade. Moored in the river is the Resnova Floating Inn, good for lunch, dinner or just a drink. They have a free water taxi (☎ 07770 628967) though you can moor up against her. The Cherub, an

Dartmouth

St Saviour's Church was rebuilt in the 1630s and incorporates timber work from the captured flagship of the Spanish Armada. Be sure to see the superb medieval ironwork depicting the elongated lions of Edward I and the tree of life. Other buildings of note include Agincourt House built for a merchant in 1415 and Tudor House whose facade dates from 1635 despite its name. The Butterwalk is a shaded timber-framed arcade built in 1635-40. The four-storey building above overhangs the street and is supported on eleven granite columns. Although badly damaged by bombs in 1943, it has been restored beautifully and is encrusted with wooden carvings. A visit to the Dartmouth Museum housed here would allow you to see inside. The King's Room has original wooden panelling and plaster ceiling and other rooms are richly decorated. The museum has a collection of model ships, including a Chinese craft made out of ivory and a man of war constructed from bone by French prisoners. There is also a room dedicated to local man Thomas Newcomen (1663-1729) who invented the steam piston used to pump water out of mines, a forerunner of James Watt's steam engine. An original Newcomen engine can be seen in action in the garden next to the Tourist Information Centre.

excellent pub with good bar food, was already 300 years old when frequented by Francis Drake.

Buses and ferries are the only form of public transport from Dartmouth and some journeys are best taken by taxi. From Kingswear you can take the steam train but this is more for pleasure than expediency.

Interest

Dartmouth has a rather sophisticated, slightly isolated, feel, perhaps because it has no beach and there are few cars as no one is driving through to get somewhere else. In the summer there is a good holiday atmosphere and there are plenty of things to do. First and foremost, perhaps a visit to the Britannia Royal Naval College whose red brick facade designed by Aston Webb, who also designed the facade of Buckingham Palace, looks majestically over the town. British naval officers are trained here. Dartmouth Tourist Information Centre (Mayors Avenue ① 01803 834224) has details of tours which run most Wednesdays and Sundays from Easter to October and last 2 hours. You are warned ahead about the highly polished wooden floors!

Dartmouth has a long maritime history beginning with the Normans. In the 12th century the Second and Third Crusades gathered and left from here and, incredibly, some buildings have survived, with restoration, from the 14th century. The timber-framed Cherub Inn in Higher Street dates from 1380.

Bayard's Cove, just beyond the lower ferry towards the river mouth, has some beautifully restored 18th-century houses behind a cobbled quay that was used as a film set for *The Onedin Line*. Dartmouth castle, beyond, is well worth a visit. Built at the end of the 15th century, it had the most advanced military design at the time with large guns, such as serpyntynes and murderers, mounted inside and fired through rectangular ports.

The Flavel Arts Centre is the venue for films, theatre and live music. The Royal Regatta on the last weekend in August is very lively, with displays by the Red Arrows and helicopters from the Royal Navy who hover above the river sending alarming amounts of spray onto craft just a few feet below. Fireworks on the last night are usually magnificent. A Food Festival in early October is an altogether more stately affair.

From Kingswear you can take the Paignton and Dartmouth Steam Railway on a 7M journey to Paignton. Running initially along the eastern bank of the Dart, the line continues along the Tor Bay coast.

The Paignton & Dartmouth Steam Railway

Dartmouth

- 🚌 Buses to Totnes
- ⇌ Paignton & Dartmouth Steam Railway, from Kingswear by the marina
- 🚢 Upper Ferry (by Dartmouth Marina) to Bridge Road

  Lower Ferry to and from Kingswear
- 🚗 United Rental, Wills Road, Totnes TQ9 5XN
  ☎ 01803 864651
- 🛒 Somerfield, 19 Fairfax Place, Dartmouth TQ6 9AB

  M&S Simply Food, Mayor's Avenue, Dartmouth TQ6 9NF

  Various small shops, grocers and delicatessen throughout the town

- 🍴 Restaurants, pubs and cafés: along Embankment (several top-class), Foss St, Fairfax Place, Lower St
- ℹ Tourist Information Centre, The Engine House, Mayor's Avenue, Dartmouth TQ6 9NG
  ☎ 01803 834224
- ⚓ Darthaven Marina, Brixham Road, Kingswear TQ6 0SG ☎ 01803 752242

  Dart Chandlers, Noss-on-Dart Marina, Bridge Road, Kingswear TQ6 0EA ☎ 01803 833772

  Shipmates, 2 Newcomen Road, Dartmouth TQ6 9AF ☎ 01803 839292
- ✚ Dartmouth & Kingswear Hospital, Mansion House St, Dartmouth TQ6 9BD
  ☎ 01803 832255

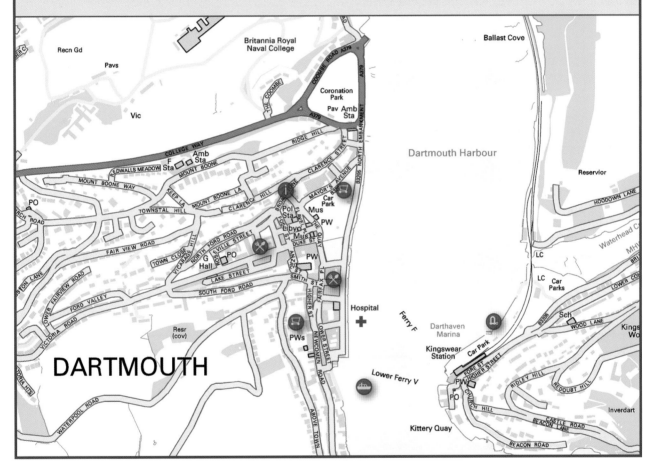

⚓ Ⓥ Dittisham to Totnes

The River Dart comes into its own upstream of the Upper Ferry where the scenery is stunning. These upper reaches are home to many birds and animals, including kingfishers, curlews, egrets, seals and otters. It is possible to navigate all the way to the Elizabethan town of Totnes but depth is in decreasing supply the further you go, so tide calculations are essential. If your boat can dry out there are some perfect spots to anchor, paradise on top of mud.

Navigation

You can reach all the way up to Totnes within HW+/-2. The common advice for rivers applies in ample doses here: keep to the outside of bends, where the flow of water creates greater depths. Turning space can be tight along many stretches. As a rule of thumb, if you have enough water at the Flat Owers buoy you will be able to get to Totnes. The difficult patches are between Blackness Point, after Stoke Gabriel and the start of the Home Reach. At all times monitor depth and make corrections for any tide and wind pushing you from your ground track.

From Dittisham:

- You can get round the river bend at all states of tide on the east side of the Flat Owers. Follow the line of boat moorings, keeping to the inside of the river where the channel is deeper, until you have passed Galmpton (pronounced 'Gamp-ton') Creek and the two boathouses.

- It is possible to sail on the west side of the Flat Owers when the tide is high. Aim at the first boathouse (Waddeton) on a bearing of 20°. This will take you close to Flat Owers red buoy R1. When you pass R1 turn to port on a bearing of 310° aiming at the second boathouse (Sandridge) until depths reach 2.3m (+ tide). You are now back in the main channel.

- From the Sandridge Boat House aim at the red beacon on Blackness Point, past Dittisham Mill Creek. Keep to the left side of the track where there is a deep pool. This is a good anchorage except in northerly winds.

- At Blackness Point begin to steer for the north side (starboard going upstream) of the river, aiming for the first boat mooring.

- At the first boat mooring turn northeast towards the first of the moorings near Stoke Gabriel. You cross the first shallow patch to reach the Long Stream channel. Keep to the inside of the river alongside the moorings, where water is deeper.

- Pass the beacons that mark the entrance to Stoke Gabriel. The DHNA visitors' buoys are set before the entrance beacons. Even if you have sufficient water do not attempt to enter the Stoke Gabriel Mill Pool as it is barred by a cill.

- After the last of the Stoke Gabriel moorings aim for the White Rock (grey rock with some white paint on it) almost directly west. This is the second shallow patch to cross.

Continues (See plan p.85)

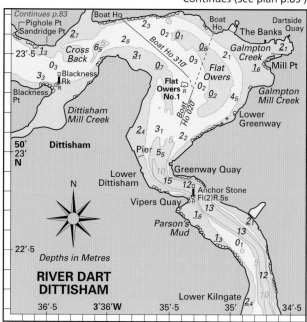

- Your next target is red buoy R2 in front of Bow Creek. This is a good anchorage in mud. Bow Creek leads to the quay (and pub) at Tuckenhay, which dries 1.6m.

- From Bow Creek the river turns northeast, past R2 and G3, and becomes narrow, easier to navigate while underway but tight for turning.

- The next bend, towards the northwest, is at Duncannon where there is a deep patch 6.7m and some moorings; stay close to the moorings. R4 marks the shallow inner part of the bend, to port going upstream.

- Keeping to the outside of the river bend you reach Hackney Creek where depth decreases. A red post marks the turning point.

- Now on a southwest heading you aim for the R6/ G5 R8/G7 buoy pairings and aim for the outside of the next bend. Depth begins to increase and reaches 8m below the cottage and boat house.

- Turn northeast and move to the east side of the river (starboard going upstream). This section is called Sharpham Reach. Anchorage is good in a line between the red R9 and the west side boathouse.

- Keeping to the outside of the river pass R10, R12 and R14 as the river turns northwest around Sharpham Point.

- You are now in Fleet Mill Reach where your only guidance becomes the river banks. Keep in the centre of the stream.

- Keep to the outside of the river until the red post in front of Berry Rock. This is your last navigation mark before Totnes.

- Turn north and then northwest around the stone wall.

- You are now in the Home Reach, a long straight section that leads you right to Totnes, to the pub and public quays.

Dittisham and the River Dart to Stoke Gabriel

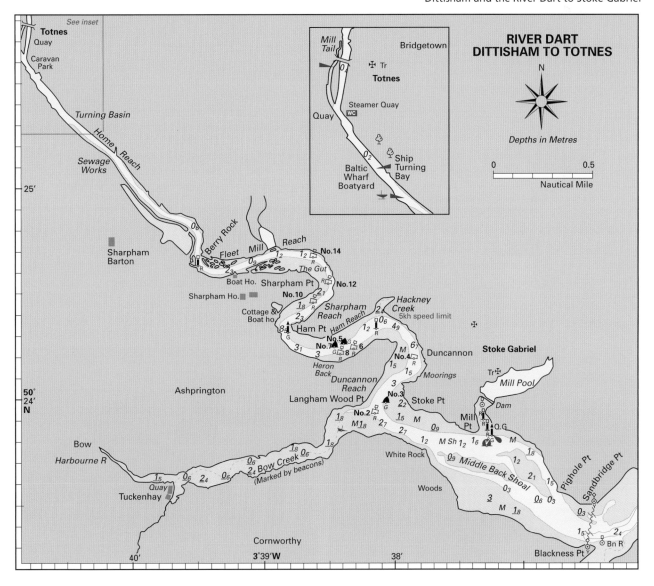

⚓ Anchor Stone

Immediately south of Anchor Stone is a popular anchorage. Stay west of a line between the rock beacon Fl(2)R.5s and the first mooring downstream to remain outside of the main channel. Survey depth to avoid grounding on Parson's Mud.

Ⓥ Dittisham

There are 23 visitors' buoys in the Dittisham river bend: 5 for LOA greater than 45ft, 3 for up to 45ft and the remainder for 30ft or less. This spot is idyllic but in the summer you may need to raft up. There are short-stay dinghy berths at the end of Dittisham pontoon and a water taxi is operated by the Dittisham to Greenway ferry (VHF10 ☎ 01803 844010).

Dittisham is a small village with a shop, a café and a pub, which runs a most unorthodox and enjoyable quiz on Thursday evenings. The Greenway Jetty is privately owned and permission to land should be sought from the ferry on VHF10. From here it is possible to walk up hill to the Greenway Estate.

Once the holiday home of Agatha Christie, it is now administered by the National Trust.

⚓ Blackness Point

As the river turns west after Dittisham there is a good anchorage between Dittisham Mill Creek and Blackness Point (red beacon). Beware of the mooring tackle upstream. The depth here are 3.2m, which accommodates boats at all states of tide. Holding is good in mud but the tide is strong. The anchorage should be avoided in strong northerly winds.

Ⓥ Stoke Gabriel

The DHNA provide 3 visitors' buoys at Stoke Gabriel for boats up to 33ft. They are marked SV 1, 2 and 3. Anchorage here is very tight even if you can dry out.

Approach to Totnes and at the Steam Packet quay

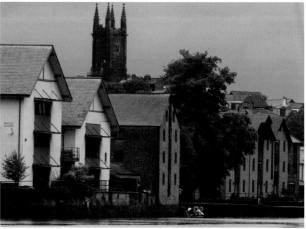

⚓ Bow Creek

Further upstream, before Bow Creek, it is possible to anchor without obstructing the main channel. There is just about enough water to keep afloat if you draw less than 2m. Along Bow Creek you can reach Tuckenhay Quay and the pub (dries 1.5m).

Ⓥ Totnes

The very determined can reach Totnes between HW+/- 2. A ferry makes the same journey. The Packet Boat Inn has a single berth on St Peter's Quay (phone ahead ☎ 01803 863880) and is easier to attach to (rings on the side of the wall) than the public quay just beyond

(rings on top), but at both you will dry out. As with the shipyard quay earlier, there is a concrete lip at the top of the quay which can catch boats as they rise, and during a strong spring tide you will rise quite high, so it may be worth weighing down the fenders to keep your hull protected. It is also possible to anchor and set a line back to the island: you may just remain afloat.

Quayside at Dittisham

Food & transport

Dittisham has a well stocked independent grocery store uphill from the river bank and two good places to eat overlooking the Dart. The Anchorstone Café, open daily 9.30am-5pm from Easter to end of October, serves hearty bacon sandwiches for breakfast and a splendid fish platter at lunchtime comprising Start Bay crab and lobster, Galmpton mussels and River Dart oysters. Opposite, the Ferry Boat Inn has views of the river if you arrive in time to get a window table. On Thursday evenings it is host to an idiosyncratic pub quiz, all welcome.

In Stoke Gabriel a couple of pubs serve food. The Castle Inn has a reasonable menu but Church House Inn serves just bar snacks and does not admit children.

Totnes is a small town with plenty of shops and restaurants. A large Morrisons supermarket is in walking distance of the quay and an Elizabethan market takes place each Tuesday morning, May to September. Effings, 50 Fore Street, is an excellent deli, with a couple of tables for lunch. For those feeling especially lazy there is the very convenient single berth against the terrace of the Steam Packet Inn on St Peter's Quay. In town Rumour, restaurant and wine bar, in the High Street is good.

Totnes train station is about a 15-minute walk from the quay. It is on the main line with a fast and frequent service to all major cities in the UK.

Interest

Dittisham (pronounced Ditsum) is a quiet village though not long ago it boasted seven inns and cider houses. A steep walk uphill takes you past some pretty homes and gardens. The church of St George dates from 1333. The village is famed for the Plowman plum, a unique variety which may have originated in Germany, its name a corruption of Pflaumen Baum. There are still extensive plum orchards round about and the fruit can be bought fresh when ripe in July/August, though the season only lasts about 10 days. Should you arrive out of season, Plowman plums are also the basis of a liqueur made by Bramley and Gage.

The Greenway Estate, a short walk uphill from the quay, was once owned by the Gilberts - a late 16th-century Tudor mansion was built for Sir John whose son Sir Humphrey took possession of Newfoundland for Elizabeth I. In 1926 it was bought by Agatha Christie as a holiday retreat (see 'Literary West Country' on page 37). Although she did not write here, the grounds are used as the setting for some of her murders. The girl guide Marlene Tucker is found strangled in the boathouse and Amyas Crale, the artist, dies in the garden having drunk beer laced with hemlock. Christie's son-in-law Anthony Hicks was a very talented gardener and there are 2,700 significant trees and woody plants to see, each of which is tagged. The estate, a massive 278 acres, is now administered by the National Trust and there are guided walks giving specialist information about the collection of tender and rare plants, and a good café. If birds are of interest you may enjoy the Dawn

Royal Navy flying during Regatta

Chorus Walk which starts at 5.30am and ends with breakfast (information ☎ 01803 842382). Permission to land at Greenway Quay is required from the ferry on VHF10. The idyllic looking Ferry Cottage is still owned by the family.

Stoke Gabriel is predominantly residential. Nearby you may see men salmon fishing during the season 15th April - 15th August. Having been feeding off the coast of Greenland, salmon return to spawn in the upper reaches of the Dart. Although they are still caught commercially the numbers taken are strictly limited. Fishermen used to repair their nets on the quay in Stoke Gabriel, now a carpark and picnic meadow. There is small café with restricted opening hours. A dam was constructed across the creek in Norman times to create a mill pond that would power a tidal corn mill. Today the pond is a haven for wildlife. There has been a church at Stoke Gabriel since Norman times, though the present building dates from the 13th century. The yew tree in the churchyard is thought to be over 1300 years old. Legend has it that if you walk around it backwards seven times you will be granted a wish. The orchard next to the church is one of the last remaining ancient church apple orchards in Devon. Church House Inn was built to accommodate the masons who constructed the church. It doubled as a Courthouse and the stocks are still there.

Totnes is sometimes talked of as the hippie capital of Devon. This is the place for rebirthing, reiki, reflexology, even therapy using raw vegetable juice, and all paid for using their alternative currency, the Totnes Pound. Launched in 2007, the Totnes pound can be exchanged for Sterling at various issuing points which then attract discounts when they are spent with participating businesses. Only paper money is available at present (printed locally of course) but a steering group are looking into some form of plastic card and are in discussion with Co-op UK about setting up an Industrial and Provident Society.

The small museum in Fore Street tells the history of the town and the life of Charles Babbage (1791-1871), who went to school here for a short time before going on to design an 'analytical engine' based on punched cards and the forerunner of our modern computer. A footpath follows the ramparts of

the old town walls and the Guildhall is medieval. The splendid church of St Mary dates from the 15th century and has an exceptional rood screen carved out of Beer stone (see 'The Jurassic Coast' on page 42). Nearby, the remarkably intact Norman castle was built to a motte-and-bailey design.

From Totnes a short bus or taxi ride would take you to Dartington Hall, the previous home of American millionairess Dorothy Elmhurst and now an arts and educational establishment with delightful gardens full of sculptures. The 14th-century great hall houses a literary festival in July and occasional concerts. Slightly nearer Totnes the Cider Press Centre is home to Dartington Glass. There is a Cranks Wholefood restaurant here, an excellent kitchen shop and a gallery selling upmarket crafts and jewellery.

The South Devon Railway runs steam trains from Totnes to Buckfastleigh, where you can visit the Dartmoor Otter Sanctuary and Butterfly Farm and Buckfast Abbey, a mile beyond.

Dartmouth during Regatta

⚓ Start Bay

Start Bay forms part of the South Devon Heritage Coast. It offers good anchorages in open bays with protection from the west. Here are some of the best west country beaches, most notably Blackpool Sands, an idyllic cove backed by steep wooded cliffs. Further west 3 miles of shingle, known as Slapton Sands, were used for rehearsing the D-Day landings. Behind is the largest natural lake in southwest of England. Designated a National Nature Reserve, this is place to see rare Cetti's warblers and numerous glow worms.

Approach & navigation

The approach to all of the beaches is straightforward and anchorage in sand and shingle is good in westerly conditions, though rolly. This is not the place to be with strong wind from the east.

Skerries Bank rises to the east and must be avoided in bad weather, when rough seas break over the bank. Depth can be as little as 2.1m.

Around Start Point the tide creates confused water and overfalls. The race should be given clearance of at least 2M in bad weather. In settled conditions it is possible to sail close to the shore, keeping a good distance to avoid Start Rocks, the Black Stone island and Sleaden Rock. Tide near the Point can be very strong (more than 3.5 knots). This inshore passage, close to shore, should be taken only with local knowledge at hand.

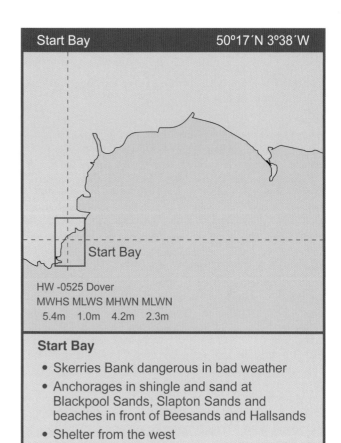

Start Bay   50°17′N 3°38′W

HW -0525 Dover

MWHS	MLWS	MHWN	MLWN
5.4m	1.0m	4.2m	2.3m

Start Bay

- Skerries Bank dangerous in bad weather
- Anchorages in shingle and sand at Blackpool Sands, Slapton Sands and beaches in front of Beesands and Hallsands
- Shelter from the west

⚓ Anchorages

Start Bay has anchorages that are picturesque and quiet: you may well be there alone. However, the open nature of the bay and the tidal stream, flowing north-south, mean your boat is likely to lie parallel to the shore and the slightest swell results in an uncomfortable night as the waves hit side on.

Blackpool Sands at the northern end of the bay is a privately managed beach which is very popular with tourists. Anchorage is good, shingle and sand, and the cliffs offer shelter from the west to northeast.

Further south along Slapton Sands up to Limpet Rocks it is quite exposed.

Below Limpet Rocks, the cliffs beyond Beesands and Hallsands offer better protection from the prevailing winds. This is a really pretty spot.

Food & Transport

The village of Torcross caters well for tourists and has a restaurant, café and pub. There is also a post office and village store. The Venus Café at Blackpool Sands serves good quality, simple food. It is open for dinner in the summer (☎ 01803 770209). Slapton, half a mile inland, has two pubs and a village shop.

Transport is limited to a few buses and taxis.

Interest

Slapton, a picturesque Devon village with houses made of stone, is well worth the walk inland. Slapton Ley National Nature Reserve is a freshwater lagoon separated from the sea by a narrow shingle bar. It teems with birds in spring when house martins,

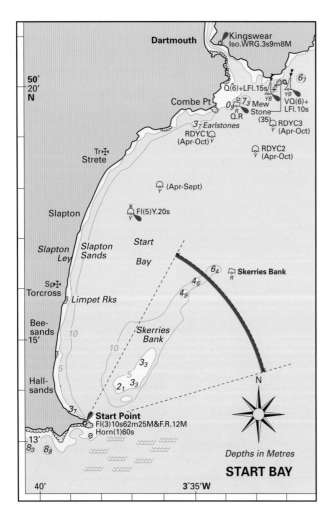

START BAY

Depths in Metres

US Sherman tank from D-Day practice at Slapton Sands

sand martins, swallows and swifts return from their migration and this is the place to see and hear the secretive reed warbler and the great crested grebe. In summer hundreds of thousands of midges take to the air in huge spiralling smoke-like plumes to provide 99% of the diet for Cetti (pronounced Chetty)'s warbler, a rare bird often seen here skulking in the reeds. Luckily the midges are not attracted to humans. Guided walks exploring this habitat and those that live here, including badgers and a breeding population of dormice, start from the Field Studies Centre in the village (☎ 01548 580685 or 01548 580466, booking essential).

Slapton Sands was considered the ideal place for American troops to rehearse for the D-Day landings on the beaches of Normandy. 750 families and all livestock in six parishes were evacuated to make way for the thousands of US servicemen that arrived

during the winter of 1943. Many families were never to return. The exercise, named Exercise Tiger, was top secret: the beach was mined, bounded by barbed wire and patrolled by sentries. On 28 April 1944 German E-boats staged a surprise attack, killing 639 American serviceman aboard their landing craft and in the mayhem many others died through so-called 'friendly fire'. At Torcross there is a memorial erected by the US Government alongside a Sherman tank that was recovered from the sea in 1984.

As you sail by Hallsands the dejected remains of a village can be seen. Ill-conceived dredging for shingle, bound for the naval dockyards at Plymouth, around 1900 progressively undermined the shoreline and in 1917 a severe storm left just one of 37 houses standing.

Huge numbers of spider crabs spawn in Start Bay every summer. Many are exported to France and Spain.

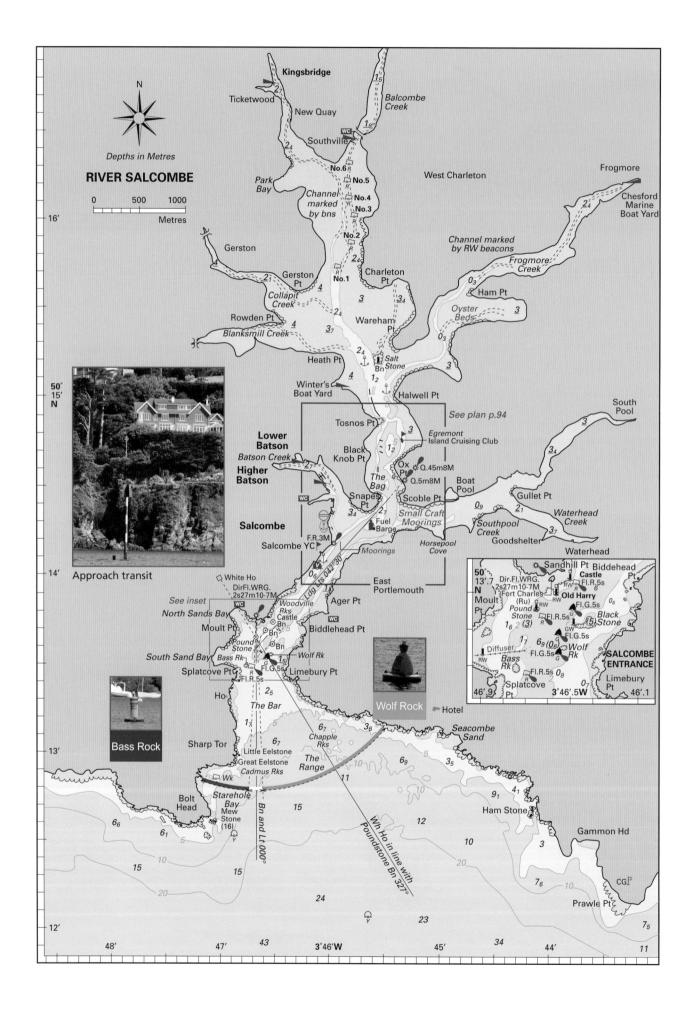

N

Depths in Metres

RIVER SALCOMBE

0   500   1000
Metres

Kingsbridge

Ticketwood

New Quay

Balcombe Creek

Southville

WC

West Charleton

Frogmore

No.6

No.5

No.4

No.3

Channel marked by bns

No.2

Chesford Marine Boat Yard

Park Bay

Gerston

Channel marked by RW beacons

Frogmore Creek

Gerston Pt

No.1

Charleton Pt

Ham Pt

Oyster Beds

Collapit Creek

Rowden Pt

Wareham Pt

Blanksmill Creek

Heath Pt

Salt Stone Bn

South Pool

Winter's Boat Yard

Halwell Pt

See plan p.94

Tosnos Pt

Egremont Island Cruising Club

Lower Batson

Black Knob Pt

Batson Creek

Ox Pt Q.45m8M

Q.5m8M

Higher Batson

The Bag

Boat Pool

Gullet Pt

Snapes Pt

Scoble Pt

Small Craft Moorings

Waterhead Creek

WC

Salcombe

Fuel Barge

Southpool Creek

Goodshelter

F.R.3M

Salcombe YC

Moorings

Horsepool Cove

Waterhead

East Portlemouth

Approach transit

White Ho
DirFl.WRG.
2s27m10-7M

Sandhill Pt

Biddenhead Pt

50°
13'.7
N

Dir.Fl.WRG.
2s27m10-7M

Castle
Fl.R.5s

Fort Charles
(Ru)

Old Harry
Fl.G.5s

Moult Pt

See inset

North Sands Bay

WC

Woodville Rks
Castle Bn

Ager Pt

Pound Stone

Fl.R.5s

Black Stone

Moult Pt

Bn

Biddlehead Pt

Pound Stone

Bn

South Sand Bay

Bass Rk

Wolf Rk

Fl.G.5s

Wolf Rk

Splatcove Pt

Fl.G.5s

Limebury Pt

Fl.R.5s

Diffuser

Bass Rk

Ho

Fl.R.5s

Splatcove Pt

Limebury Pt

The Bar

Wolf Rock

Hotel

SALCOMBE ENTRANCE

3°46'.5W

Sharp Tor

Little Eelstone

Chapple Rks

Seacombe Sand

Great Eelstone
Cadmus Rks

The Range

Ham Stone

Wk

Bolt Head

Starehole Bay

Mew Stone (16)

Bn and Lt.000°

Gammon Hd

Wh Ho in line with Poundstone Bn 327°

Prawle Pt

CG

Bass Rock

Salcombe and Kingsbridge

Salcombe and Kingsbridge are accessed by crossing a sand bar that is thought to have inspired Lord Tennyson's famous poem 'Crossing the Bar'. The harbour is sheltered but the entrance can be very choppy in strong wind against tide.

Salcombe now caters primarily for the holiday trade. It is a very popular sailing destination and there can be five boats to a buoy in August. Pretty houses line the waterfront and there are numerous good places to eat, plus several galleries and many boutiques. Kingsbridge, 5M upstream, is a busy market town that can be reached by ferry.

Approach & entrance

The entrance to Salcombe should not be attempted in bad weather or strong southerly winds against the ebb. It is advisable to enter at night only in settled conditions. The Bar at the entrance takes you over 1.3m.

In settled weather entering Salcombe presents no problems. There is plenty of space in front of the entrance to the southeast, but not to the west, so it is essential not to be in the red sector or the sectored entrance light.

- Approach the entrance on a bearing of 327°, which is a transit between a white house on the hill and Poundstone Beacon. This gives ample clearance on both sides.

- Once you have passed Bolt Head move from the green sector to the white sector of the entrance beacon DirFl.WRG.2s (red and white diamond). The beach at Starehole Bay, immediately north of Bolt Head, is a good place to aim for.

- Turn due north when in the white sector of entrance DirFl.WRG.2s red and white diamond (transit with Poundstone Beacon, red and white post). This is around 400m from Bolt Head.

- Continue on the leading line, passing red Fl.R.5s to port which marks Bass Rock (submerged).

- Still on the leading line pass green Fl.G.5s to starboard on Wolf Rock. You are through the bar and depth begins to increase.

- Turn northeast towards the space between Poundstone Beacon (red and white post) and Blackstone beacon (green and white), leaving to port two red and white beacons marking rocks off Sandhill Point.

- Continue on a course of 42° towards two Q leading lights (5m and 45m heights) along the fairway.

To continue to Kingsbridge (HW +/-2.5, boats of draught less than 2m, length 11m):

- Remain on the fairway on a course of 42°. Salcombe is on your left with cottages and a hotel looking down on you and visitors' buoys to port.

- Keep going between further visitors' buoys sited in front of the large opening to port which is full of small boat moorings.

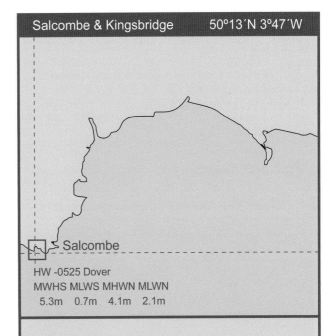

Salcombe & Kingsbridge   50°13′N 3°47′W

HW -0525 Dover
MWHS MLWS MHWN MLWN
5.3m   0.7m   4.1m   2.1m

Salcombe

- Approach: dangerous in bad conditions
- Entrance: bar 1.3m
- Visitors' buoys: 15 marked 'V' in entrance fairway and past town quay
- Normandy Pontoon - loading only, 1m
- Visitors' pontoon at The Bag - deep berths
- Drying moorings up to 6m
- Harbourmaster VHF14 ① 01548 843791 Fax 01458 842033
- salcombe.harbour@southhams.gov.uk
- www.salcombeharbour.co.uk
- Yacht taxi VHF12 - ① 07807 643879
- Fuel barge VHF06 ① 07801 798862/01548 843838. Easter - 30 Sep 0830-1700. 1 Oct - Easter 0830-1700, closed Sat/Sun
- Repairs: consult harbourmaster
- Showers and laundry at Salcombe Yacht Club ① 01548 842593 www.salcombeyc.org.uk

- Go past the fuel barge and begin to turn north (do not continue on what appears to be the continuation of the fairway at high water), around Snapes Point and into The Bag.

- Continue north through The Bag past visitors' and residents' pontoons to port and the intriguing floating Egremont Island Cruising Club to Starboard.

- There are shallow patches at the north end of The Bag, best navigated by a close watch on depth. Round Tosnos Point and rocks extending, remaining mid stream.

- Pass further residents' pontoons to port.

- Leave Salt Stone beacon to starboard. This is a good area for anchoring in sufficient water for most boats.

- Remain midstream (2.4m) keeping an eye on depth in case you stray to either side. Your target is the first red R1

- After R1 the course dries. The deepest section is marked by red buoys R2, R3, R4, R5 and R6 to Kingsbridge. Continue to the visitors' pontoon (second pontoon, after New Quay) or the wall on port side. Both dry.

⚓ Ⓥ Salcombe

There are four visitors' buoys in the entrance fairway and a further eleven between the town pontoon and the fuel barge. In the summer visitors' buoys can have several boats attached. It is always worth talking with the harbourmaster on VHF14 as there may be a spare residents' mooring. The Normandy pontoon attached to the shore may be used by visitors for short stays, to take in water and load/unload.

The visitors' pontoon in The Bag is often sheltered from swell.

You can anchor on the eastern side of the fairway but not beyond. Further on past The Bag, where the stream forks, there is a quiet anchorage around Salt Stone.

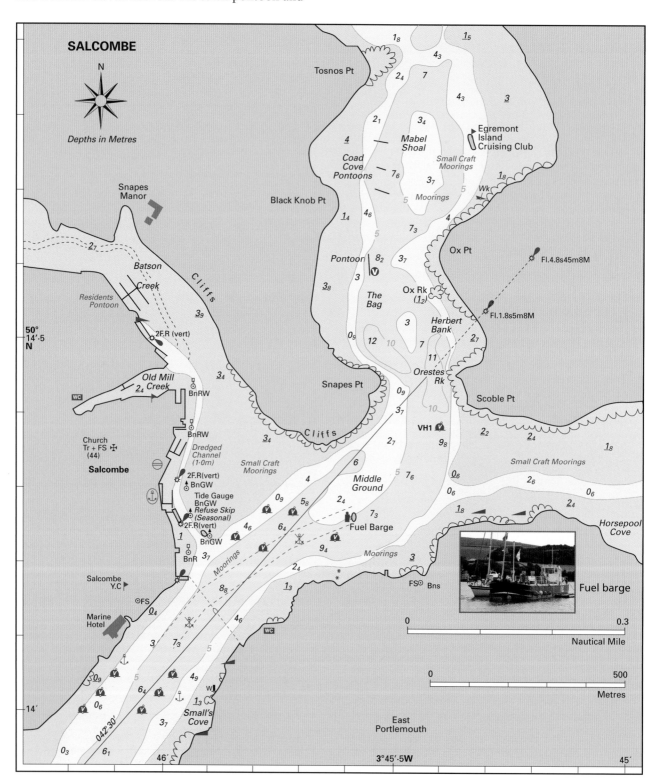

Fuel barge

⚓ Kingsbridge

All berthing at Kingsbridge dries. The second pontoon after New Quay and the wall on the port side accept visitors.

Food & Transport

Salcombe has many small shops selling food, including pasties. There are bakeries, an off-licence and a small greengrocers. Salcombe Deli in Fore Street is excellent. It has a selection of gourmet ready meals and sells frozen scones which taste homemade after briefly heating in the oven. (Clotted cream and jam are easily sourced!) The Boat Yard in Island Street sells live, and cooked to order, crabs and lobsters. Across the water in East Portlemouth The Venus Café serves simple, high quality food looking onto the beach (Open daytime only. ☎ 01548 843558).

The nearest train station is at Totnes. A bus runs hourly (not Sunday) between Salcombe (Gould Road/ Shadycombe Road, north end) and Kingsbridge (Quay) and there is also a ferry. From Kingsbridge there are buses on to Totnes, Dartmouth, Exeter and Plymouth.

Interest

The Salcombe-Kingsbridge 'estuary' is a ria, formed when the sea level rose more than 100m during the last ice age. Today no river flows into the sea inlet, which is especially sheltered and home to some very rare plants and animals including a sea-slug thought to be found nowhere else. Designated a Marine Site of Special Scientific Interest in 1987 and a marine Nature Reserve in 1992, there are eelgrass beds that support seahorses (see 'Seahorses' on page 109) and the very rare fan mussel which can grow to over 1ft in diameter.

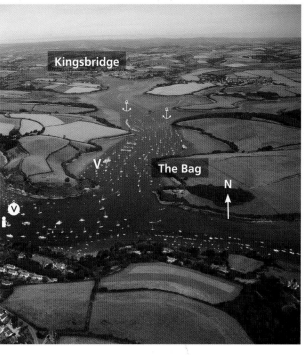

Salcombe

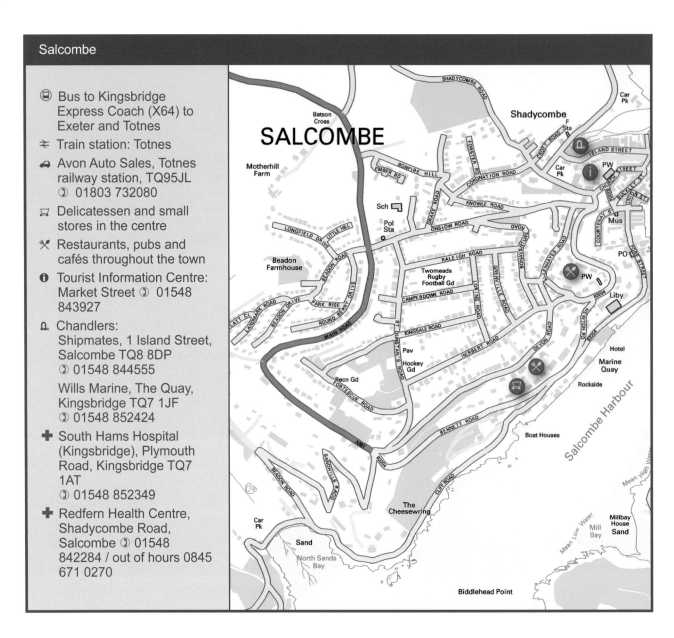

🚌 Bus to Kingsbridge
Express Coach (X64) to
Exeter and Totnes

🚆 Train station: Totnes

🚗 Avon Auto Sales, Totnes
railway station, TQ95JL
① 01803 732080

🍴 Delicatessen and small
stores in the centre

✕ Restaurants, pubs and
cafés throughout the town

ℹ️ Tourist Information Centre:
Market Street ① 01548
843927

⚓ Chandlers:
Shipmates, 1 Island Street,
Salcombe TQ8 8DP
① 01548 844555

Wills Marine, The Quay,
Kingsbridge TQ7 1JF
① 01548 852424

✚ South Hams Hospital
(Kingsbridge), Plymouth
Road, Kingsbridge TQ7
1AT
① 01548 852349

✚ Redfern Health Centre,
Shadycombe Road,
Salcombe ① 01548
842284 / out of hours 0845
671 0270

Please do not drop anchor in eelgrass designated areas.

The small Salcombe Maritime Museum has some technically accurate paintings of ships that were trading out of Salcombe during the Victorian period and much information about nearby wrecks. Lord Tennyson's poem 'Crossing the Bar' begins 'Sunset and evening star and one clear call for me! And may there be no moaning of the bar when I put out to sea.' The moaning is thought to refer to the sound of water breaking over the bar, a situation that was recognised as dangerous. In 1916 the Salcombe lifeboat, a rowing boat in those days, capsized here with the loss of 13 lives.

You are likely to see the Salcombe yawl, a traditional small two-mast fishing boat, competing in various races throughout the summer. For those who enjoy walking there is easy access to the South West Coast Path and the Tourist Information and Harbour Office has an excellent booklet describing six self-guided walks.

Kingsbridge, 5M upstream, is rich in architecture. There are fine Tudor and Georgian buildings and the Shambles is an Elizabethan colonnade. If you are interested in china then you should visit the Cookworthy Museum of Rural Life, housed in the 17th-century grammar school. Cookworthy was born in Kingsbridge in 1705 and worked as an apothecary in Plymouth before becoming the first person in Europe to make hard paste porcelain (see 'China Clay' on page 152).

Those with an interest in plants should find time to visit Overbeck's (Salcombe ferry to South sands and then a strenuous half-mile walk uphill), once the home of an eccentric German chemist. There are seven acres of rare and exotic plants that thrive in this sheltered microclimate including Chusan palm trees, banana trees, olive groves and fuchsias from South America. The Edwardian house (now in the hands of the National Trust) is filled with his lifelong enthusiasms, including huge collections of beetles and butterflies, but he is best known for an electric shock device which he claimed stopped and reversed the ageing process. There are guided walks, and talks, and a tearoom for refreshments.

Cream teas

No one should visit the West Country without enjoying a cream tea: after all, when in Rome! It is said that clotted cream exists nowhere but in Devon, Cornwall and the Lebanon as Phoenicians, seeking Cornish tin, took the recipe home 500 years ago. It is made by leaving creamy milk to stand until the fat has risen to the surface. Gently heating for an hour then causes a thick, delicious crust of cream clots to form. Six pints of milk produces about half a pound.

An early account of the serving of cream teas comes from Tavistock's Benedictine Abbey. Established in the 10th-century it was badly damaged in 997AD by marauding Vikings but during the rebuilding local workers were served bread, clotted cream and strawberry preserves. Cream teas were apparently enjoyed so much that the monks continued to serve them to passing travellers until the Abbey's unhappy demise when Henry VIII dissolved the Monasteries in 1539. Incidentally not only was the cream tea 'born' in Tavistock but so too was Sir Francis Drake.

These days there is much friendly rivalry between Devon and Cornwall, not just as regards who produces the best cream but also whether the scones should be buttered and whether the jam or cream should be on top. In fact the traditional Cornish cream tea was served on a Cornish split, a slightly sweet bread roll that was buttered then coated in jam and topped with a spoonful of clotted cream. In Devon scones are used, without butter, and the jam goes on top.

Although the West Country is full of gorgeous venues for cream teas ashore, scones are very easy to make on board and you will have no difficulty sourcing clotted cream and jam. Scone ingredients can be taken to the boat already combined (except for the milk and egg) as it stores well in the fridge.

This is our favourite recipe. Leave out the ginger if it is not to your liking.

Scones (makes about 8)

Mix   225g (8oz) self raising flour
           1 teaspoon baking powder
           1 teaspoon ground ginger
           40g (1.5oz) caster sugar

Rub in 50g (2oz) butter

Add   2-3 pieces of preserved ginger, chopped
           1 egg
           3-4 tablespoons milk

Bind the mixture then roll out to a thickness of 2cm. Cut out the scones and brush with milk. Bake for 10 minutes in a hot oven (Gas mark 7).

West Devon

Bigbury Bay, River Yealm, Plymouth and the rivers flowing to Plymouth Sound

West Devon

Bigbury Bay, River Yealm, Plymouth and the rivers flowing to Plymouth Sound

WEST DEVON

From Bolt Head to Rame Head there are some very different sailing experiences to be had. You can be alone in a pristine natural environment surrounded by trees and listening just to bird song while not far away in Plymouth, the biggest city in the West Country, is a huge man-made industrial landscape.

Bigbury Bay and the river Avon have the feel of yesteryear. It's not just the Art Deco hotel on Burgh Island and its associations with Noel Coward, the Duke of Windsor and Mrs Simpson, but land abutting the Avon estuary (much still in private hands) has seen little development. Thatched boathouses line a route that is a must for those craving tranquillity and the means to dry out. From Bantham there is a delightful circular walk along the riverbank and the area is especially rich in bird life, attracting all sorts of waders, gulls and wildfowl.

Further west the River Yealm is a designated Area of Outstanding Natural Beauty and Site of Special Scientific Interest. Sheltered and picturesque, this is a popular sailing destination. Newton Ferrers and Noss Mayo, just above the mouth of the estuary, are small and welcoming communities. Both have a pub with a quay that dries.

In terms of character Bigbury and the Yealm are a million miles away from Plymouth Sound, that vast and busy expanse of water just a short sail further west. It is one of the finest deep-water anchorages in Europe and its development was supported by Sir

Francis Drake when he was Mayor of Plymouth. It was here that Drake landed after circumnavigating the world, and from here he set sail against the Spanish Armada in 1588. Today Devonport is a British naval base and warships are generally in evidence, but don't let that put you off as there are delightful anchorages and excellent marinas with easy access to all the city has to offer. Although Plymouth was almost completely destroyed during the second world war some gems remain, including the Royal Citadel and a couple of limestone and timber-framed Elizabethan houses. Smeaton's tower, once the Eddystone Reef lighthouse, affords splendid views of the Sound and the Church of St Andrew's has six wonderful stained glass windows designed by John Piper. The aquarium is an excellent introduction to marine life in the West Country and around the world, and houses a collection of seahorses. Those interested in china should head for the City Museum and Art Gallery where the discovery of porcelain by Devon man William Cookworthy is explained. Joshua Reynolds was born nearby and Beryl Cook was a resident until her death in 2008, and their work is often exhibited. Others may prefer mixing botanicals to create their own flavour of gin during a tour of Black Friars Distillery, while everyone can wander around the Barbican district to eat and drink and spend time where so much history was made.

Upstream of Plymouth there are a few miles of industrial landscape, but here too is the magnificent

Bantham

Lighthouse at the Plymouth breakwater

Royal William Victualling Yard. Open to the public after more than 150 years, these buildings constitute the finest and most complete early 19th-century industrial complex in the country. In time 30 or so yachts will be accommodated in the inner basin on a pay and display basis but for now there is a waterbus from the Barbican (summer only).

Although this is generally a busy waterway, there are quiet anchorages upstream. Off Cawsand, a medieval village within the Sound, is also a delightful place to be.

Sir Frances Drake looking out from the Hoe

Royal William Victualling Yard

Burgh Island

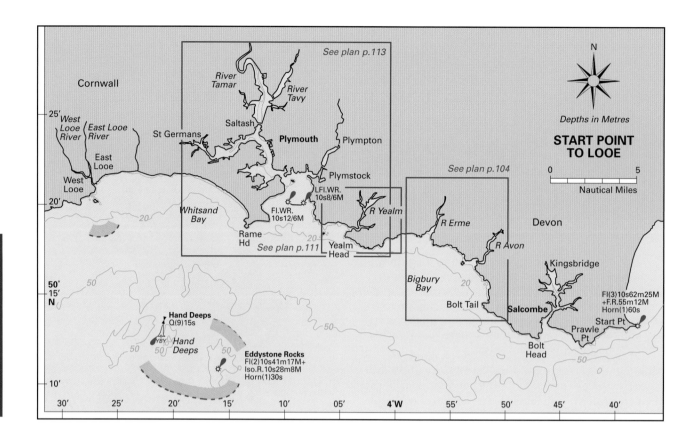

Sailing between Bolt Head and Rame Head

The large bay that stretches from Bolt Head to the Lizard spans Devon and Cornwall, with Plymouth sitting astride the county boundary. This coast has numerous places for secure berthing and a wealth of anchorages in picturesque locations.

In west Devon, Bigbury Bay opens out after passing Bolt Tail. This part of the county is remote and untouched by large development but is not the easiest for a yacht as swell is an almost constant feature and the rivers dry for much of their accessible course. With good planning and calm weather, especially in a boat than can dry out, there is little to rival the River Avon for tranquillity and a sense of adventure. The entrance should not be attempted in bad weather, and there is a risk of not being able to leave if conditions change, but the reward on a lovely day is immense. Outside Hope Cove or anchored off Burgh Island is also idyllic, but the prevailing southwesterlies in such open space create swell that rarely makes an overnight stay possible. The visitor who makes it can reminisce about pilchard fishing in the aptly name Pilchard Inn situated on Burgh Island.

Immediately west of Bigbury Bay, 14M from Bolt Head, the River Yealm is a favourite destination for nearly all West Country cruisers, with Newton Ferrers welcoming visitors. The river is completely sheltered, with buoys and pontoons, and there are enjoyable excursions to be had by dinghy. The entrance has a sand bar, no problem in good weather but not something to negotiate in strong westerly winds.

The entrance to Plymouth Sound is 16M from Bolt Head. This large natural harbour, together with rivers Tamar and Lynher, offers a wealth of berthing options

in several high-standard marinas, swinging moorings and anchorages. The marinas give immediate access to Plymouth and all that it has to offer, plus good support for sailors. Close to the entrance, Cawsand is a good anchorage in westerly conditions, while several places in the Sound offer protection from the east. Upstream the rivers make for long passages towards quiet spots away from the industrial landscape.

Initial shelter

Plymouth is an all-weather harbour, accessible day and night and with extensive options for berthing. The River Yealm can be considered as an initial destination in good weather.

Emergencies

The RNLI stations are at Salcombe and Plymouth, with a beach lifeguard in Bigbury Bay. The main lifeboat is based at Plymouth.

The Maritime Safety Co-ordination Centre (MRCC) is based at Falmouth and monitors Channel 16, MF 2182kHz and DSC Channel 70. Coast radio stations (Coastguard), at Portland and Brixham, transmit Maritime Safety Information (see appendix for timings). There are volunteer Coastguard Rescue teams at Hope Cove, Bigbury, River Yealm, Plymouth, River Tamar and Rame Head.

Plymouth has significant medical facilities.

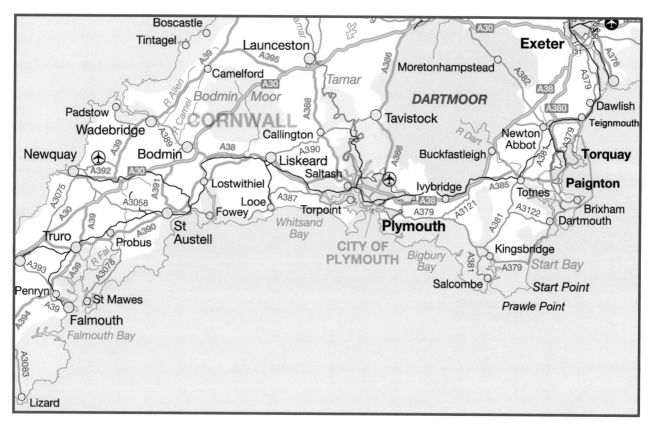

Provisioning

Plymouth is a large city and access to its many supermarkets, shops, pubs, restaurants and cafés is easy from any of the marinas. Newton Ferrers has a village store and several pubs accessible by dinghy. Some of the small villages within Bigbury Bay have shops but they are not within easy reach. The Pilchard Inn on Burgh Island serves good food.

Repairs and chandleries

In Plymouth there are boat lifts at Plymouth Yacht Haven, Queen Anne's Battery Marina, Sutton Harbour and Mayflower Marina. All the main marinas have access to specialist services, including mechanical, rigging and electronic expertise. The chandleries at Plymouth Yacht Haven, Queen Anne's Battery and Mayflower Marina are large and very well stocked, the best in the West Country. Their boat yards also offer extensive yacht services.

Fuel

- Queen Anne's Battery: pontoon close to Sutton lock (diesel and petrol).

- Mayflower Marina: pontoon shoreside of the marina (diesel and petrol).

Transport

High speed trains stop at Plymouth and connect the city to the rest of the UK. Plymouth airport handles national and some international flights.

There are buses and coaches from Plymouth to most seaside towns and large cities in the country.

Passages

The distance from Prawle Point to Plymouth is 18M, with only some disturbance of the water off Prawle Point.

From the entrance of Plymouth Sound to Fowey it is 19M. Keep clear of Rame Head and Looe Island to avoid confused seas.

The distance from Fowey to the seaward side of Falmouth Bay is 19M. Beware of Guineas Rock and then the headland of Dodman Point, with The Bellows to the south, and The Bizzies.

The long passage from Prawle Point to The Lizard is 58M. It should be timed to reach the Lizard with a fair tide. If proceeding on to the Isles of Scilly this is the significant tidal gate of the passage, but if going on to round Land's End a more complex calculation is needed. Aim to pass well south of The Lizard, a good 5M off in good weather and more if conditions are difficult.

The Eddystone Rocks (Fl(2)10s41m17M and Iso.R.10s28m8M) and Hand Deeps (Q(9)15s) stand 9M SSW of Plymouth Sound. They are well marked and must be given a wide berth.

There is plenty of shipping heading for Land's End and also significant naval activity off Plymouth. Naval firing practice takes place across Megavissey Bay.

There are inshore fishing boats operating out of Looe, Polperro and Mevagissey. Look out for fishing pots in anything up to 50m.

Bigbury Bay

Bigbury Bay has a number of anchorages in settled weather, offshore winds or easterlies. The rivers Avon and Erme are stunning settings but both dry and should not be attempted when the wind is onshore.

This corner of Devon attracts many holidaymakers but the drive through narrow lanes, with few passing places, means that by the time the sea is in sight tempers can be frayed. Needless to say, the best way to arrive is by boat! Hope Cove and Bigbury-on-Sea have splendid beaches, the latter is very popular with surfers and windsurfers. Burgh Island is tethered to Bigbury by 250 metres of golden sand. A sea tractor criss-crosses the isthmus when the tide is in.

Hope Cove

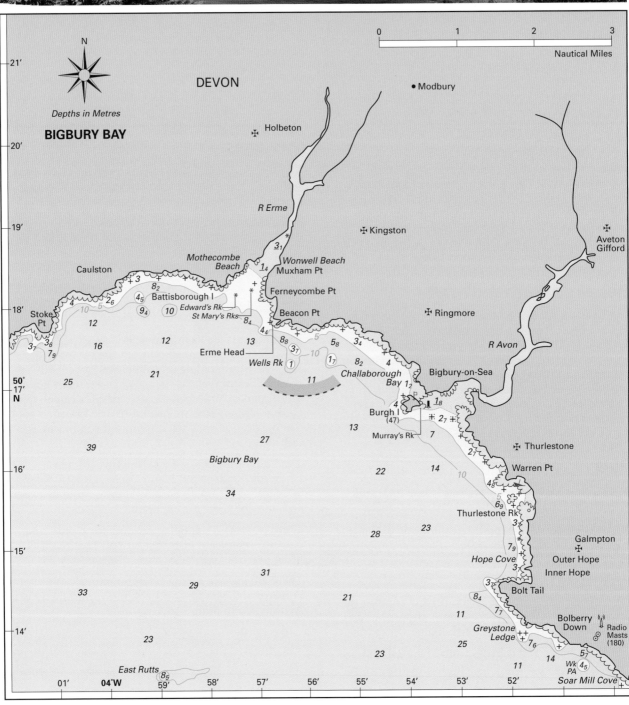

⚓ Hope Cove

A pleasant anchorage but use only in very settled conditions, easterlies or wind offshore. Head for the centre of the bay on 130° and anchor WSW of the pier, allowing for Bass Rock which extends from the pier head. Beware Goody Rock (cleared by 60° on pier head) and stay clear of moorings.

Treat with caution in the prevailing southwesterlies and keep a wide berth in strong conditions.

Food and transport

There are two pubs in the cove, Hope Inn and Anchor Inn. Hope Cove and Thurlestone are served by local buses.

⚓ Burgh Island

Home to the Art Deco Burgh Island Hotel, the island is joined to the shore by a tidal strip of sand about 250m long. Anchorage is possible north or south of the strip, exposed to the prevailing southwest and bouncy except in very calm conditions. Murray's Rock to the east of the island is marked by an unlit beacon.

Food and transport

The Pilchard Inn on Burgh Island has excellent food. It is owned by the hotel and they share a kitchen. The hotel is open to residents only and to those using its formal restaurant.

Bigbury-on-Sea has a post office and a couple of general stores. The Venus Café has good quality food (☎ 01548 810141). There are outdoor showers and toilets in the car park. Public transport is limited to an infrequent bus between Bigbury (inland) and Plymouth.

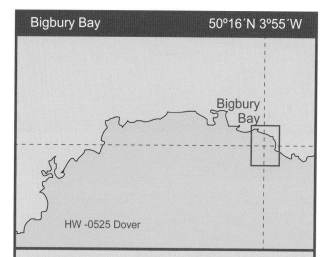

Bigbury Bay	50°16′N 3°55′W

HW -0525 Dover

Hope Cove

- Settled, offshore or easterly winds only
- ⚓ WSW pier, stay clear of Bass Rock and moorings

Burgh Island

- ⚓ Exposed, unlit Murray's Rock east of island

River Avon

- Dries, sandbar, narrow channel; sheltered
- Enter HW-1, settled conditions, never in onshore winds; beware Murray's Rock
- Harbourmaster ☎ 01458 561196
- Small workshop at Bantham

River Erme

- Dries, enter HW
- Enter: settled conditions, never approach with onshore winds. Beware Wells Rock and Edwards Rock

Bigbury Bay

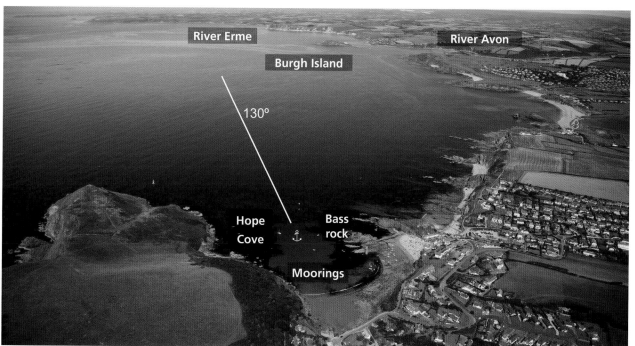

River Erme

River Avon

Burgh Island

130°

Hope Cove

Bass rock

Moorings

⚓ River Avon

The River Avon is one of the best destinations in the West Country if you can dry out. It is very sheltered but wind from the southwest may make it impossible to leave!

The entrance needs to be treated with great care and is best with some local knowledge or preceded by a reconnaissance trip in the dinghy. Depth sounding essential.

Approach & entrance

- DO NOT attempt in onshore winds or unsettled conditions.

- Best approach at HW-1 as the stream runs fast in the entrance channel.

- BEWARE unlit Murray's Rock SE of Burgh Island and further east Blind Mare which has only 1m of water above it at low water springs.

- Keep close to the island. The edge of the sandbar is on a transit between the right-hand chimney of the large farmhouse on the skyline of Mount Folly and the white house immediately below. Both houses are on the east side of the cluster of buildings.

- Pass through the entrance (DRIES) leaving Bantham Sands to starboard.

- The channel is narrow and runs close to Mount Folly at the entrance, with about 1m depth.

- It is best to ignore the painted white entrance marker, which is not correctly sighted for the channel. Better to use your judgement and the depth gauge.

Burgh Island and River Avon entrance

WEST DEVON

BIGBURY BAY

- Before you reach Lower Cellars, you will cross patches of sand that dry and shift frequently. A buoy may mark the shallows.

- Continue between Lower and Upper Cellars, keeping south, towards the entrance where there is a red painted/thatched boathouse. A shingle bank that extends from Cockleridge is closed to your port side.

- The river widens and deepens in front of the thatched boathouse, with depth of 1.8m. Anchoring is possible for limited periods only as you may drag due to poor holding and strong current on the ebb.

- Stay to the south/east side of the river on starboard and pass the harbourmaster's beautiful thatched boathouse.

Anchor beyond the moorings. The river continues to flow but it is shallow everywhere so expect to dry out. The bottom is sand.

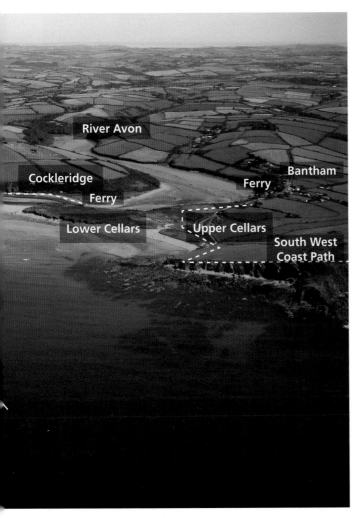

Food and transport

The village of Bantham is owned by Evans Estates, who also run the car park. The Sloop Inn in Bantham and the Fisherman's Rest at Aveton Gifford (access by dinghy) are good places to eat. Just off the tidal road, on the approach to Aveton Gifford, the Oyster Shack is thoroughly recommended (℡ 01548 810876).

Transport is very limited but bus no. 93 runs along the A379 between Kingsbridge and Plymouth.

A ferry crosses between Bantham and Cockleridge Farm, March to end of September, linking the South West Coast Path across the river.

Interest

Most of Burgh Island's 28-acres have public right of way and a visit is recommended. A short, steep climb uphill takes you to a vantage point with magnificent views back along the coast, though Bigbury-on-Sea is rather an eyesore, and across the water. The sea here once supported huge shoals of pilchards and there are still the remains of a Huer's Hut on the crest of the island. Hue is old French for shout and the term 'hue and cry' has passed into the language. No guesses for how the 14th-century Pilchard Inn got its name.

A hotel was first built on Burgh Island in 1895 for the music hall singer George Chirgwin. Struck by the views on offer he is said to have exclaimed, 'If the world is a stage this is its private box.' In 1927 he sold the property to Archibald Nettlefold, a starstruck industrialist who had recently married an opera singer. Wanting to provide his wife and her fashionable friends with a place to drink cocktails and dance to jazz, he asked the architect Matthew Dawson to design him a private holiday home. For a while it was known as the 'jet-set isle' with guests that included Noel Coward, Gertrude Lawrence, the Duke of Windsor and Mrs Simpson, but it was soon converted into a hotel. Agatha Christie wrote six of her books here (see 'Literary West Country' on page 37). *And Then There Were None*, her most popular book, and *Evil Under the Sun* were both set on the island. It is possible to walk across the causeway when the tide is low, but at high tide the journey is made by sea-tractor. This unique piece of machinery was built by Beare & Sons of Newton Abbot and can operate in up to 7ft of water.

Bantham was a base for processing pilchards until overfishing exhausted supplies in the late 19th century. Its modern thatched boathouse is home to the harbourmaster and is also a workshop for building clinker boats. The river is a magnet for birds.

⚓ River Erme

The river Erme is as picturesque as the river Avon but it dries completely and is open to the southwest without any protection. The river is private so anchoring is possible only at the entrance and should be considered only in settled conditions.

Approach & entrance

Anchorages at the mouth, off Mothecombe Beach and Wonwell Beach.

DO NOT attempt in onshore winds or unsettled conditions.

HAZARDS:

- Wells Rock (1m) 1M SE of entrance.
- Edward's Rock (1m) 250m south of Battisborough Island.
- E and W Mary's Rocks in the mouth.

Access near HW from SW between Battisborough Island and W Mary's Rock (dries 1.1m). Keep to the west side and aim for Owen's Hill.

Sound in (depths from 5m to 1m as you go in). Sandy bottom.

Interest

Situated within an Area of Outstanding Natural Beauty the River Erme is owned by the Flete Estate. It offers those rare treats of solitude and tranquillity. Exploration by dinghy is great fun but do consider rowing to preserve the peace! Swimmers and canoeists often use the river, which is also a haven for birds. There are no facilities or links with mainland

transport. The nearest place for food is the Dolphin Inn in Kingston, a mile inland.

The Dolphin Inn, Kingston

River Erme

Seahorses

Two species of seahorse exist around the British Isles and according to Neil Garrick-Maidment of the Exeter based Seahorse Trust, the West Country is a hot spot. The short-snouted, stocky-looking *Hippocampus hippocampus* favours the north-facing shoreline, usually living on open sand, while the spiny seahorse, *Hippocampus guttulatus*, prefers the fast-flowing estuaries of the south where it lives camouflaged amongst seagrass and algae. Although seahorses are most likely to be found in shallow water, some live at great depths. One pulled ashore in a shrimp pot a mile off Dartmouth came up from 257 feet.

Seahorses are fish. They live in water, breath through gills and have a swim bladder, but they are not covered in scales. Instead they have an exo-skeleton of external, bony plates fused together and covered in flesh. They are poor swimmers, relying on a tiny dorsal fin that beats up to 70 times a second. The small pectoral fin either side of their head gives them stability and helps with steering, but is not used for propulsion.

Seahorses live on small crustacea (such as mysis shrimp) and plankton but they have no ability to chew so some lucky prey sucked in through their snout will pass through unscathed. Their eyes work independently so they can look both forwards and backwards at the same time. This is useful when, as fry, they need to find 3,000 pieces of food every day.

Seahorses pair for life and the female passes her eggs to the male to fertilise and carry. Known as 'reverse pregnancy', this is unique in the animal kingdom. Gestation takes about 4 weeks. Of the 500 or so fry that are produced by our native species only one or two will survive to adulthood. Without predation they can expect to live about ten years.

Since April 2008 both the short-snouted and the spiny seahorse have been fully protected by the Wildlife and Countryside Act, but they are at greater risk than ever before because of an increase in anchor damage to their habitat. However, we should also consider the broader picture. 'Seagrass is the rainforest of the sea. It stops erosion, stores carbon dioxide and is a nursery for numerous marine animals as well as being a seahorse habitat. Once a mat of roots have been wrenched from the sand there is often no going back because crabs excavate further and swirls of water create a vortex washing away more and more of the root system', says Neil. Many people are now pinning their hopes on the 2009 Marine and Coastal Access Bill with its intention to 'halt deterioration in ... marine biodiversity and promote recovery'. No doubt in time advice about anchoring will become available.

Until then we are all urged to write to the Crown Estate and Natural England asking that they replace their old moorings with those that are environmentally friendly. Most buoys in the West Country drag chain but newer moorings screw into the seabed with chain that floats. Apparently many boat owners have already written letters asking for change. Contact details are given below.

If you like to dive, Tor Bay is a good place to see seahorses as both our native species can be found just 100-200 yards from the shore. They are also in the River Tamar and on the inside of Drake Island in Plymouth Sound. Those who would like to see them without getting wet should head for the National Marine Aquarium in Plymouth.

Contact details: The Crown Estate, 16 New Burlington Place, London W1S 2HX; Natural England, 1 East Parade, Sheffield S1 2ET; www.theseahorsetrust.com

River Yealm

As sheltered as the river Avon but with the advantage of depth, the Yealm is a five-star destination. Not surprisingly, it is often very crowded both with cruising boats and with daytrippers from Plymouth. Newton Ferrers on the south side of the estuary, is the larger community. Noss Mayo, on the north side, is much smaller. Both have quaint fishermen's cottages which line the riverbank, but there are plenty of new houses too. This is a prime spot for second homes and more than half of the population are beyond retirement age.

The estuary has a main channel and a number of creeks with trees down to the water's edge. Magnificent views can be had from the two pubs on the shoreline.

Approach & entrance

Straightforward entrance except in strong west/southwesterlies. Dangers include Slimers, east of Great Mewstone, and Ebb Rocks, west of Yealm Head. You will need to clear the entrance sandbar on a dogleg course. Inside there are many resident boats and moorings.

- Approach from west/southwest between bearings of 10° and 30° to clear Slimers and Ebb Rocks.

- Turn towards entrance buoy Fl.R.5s when abeam.

- Use transit beacons (white triangle top black stripe) on a bearing of 89° to clear Mouthstone Ledge. This transit does NOT clear the sandbar.

- To clear the sandbar leave the two red buoys Fl.R.5s and R to port. The gap between the sand bar and the shore is quite narrow but perfectly adequate.

- When the second red buoy is to port aim towards the RW beacon high on the north bank (white rectangle top, red stripe) on a bearing of 47°.

- Depth from the buoy to Misery Point is 1m during springs. Once past the Point depth will begin to rise to 3m or deeper dring MLWS.

- After a southeast turn the first visitors' buoys appear.

- To access a second set of visitors' buoys and the visitors' pontoon at Yealm Pool: leave the red buoy to port 300m later in order to clear a drying spit.

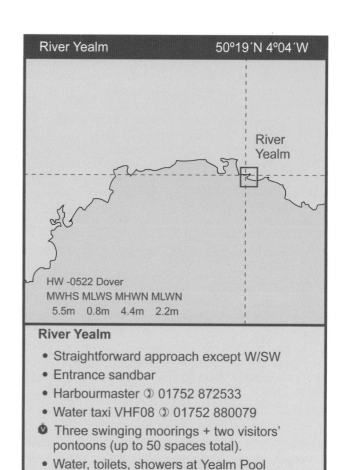

River Yealm   50°19′N 4°04′W

HW -0522 Dover

MWHS	MLWS	MHWN	MLWN
5.5m	0.8m	4.4m	2.2m

River Yealm

- Straightforward approach except W/SW
- Entrance sandbar
- Harbourmaster ☎ 01752 872533
- Water taxi VHF08 ☎ 01752 880079
- Three swinging moorings + two visitors' pontoons (up to 50 spaces total).
- Water, toilets, showers at Yealm Pool
- Landing Newtown Ferrers and Noss Mayo
- Yealm Yacht Club ☎ 01752 872291

- As the river turns north continue on to reach the final set of visitors' moorings. There is space to turn beyond these buoys in 3.5m.

Berthing & facilities

Visitors' pontoons are at the Yealm Pool river bend (25 boats) and 0.3M upstream (20 boats), past the Yealm Hotel. There is a visitors' mooring just beyond Misery Point (large boats), and two further moorings in the pool (3 boats each). Unless it is very quiet you expect to be rafted up.

There is a pontoon (all states of tide) on the south side of Yealm Pool for short stops. Showers, toilets and tap water available.

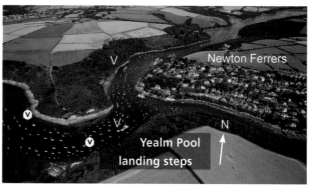

River Yealm at the pool and Newton Ferrers

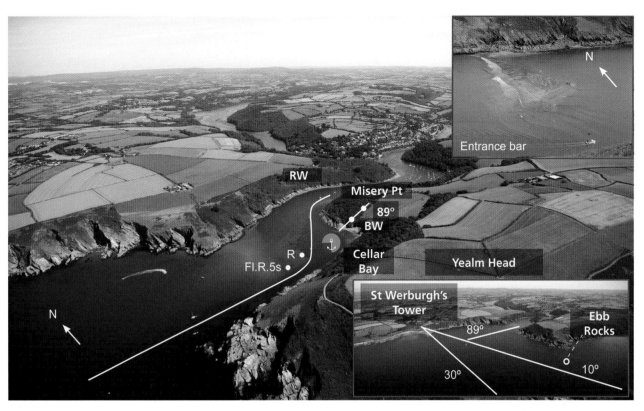

RW

Misery Pt

89°

BW

R

Fl.R.5s

Cellar Bay

Yealm Head

Entrance bar

N

St Werburgh's Tower

89°

Ebb Rocks

30°

10°

Entrance to the River Yealm

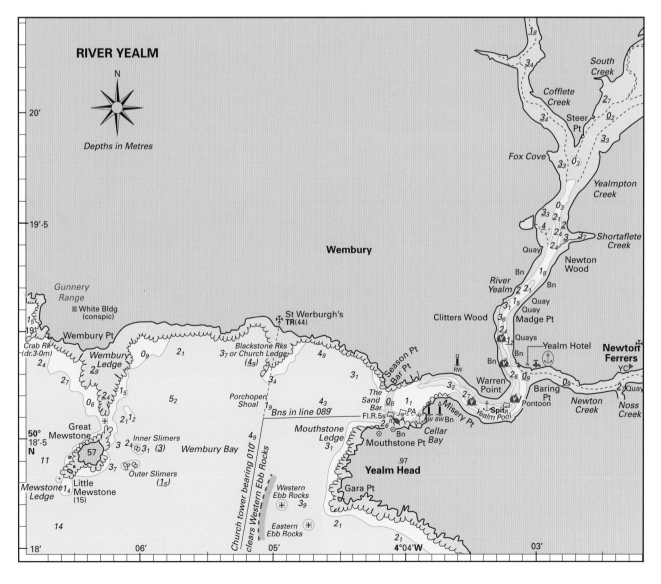

RIVER YEALM

N

Depths in Metres

20'

19'·5

19'

50°
18'·5
N

18'

06'

05'

4°04'W

03'

South Creek

Cofflete Creek

Steer Pt

Fox Cove

Yealmpton Creek

Shortaflete Creek

Quay

Newton Wood

Bn

River Yealm

Bn

Clitters Wood

Quay
Quay
Madge Pt

Quays

Yealm Hotel

Newton Ferrers

YC

Bn

Warren Point

Baring Pt

Newton Creek

Noss Creek

Spit

Pontoon

Yealm Pool

Quay

Wembury

Gunnery Range

White Bldg (conspic)

Wembury Pt

St Werburgh's TR(44)

Blackstone Rks or Church Ledge (4₉)

Season Pt

Bar Pt

RW

Crab Rk (dr.3·0m)

Wembury Ledge

Porchopen Shoal

Bns in line 089°

The Sand Bar

Fl.R.5s

PA

Misery Pt

Cellar Bay

Bn

Great Mewstone

Inner Slimers (3)

Wembury Bay

Mouthstone Ledge

Mouthstone Pt

Yealm Head

Little Mewstone (15)

Outer Slimers (1₅)

Mewstone Ledge

57

Church tower bearing 010° clears Western Ebb Rocks

Western Ebb Rocks

Eastern Ebb Rocks

Gara Pt

.97

⚓ Anchorages

Cellar Bay just after the entrance sandbar is the only location for anchoring unless you can dry out. It is exposed to west/southwesterlies.

Newton Creek allows access to Newton Ferrers and Noss Mayo though the quays dry 2.7m. If you can dry out and there is space, you can anchor close to shore (avoid the two causeways and the cables at Noss Creek). There is a quay at Bridgend, right at the end of Newton Creek, which can be reached an hour from high water.

Upstream and just beyond the second set of visitors' pontoons on the port side, opposite Madge Point, there are posts for scrubbing. Anchoring is not permitted beyond this point (oyster beds). At high water you can explore beyond the fork into Cofflete Creek, northwest, and Yealmton Creek, northeast and other times make excursions by dinghy.

Food & transport

Newton Ferrers has a Co-operative, a post-office, a butchers and a pharmacy. There are no shops in Noss Mayo. The Ship Inn, Noss Mayo, has a good reputation for food and is well stocked with local and regional beers. The Dolphin Inn in Newton Ferrers has a terrace with splendid views of the creek.

There is a bus that goes from Newton Ferrers and Noss Mayo to Plymouth and Kingsbridge. The nearest train station is at Plymouth.

Visitors' buoy at the pool in the Yealm

Cawsand, a great spot for anchoring in westerlies

⚓ Cawsand

A popular anchorage on the western side of Plymouth Sound in Cornwall, Cawsand is a delightful medieval village with old colour-washed cottages and narrow winding streets. There are several pubs and a couple of shops for provisioning. Ample room for anchoring in platform shelving from 3m to 9m. Good holding. Stay clear of local moorings. Anchoring is prohibited south of 50°19´.6N (Pier Cove level). There are ferries each day to and from Plymouth Barbican.

Plymouth Sound

Plymouth, a large naval and commercial port, offers shelter and extensive facilities. Several marinas, and a few anchorages, can accommodate visitors in quantity but in the summer it can get very busy.

The city of Plymouth has plenty to offer. There are historic houses to visit and an excellent museum and art gallery. A tour of HM Naval Base Devonport usually includes stepping aboard a warship and sometimes a nuclear submarine. Nearby the National Maritime Aquarium is the largest in the UK, housing over 4,000 marine animals in habitats that range from the west country to coral reefs.

Approach & entrance

The approach to the Sound is straightforward with few dangers but it can difficult at night, given the sheer quantity of lights. The mile-long breakwater is not obvious from a distance but can be located from the lighthouses and central fort.

Give way to large ships (restricted in ability to manoeuvre). Warships have right of way in the main and DW channels. Keep at least 50m off berthed warships and 100m off berthed submarines. Do not pass within 200m or cross astern within 800m of submarines underway.

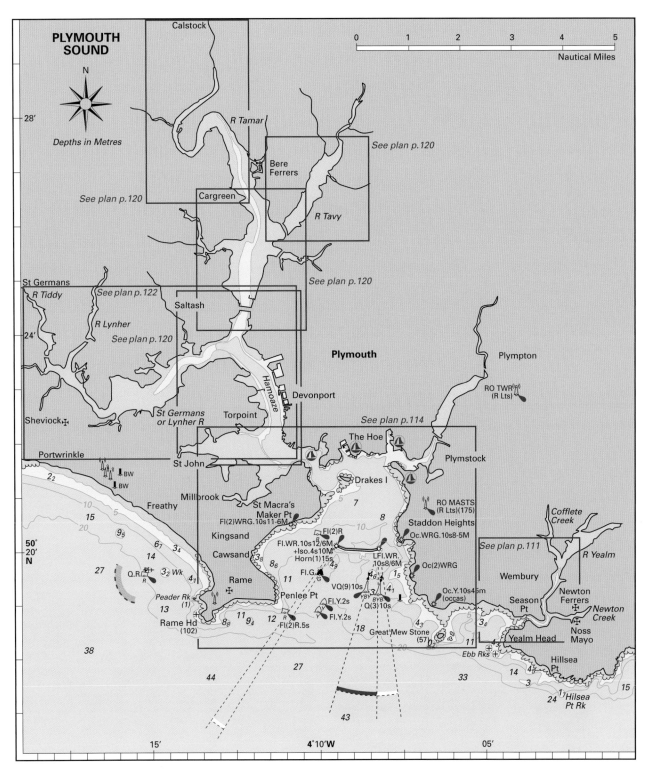

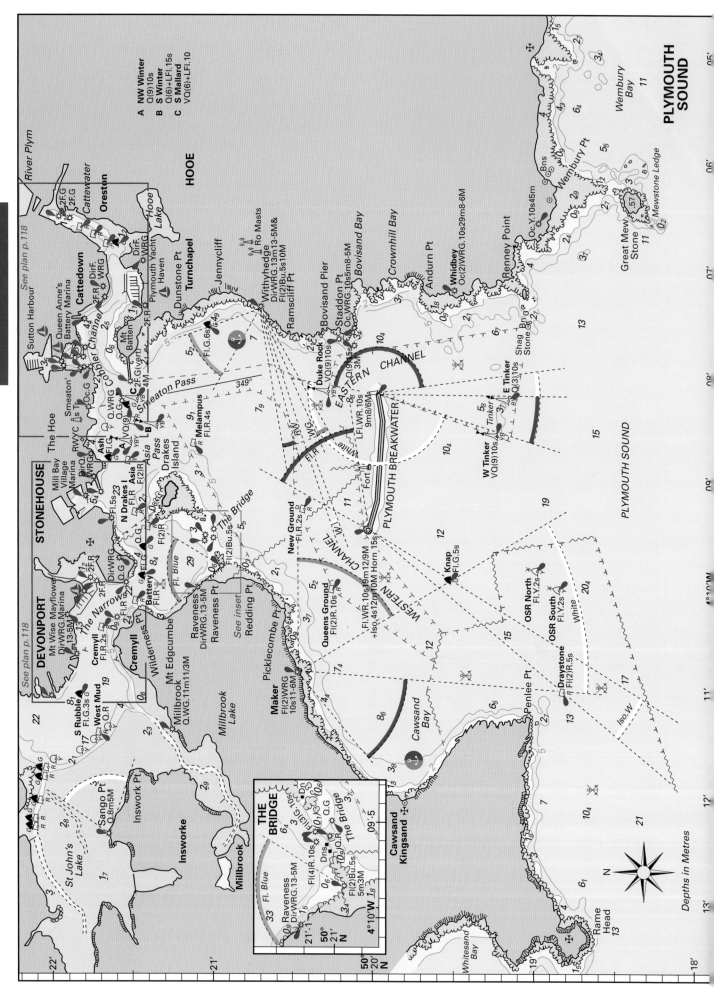

PLYMOUTH SOUND

A NW Winter Q(9)10s
B S Winter Q(6)+LFl.15s
C S Mallard VQ(6)+LFl.10

River Plym

Oreston

Cattewater

Cattedown

HOOE

See plan.118

Sutton Harbour

Queen Anne's Battery Marina

2F.G
2F.G

DirF.
DirF.
WRG

DirF.WRG

Hooe Lake

Mt. Batten

Cobbler Channel

Plymouth Yacht Haven

Dunstone Pt

Turnchapel

Jennycliff

Withyhedge
DirWRG.13m13-5M&
Fl(2)Bu.5s10M

Ramscliff Pt

Ro Masts

Bovisand Pier

Bovisand Bay

Crownhill Bay

Wembury Bay

Staddon Pt
Oc.WRG.10s5m8-5M

Andurn Pt

Whidbey
Oc(2)WRG.10s29m8-6M

Renney Point

Wembury Pt

Mewstone Ledge

Great Mew Stone

Shag Stone

Oc.Y.10s45m

EASTERN CHANNEL

Duke Rock
VQ(9)10s

Fort

Mt Batten

Smeaton Pass

349°

Melampus
Fl.R.4s

White

LFl.WR.10s
9m8/6M

PLYMOUTH BREAKWATER

E Tinker
Q(3)10s

W Tinker
VQ(9)10s

PLYMOUTH SOUND

The Hoe

STONEHOUSE

Mill Bay Village Marina

RWYC

Smeaton

Ash
Fl.G

A
B
C

Drakes Island

Asia

N Drakes
Fl.R

New Ground
Fl.R.2s

Knap
Fl.G.5s

OSR North
Fl.Y.2s

OSR South
Fl.Y.2s

White

DEVONPORT

Mt Wise Mayflower
DirWRG.Marina

Cremyll
Fl.R.2s

Cremyll

Mt Edgcumbe

Millbrook
Q.WG.11m11/3M

The Narrows

Battery
Fl.R

Wilderness Pt

Raveness Pt

Raveness
DirWRG.13-5M

Redding Pt

Fl. Blue

Pickelcombe Pt

Maker
Fl(2)WRG
10s11-6M

Queens Ground
Fl(2)R.10s

Fl.WR.10s19m12/9M
+Iso.4s12m10M Horn 15s

WESTERN CHANNEL

Cawsand Bay

Penlee Pt

Draystone
Fl(2)R.5s

Iso.W

Millbrook Lake

See plan.118

West Mud
Q.WG.11m11/3M

S Rubble
Fl.G.3s G

West Mud
Q.R

Sango Pt
Q.8m5M

Inswork Pt

St John's Lake

Insworke

Millbrook

THE BRIDGE

Fl. Blue

Raveness
DirWRG.13-5M

The Bridge

Q.G

Fl(2)Bu.5s
5m3M

Kingsand

Cawsand

Rame Head

Whitesand Bay

Depths in Metres

N

114 THE WEST COUNTRY

Outer approach - from the west

- Approach Plymouth Sound from the west in strong westerlies.

- This is the primary route used by large ships (DW channel).

- Aim at the Maker Point lighthouse Fl(2)9. WRG.10s. The white sector between 4° and 330° reaches west to the Draystone buoy Fl(2)R.5s and east to the Knap buoys Fl.G.5s (clears the Draystone rocks and the Knap shallows 4.5m).

- In order to be clear of Draystone, do not stray west of the white sector of the breakwater west lighthouse Fl.WR.10s and Iso.4s.

- Once you have passed the Knap buoy Fl.G.5s to starboard you can safely turn towards the west side of the breakwater.

- From the breakwater edge there are no further dangers for yachts but you must conform to the rules concerning large vessels in the main channel.

Outer approach - from the east

- Avoid this approach in strong SW/S conditions unless you are very familiar with the dangers.

- DANGERS:
  - Shag Stone, unlit beacon.
  - Tinker shoal (3.5m), breaks in heavy weather, marked by cardinals W Tinker VQ(9)10s and E Tinker Q(3)10s.

- East breakwater lighthouse LFl.WR.10s red sector covers Tinker danger.

- You may approach either side of Tinker as yachts do not need to follow the channel.

West of Tinker:

- Remain in the white sector of Fort Bovisand light Oc.WRG.10s between 38° and 50°.

East of Tinker:

- Remain in the white sector of the east breakwater lighthouse LFl.WR.10s between 354° and 1°.

- Pass between Shag Stone (unlit beacon) and E Tinker cardinal Q(3)10s. It is best to take a line close (and east) to the transit between E Tinker and the east breakwater lighthouse. This avoids some shallow patches to the east (3m) and keeps you well off a lee shore in westerlies.

- Around 0.3M short of the east breakwater lighthouse you will intersect the white sector of Fort Bovisand light Oc.WRG.10s. Turn towards it on a course between 38° and 50°.

At the breakwater edge east:

- Shortly before you are abeam the east breakwater lighthouse you will intersect the white sector of the Whidbey light Oc(2)WRG.10s. Turn to 318° from the light.

- Leave to port the west cardinal W Staddon Q(9)15s and then Duke Rock VQ(9)10s.

- Once past Duke Rock there are no immediate dangers for yachts but you must conform to the rules concerning large vessels in the main channel.

Directional lights

Directional WRG lights define all the main channels: Whidbey 138.5°, Staddon Pt 44°, Withyhedge 70°, W Hoe 315°, Western King 271°, Ravenness 225°, Mount Wise 343°. Millbay 48.5° and Ocean Court 85° not 24h.

Plymouth Sound

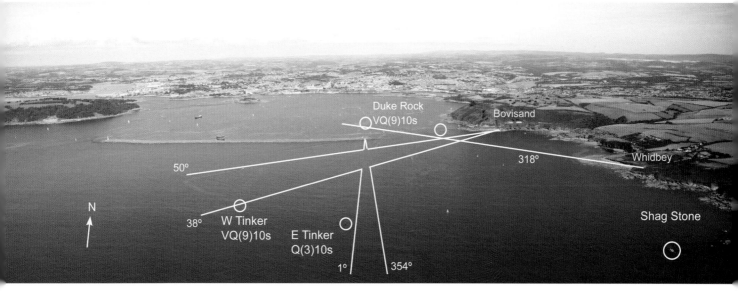

Smeaton Pass to Cattewater

Once you are in the harbour and clear of Duke Rock to the east you can reach Cattewater through the Smeaton pass. This is straightforward:

- Large ships and the ferry use this the channel so beware.

- Follow the leading lights on 349°:
  - Oc.G on the shore at the edge of the Citadel walls
  - Mallard Shoal white column in the water Q.WRG / Fl.5s(in fog) and
  - S Mallard cardinal VQ(6)+LFl.10s.

- Go through Q.R and Q.G that mark the channel and past the white column.

The dredged channel (5m) opens to starboard into Cattewater where there are marinas (Sutton Harbour, Queen Anne's Battery and Plymouth Yacht Haven).

To port you can proceed along Drake Channel.

Asia Pass to Drake Channel

Asia Pass is 0.1M wide immediately west of Smeaton Pass and Winter Shoal (2.9m).

- Make way between Fl(2)R.5s to port and cardinals S Winter Q(6)+LFl.15s and NW Winter VQ(9) to starboard.

The Bridge to the Narrows

The narrow pass (15m wide, 1.3m minimum depth) to the west of Drake's Island is clearly marked by lit beacons. The Bridge is a great shortcut but the tide is

The Bridge
327°/147° to tall blue/white building

strong and there is no room for error either side so it should only be used in good conditions.

Coming into harbour the beacons are in this order: No.1 Q.G to starboard, No.2 Q.R to port, No.3 Fl(3) G.10s to starboard, No.4 Fl(4)R.10s to port. The beacons have tide gauges showing height above CD.

- STRONG TIDE 346°/1.6kn at HW-4 and 150°/2.4kn at HW+4.

- Drying ROCKS close to the sides of the channel.

- The channel is aligned 327°/147° to the conspicuous blue and white building on the left side of a cluster of buildings in Devonport.

Drake Channel

Drake Channel is wide, deep and well marked. Your concerns will be traffic and the strength of the tide, more than 2kn in places.

It is possible to anchor below the Hoe in the centre and at Barn Pool west but the main destinations are the marinas in Cattewater, Mill Bay, Devonport and the yacht clubs upstream in the River Tamar.

Plymouth Sound past the breakwater

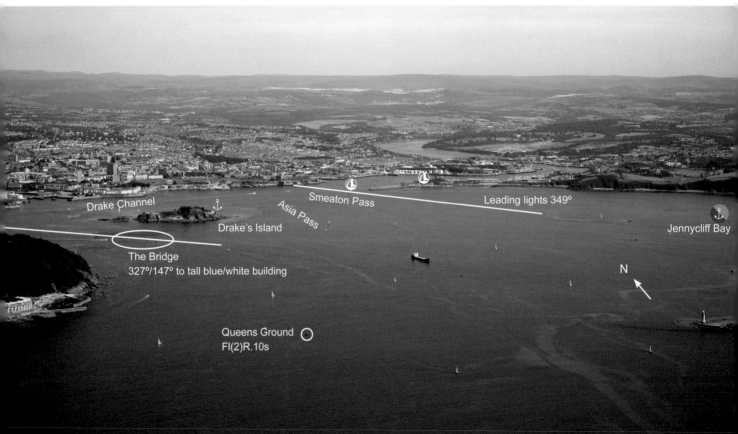

Lynher
Torpoint
Southdown
Barn Pool
Narrows
Drake's Island
N
Mayflower
Sutton
QAB
Plymouth Yacht Haven

⚓⊕ The Sound - east to west

⚓ The anchorage in Jennycliff Bay has ample room close to shore (2m minimum depth). It offers protection from easterlies and is best towards the south side. Stay clear of the buoy Fl.G.6s (and a wreck between the buoy and the shore).

Having rounded Mallard there are several marinas in Cattewater. ⊕ On the southern side, Plymouth Yacht Haven is large and straightforward with plentiful spaces for visitors along both sides of the outer pontoon. West of the visitors' spaces is a patch that dries 0.3m. Facilities include a lift and fuel. Access to Plymouth is via the ferry from Mount Batten.

Deeper into Cattewater, Yacht Haven Quay (run by the same company as Plymouth Yacht Haven) has a pontoon in 1.2m, with dry storage ashore.

⊕ Queen Anne's Battery Marina on the Plymouth side has a visitors' pontoon behind the high wall. This is a popular marina run by MDL. It has a very well stocked chandler, yard services and fuel, and from here you can walk into the city.

⊕ Sutton Harbour Marina is reached through a lock with floating pontoons (24h operation) that keeps 3.5m in the basin. You need to contact the marina to open the lock whenever it is not free flow (HW+/-3). Arrange a berth ahead. The pontoons of West Pier and Guy's Quay are private.

⚓ You can anchor on the northern side of the channel in the bay between the Grand Parade and the Hoe. This is not a quiet spot however and is only sheltered from northerlies.

Mill Bay Marina Village is small and private (apartment berths). Possible for MDL berth holders.

⚓ Further west Drake's Island provides shelter from the southwest. Stay in at least 3m charted depth to

Sutton
QAB
N

Queen Anne's Battery and Sutton Harbour

avoid drying rocks closer in and a charted obstruction (0.9m) north of the pier.

⚓ Barn Pool on the west side of The Narrows protects from southwest/west. This is a pleasant location with Mount Edgcumbe Country Park as a backdrop. Avoid the foul southern end and arrange a trip line for the anchor just in case.

⊕ Mayflower Marina is on the east side of The Narrows. Opposite is the magnificent 19th-century naval victualling yard, now open to the public. The tide runs very hard along this stretch so steering may be difficult when in full flow. Facilities include a lift, fuel (behind the pontoons in 1.5m depth) and a very well stocked chandler. This is a popular destination for visitors.

Mayflower

N
⊕

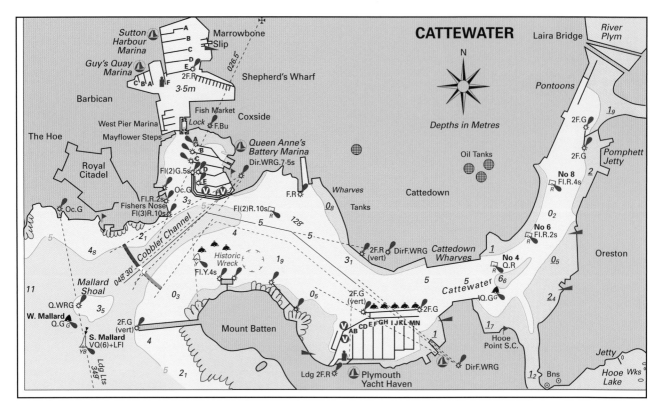

Queen Anne's Battery and Sutton Harbour

Cattewater and Plymouth Yacht Haven

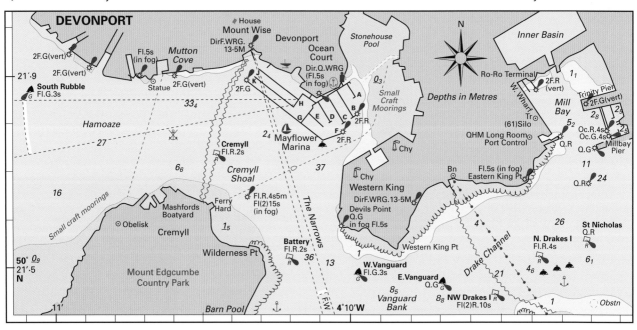

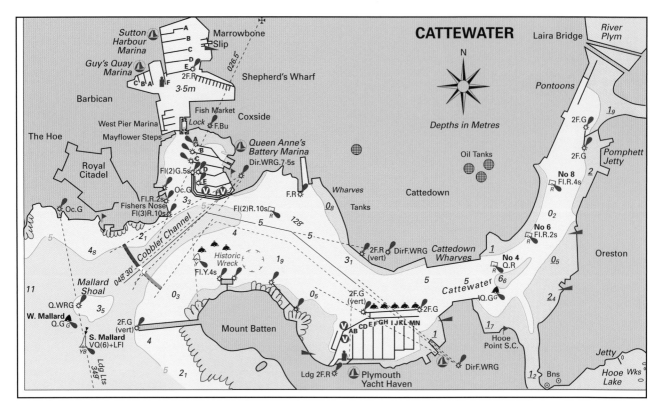

WEST DEVON

PLYMOUTH SOUND

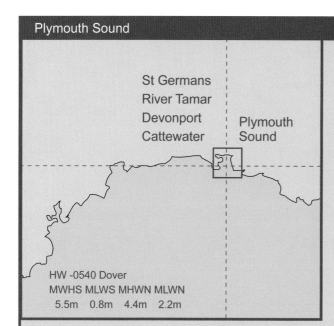

St Germans
River Tamar
Devonport
Cattewater

Plymouth
Sound

HW -0540 Dover
MWHS MLWS MHWN MLWN
5.5m   0.8m   4.4m   2.2m

Plymouth Sound

- Straightforward approach, many lights at night
- Smeaton Pass, Asia Pass, Bridge (strong tide) to main Drake Channel

CATTEWATER
Plymouth Yacht Haven Marina

- Visitors: outer pontoon west
- 450 berths, dredged 2.2m
- 01752 404231 Fax 01752 484177
- VHF 37 / 80
- www.yachthavens.com
- Water and electricity at the pontoons
- 65-ton travel lift
- Extensive yard services, chandler
- Showers, laundry, car park
- Mount Batten ferry to the Barbican ☺ 07930 838614

Queen Anne's Battery Marina

- Visitors: alongside pontoon at the wall
- 235 berths, 40 visitors, dredged 2.2m
- 01752 671142 / 07740 806039
- VHF 80
- www.queenannesbattery.co.uk
- Water and electricity at the pontoons
- 25-ton travel lift
- Extensive yard services, large chandlery
- Showers, laundry, car park
- Fuel: end of pontoon E near lock

Sutton Harbour Marina

- 467 berths incl. visitors', 3.5m depth
- 01752 204702
- Lock 24h: VHF 12 for entry and berth
- www.suttonharbourmarina.co.uk
- Water and electricity at the pontoons
- 25-ton travel lift

NARROWS
Mayflower Marina

- Visitors: outer pontoon
- 396 berths, 40 visitors, 3.5m depth
- 01752 556633 / 07840 116853
- VHF 80
- www.mayflowermarina.co.uk
- Water and electricity at the pontoons
- 33-ton travel lift
- Extensive yard services, chandlery
- Showers, laundry, car park
- Fuel behind marina (1.5m depth)

HAMOAZE
Southdown Marina

- 35 berths inc visitors, 2m depth
- Access HW+/-4
- 01752 823084   office@hugginsmarine.com
- www.southdownmarina.co.uk
- Showers, laundry, water taxi

Torpoint Yacht Harbour

- 70 berths, 2m depth
- 100 moorings
- 01752 813658 office@torpointyachtharbour.co.uk
- www.torpointyachtharbour.co.uk
- Showers, laundry, water taxi

River Tamar

- Weir Quay Boatyard moorings
  01822 840474

Anchorages - shelter
- Cawsand - W / SW
- Jennycliff Bay - E
- Drake's Island - W / SW
- Barn Pool - W / SW, patches foul
- St Germans River - several
- Cargreen - open, moorings

WEST DEVON

PLYMOUTH SOUND

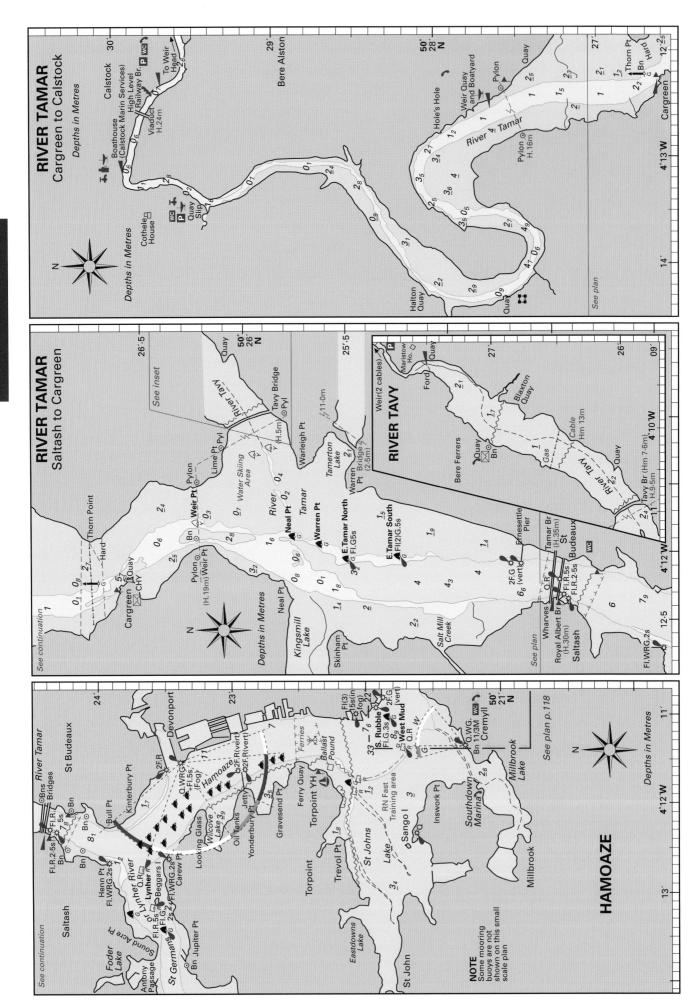

RIVER TAMAR
Cargreen to Calstock
Depths in Metres

Calstock

Boathouse (Calstock Marin Services)

To Weir Head

High Level Railway Br.

Viaduct H.24m

Bere Alston

Cothele House

Quay Slip

Hole's Hole

Weir Quay and Boatyard

Pylon

Thorn Pt

Hard

River Tamar

Pylon H.16m

Halton Quay

Quay

See plan

Cargreen

50° 28′ N

4°13′W

RIVER TAMAR
Saltash to Cargreen

Depths in Metres

Thorn Point

Hard

Cargreen Quay CHY

Weir Pt

See inset

Quay

River Tavy

Tavy Bridge

Pyl

Lime Pt

Pylon (H.19m) Weir Pt

Water Skiing Area

Neal Pt

River Tamar

Warleigh Pt

Warren Pt

Tamerton Lake

Warren Bridge Pt (2.5m)

Neal Pt

Kingsmill Lake

E. Tamar North

E. Tamar South Fl(2)G.5s

Ernesettle Pier

Skinham Pt

Salt Mill Creek

2F.G (vert)

Tamar Br (H.35m)

Budeaux

Wharves

Royal Albert Br (H.30m)

Saltash

Q.R

Fl.R.5s

Fl.R.2.5s

Fl.WRG.2s

RIVER TAVY

Maristow Ho.

Quay

Ford

Blaxton Quay

Bere Ferrers

Quay

Bn

Gas

Cable Hm 13m

Quay

River Tavy

Tavy Br (Hm 7.6m) H.9.5m

Weir (2 cables)

50° 26′ N

4°10′W

4°12′W

HAMOAZE

River Tamar

St Budeaux

Devonport

Saltash

Foder Lake

Antony Passage

St Germans

Henn Pt Fl.WRG.2s

Sound Acre Pt

Lynher River

Lynher

Beggars I

Carew Pt

Bn Jupiter Pt

Bull Pt

Kinterbury Pt

Looking Glass

Wilcove Lake

Oil Tanks

Yonderberry Pt

Gravesend Pt

Ferry Quay

Torpoint YH

Ferries

Ballast Pound

Hamoaze

Q.WRG Fl.5s (Fog)

2F.R(vert)

2F.R(vert)

2F.R(vert)

Fl(3) 15s (in fog)

S. Rubble Fl.G.3s

33 — 7.6

West Mud Q.R

2F.G (vert)

RN Fast Training area

Torpoint

Trevol Pt

St Johns Lake

Sango I

Inswork Pt

Q.WG. Bn 11/3M Cremyll

Southdown Marina

Millbrook Lake

Millbrook

Eastdowns Lake

St John

50° 21′ N

4°12′W

See plan p.118

Depths in Metres

NOTE Some mooring buoys are not shown on this small scale plan

Upstream from Plymouth

Hamoaze

Having gone through the Narrows the area aptly named West Mud opens up, well marked by channel buoys. ④ Southdown Marina in Millbrook Lake can only be accessed between HW+/-4. Visitors can make use of the pontoon (2m), moorings or a drying quay.

④ At the northern end of the drying area is Torpoint Yacht Harbour. It can be accessed at any time but visitors' berths are only be arrangement.

The Torpoint Chain Ferry is a multi-boat facility that runs constantly. Take due care, particularly when the tide is in full stream.

The stretch of water up to St Germans or Lynher river is home to HM naval base Devonport and a very busy place. Expect to see various warships, including submarines and the occasional aircraft carrier.

⚓ River Tamar

The River Tamar is navigable for 12M with tide, up to Gunnislake and its weir. Because of depth restrictions, only small boats are likely to go beyond Calstock. ⚓ The best anchorage is at Cargreen (2-5m but beware of moorings), with a possible one at Calstock (0.7m).

Immediately beyond the bridge on the western side it is often possible to tie up at the pontoon of the Saltash Sailing Club (survey depth), for a short stay. Overnight on at one of the club moorings is by arrangement.

- Depths upstream:
  - 1.6m west side of the River Tavy
  - 0.6m at the bend before Cargreen
  - 0.1m just beyond Cargreen
  - 0.1m to 4.7m to Calstock.

- Stay in the wide channel, passing the moorings for large ships, up to the first green buoys marking the opening to starboard towards the River Tavy. E Tamar South and North are lit Fl.G.5s but the next two, Warren Pt and Neal Pt, are not.

- Keep close to the three green buoys, leaving them to starboard, to avoid shallows and drying patches. This is particularly important around Neal Point where the channel narrows.

- Once you are just past the third Neil Point green buoy aim directly for the beacon by the electricity pylon (west side). This will give you at least 1.6m plus tide. Clearance under the cables is marked as 19m, more on the sides.

- From under the cables aim towards the quay at Cargreen, keeping to the centre of the channel (0.6m plus tide).

- There are many moorings at Cargreen. Those that used to belong to the pub (closed) are now private. Anchor among the moorings in 2-5m.

- Stay in the centre between the moorings to continue on to Weir Quay Boatyard, which is to starboard just passed a second set of power cables (16m). Call the boatyard ahead if you want to pick a mooring.

- From here to Calstock proceed on a rising tide, keep to the outside of the channel and monitor depth. A good guide is HW+/-3 but make appropriate tide calculations on the day.

The River Tamar before and after the road suspension bridge

⚓ St Germans or Lynher river

Having passed the busy Devonport naval yard, the St Germans or Lynher opens to your left, around 0.8M before the high bridge. Here it is splendidly calm and rural. ⚓ You can go as far as Dandy Hole on the tide. Beyond this, to the quay by the viaduct, the course dries.

- Depths upstream:
  - 2-5m up to Sand Acre (opposite Forder Lake)
  - 1.3-3m to Ince Castle
  - Dry-1m to Dandy Hole
  - 5m Dandy Hole pool
  - Dries to St German's Quay by the viaduct.

- Enter the channel by rounding the entrance Lynher Q.R.

Upstream rivers (St Germans and Lynher)

St Germans

Dandy Hole

N

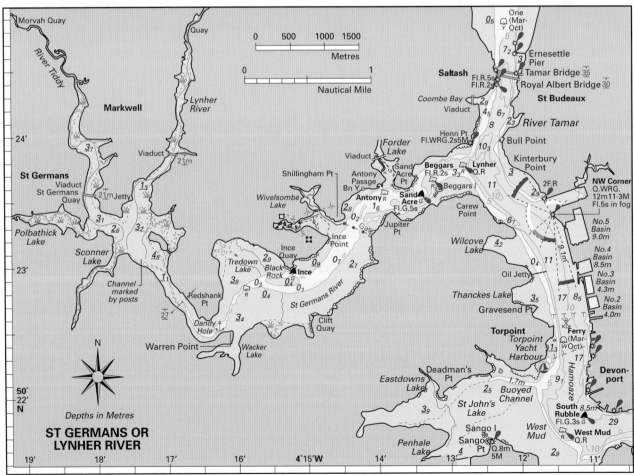

ST GERMANS OR LYNHER RIVER

Depths in Metres

- ⚓ Anchorage on the north side of Sand Acre, north of Beggars red and Sand Acre green buoys. Foul ground reported, use a trip line.

- Turn south towards the local moorings and buoy, Sand Acre Fl.G.5s, to complete the first mile. The pontoons at Jupiter Point belong to the Navy.

- Turn west towards Anthony Red, close to the northern shore and Forder Lake. Local moorings and underwater cables.

- You can anchor on the northern side before Shillingham Point to avoid further underwater cables.

- ⚓ Continue to Ince Point where you can anchor in 2.5m. The point is marked by a green buoys, stay close to it and to the northern side.

- A final red buoy marks the edge of the channel. When all is covered by the tide the buoy is in the centre of a very wide expanse of water.

- ⚓ Head from the red buoy on a southwest course towards the sharp river bend at Dandy Hole. Here you can anchor in peace, in up to 5m.

- From here to St German's Quay by the viaduct the course dries. Dry berthing at the quay by arrangement only.

St Germans or Lynher river from Hamoaze

St German's Quay by the viaduct

Drake he was a Devon man

On Plymouth Hoe stands a statue to the greatest of mariners, Sir Francis Drake. He combined all the best and worst aspects of an adventurer of his time but set a course for England centred on maritime prowess that would ultimately lead to the development of the British Empire. As a pirate, and as an admiral, his life was bound up in the ongoing, expensive and bloody tit-for-tat with the Spanish empire.

Drake was born in Tavistock around 1540, the son of a farmer. By the age of 23 he had made one of the first slaving voyages to the New World aboard a fleet of ships owned by his relatives in Plymouth. Five years later the fleet was attacked by Spanish boats in the Mexican port of San Juan de Ulua, the viceroy of Peru, Don Martín Enríquez reneging on an earlier agreement to let them be. Having lost all but two boats Drake vowed lifelong revenge saying 'I would not wish to take anything except what belongs to King Philip and Don Martín Enríquez... I am not going to stop until I collect the two millions which my cousin, John Hawkins, lost at San Juan de Ulua'.

After two minor voyages to the West Indies Drake's first independent enterprise was an attack on the port of Nombre de Dios in 1572, a Spanish colony on the Panama isthmus. It was from here that gold and silver, mined by the Spanish in Peru, was stored awaiting the galleons that would take it home. Here too were warehouses full of merchandise from Seville left for distribution throughout the Americas. Although the raid failed, Drake was hurt and they left without any treasure, he was soon rich beyond his wildest dreams after plundering more than 20 tons of gold and silver from a mule train destined for the port.

Drake's exploits made him a celebrity at Court and his next venture was financed by the Queen and private investors, in a 'joint-stock' initiative to which Elizabeth contributed one thousand crowns. Although there was to be nothing incriminating in writing, the intention was to attack Spanish towns and vessels along the Pacific coast of South America and claim a place for England in the profitable spice trade. Drake left in 1577 with six ships. For navigation he had just a few charts, a translation of Cortes' *Art of Navigation*, Pedro Medina's *Arte de Navegar* and an account of Magellan's earlier voyage around the world. Three ships were lost by the time they reached San Julián, now in Argentina, and here Drake executed Thomas Doughty for agitating against his authority, a sign of his ruthless nature but also of a leader taking decisive action. The following autumn another ship was lost and a second returned home, leaving just Drake and his crew aboard the *Pelican*.

It seems likely that Drake then sailed through the Magellan Strait though driven south by storms he made two important observations. First, that there was a more southerly passage from the Atlantic to the Pacific (now called Drake's Passage) and second, that the land there was a scattering of islands and not another continent. Renaming his ship the *Golden Hind* (a detail from the coat of arms of Sir Christopher Hatton one of his principle benefactors) he continued on and near Lima captured the Spanish treasure ship *Nuestra Señora de la Concepción*. Gold, silver and jewels estimated at £126,000 were taken, half the annual revenue of the English Crown. Drake's fame and a handsome return for investors assured it was time to come home. He headed north, reaching 38°, and ashore claimed the first overseas territory for England, now in California. Preparing for the long passage he was well aware of the difficulty that Magellan's successor, Elcano, had faced when sailing west across the Pacific. Following a northern route Drake made use of the seasonal trade winds and reached the Spice Islands after 60 days. He then sailed across the Indian Ocean and around the Cape of Good Hope arriving back in Plymouth on 26 September 1580 to a hero's welcome. The *Golden Hind* was full to the gunwales with treasure, his investors were to receive a return of 4,700%, and he had become the second man ever to circumnavigate the world.

A few years ashore followed, during which Drake became mayor of Plymouth and an MP, sitting on Parliamentary committees that dealt with the importation of fish, the preservation of Plymouth harbour, the maintenance of the navy and the licence given to Raleigh for the establishment of a colony in Virginia. He was knighted in 1581 and the same year Philip of Spain became King of Portugal which created a joint naval resource six times that of England. England was fast moving away from Catholicism and there was continuing resentment associated with the Treaty of Tordesillas in which the Pope had granted to Spain territories to the west and to Portugal territories to the east. In an ongoing escalation of enmity against King Philip and the Pope the English supported the Dutch rebellion against Spain and defeated a Papal expedition designed to support an uprising against the crown in Ireland. The desire for war was already reaching a crescendo when an English vessel returned home containing an official document in which Philip instructed the Spanish to capture English boats.

In 1585 Drake again sailed to Spain in another joint-stock venture, the Queen contributing two vessels. The purpose was the righteous release of English ships and crew but with authority to recoup losses by any means, in other words leeway for any plunder or piracy Drake felt fit to undertake. The expedition ended in the Caribbean where Drake captured Santo Domingo, a key Spanish town for which he was paid a large ransom. There was no affront the English could have chosen that would anger Philip more.

Spanish plans to attack England directly were soon evident and Drake set off to destroy the Spanish fleet in Cadiz. Itching for action, he attacked before all his boats had arrived thereby inflicting much less damage than he might have. Aware of the continual need for financial return he moved on to the Azores, where he again captured significant booty. The trip was not a naval success, but it delayed Spanish preparations for a year and enabled the English to better their defences.

The great Spanish Armada under the command of Admiral Medina Sidonia left Coruña on 12 July 1588. The intention was to sail to Holland, pick up the Duke of Parma's soldiers and then invade England. With 73 vessels the fleet was huge but beset with many problems, not least needing to proceed at the speed of its slowest vessels (galleys) and having greatly underpowered armoury. The English fleet consisted of a disparate array of boats but at least they were sailing boats, more easily able to capture the windward position. Under the command of Howard of Effingham, counselled by Drake, Hawkins, Frobisher and Fenner, this fleet was ready to defend the realm.

Among the many myths of the great event, Drake's personality has been immortalised in a painting that shows him calmly playing bowls on Plymouth Hoe with the Spanish Armada already in sight. In fact there were a number of separate battles in which neither side took great losses because they both failed to capitalise on their strengths. The Spanish, heading first to Holland, did not attack Plymouth when it would have been to their advantage. The English, wary of so many Spanish soldiers ready for boarding, kept their distance, thus failing to take advantage of their superior gun power. (Nelson, in a different era, would have caused devastation by continuous fire at close quarter.) Drake's valuable contribution was to attempt to drive the Spanish fleet aground off the Isle of Wight, thus keeping them moving on without any respite. At Calais the English caused mayhem amongst the Armada by deploying fireships and, in panic, many Spanish captains cut their anchors and sailed away. At Gravelines, in Belgium, the English finally got close enough to fire their guns with good effect, but having destroyed only four ships they ran out of ammunition! Neither side can be proud of this naval battle and the loss of men was horrific. The Spanish died in greatest numbers sailing home via Scotland and Ireland after failing to make contact with Parma, and many English sailors went on to die of disease. However, England was safe and Spain had taken a significant blow to both its pride and finances.

England then decided to attack Spain in a counter-armada under Drake's command. Leaving in 1589 the intention was to destroy any Spanish ships that remained, land in Portugal where soldiers on board, under the command of Norris, would reinstate Dom Antonio as King, then sail on and take the Azores. This would split the great Spanish/Portuguese empire and provide a base in the Atlantic from which to attack ships returning from the New Indies. In fact the expedition was as much a disaster for England as the Armada had been for Spain.

Weather, indecision and bad tactics diverted Drake from Santander where the remaining Spanish ships were anchored, so they were not destroyed. A battle was won at Coruña where they re-victualled, but with twelve thousand men most of the food was consumed during the next three weeks holed up in harbour due to bad weather. They did eventually sail to Lisbon but neither rebellious locals nor the army on board took the appropriate initiative so there was no uprising. More than half the men died and returning home many ships were lost at sea. Neither Spain nor England had been able to deliver the other a decisive blow.

Drake's final voyage, in 1595, was commanded jointly with his cousin John Hawkins and once again they set off to attack Spanish towns and ships in the Caribbean. However, things went badly wrong. The towns now had extensive fortifications and the Spanish had intelligence about Drake's plans. Sending out a fleet of fast new warships the Spanish arrived first, Drake had lost his earlier daring and the voyage was marked by losses. Anchored off the Caribbean, Drake then submitted to dysentery and died. He was 55.

Drake's role in English history should not be underestimated. He proved that a daring maritime attitude could serve the country well; he set the pattern for joint-stock operations and provided many of the funds investors used to establish the East India Company, which extended Britain's territory throughout the world. War with Spain ended with the Treaty of London, signed at Somerset House in 1604. About a hundred years later the Bank of England was created, as a joint stock operation, to raise funds for the Royal Navy.

In the harbour at Brixham there is a replica of the *Golden Hind* that can be visited. Drake's drum, the subject of legends, can be seen at Buckland Abbey, his former home near Plymouth (National Trust).

'Drake he was a Devon man, an' ruled the Devon seas,
(Capten, art tha sleepin' there below?),
Rovin' tho' his death fell, he went wi' heart at ease,
An' dreamin' arl the time o' Plymouth Hoe,
Take my drum to England, hang et by the shore,
Strike et when your powder's runnin' low;
If the Dons sight Devon, I'll quit the port o' Heaven,
An' drum them up the Channel as we drummed them
long ago.'   *Henry Newbolt*

Plymouth area

Food & transport

Plymouth is a large city that is easily accessed from the marinas.

The railway station is at the northern end of town (North Road), best reached by taxi. The bus station at Bretonside is close to Sutton Marina and about a mile walk from QAB (best route via the Barbican).

There is a ferry terminal at Mill Bay, on the northern side of Drake Channel, close to Mayflower Marina where there are services to Roscoff (daily) and Santander (weekly). There are numerous restaurants and pubs in the Barbican district close to QAB and Sutton Harbour. The Barbican Leisure Park has restaurants and a cinema. Blackfriars Distillery houses both Tanner's Barbican Kitchen, a good restaurant, and the Refectory, a stylish cocktail lounge set in a medieval hall with a stunning vaulted ceiling.

If you are berthed at Plymouth Yacht Haven then the Bridge bar/restaurant is nearby.

The Mayflower Marina restaurant, Astra's, is very popular. At busy times booking is required (☎ 01752 500008).

If you are anchored at Cawsand, a dinghy trip ashore gives access to a number of pubs plus a couple of shops for provisioning. A motor launch runs from Cawsand to the Mayflower Steps four times daily, May-Sept.

From Southdown Marina it is only half a mile to the village of Millbrook where there is a convenience store and pubs serving food.

Torpoint Yacht Harbour is on the edge of Torpoint, which has a Somerfield supermarket (Anthony Road, north of the chain ferry) and plenty of shops. The Torpoint Mosquito Sailing Club has a restaurant and bar and welcomes visitors.

In the St Germans or Lynher River it is self-catering unless you can reach the village where the Elliott Arms serves food.

The Crooked Spaniard pub at Cargreen closed in 2009 (buoys now private) but there is a post office and grocers. The Cargreen Yacht Club in the village welcomes visitors to its bar and showers.

The Promenade, Plymouth

Interest

Plymouth has its origins in the 'little fishe towne' of Sutton which was owned, until 1439, by the Dominican order of monks from Plympton Priory. Today it is the largest city in Devon and Cornwall, and the most important with respect to maritime history, but heavy bombing during the second world war has left little of historic interest. Fifty nine air raids damaged or wiped out nearly 12,000 houses and much of the city centre has been reconstructed. What's left of the old city, around Sutton Harbour and the Barbican (where even the stone road surface is listed as being of historical importance) is full of character, but this is combined with a roughness that warrants a field hospital on Saturday nights in the summer.

The name barbican comes from *barbecana*, medieval Latin for the fortified outpost of a city. Here limestone and timber-framed jettied houses hang towards each other along narrow lanes. The Elizabethan House is worth a visit. The former home of a ship's captain, it is packed with carved oak furniture including two fantastic beds: a canopied tester and a Brittany box bed with sliding door. Nearby Black Friars Distillery is housed in monastery buildings dating back to 1431. Plymouth gin, produced here since 1793, is distinguished by a relatively weak juniper taste and a higher than usual proportion of botanicals, including orris and angelica root. It comes in two strengths. The original is 41.2% alcohol by volume. However, navy strength is 57% alcohol by volume (100° English proof). At this strength it can be spilt on gunpowder without preventing the powder from igniting. The company is now owned by Pernod Ricard. Visitors can watch the distillery in action and make gin to their own taste by varying the proportion of botanicals. The oldest part of the site houses the Refectory cocktail bar in a medieval hall which has a stunning vaulted ceiling. Tanner's Barbican Kitchen, also in the same building, is a popular place to eat.

Plymouth's trawler fleet is based at Sutton harbour, where there is also an early morning fish market. In 1620 the Pilgrim Fathers set sail from here aboard the *Mayflower*. At Mayflower Steps there is an inscription listing the names and occupations of the 102 people on board. Later known as Puritans, they left because their protestant faith had brought them into conflict with King James I. Their intention had been to establish a colony in Virginia, though after 66 days they landed near to Cape Cod where they founded New Plymouth. It was also from Sutton Harbour that Raleigh and Granville launched their (failed) attempts to colonise Virginia, and Captain Cook and Charles Darwin left on their great expeditions. During the 19th century thousands of colonists and convicts left the harbour bound for Australia. More recently it was here that Sir Francis Chichester began and ended his round-the-world solo navigation aboard *Gipsy Moth IV*.

The National Marine Aquarium on the water front is well worth a visit. Over 4,000 marine animals are exhibited: over 400 species, in 50 different habitats ranging from the west country coast to coral reefs.

Plymouth

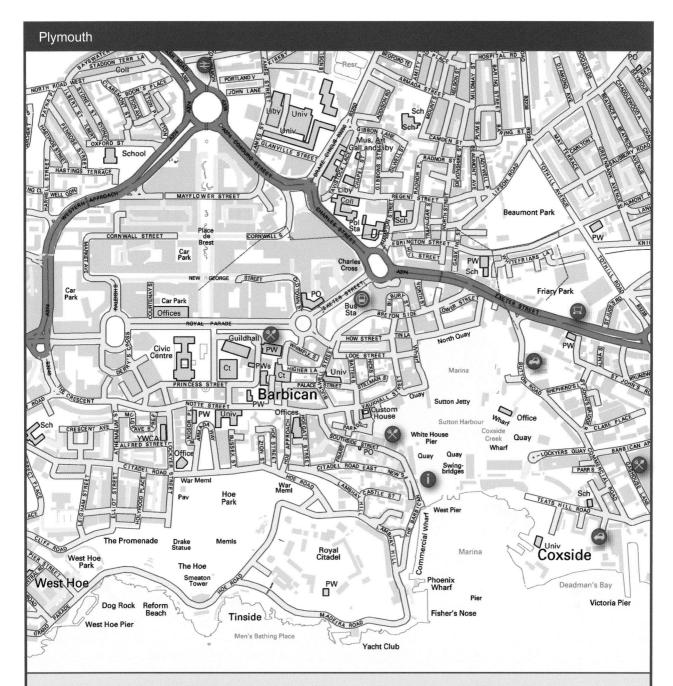

🚌 Bus/coach station: Bretonside, Plymouth, PL4 0BG

🚉 Train station: North Road, Plymouth PL4 6AB ① 0845 7000125
Main line to Penzance, Bristol, London

🚗 Avis: 20 Commercial Road, Coxside PL4 0LE ① 01752 221550

Hertz: Sutton Road PL4 0HN ① 01752 207207

Europcar: (Plymouth Railway Station) North Road PL4 6AB ① 01752 668004

🚢 Ferry to Roscoff and Santander

🛒 Co-operative: Alma Street off Exeter Street; Southside Street Barbican

🛒 Co-operative, Tesco, Lidl, Sainsbury's: centre between Royal Parade, Exeter Street, Charles Street

🛒 Somerfield, Anthony Road , Torpoint

🍴 Restaurants, pubs and cafés:
- Shopping centre near QAB, Barbican Approach/Gashouse Lane
- Mayflower Steps/Barbican area
- Royal Parade

ℹ Tourist Information Centre: 3-5 The Barbican, Mayflower Steps PL1 2LR ① 01752 306330

⚓ Chandlers: extensive at QAB, Plymouth Yacht Haven and Mayflower marinas

⚓ Weir Quay up the River Tamar

✚ Mount Gould Hospital, 200 Mount Gould Road, Plymouth PL4 7QD ① 0845 1558085

✚ Derriford District Hospital, Derriford Road, Plymouth PL6 8DH ① 01752 777111

Sunk within 2.5 million litres of water, the Atlantic ocean exhibit contains the wreck of a bi-plane with nurse sharks sheltering under the fuselage. There are 15 species of shark and ray in all, including the coral cat shark, sand tiger sharks and the starry smooth hound. Species of jellyfish, moon jellies, Japanese sea nettles and upside-down jellies are displayed in a round 'kreisel' tank to prevent them damaging themselves. The place buzzes with the energy of dedicated scientists who care. Talks throughout the day are hugely informative (for example, the Loggerhead turtle housed in the aquarium since being washed up on a Cornish beach in 1990 can nap underwater while holding its breath for an hour) and youngsters get to handle crabs and starfish displayed in open top tanks.

The best view of the Sound is from the grassy esplanade known as the Hoe (coming from Saxon for 'high place'). Higher still, by about 70ft, an even better view can be had from the lantern room in Smeaton's Tower. This former lighthouse was built on the Eddystone Reef in 1759. When it was replaced in 1882 the top two-thirds were reassembled here. The Sound is an exceptionally fine deep-water harbour but for many years it suffered from exposure to the prevailing southwesterlies, the breakwater not being completed until 1847. From the 13th century on it was used increasingly as a place of assembly for military expeditions. It was from here on 19 July 1588 that Drake set sail to defeat the Spanish Armada (see 'Drake he was a Devon man' on page 125). He was mayor of Plymouth for a while and, along with his cousin Sir John Hawkins, helped establish the port's supremacy. A statue of Drake adorns the Hoe. The 6.5-acre island named after him was fortified in the 16th century to defend the only deep-water channel to Devonport. It is now in private hands but has been left to decay, its four grade II listed buildings now on the 'at risk' register. The owner, Dan McCauley, said recently 'The grass must be four feet high and there are seagulls nesting in the rooms, but otherwise it's in fine condition.' His stated intention is to turn Drake's Island into a luxury holiday resort.

East of the Hoe is the Royal Citadel, a huge fortress with walls 70ft high. It was built using local limestone in 1665 in response to a threatened Dutch invasion. The gateway, designed by Sir Thomas Fitz and made of Portland stone, is one of the best examples of English Baroque architecture in the country. It was originally approached by a drawbridge over a dry moat that was filled in in the 1880s to create a garden. Since 1962 the Citadel has been occupied by 29 Commando Royal Artillery but there are guided tours which include the garrison church of St Katherine-upon-the-Hoe. Those interested in cannons will be in their element as there are no less than 113. Unusually, some were positioned pointing towards the city in an attempt to intimidate the populace who sided with Parliament, not the Crown, during the English Civil War.

In the city centre there are also good things to see. The timber-framed Merchant's House in St Andrew's Street is the former home of William Parker, an Elizabethan privateer and mayor of Plymouth. Built in 1608, it now houses four small museums including a Victorian schoolroom and a reconstructed pre-war pharmacy. Nearby the Mission is a good place for lunch. Housed in a former methodist church where the families of local fishermen came to pray for their safe return, it has original stained glass windows, a splendid wooden ceiling and ecclesiastical furniture. The church of St Andrew's acts as Plymouth's

WEST DEVON

PLYMOUTH AREA

cathedral. The original 15th-century building was destroyed by a single bomb in 1941 but it has been reconstructed in the perpendicular style. Six absolutely splendid stained glass windows designed by John Piper are the major attraction. Prysten House just south of the church is the former home of Thomas Yogge, a rich wine merchant. The three-storied stone built property from 1498 has an impressive inner courtyard with open timber galleries. The hall, with fine timber roof and granite fireplace, belongs to the church and is used for community functions. The City Museum and Art Gallery has a small but excellent display of porcelain and describes the role played by local man William Cookworthy in its discovery (see 'China Clay' on page 152). The work of local artists is often exhibited, including Joshua Reynolds, who was born in Plympton in 1723, and Beryl Cook, who lived in Plymouth most of her adult life and died here in 2008. There are lunchtime talks most Tuesdays which, although free, require a ticket (☎ 01752 304774).

The Royal Naval Dockyard was founded by William III in 1691. Set on Bunker's Hill, Devonport, its initial 5-acre site has since grown to 330 acres. A 100ft-column commemorates the renaming of Plymouth Dock 'Devonport' on 1 January 1824. HM Naval Base Devonport can be visited on guided tours which take 2.5 hours (Monday-Thursday, 10am and 1pm, ☎ 01752 552326). Depending on operational and security constraints it may be possible to tour either a warship or a nuclear submarine. Some fine 19th-century buildings remain nearby, including Plymouth Town Hall, built in 1823 and modelled on the Parthenon.

The highly visible Tudor house on the Rame peninsula is part of Mount Edgcumbe estate, now jointly owned by Cornwall County and Plymouth City Councils. The gardens are of special historic interest, Grade I listed, and home to the National Camellia Collection. There is landscaping from 1750-1820 in the Italian, English and French style and some contemporary planting, including a Jubilee Garden from 2003. The estate of over 860 acres covers the whole eastern side of the Rame peninsula and is much favoured by walkers. Cawsand and Kingsand can be reached in about 2 hours, which with good timing coincides with a ferry back to Plymouth's Mayflower Steps. In 1515 King Henry VIII gave Sir Piers Edgcumbe permission to keep deer and those that roam free today are direct descendents. Although the house looks magnificent the original was destroyed by German incendiary bombs in 1941. Restoration began in the 1950s. The Orangery dating from 1760 is now a licensed

restaurant. The quayside at Cremyll can be reached by ferry from Admiral's Hard, Stonehouse, near to the Royal William Victualling Yard.

Two trips are worth taking further afield. Saltram House belonged to John Parker, a lifelong friend of Joshua Reynolds through whom he met both Robert Adam and Thomas Chippendale. Following a fire the house was reconstructed and today contains some of the finest 18th-century rooms in the country, furnished with Chippendale furniture, Reynolds portraits and an impressive collection of porcelain. Scenes from Ang Lee's film of Jane Austen's *Sense and Sensibility*, starring Kate Winslet and Emma Thompson, were filmed here. The house is in the hands of the National Trust and can be reached by Plymouth Citybus. Near Saltash is Cotehele, a Tudor house festooned with tapestries and textiles from the period. Also in the hands of the National Trust, it is 14M from the city centre but well worth the effort required to get there.

John Piper stained glass window, St Andrew's Church

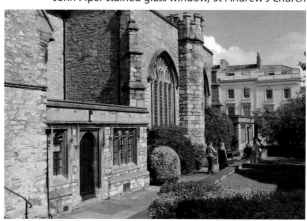

Arriving at Cremyll quayside for Mount Edgcumbe

Magnificent Georgian buildings on a peninsula jutting out into the River Tamar were designed to provide victuals for the Royal Navy. Built between 1826 and 1835, to a design by Sir John Rennie (1794-1874), they constitute the finest and most complete early 19th-century industrial complex in the country. Plymouth was a special target during the second world war, because of its naval presence, and the blitz was so extensive it is remarkable that they survived unscathed. Although closed to the public for more than 150 years, the yard is now in private hands and visitors are welcome though as yet there is little to see. Cafés, galleries, a hotel and restaurants are planned. There are 30 berths for yachts, some of which are available for visitors (☎ 07152 659252/07979 152008). Urban Splash, the Manchester-based development company, has been converting some of the buildings into luxury apartments and work is ongoing. The Ministry of Defence is planning a visitor centre in the former bakery and its twice-daily tours of the naval base will eventually leave from here.

The buildings seaward are the most impressive and there is ceremonial access between a pair of cast iron gates embellished with crossed fouled anchors. Visitors can arrive by waterbus, twice daily from the Barbican in the summer. A tunnel, which allowed light provisions to be taken out to ships in the Sound when ebb tides made access to the basin difficult, has been blocked off. The basin, 200ft

by 250ft, was designed for deep-water hoys and barges. The swivel bridge over the entrance was constructed by the Horseley Iron Company and added as an afterthought to improve circulation of traffic around the yard.

The site is 16 acres in all, 6 having been reclaimed from the sea. Entrance from the land is via Cremyll Street, where a granite gateway in the Greco-Roman style supports a huge statue of King William IV surrounded by the heads of 4 oxen. Up to 100 bullocks were slaughtered at the yard every day, the meat then layered in wooden barrels and salted. 100 coopers manufactured kegs and barrels for the transport of meat, biscuits, salt, beer, spirits, fresh water and gunpowder. Everything was devised on an industrial scale. For example, the bakery, brought into use in 1843, was capable of grinding 100 bushels (270,000lbs) of corn every hour using 27 millstones driven by two 40hp steam engines. The brewhouse was capable of producing 30,000 gallons of beer per day, though by the time of its commission in 1831 fresh water could be taken to sea, so just small quantities of alcohol were produced for the Naval Hospital and the Royal Marine Infirmary!

At its height over 250 men were employed at the yard but from 1985, when the RN entitlement to a tot of rum ended, the buildings were used just for storage. The yard finally closed in August 1992 after Michael Heseltine, as Minister of Defence, announced that a scheduled ancient monument should be used for greater glory. In 2003 the yard, its buildings and associated features became Grade I listed.

In the early days provision of victuals to the Navy was rather haphazard. There were many different suppliers, no central purchasing and on no two ships was food the same. Henry VIII changed this, specifying a diet and rate for which it was to be purchased. In 1545 each man was provided with a pound of biscuit and a gallon of beer a day and 200 'pieces of flesh' (salt beef or stock fish) fed 100 men on four days of the week. This worked out at a cost of 18d per day per man. Ships were expected to carry provisions for 2 months. By 1550 Edward Baeshe had the title of 'General Surveyor of the victuals of the seas' for which he was paid £50 a

ROYAL WILLIAM
VICTUALLING YARD
COMMISSIONED TO BE BUILT IN 1824
IN THE REIGN OF KING GEORGE IV
WITH THE SOLE PURPOSE OF SUPPLYING
VICTUALS TO HIS MAJESTY'S NAVY.
COMPLETED IN THE REIGN OF KING WILLIAM IV
FROM WHOM THE YARD TOOK ITS NAME ON
3RD DECEMBER 1833.
ARCHITECTS: SIR JOHN RENNIE
AND MR. PHILIP RICHARDS.

year. By the time of the Spanish Armada James Quarles was in charge. His chief clerk, Marmaduke Darrell, was sent to Plymouth to supervise victualling for the fleets of Lord Howard and Sir Francis Drake. Sir John Hawkins, a mariner and merchant, and his brother William were given the contract. Their victuals were considered especially good and included live animals (sheep and pigs), apples and pears. It was Hawkins, in 1597, who requested payment for 300 bolts of canvas 'to make hanging cabones or beddes … for the better preservation of (the sailors') health' and which led to the introduction of hammocks. His family built a new conduit to improve the water supply to Plymouth and her ships and founded the town's flour mills. As a result Plymouth became known for its ability to supply the fleet. Years later the King William Victualling Yard was built for just this task.

East Cornwall

Looe to Lizard Point

East Cornwall

Looe, Polperro, Fowey, Mevagissey, Falmouth and the River Helford

Looe Bay to the Helford River contains Cornwall's two most favoured sailing destinations, Falmouth and Fowey, but there is much else besides. Tiny picturesque harbours whose origins lie in a thriving fishing industry are now characterful holiday destinations and there are numerous small coves and sandy beaches to delay you.

With no roads, no shops and no traffic, those seeking solitude might like to spend a day on Looe Island. Run by Cornwall Wildlife Trust, this bird sanctuary, a mile in circumference, is home to a large colony of black-backed gulls. Animal lovers might also like to observe the rehabilitation of injured seals at the seal sanctuary in Gweek on the Helford Estuary. Shark fishing trips leave from the quay at Looe for those with less green credentials.

Fowey is a busy harbour with both pleasure and commercial craft. China clay is still mined nearby for export. The town has a relaxed holiday feel with boutiques, delis and numerous restaurants. It is here you should come if you want to be sociable! The Royal Regatta in August is a particular draw, as is the Daphne du Maurier Festival of Arts and Literature in May. *Rebecca* and *Frenchman's Creek* make good holiday reading and the eponymous creek can be found on the Helford River.

A visit to Charlestown will provoke nostalgia. The harbour, designed by John Smeaton who was also responsible for the third Eddystone lighthouse, has evaded development and the inner floating basin is home to a fleet of square-rigged sailing ships. It still looks much like an 18th-century working dock

and scenes from *The Onedin Line* and *Poldark* were filmed here. Inland, a trip to the China Clay Country Park Mining and Heritage Centre is hugely informative and buses run from St Austell to the Eden Project and The Lost Gardens of Heligan.

Mevagissey is a quintessential Cornish fishing village and a very popular tourist destination. Portmellon is a delightful small cove and Goran Haven an attractive anchorage in fine weather. Veryan Bay and Gerran's Bay have Heritage Coast status in recognition of their natural beauty.

Falmouth is a huge natural harbour where the Royal Navy has a presence and there are dry docks enabling repairs to ships of up to 100,000 tons. Although this might suggest a destination with little appeal, the estuary has lots to offer. From marinas in the town it is just a brief walk to numerous shops and restaurants and upstream there are quiet anchorages away from the bustle. The National Maritime Museum, opened in 2003, houses an internationally acclaimed collection of small boats in an architecturally impressive building. St Mawes, Flushing and St Just are gorgeous communities on the pristine Roseland Peninsula and Cornwall's only city, Truro, can be reached in small-draught vessels or by ferry. Truro is full of splendid Georgian architecture and home to England's most recently built cathedral.

The Helford River has few facilities but more than compensates with splendid solitude and the opportunity to visit some magnificent gardens. From here the Duchy of Cornwall supplies many a posh London restaurant with oysters.

The old lifeboat station at the Lizard

Charlestown

The Lizard

Alexander von Humboldt visiting Falmouth

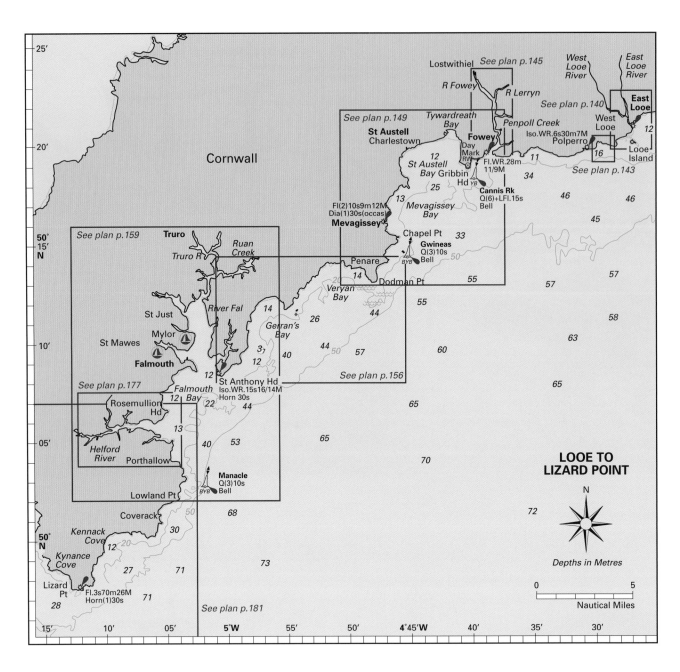

Sailing from Rame Head to the Lizard

The large bay that stretches from Bolt Head to the Lizard spans Devon and Cornwall. There are numerous places for secure berthing and a wealth of anchorages in picturesque locations.

Immediately after Rame Head, Whitesand Bay is exposed and has a dangerous wreck to the east. The area between Tregantle Fort and Portwinkle is used for firing practice.

Looe harbour, in Cornwall, is only for boats that can dry out. The town is popular with tourists.

A short distance westward is Polperro. There are two pairs of fore/aft buoys at the entrance and a single space in the inner harbour quay. Check before arrival and never approach in onshore conditions.

The River Fowey is a popular sailing destination. There are plenty of buoys and three visitors'

pontoons. The harbour is well lit and can be accessed in all conditions, although a strong southwest against the ebb creates swell which can make the berths uncomfortable.

Charlestown is the only harbour in St Austell Bay. The entrance is difficult and there is a lock. Looking much as it did in Georgian times, it is often used as a film set and is home to a number of tall ships. Arrangements must be made ahead.

St Austell Bay has a number of safe anchorages but open conditions mean there should be a plan of retreat if the weather turns.

Mevagissey is a quintessential Cornish village with a busy fishing harbour. Visitors can use buoys towards the entrance (fore and aft) and, subject to permission, the harbour wall. Do not attempt the entrance in

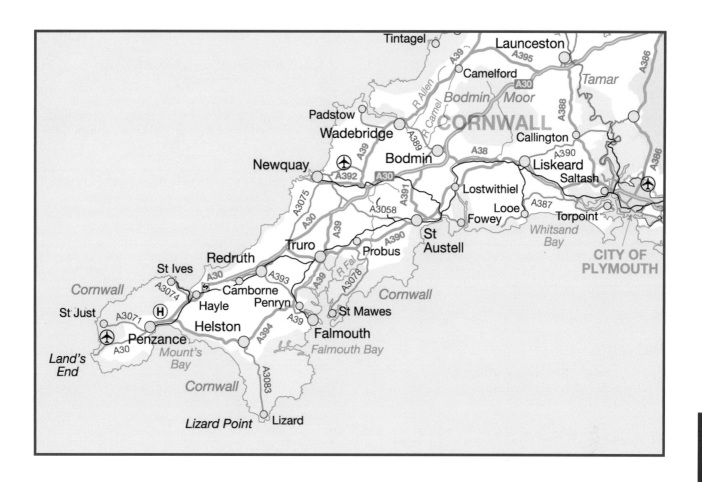

strong easterlies. The anchorage at Gorran Haven, further south, is a delight.

Falmouth Estuary is huge. Meandering 10M inland, it has a shoreline of over 60 miles. There are marinas within walking distance of the bustle of Falmouth town and quiet, remote anchorages beside wooded river banks further upstream. Across the bay, there are places to anchor and swinging moorings at St Mawes. The entrance to St Just is a wonderful place to drop anchor, while Mylor Yacht Harbour provides buoys and pontoons on the western side. From here anchorages and Truro Harbour Authority pontoons alternate up the river to Truro, Cornwall's county town.

The Helford River becomes uncomfortable in strong easterlies but is a deservedly popular sailing destination. This pristine marine environment has plenty of opportunities for berthing and dropping anchor. Boats that dry can enjoy a number of muddy creeks, alone but for the sound of tawny owls.

Initial shelter

Falmouth and Fowey are all-weather harbours, accessible day and night. Falmouth has extensive options for berthing.

Emergencies

There are RNLI stations at Plymouth, Looe, Fowey, Falmouth and The Lizard. The main lifeboats are at Plymouth, Falmouth and The Lizard.

The Maritime Safety Coordination Centre (MRCC) is based at Falmouth and monitors Channel 16, MF 2182kHz and DSC Channel 70. The coastal radio stations (Coastguard) at Falmouth and Brixham transmit Maritime Safety Information (see appendix for timings).

Falmouth has significant medical facilities.

Provisioning

Falmouth is a large town with access to supermarkets, shops, pubs, restaurants and cafés from the harbour. St Mawes, across the bay, is very small but has a Co-operative and places to eat.

The Helford is limited but there are pubs on both sides of the entrance.

Fowey is a medium-sized town with food shops and numerous restaurants.

Mevagissey, Looe and Polperro have small shops and some places to eat, subject to being able to get ashore.

Repairs and chandleries

In Falmouth there are boat lifts at Port Pendennis, Falmouth Yacht Marina and Mylor Yacht Harbour.

Falmouth and Mylor are the best for boat services and chandlery. Fowey has a small but well stocked chandler.

Fuel

- Looe: east quay (diesel)
- Fowey: Polruan Quay (diesel)
- Mevagissey: Victoria Pier (diesel)
- Falmouth: Visitors' Yacht Haven town marina and Falmouth Yacht Marina (diesel and petrol)
- Mylor: Mylor Yacht Marina (diesel and petrol).

Transport

High speed trains from London and Bristol stop at Liskeard, Lostwithiel, St Austell and Truro, which has a large main station. There are branch lines to Looe and Falmouth.

Buses are numerous and connect all the seaside towns.

Newquay airport handles mainly domestic flights.

Passages

From Plymouth to Fowey it is 19M. Keep clear of Rame Head and Looe Island where the tide creates confused seas.

The Eddystone Rocks, Fl(2)10s41m17M & Iso.R.10s28m8M, and Hand Deeps, Q(9)15s, stand 9M SSW of Plymouth. They are well marked and must be given a wide berth.

The distance from Fowey to the seaward side of Falmouth Bay is 19M. For this passage care should be taken with the Gwineas Rock and then the headlands of Dodman Point, with The Bellows to the south, and The Bizzies.

The long passage from Prawle Point to The Lizard is 58M, or 12 hours at 5 knots. This must be timed correctly to reach the Lizard with a fair tide. If proceeding on to the Isles of Scilly this is the significant tidal gate of the passage, but if going on to round Land's End a more complex calculation is needed. Aim to pass well south of The Lizard, a good 5M off in good weather and more if conditions are difficult.

There is plenty of shipping traffic heading for Land's End and also significant naval activity off Plymouth, a Royal Navy base. Naval firing practice takes place across Megavissey Bay.

Inshore fishing boats operate out of Looe, Polperro and Mevagissey. As ever maintain a look out for fishing pots in anything up to 50m.

Percuil

Mevagissey

Percuil near St Mawes

Mylor

⚓𝓥 Looe

Drying harbour, sheltered but uncomfortable inside in SE winds. Dangerous in strong southeasterlies when the sea breaks at the entrance. Strong tidal stream, very strong on the ebb during springs. Eddy on the flood to beyond visitors' berths.

A 7-span Victorian road bridge connects the two parts of the town which straddles the merged East and West Looe rivers. Looe is a popular tourist destination with a crowded fishing harbour.

Approach & entrance

To clear the bar approach the entrance at HW+/-1. The harbour dries except along the eastern wall, which is used by the many fishing boats.

Anchor outside in front of the beach if you need to wait for HW.

- CURRENTS: time your entrance with care to avoid strong currents, particularly on the ebb and during spring tides.

- DANGERS:
- Ranneys 500m SE of Looe Island, marked by the south cardinal Q(6)+LFl.15s
- Overfalls south of the Ranneys
- Unmarked Limmicks rocks 0.3M NE of entrance
- Many rocks between entrance and Looe Island.

- From the west, keep well clear of Looe Island and the Ranneys reef and its overfalls. East of 4°25′W and south of 50°19′N is a conservative but comfortable guide.

- From the east, Knight Errant Patch has a few shallow spots (5m) which can be turbulent.

- Keep in the white sector of the Banjo Pier light (between 263° and 313°) Oc.WR.3s.

- The deepest water is in the centre between the pier and the western cliff.

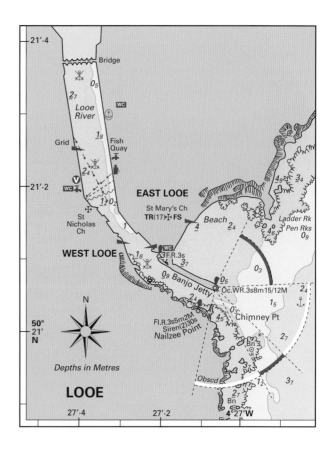

Berthing & facilities

𝓥 The visitors' berths (marked Visitors) are on the western quay after the ferry steps. Up to 3 boats abreast, dries to 3m. A fender board is required if next to the wall.

⚓ Anchorage outside in 2-3m sand and mud, sheltered from W but open from E to SSW. Avoid in strong E / SE. Anchorage prohibited in the harbour.

Food & transport

There are numerous cafés, restaurants and pubs and a Somerfield supermarket. Trawlers on the Quay, in East Looe, is a good place to eat seafood which often includes a trio of fish from the day's haul.

Buses run from a stop near the bridge to Polperro, Liskeard and Plymouth. The Looe valley train to Liskeard is very popular with tourists (summer only).

Interest

Looe has been a popular tourist destination for many years. It was here that the leisured classes came during the Napoleonic War. Bathing machines were available by about 1800. These small huts were used for changing, then pulled into the water by horses. The bather would emerge down some steps while all the time being shielded from public view. Thus, we are told, 'the most refined female is enabled to enjoy the advantages of the sea with the strictest delicacy.'

Tourism grew considerably with the establishment of the railway and the short 8.75M single track to Liskeard is a delightful journey which follows the East Looe river for much of its course. Opened in 1860, it has been operated by First Great Western since 2006. New 1950s-style chocolate and cream signs encourage nostalgia, which can be furthered by a trip to the Magnificent Music Machines Museum, just a short walk from the St Keyne Wishing Well Halt. Here polyphons, phonographs and player pianos can be heard, together with the mighty 1929 Wurlitzer organ from the Regent Theatre, Brighton. With 693 pipes and real percussion including a xylophone, glockenspiel and tubular bells, the organ provided the soundtrack for numerous silent films. The museum is open in summer only and tours take an hour.

Of the two settlements East Looe is the more attractive. Laid out in a grid fashion, it is an example of an early 'planted borough', i.e. a new town developed according to a plan. Many houses were built above a cellar, used to process pilchards, and some still use an outside stone staircase to accommodation above. West and East Looe were renowned examples of rotten boroughs, so called because they had unfair representation in Parliament. Until the Great Reform Act of 1832 each borough was entitled to elect two MPs, which East Looe did with only 167 houses and 38 voters. No one is

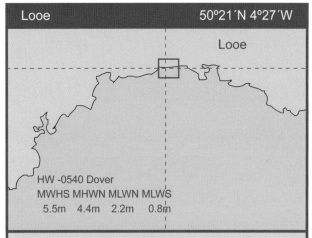

Looe	50°21′N 4°27′W

Looe

HW -0540 Dover

MWHS	MHWN	MLWN	MLWS
5.5m	4.4m	2.2m	0.8m

Looe

- Dangerous in strong SE
- HW+/-1 to clear bar; rock dangers
- Visitors' berths W quay (dries 3.3m sand)
- ☎ 01503 262839 / 07918 7289550
- Water tap west quay
- Diesel east quay

suggesting Looe could be bought, of course, but this, along with thinking very little, is how Sir Joseph Porter became Ruler of the Queen's Navee in *H.M.S. Pinafore* by Gilbert and Sullivan:

> *I grew so rich that I was sent*
> *By a pocket borough into Parliament.*
> *I always voted at my party's call,*
> *And I never thought of thinking for myself at all.*
> ...
> *I thought so little, they rewarded me*
> *By making me the Ruler of the Queen's Navee!*

The Monkey Sanctuary in walking distance of the harbour is a place of rescue for Barbary macaques, Capuchin, Woolly and Patas monkeys and is well worth a visit. Rare lesser horseshoe bats (named after the shape of their nose) can also be observed in their cellar roost-site thanks to a pan and tilt camera and infra-red lighting. There are also meadows, ponds, a Victorian border garden and forest to wander around, and an excellent vegetarian café.

Looe Banjo Pier and harbour

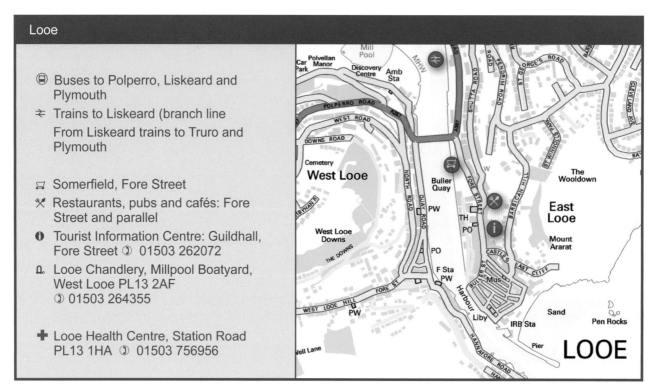

Looe

Buses to Polperro, Liskeard and Plymouth

Trains to Liskeard (branch line From Liskeard trains to Truro and Plymouth

Somerfield, Fore Street

Restaurants, pubs and cafés: Fore Street and parallel

Tourist Information Centre: Guildhall, Fore Street ☎ 01503 262072

Looe Chandlery, Millpool Boatyard, West Looe PL13 2AF ☎ 01503 264355

Looe Health Centre, Station Road PL13 1HA ☎ 01503 756956

There is a very rewarding 5M walk along the South West Coast Path from Looe to Polperro and there are boat-trips to St George's Island, also called Looe Island, about 1M offshore. Bought by the Atkins sisters in 1965, the island was their home for over 40 years and Evelyn wrote two books about it: *We bought an island* and *Tales from our Cornish island*. Now owned by Cornwall Wildlife Trust, it is a designated bird sanctuary with a huge colony of black-backed gulls. Dogs are not permitted. In 2008 the island was filmed as part of Channel 4's Time Team programme and excavations unearthed the burial of a adult man and a hoard of Roman coins.

Banjo Pier in East Looe has a rounded end making it look like a banjo. It was designed by Joseph Thomas (1838-1901).

Polperro
Fore/aft mooring buoys outside the wall. Inset: view along the quay towards inner harbour and visitors' berths.

EAST CORNWALL

LOEE

⚓ⓥ Polperro

Small drying harbour, protected by a storm gate in bad weather. Dangerous to approach in S / SE conditions. Mooring buoys in entrance channel, best used fore and aft.

Polperro is an exceptionally quaint fishing village but its charm is inversely proportional to the number of tourists.

Approach & entrance

The entrance, nestled between cliffs, is narrow and difficult to distinguish from a distance. Guide yourself visually by the measured mile beacons between Polperro and Looe (western transit set about 1M east of the entrance) or, coming from Fowey, the Udder Rock south cardinal (2M from the entrance).

Entrance is closed by a storm gate in bad weather. If it is closed the FW light on west pier shows FR (black ball in daylight).

DANGEROUS to enter in S / SE conditions.

- HAZARDS:
- The Polca Rock (1m) about 200m SW of Spy House Point, close to entrance transit.
- The Raney Reef which extends from Peak Rock (ragged rock west of entrance).

- From the west: approach between Polca Rock and Raney Reef, best judged by keeping charted depth of at least 7m. Turn towards the harbour entrance once you can see the transit formed by the ends of the east and west pier (310°).

- From the east, clear The Polca rock by using the outer/west pier transit.

The light at Spy House Point shows a white sector from 288° to 60°.

Berthing

Two spaces for visitors, up to 10m LOA, alongside at the east wall inside the harbour, which dries 2m. The gap through the gate is very narrow.

ⓥ There are four buoys outside. Tie up fore and aft to avoid swinging across the channel and towards the rocks. ⚓ Anchorage in the inlet in offshore winds.

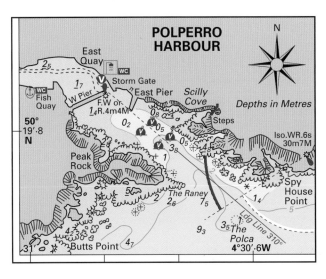

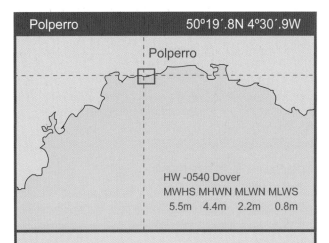

Polperro	50°19′.8N 4°30′.9W

HW -0540 Dover

MWHS	MHWN	MLWN	MLWS
5.5m	4.4m	2.2m	0.8m

Polperro

- Approach dangerous in S/SE
- Entrance narrow, difficult to spot
- Inner east quay wood piles: 2 boats up to 10m LOA - dries 2m
- Four buoys in entrance: tie fore and aft to avoid swinging into the channel
- Harbourmaster VHF10 ☎ 01503 272809 or *Girl Jane* fishing boat ☎ 01503 272423

Food & transport

Polperro caters exceptionally well for tourists and there are numerous places to eat and drink. Buses link the village with Looe.

Interest

The price Polperro pays for being exceptionally pretty is that it is usually overrun by tourists. There are narrow lanes and alleyways and tightly packed houses that ramble delightfully down to the sea. It is still a fishing village but most of all it caters for visitors, with an almost unbroken stream of gift shops and cafés. The Polperro Heritage Museum of Smuggling and Fishing (Easter to October), housed in the old pilchard factory on the east of the harbour, is worth a brief visit. In good weather a walk along the South West Coast Path to Fowey, 5M away, is not to be missed. This is one of the most scenic stretches in the whole of Cornwall and provides access to some beautiful, secluded, sandy beaches.

Polperro

⏱ Fowey

Sheltered harbour which can be entered in all conditions day and night. The lower harbour is subject to swell in strong south/southwesterlies.

Fowey (pronounced 'Foy') and Polruan, opposite, are small picturesque communities and popular tourist destinations. There are plenty of places to eat, drink and hang out with the 'in crowd'.

Approach & entrance

Straightforward entrance in all conditions and state of tide. However, in strong SW winds against an ebb tide, the entrance can be choppy.

- HAZARDS:
  - Cannis Rock 1.5M SSW of entrance, marked by a south cardinal Q(6)LFl.15s
  - Punch Cross Rocks on the eastern side of the entrance, marked by a beacon (unlit)
  - Udder Rock 3M E of entrance, marked by a south cardinal VQ(6)+LFl.10s.

- Fowey is a busy port exporting clay. Beware of large ships at the entrance.

- Keep in the centre of the channel. At night stay in the white sectors of the entrance light LFl.WR.5s and Whitehouse Point Iso.WRG.3s (22° to 32°) inside the harbour.

- Keep clear of Punch Cross Rocks lying to starboard at the entrance (marked by an unlit post and triangle beacon). At night pass between entrance lights FL.G.5s and Fl.R.2s.

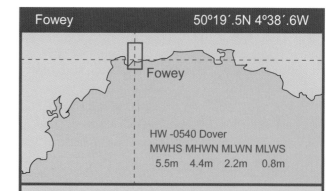

Fowey   50°19´.5N 4°38´.6W

Fowey

HW -0540 Dover

MWHS	MHWN	MLWN	MLWS
5.5m	4.4m	2.2m	0.8m

Fowey

- Straightforward approach & entrance in all conditions

- Ⓥ Visitors' berths and moorings:
  - Polruan Quay short stay
  - Moorings and pontoon at Pont Pill
  - Pontoon and moorings east beyond Penleath Point
  - Temporary pontoon at Albert Quay
  - Pontoon east past Bodinnick
  - Berrills boatyard short stay
  - Pontoon south side at Mixtow Pill
  - Mooring at Wiseman's Reach

- Harbourmaster/harbour patrol VHF12 ☎ 01726 832471

- Water at Berrils and Mixtow Pill pontoons (also showers)

- 🛢 Diesel from Polruan Quay

- 🔧 C Toms & Son Boatyard Polruan ☎ 01726 870232; Fowey Marine Engineers, Fowey ☎ 01726 832806

- Royal Fowey Yacht Club ☎ 01726 832245 Fowey Gallants Yacht Club ☎ 01726 832335

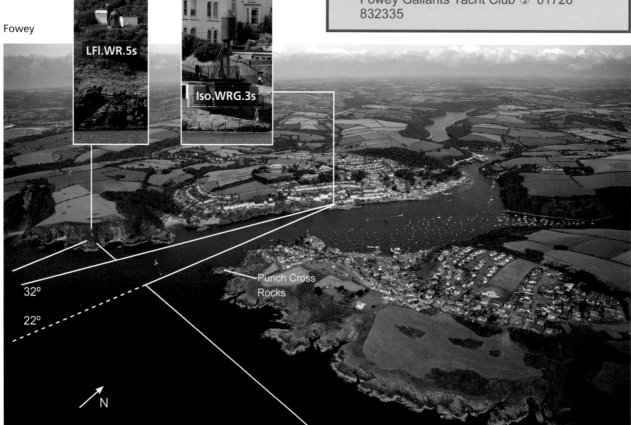

Fowey

LFl.WR.5s

Iso.WRG.3s

Punch Cross Rocks

32°

22°

N

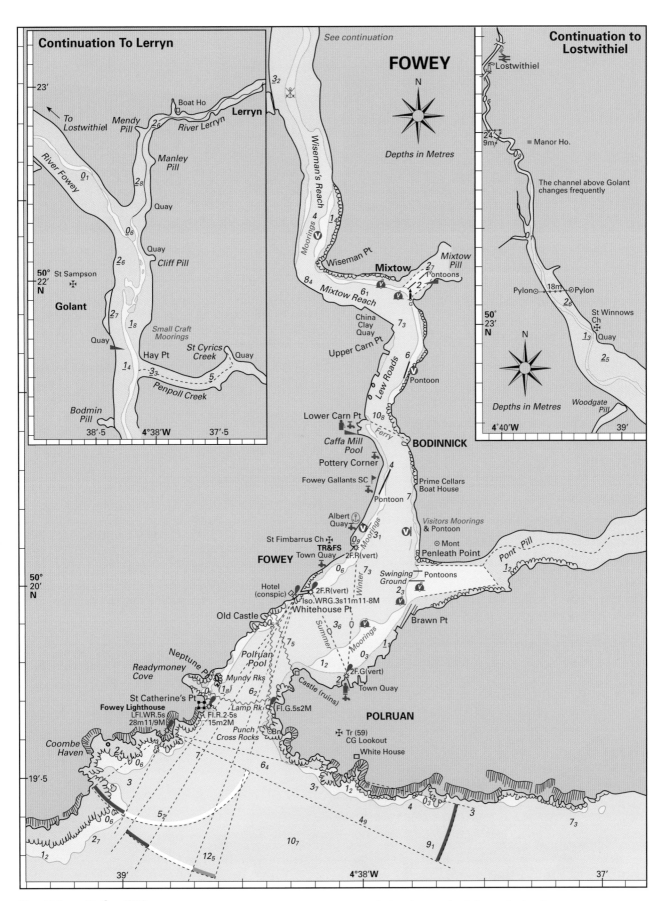

Berthing & facilities

The lower harbour can be uncomfortable in strong south or southwest conditions, when there is swell. Swell can extend as far as Bodinnick, with the lower reaches becoming very bouncy on the ebb.

Permission is required from the harbourmaster to anchor off Polruan and in Pont Pill. Ship movements and the availability of pontoons and moorings will be taken into account. Anchoring is not allowed in front of Pont Pill or in the channel from Pont Pill to Wiseman Point as the area is used by ships to swing.

Gribbin Head, conspicuous mark at the Head

South cardinal marking Cannis Rock

There are several options for berthing in the lower harbour:

- Visitors' moorings off Polruan and Pont Pill, for boats up to 12m LOA. All buoys are white and marked FHC Visitors.
- 40m pontoon and fore/aft moorings in Pont Pill, which provide more shelter in W / SW conditions.
- 40m pontoon east side, just beyond Penleath Point.

In addition a number of pontoons are available for short stays:

- Albert Quay Pontoon. The harbourmaster's office is nearby and there is a water tap .
- Shipyard pontoon in Polruan. Fuel and water.
- Summer pontoon, all states of tide, Polruan side.
- Berril's Boatyard pontoon can be used for up to 2h. Stream side, all states of tide.

The Royal Fowey Sailing Club in Fowey welcomes visitors. It has showers, a bar and restaurant.

Fuel is dispensed from the *Fowey Refueller* barge at the entrance to Pont Pill.

Fowey

Ⓥ Lew Roads & Mixtow Pill

Upstream from Fowey and Polruan the channel narrows but continues to be deep. Do not anchor anywhere along this stretch as it is used by large ships. Two further pontoons can be used by visitors.

- East side pontoon between Boddinick and Mixtow Pill.
- 135m pontoon (2m) in Mixtow Pill, quiet, sheltered and linked to shore. Visitors on the south side. The end of the pontoon is very shallow.

There are showers and a fresh water tap at Mixtow.

⚓ Wiseman's Reach & upstream

Beyond Mixtow Pill and the clay loading area, the river turns north. At the beginning of Wiseman's Reach it is still deep. Ⓥ There is a visitors' buoy 30m north Wiseman's Point. The reach is full of small boat moorings with no space for anchoring.

Beyond Wiseman's Point the river dries. However, on the flood, it can be explored by shallow-draught boats all the way to Lostwithiel.

Golant (1.5M north) is a good destination if you can dry out and find space to anchor among the many moorings. Bottom is mud and sand. There is a quay on the west bank just before the village.

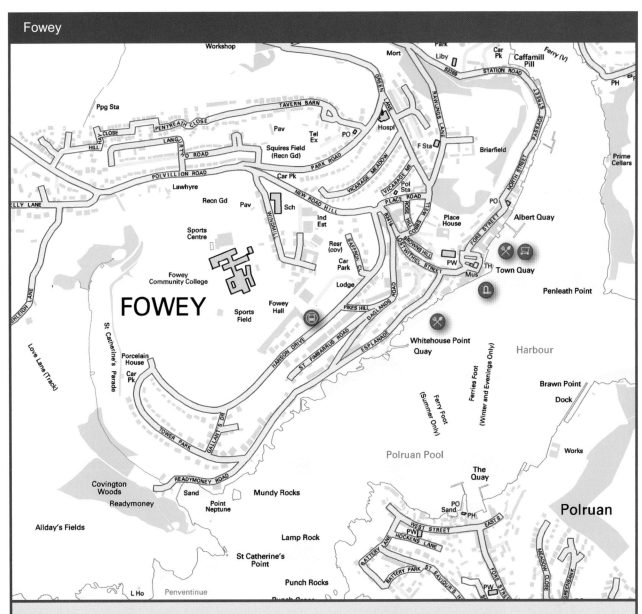

Fowey

- 🚌 Buses to Polperro and Looe from Hanson Drive
- ⇌ Train station at Lostwithiel and Par
- ⛴ Ferry Fowey-Polruan and Fowey-Bodinnick
- 🛒 Minimarket, numerous groceries and delis in Fore Street
- 🍴 Restaurants, pubs and cafés: Esplanade, Fore Street and Passage Street

- ❶ The Ticket Shop & Daphne du Maurier Literary Centre/Tourist Information Centre
  5 South Street, Fowey PL23 1AR
  ☎ 01726 833616
- ⚓ Upper Deck Marine, Albert Quay, Fowey PL23 1AQ ☎ 01726 832287 (well stocked)
- ✚ Fowey Hospital, Park Road, Fowey PL23 1EE
  ☎ 01726 832241

Beyond Golant the river forks. The creek northeast towards Lerryn dries 2.8m but the village creek can be reached by dinghy.

The main river going northwest is a mere trickle at low water and the channel shifts frequently but you can get as far as Lostwithiel. This takes you past the lovely St Winnow church and under some less lovely electrical cables (18m clearance).

Food & transport

Fowey caters well for tourists and has many places to eat and drink. There are also small grocery stores, delis, and an excellent fishmonger. The Royal Fowey

Yacht Club welcomes sailors to its bar and restaurant (check times).

Public transport is very limited but there are buses to St Austell and Par railway station (main line on to Penzance, Newquay, Plymouth, Bristol and London Paddington). A vehicle and foot ferry crosses the river to Bodinnick and Polruan and, weather permitting, there is a foot ferry to Mevagissey (May to October).

Polruan, Golant and Lerryn each have a post office and general store. Cornish Knocker and Cornish Blonde, two well-known local beers, are served at the Ship Inn, Lerryn.

EAST CORNWALL

FOWEY

Interest

Fowey is a natural deep-water harbour where trade with Europe developed from medieval times. 160 archers defended the harbour in the early 14th century but were relieved of duties by 1380 when a chain was slung between two square blockhouses built across the estuary. This method of defence was popular for a while; it was also deployed at the entrance to the River Dart. Fowey supplied 47 vessels for the Siege of Calais in 1346 (in comparison to 25 provided by London) and 700 local men participated. In return the town was attacked twice, first in 1380 and then again in 1467.

Once the Cornish mining industry was established, rival harbours were built along the coast at West Polmear (later renamed Charlestown) and Par (see 'The mining industry' on page 174 and "China Clay" on page 152) and Fowey declined in importance until the Fowey Harbour Commissioners, established by an Act of Parliament in 1869, began a programme of redevelopment. In the same year the broad gauge Lostwithiel and Fowey Railway and the standard gauge Cornwall Minerals Railway opened and Fowey's supremacy over the shallow artificial harbours nearer to the mines and china clay works was secured. About 3 million tonnes of china clay are still exported from Devon and Cornwall each year and much of it is shipped from Fowey. There is a loading base on the west side of the river 1M upstream, and should you moor in Mixtow or Wiseman's Reach this is the mysterious fine white dust that settles on the decking.

The Sawmill Studios at Golant are based in a pretty 17th-century watermill on the edge of the river. It is kitted out with the very best technology and Oasis, The Verve, The Stone Roses and Muse have all recorded here.

In Fowey itself the parish church of St Fimbarrus is worth a visit. Although extensive restoration took place in the 19th century, its 14th-century origins give it Grade I listed status. The tower, in four stages with buttresses and bands of ornament, is the second tallest in Cornwall. The wagon roof is 15th-century. Inside there is a Norman font made of Catacleuze stone and a pulpit made from the panelling of a Spanish Galleon.

Fowey is an enjoyable place to mooch. Houses with cellars where pilchards were processed still make use of external staircases. Narrow lanes, steep alleyways and medieval merchants' houses line the waterfront in a community with character. Polruan blockhouse, visible at the harbour entrance, may be visited on foot. The blockhouse at Fowey is in ruins and not accessible.

The romantic novelist Daphne du Maurier spent most of her adult life here. She lived for a while at the Ferryside house in Bodinnick where a figurehead from a wrecked 19th-century schooner, *Jane Slade*, is displayed on a beam below what used to be her bedroom. Du Maurier found the figurehead in Pont Creek and based her first novel, *The Loving Spirit*, on her research into the life of the real Jane Slade, whom she renamed Janet Coombs. The story follows the

Polruan

lives of a Cornish boatbuilding family across four generations and its setting is unmistakably that of Polruan. In 1943 du Maurier moved to Menabilly, the Elizabethan ancestral home of the Rashleigh family two miles west of Fowey. The house was in a dilapidated state which she restored and made famous as the setting for *Rebecca* (see 'Literary West Country' on page 37). Since 1997, Fowey has hosted a Daphne du Maurier Festival of Arts and Literature in May.

There are a number of splendid walks from Fowey and Polruan (details from the Tourist Information Centre). The Saints Way goes to Padstow, 30 miles northwards. Far more manageable is Hall Walk (3 miles) starting at the Polruan blockhouse. Head first to Pont Pill and then Bodinnick, where the path meanders through woodland before opening out to some fine vistas across the water. A longer walk can be had by continuing on as far as Golant. South of Polruan the coastal walk to Lantic Bay is also a delight, with signs that are easy to follow. The red and white striped day marker at Gribbin Head (National Trust) can be visited on some Sundays in the summer. It was erected in 1832 in order to distinguish The Gribbin from St Anthony Head at the entrance to Falmouth. Although the two headlands are miles away from one another they look quite similar from the sea and were often mistaken with disastrous consequences. Located on the South West Coast Path, the daymark is a 30-40 minute walk from Hamblands car park at Menabilly. Steep, narrow stairs ascend 84ft to a lookout with magnificent views out to sea.

Fowey is especially lively in the third week of August when it hosts a Royal Regatta. After all the races the grand finale usually includes a fly-past by the Red Arrows and a fantastic firework display.

The town pontoon and Daphne du Maurier's Ferryhouse

St Austell Bay and Mevagissey Bay

The bays of St Austell and Megavissey offer shelter in a variety of anchorages and inside the protection of two harbours.

St Austell Bay is wide and slowly shelving, which helps to absorb some of the swell. There are several sandy beaches which are workable as anchorages in westerly conditions, as well as the small cove at Polkerris which is good in easterlies. Charlestown harbour is only practical in the most moderate westerly conditions, but well worth a visit even if only by dinghy from an anchorage outside.

Mevagissey has a small harbour, well protected and very picturesque. It is the destination for boat trips from Fowey. The beach at Pentewan and the small cove of Portmellon can be good anchorages. Gorran Haven is a delightful anchorage further south.

There are few dangers in the bays, and none more than 200m away from the coast. Beware the Kilyvarder Rock in Par Sands. On passage from the east you need to pass south of Cannis Rock, marked by a south cardinal off Gribbin Head. From the south there are tidal races off Dodman Point and you need to pass east of Gwineas Rock, marked by a cardinal.

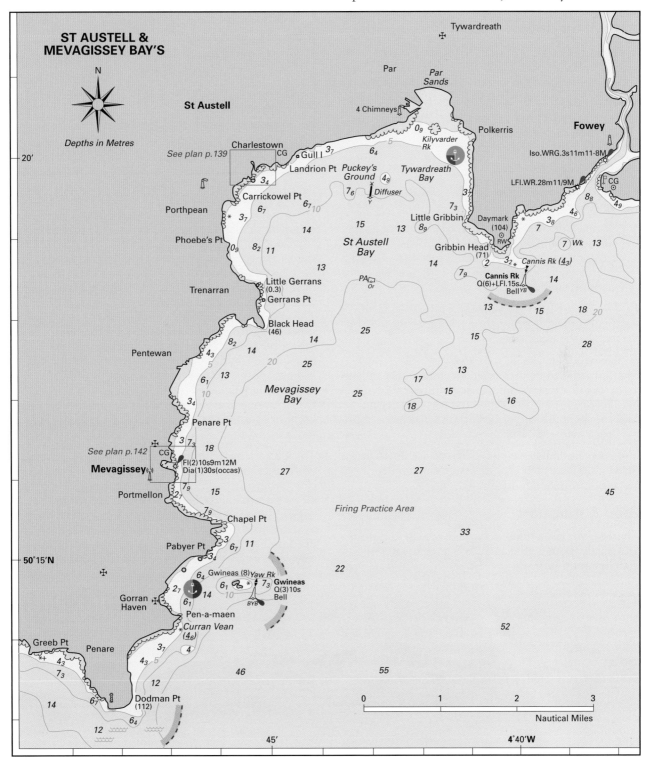

St Austell Bay

⚓ Polkerris

Small drying harbour in the northeastern corner of St Austell Bay. There is a large area of 1.5m depth good for anchoring in easterlies and in calm conditions. If you can dry out the small harbour wall will give protection from southerly swell. Arrive in good weather unless you are familiar with the layout as there is little space.

⚓ Par Sands

Par Sands is a commercial clay port. The approach dries completely. Only for emergency.

⚓🕐 Charlestown

In the northwest of St Austell Bay, Charlestown used to be a clay port and is interesting to visit. The approach dries and the entrance to the outer basin is very narrow. The inner basin can be entered HW+/-2.

- DO NOT ATTEMPT in anything other than calm conditions and westerlies. DAY ENTRY ONLY.

- Enter only after having made arrangements with the harbourmaster.

- 15m wide entrance gate and DANGERS immediately to either side.

- Approach the outer basin on 287° transit of gable end cottage and white mark in outer basin. Under no circumstances go beyond the entrance gate towards the beach - a submerged training wall/reef extends from the gate.

V Pick up the buoy 300m south of the harbour if waiting for the tide or for the harbourmaster to open the lock to the inner basin.

⚓ The wide expanse in front and south of Charlestown can be used as an anchorage, but only in westerlies or calm conditions. Stay at least 200m from the shore to get enough depth and to avoid drying rocks at the south end of Porthpean's beaches and off the beach below the Ropehaven cliffs.

The outer basin has plenty of steps to use if you arrive by dinghy. Time your stay to ensure enough depth (drying 1.2m in sections).

Food & transport

Charlestown has a number of places to eat and drink. St Austell, about a mile away, is a large town with mainline train station.

Charlestown's outer basin

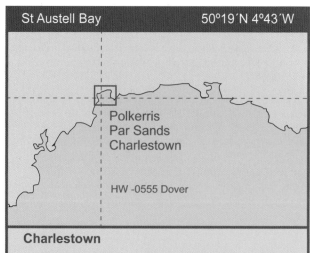

Polkerris
Par Sands
Charlestown

HW -0555 Dover

Charlestown

- Difficult entrance that needs to be arranged with the harbourmaster in advance
- ONLY ATTEMPT in calm westerlies
- **V** Visitors in inner basin behind lock, by arrangement
- Harbourmaster ☎ 01276 70241 VHF14/16 only when vessel expected
- www.square-sail.com

Interest

St Austell Bay is historically associated with the shipment of clay, copper and tin from nearby mines. Charlestown was a working port until the 1990s and is well worth a visit if you like a sailing challenge. The harbour is a reminder of a bygone age, a Georgian port lined with granite cottages. It was built in the late 18th century by local businessman Charles Rashleigh. The village was originally called West Polmear until it became known as Charles's town before being officially renamed Charlestown in honour of its benefactor. Developing the harbour was an obvious business opportunity. Over four months in 1813, 49 ships had exported nearly 4,000 tons of copper from just one nearby mine called Crinnis. Today the harbour is owned by Square Sail Shipyard Ltd, who use it for berthing their tall ships. It is Grade II listed.

The Charlestown Shipwreck and Heritage Centre is worth a brief visit. A tunnel, used until 1972 to bring clay to the port, takes you to a platform with splendid views over the harbour. If you are interested in the engraving of whalebone and walrus tusks, known as scrimshaw, there are good examples here. First produced by 19th-century whalers, who might be at sea for more than a year, they typically depict images

EAST CORNWALL

ST AUSTELL BAY

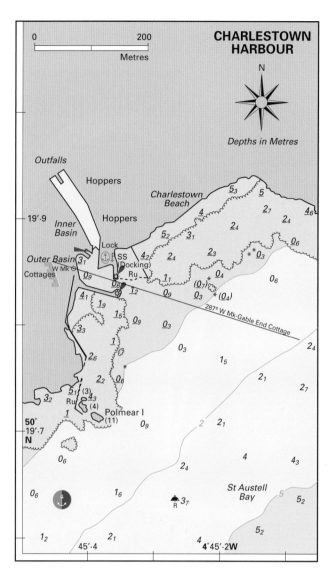

CHARLESTOWN HARBOUR

N

Depths in Metres

0   200
Metres

Outfalls
Hoppers
Charlestown Beach
Hoppers
Inner Basin
Outer Basin
Cottages
Lock
SS (Docking)
Ru
287° W Mk-Gable End Cottage
Polmear I
Ru
St Austell Bay

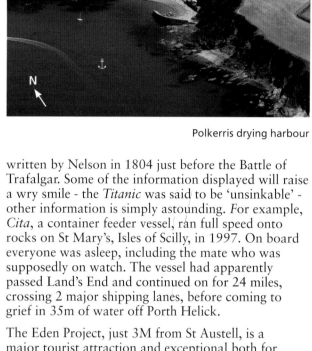

Polkerris drying harbour

of their sweethearts and their gardens at home along with pictures of ships, whale hunts and mythological figures. The centre also contains much memorabilia from ships such as *HMS Victory* and there is a letter

Charlestown

written by Nelson in 1804 just before the Battle of Trafalgar. Some of the information displayed will raise a wry smile - the *Titanic* was said to be 'unsinkable' - other information is simply astounding. For example, *Cita*, a container feeder vessel, ran full speed onto rocks on St Mary's, Isles of Scilly, in 1997. On board everyone was asleep, including the mate who was supposedly on watch. The vessel had apparently passed Land's End and continued on for 24 miles, crossing 2 major shipping lanes, before coming to grief in 35m of water off Porth Helick.

The Eden Project, just 3M from St Austell, is a major tourist attraction and exceptional both for its engineering and for the million or so plants that are contained in 3 different climatic zones. Housed in a 160-year-old exhausted china clay quarry, huge biomes, looking like giant golf balls, use triple-glazed thermoplastic bubbles to imitate the rainforest and warm temperate conditions associated with the Mediterranean. Even the soil has been custom-made with the help of academics from Reading University. The scale is breathtaking. The Tower of London can fit inside the rainforest biome and many plants are now so huge that they have to be pruned by abseilers. Further afield The China Clay Country Park Mining and Heritage Centre, 2M north of St Austell, is worth a visit (see 'China Clay' on page 152).

The English so admired 17th-century Chinese porcelain that the word 'china' became a synonym and all over Europe the hunt was on to identify its secret ingredients. William Cookworthy, the son of a Quaker weaver from Kingsbridge in Devon, was the first to do so in England. Apprenticed to a 'chemist and druggist' in London, he eventually owned a very successful apothecary in Plymouth and is said to have entertained Captain Cook and Joseph Banks before they sailed in *Endeavour* to Otaheite, in the Pacific Ocean, in 1769.

Cookworthy's curiosity had been aroused when he read an account of the manufacture of Chinese porcelain written in the 1740s by a Jesuit missionary. When, in 1745, some American businessmen tried to persuade him to produce English porcelain from imported Virginian clay, he began to look locally for suitable minerals and in 1746 found kaolin, or china clay as it is known, at Tregonning Hill, Cornwall. Here it was known as 'moorstone' and in 1768 Cookworthy's successful patent application, number 898, was for 'Making porcelain from moorstone, growan and growan clay'. By then he had established the Plymouth China Works, making decorated tea services, jugs and vases.

Although Cookworthy eventually found very good quality clay near St Austell, production difficulties led to financial problems and the business amalgamated with a pottery in Bristol. Cookworthy sold his financial interest to his cousin and business manager, Richard Champion, in 1774 but three years later potters from the Midlands, led by Josiah Wedgwood, objected to the patent's renewal. The ensuing legal battle crippled the company and Champion sold the formula to the Staffordshire potters in 1782. It was used for another 20 years until surpassed by the quality of bone china. The earliest piece of Cookworthy hard-paste porcelain, now in the British Museum, is a decorated blue mug bearing the Arms of Plymouth and the inscription '14 March 1768 C.F.' It is thought that the initials mean 'Cookworthy fecit' (Cookworthy made it).

By the 1800s there had been an expansion of potteries in the Midlands and clay was being used in the paper and cotton industries. By 1858 forty-two mining companies were producing 65,000 tons of china clay in Cornwall every year. Pits and tips had changed the Cornish landscape forever. Today the mining of China Clay is Cornwall's largest industry. Four companies operate pits

in Cornwall and Devon, producing almost three million tonnes of clay each year. About 70% is used in the production of paper and 20% in the production of ceramics. This fine, inert filling agent is also used in medicines, toothpaste, cosmetics, paints and plastics.

Charlestown, 2 miles from St Austell, was developed as a harbour for the transport of copper, tin and china clay. Originally a small fishing village called West Polmear, trading vessels had landed and loaded on the beach until a deep harbour with lock gates was constructed in the late 18th century by local landowner Charles Rashleigh. Designed by John Smeaton, who also designed the third Eddystone Lighthouse, it soon thronged with activity. There was boat building, rope making, brickworks, lime burning, net houses, bark houses and pilchard curing and the population of 9 in 1790 grew to 3,184 by 1911. In 1799 the port was renamed Charles's Town, which in turn became Charlestown. Today the harbour is owned by Square Sail Shipyard Ltd. One or more of their square riggers are often in the dock and can sometimes be visited.

Charlestown has largely escaped development and it is not hard for the visitor to imagine yesteryear. It was a working port, exporting china clay, until the 1990s. Today it is often used as a film set and scenes from Poldark, The Onedin Line, The Voyage of Charles Darwin and the 1993 version of The Three Musketeers were shot here. The Charlestown Shipwreck and Heritage Centre is worth a brief visit.

The China Clay Country Park Mining and Heritage Centre, 2 miles north of St Austell, is well worth a detour. Situated within the old Wheal Martyn and Gomm china clay works, a trail takes you through the processes involved in extracting clay from granite. Basically, water is used to form a slurry of minerals from which mica, quartz and granite are filtered before the clay is dried and cut into blocks. Old water wheels, a crib

hut, a blueing house, mica drags, a pan kiln and methods for transporting clay to the harbour at Charlestown are all there, with helpful explanation. The site was given Scheduled Ancient Monument status in 1979.

EAST CORNWALL

ST AUSTELL BAY

Mevagissey Bay

Home to Mevagissey, the second most important harbour in the area, the bay looks directly east and is very open so should not be considered in easterlies of any strength.

1⚓Ⓥ Mevagissey

A fishing harbour with a substantial outer pier. The inner harbour dries but there is always at least 2m to seaward at the outer harbour near the entrance. Exposed to easterlies only. Crowded inside with fishing and local boats.

Approach & entrance

Straightforward entrance in good conditions.

- DANGEROUS in strong E / SE
- DANGERS: rocky ledge from north pier
- Head for the end of the south pier (Victoria Pier) Fl(2)10s
- Keep away from the north pier to avoid the rocky ledge extending from it.

Berthing & facilities

Ⓥ Consult with the harbourmaster ahead of arrival, particularly if you are planning to use the outer moorings, which are normally fore and aft.

Ⓥ Visitors are welcome alongside the wall of the south pier, but must be prepared to leave immediately should the space be required as a temporary berth for a fishing boat.

The inner harbour dries completely, as do the edges of the outer harbour.

⚓ The anchorage off the south pier should be used only in calm conditions with offshore winds.

⚓ Portmellon

Portmellon is a small cove south of Mevagissey which can be explored in calm conditions. Keep at least 200m from the shore. Sound carefully as depth changes rapidly. The cove has a beach good for landing in a dinghy.

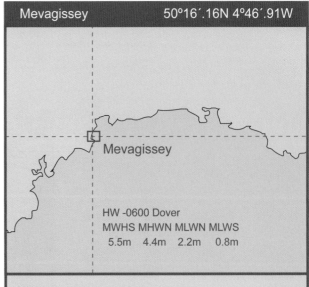

Mevagissey	50°16′.16N 4°46′.91W

HW -0600 Dover

MWHS	MHWN	MLWN	MLWS
5.5m	4.4m	2.2m	0.8m

Mevagissey Harbour

- Straightforward approach but dangerous in strong E / SE
- Busy fishing harbour
- Ⓥ South (Victoria) pier in 2m
- Ⓥ Seaward outer harbour, consult ahead
- Harbourmaster ☎ 01726 843305 (out of hours 842496)
- VHF 14/16
- meva.harbour@talk21.com
- www.mevagisseyharbour.com
- Water at the quay
- 🛢 Diesel from Victoria Pier

⚓ Gorran Haven

Further south, Gorran Haven is a delightful sandy cove protected from the prevailing southwesterlies. To the east Gwineas Rock, marked by an east cardinal Q(3)10s, must be avoided. It is perfectly feasible to pass on the inside of the rocks but do not attempt this in poor visibility or conditions of any difficulty.

⚓ Anchor in sand east of the wall. There is plenty of space and the beach shelves gradually. If you can dry out, and conditions are calm, you can settle inside the small drying harbour.

Gorran Haven

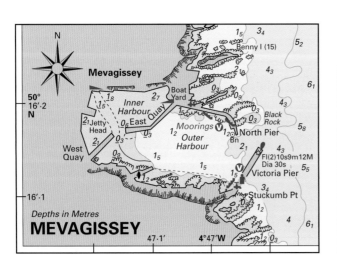

Mevagissey

Food & Transport

There are plenty of shops, pubs and restaurants at Mevagissey. Gorran Haven has an award-winning post office/village store/baker. The nearest railway station is at St Austell which can be reached by bus from Mevagissey.

Interest

The first mention of St Meva and St Issey is a written record of 1313 but of course there was a settlement here long before. Meva-ag-issey is the largest fishing village in St Austell Bay. From Tudor times small, oily fish from the *Clupeoid* family, that is, sardines and pilchards, has been its most important catch. In fact these names refer to more than 21 different species of fish and although the terms are often used interchangeably Britain's Sea Fish Industry Authority defines a sardine as less than 2 years of age and less than 6 inches long. Should it survive, it then becomes a pilchard. Sardines are named after the Mediterranean island of Sardinia, where they once lived in abundance. They arrive in the West Country in July, gradually moving from Lands End eastwards, and are caught mainly at night as they approach the surface to feed on plankton. In the past a seine boat would encircle the fish and drop a net around them, called a purse seine. With the help of 2 further boats the trapped fish would then be pulled to the beach using large capstans. A process of salting (baulking) would preserve the fish for a year or more. Oil was also extracted to be used in lamps. For many years Mevagissey provided pilchards to the Royal navy who referred to them as Mevagissey Ducks. A local delicacy is Starry-Gazey pie baked with the heads of sardines gazing skywards from a golden pastry crust.

Inside are the fish with slices of hard-boiled egg and chopped leeks.

Mevagissey has a small museum with exhibits of farm equipment, such as a cider press and horse-drawn barley thresher, and a Cornish kitchen with working cloam oven. Space is dedicated to Andrew Pears, the founder of Pears Soap, who was born in the village in 1768. The former RNLI lifeboat station is now a tiny aquarium. Nearby the World of Model Railways Exhibition has over 2,000 exhibits and a layout of 50 working trains. At the end of June Mevagissey celebrates St Peter, the patron saint of fishermen. A week-long festival includes choral concerts, floral dances and street processions. A 45-minute walk or 5-minute bus/taxi ride takes you to The Lost Gardens of Heligan. A work in progress, the gardens are being restored to their former glory after years of neglect.

The crowded Mevagissey inner harbour

Veryan Bay & Gerran's Bay

Both Veryan Bay and Gerran's Bay are completely unspoilt, with marvellous views of the coast.

Veryan Bay has a steep-to shoreline with small sandy coves. Porthluney Cove has a beach which is especially popular in the summer. In bad weather Dodman Point, to the east, is notorious for races and very disturbed water. Within the bay, Lath Rock (dries 2.1m) must be avoided. Close to shore, Shag Rock and May's Rock are among several dangers that should be taken into account. Gull Rock and The Whelps to the south, east of Nare Head, also need to be avoided although you may pass inside in good conditions. Local knowledge or detailed charts are required. Only attempt anchorage when it is absolutely calm.

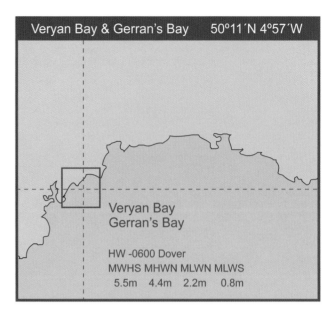

Veryan Bay & Gerran's Bay   50°11′N 4°57′W

Veryan Bay
Gerran's Bay

HW -0600 Dover

MWHS	MHWN	MLWN	MLWS
5.5m	4.4m	2.2m	0.8m

Porthscatho

Gerran's Bay is more sheltered from the prevailing southwesterlies than Veryan Bay and has slightly less chance of swell. Porthscatho is a very good destination in settled weather and offshore winds. The Bizzies shallows to the south are an area of races and overfalls. On the north side Pendower is an attractive beach backed by dunes. Beware drying Pibyah Rock, opposite the hotel.

⚓ⓥ Porthscatho

Small drying harbour with visitors' buoys and plenty of space for anchoring in 5m, good holding, sand and shingle. Very pleasant in good weather.

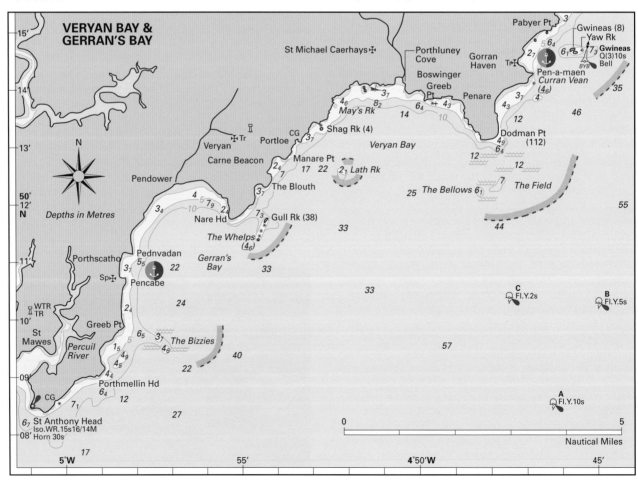

Cornish pasties

Pasties have been around for a long time. The earliest known reference, written in old French, is from a 12th-century Romance set in Cornwall by poet Chrétien de Troyes. Later Chaucer described them as 'pouches of dough' that are 'small and portable' and today, filled with pumpkin, they even make an appearance in the *Harry Potter* novels.

Tradition has it that pasties evolved as a convenient lunch for Cornish tin miners. Wrapped in cloth, the pasty's dense, folded pastry would stay warm for hours, though some mines provided an oven, necessitating the picking out of a man's initials in raised pastry so he knew which one was his. Pasties could also be reheated by placing them on a shovel over a lamp but this was discouraged following a fire below ground in 1890 when the crust of a forgotten pasty ignited.

The Cornish word for pasty is 'hogen' and the popular Cornish chant 'Oggy Oggy Oggy, Oi Oi Oi' is thought to have originated from bal maidens ('bal' is ancient Cornish for 'mining place') summoning the men to lunch by shouting 'Oggy Oggy Oggy' down the shaft. 'Oi Oi Oi' was the miners' reply. Covered in dirt, and possibly arsenic, miners could hold the pastry edge and eat the contents without touching it. The crimped knot of pastry would then be thrown away to appease the knockers, capricious spirits that could lead miners into danger.

The earliest known recipe for a Cornish pasty is held in Truro's Records Office and dated 1746. Traditionally the filling is of beef, potato, turnip or swede and onion. Meat must now make up 12.5%

of the contents, but the miners would have had a higher proportion of vegetables as meat was a luxury. A half-savoury, half-sweet pasty was eaten by some miners in the 19th century. Meat and veg on one side was separated from fruit and jam on the other by a pastry divider or a finger of stale bread; however, this meal-in-one never caught on.

The traditional pasty is hugely popular. Almost 90 million are made in Cornwall each year, with most of the ingredients locally sourced. In 2005 this included 5,700 tonnes of potatoes, 5,200 tonnes of beef, 310 tonnes of onions and 1,550 tonnes of swede. In 2011 the European commission granted the Cornish pasty 'protected geographical indication' status, meaning that only pastes made in Cornwall to the traditional recipe can be sold as Cornish pasties.

As you might imagine, pasties feature in many Cornish festivals. In Fowey a huge pasty is paraded through the streets during Regatta. Six feet long, it is carried by four men in fancy dress. In 1985 Cornwall Young Farmers spent 7 hours making a pasty 32 ft long, but even this is thought to have been surpassed by bakers in Falmouth in 1999.

Cornish ode to a pasty:

> *I dearly luv a pasty,*
> *A 'ot 'n' leaky wun,*
> *Weth taties, mayt 'n' turmit,*
> *Purs'ly 'n' honyun,*
> *Un crus be made with su't,*
> *'N' shaped like 'alf a moon,*
> *Weth crinkly hedges, freshly baked,*
> *E always gone too soon!*

Falmouth Bay

Falmouth Bay contains the Fal estuary and the Helford River and both are fantastic sailing destinations.

Seven different rivers discharge into the Fal estuary which constitutes the third-largest naturally occurring deep-water harbour after Sydney and Rio de Janeiro. It is huge, with a shoreline of over 100km and approximately 4,500 moorings, and has lots to offer: a busy town, quiet villages, idyllic creeks and that special holiday feel associated with ferries full of tourists crisscrossing the water. Falmouth grew in size in the 17th and 18th centuries when the post office made it the UK's southernmost packet ship port. Fast, armed sailing boats carried people and post from here to the Americas, the West Indies, Europe and the Mediterranean. Today it continues to be the start and finish of many a transatlantic voyage but also a sailing destination in its own right. Pendennis Castle and the National Maritime Museum are well worth a visit. Those able to navigate to the head of the Truro River can walk into Cornwall's county town and visit the impressive cathedral. On as smaller scale, the idyllic 13th-century church of St Just is so close to a creek it is reflected in the water at high tide. St Mawes across the water from Falmouth is a pretty fishing village and upstream Restronguet offers a wooded haven.

Approach & entrance

Falmouth Harbour can be approached in any conditions day and night. It is even safe, though rough, in strong southerlies against an ebb tide. The entrance is 1M wide.

The Carrick Roads are a deep buoyed channel with a wide shallow passage between the channel and the shore.

DANGER: Black Rock dries 2.1m. It is marked by an isolated danger mark Fl(2)10s in the centre of the entrance between St Anthony Head to the east and Pendennis Point to the west. DO NOT pass close to Black Rock (shallows) or between it and Black Rock Fl.R.2.5s.

Pass either side of Black Rock (beacon west, cardinal east). The east channel is used by large shipping and is favoured for any boat during a night approach. The west side is good for smaller boats, with depths of at least 6m, but does not offer the convenience of a buoyed lit channel.

To reach Falmouth as your first port of call:

East channel: leave Black Rock Fl.R.2.5s to port, then Castle green Fl.G.2.5s to starboard and go north as far as West Narrows red Fl(2)R.

West channel: leave The Governor east cardinal VQ(3)5s to port and continue north until you are between West Narrows Fl(2)R.10s and the end of the Eastern Breakwater.

Turn due west and go past the Eastern Breakwater 2F.R(vert).

Proceed past the Western Breakwater northern wall, first Q.R.5m then 2F.R(vert). The area to starboard becomes shallow but depth is at least 2.9m.

Falmouth harbour and Carrick Roads

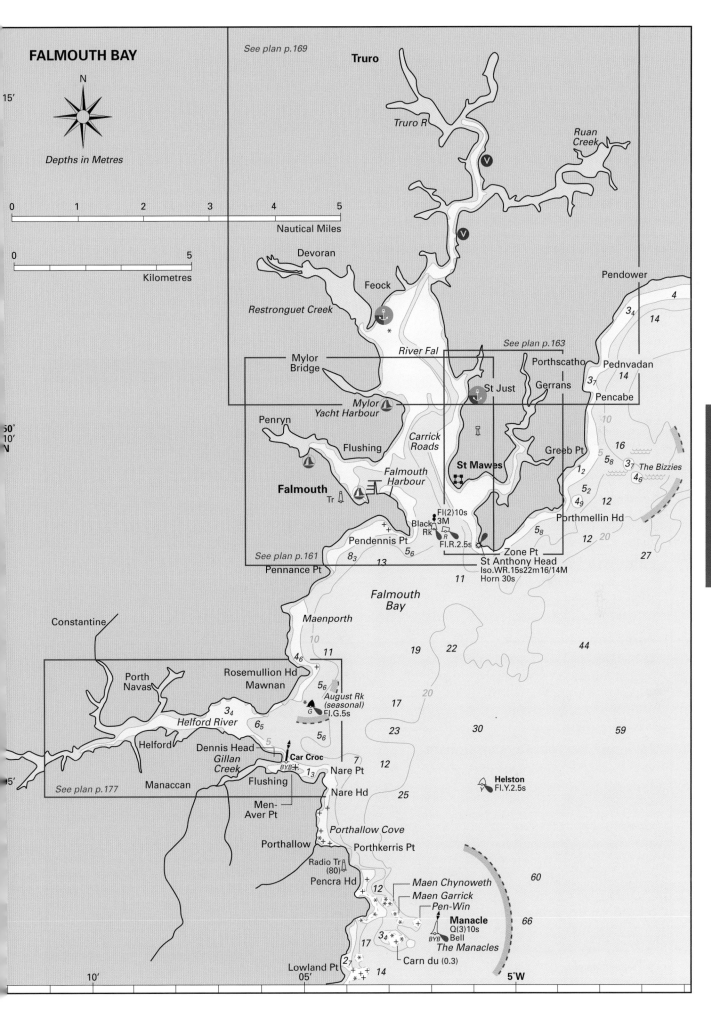

FALMOUTH BAY

N

Depths in Metres

0   1   2   3   4   5

Nautical Miles

0   5

Kilometres

15'

50°
10'
N

05'

10'

See plan p.169

Truro

Truro R

Ruan Creek

Pendower

Devoran

Feock

Restronguet Creek

River Fal

See plan p.163

Porthscatho

Pendower

4

3₄   14

Pednvadan

14

Mylor
Bridge

Gerrans

3₇

Pencabe

*Mylor
Yacht Harbour*

St Just

Penryn

Flushing

*Carrick
Roads*

St Mawes

Greeb Pt

10

16

5   5₈   3₇   *The Bizzies*

4₆

*Falmouth
Harbour*

1₂

5₂

Falmouth

Tr

Porthmellin Hd

4₉

12

Fl(2)10s
3M

Black
Rk
R
Fl.R.2.5s

5₈

12   20

Pendennis Pt

5₆

Zone Pt
St Anthony Head
Iso.WR.15s22m16/14M
Horn 30s

27

See plan p.161

Pennance Pt

8₃

13

11

Constantine

*Falmouth
Bay*

Maenporth

10

19   22

44

Rosemullion Hd
Mawnan

4₆   11

Porth
Navas

5₆

August Rk
(seasonal)
G
Fl.G.5s

17

20

3₄

Helford River

6₅

5₆

23

30

59

Helford

5

Dennis Head
*Gillan
Creek*

Car Croc
BYB

1₃

Nare Pt

7

12

25

Helston
Y
Fl.Y.2.5s

See plan p.177

Manaccan

Flushing

Nare Hd

Men-
Aver Pt

Porthallow Cove

Porthallow

Porthkerris Pt

60

Radio Tr
(80)

Pencra Hd

12

Maen Chynoweth

Maen Garrick

Pen-Win

66

Manacle
Q(3)10s
BYB   Bell
The Manacles

17

3₄

Carn du (0.3)

Lowland Pt

2₇

14

5°W

Falmouth & St Mawes

Falmouth spreads along the Penryn River and is in walking distance of Falmouth Yacht Marina, Visitors' Yacht Haven and Port Pendennis. It is a busy seaside town with narrow streets containing 18th-century houses and warehouses, and an inner basin whose quay dates back to 1670. The docks are less busy since the navy withdrew but Pendennis Shipyard employs about 300 trades people who build, refit and repair vessels up to 70 metres. The National Maritime Museum Cornwall has a permanent display of about 140 small craft and much information about the town's maritime history. The port developed significantly in the 17th century when the post office sent mail and bullion from here in packet ships bound for the Americas, West Indies and Europe. Pendennis Castle, built by Henry VIII, is well worth a visit, as is its twin at St Mawes opposite. The village of St Mawes is situated on the Roseland Peninsula, a quiet haven of narrow lanes and idyllic waterside retreats.

Approach & entrance

Approaching the visitors' spaces is straightforward, though care must be taken over shallow water. Beyond the Western Breakwater there are many boats on moorings.

For Falmouth Inner Harbour:

- From the end of the Queen's Jetty (coming off the Western Breakwater) 2.F.R(vert) turn due south. DO NOT head straight for the pontoons of Visitors' Yacht Haven as there is shallow water and numerous moorings to avoid.

- The leading line for Yacht Haven is 235° (minimum depth 1.4m).

For Falmouth Yacht Marina:

- Continue along the Penryn River in a northwesterly direction remaining in the buoyed channel, 2m minimum depth. DO NOT stray from the channel at low tide.

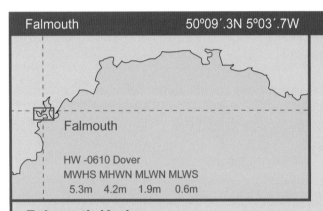

Falmouth — 50°09´.3N 5°03´.7W

Falmouth

HW -0610 Dover

MWHS	MHWN	MLWN	MLWS
5.3m	4.2m	1.9m	0.6m

Falmouth Harbour

- Straightfoward approach in all conditions
- Beware Black Rock at the entrance
- Falmouth Harbour Radio VHF12

Port Pendennis Marina

- Ⓥ 20 visitors' berths in 3-4.5m up to 70m LOA
- Inner harbour HW+/-3 residents
- VHF80 ☎ 01326 211211
  marina@portpendennis.com
- ⚓ 40-ton travel lift

Falmouth Harbour Commissioners

- Ⓥ 21 green off Prince of Wales Pier
- ⚓ Up to 200m east of Yacht Haven in 2.5m
- ☎ 01326 312285

Visitors' Yacht Haven

- 1.4m maximum depth approach on 235°
- 100 berths max 15m LOA
- 2.0/1.5m depth at berths
  Shallow path 1.2m north of pontoons
- VHF12 ☎ 01326 310991
  ☎ 07815 955263 0800-1900 in season
- Water, electricity at the pontoons; showers
- ⛽ Diesel and petrol

Royal Cornwall Yacht Club

- Ⓥ 2 visitors' moorings
- VHF Channel M ☎ 1326 312126

Falmouth Yacht Marina

- Dredged channel 2m depth
- VHF80 ☎ 1326 316620
  www.premiermarinas.com
- Ⓥ 20 visitors' spaces
- ⚓ 30-ton travel lift
- ⛽ Diesel and petrol
- Water, electricity at the pontoons; showers
- Dry berthing ashore

Penryn - Challenger Marine

- VHF80 ☎ 01326 377222
- Ⓥ 45 drying berths

Mylor Yacht Harbour

- 2m dredged approach channel
- Ⓥ 40 visitors' berths
- Ⓥ 15 visitors' moorings
- VHF Channel M ☎ 1326 372121
- ⚓ 35-ton travel lift
- ⛽ Diesel and petrol

St Mawes

- VHF12 ☎ 1326 270553
- ⚓ East of castle
- Ⓥ 15 visitors' moorings

Water Taxi

- Falmouth: VHF71 ☎ 07970 242258
  Mylor VHF Channel M

- 🔧 Marine services: extensive at Penryn, Falmouth Yacht Marina, Mylor Marina, Falmouth

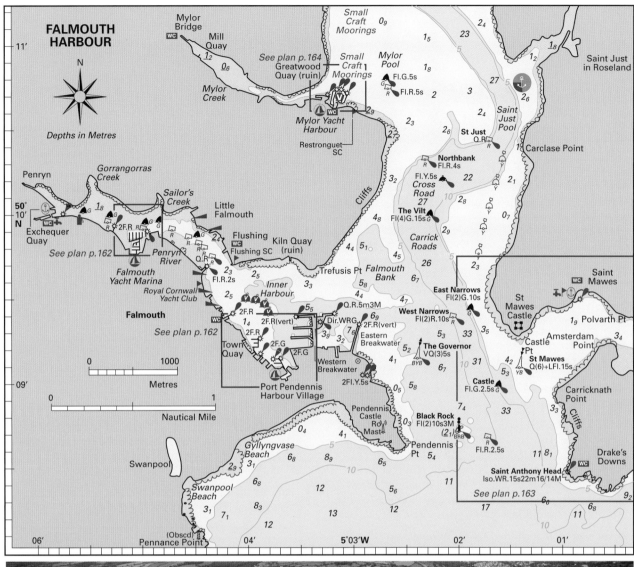

FALMOUTH HARBOUR

N

Depths in Metres

Penryn

Gorrangorras Creek

Sailor's Creek

Little Falmouth

Mylor Bridge
WC
Mill Quay

1_2

0_6

Mylor Creek

See plan p.164
Greatwood Quay (ruin)

Small Craft Moorings

Small Craft Moorings

0_9

1_5

2_4

23

1_8

Saint Just in Roseland

Mylor Pool
Fl.G.5s
G
Fl.R.5s

1_8

5

1_2

27

5

2_6

Saint Just Pool

3

2_4

Mylor Yacht Harbour
V
WC
2_9

Restronguet SC

2_3

2_7

3_2

St Just
Q.R
R

1_8

Carclase Point

Exchequer Quay
WC
See plan p.162
1_8
G
R
R
2.F.R
R R
Penryn River
G
Q.R.
R
R R

Falmouth Yacht Marina
Fl.R.2s

Royal Cornwall Yacht Club

Falmouth

See plan p.162

2_4

2_5

2_3

2_5

Flushing
WC
Flushing SC

Kiln Quay (ruin)

4_4

5_1

Trefusis Pt

Northbank
Fl.R.4s
R

Fl.Y.5s
Cross Road
27

22

2_1

2_8

10

Y

The Vilt
Fl(4)G.15s G

Carrick Roads

Y

0_7

2_9

Inner Harbour
Y Y Y
2.F.R
Dir.WRG
5_5
Q.R.5m3M
6_9
2.F.R(vert)

Falmouth Bank

4_4

5_8

4_5

4_7

26

6_7

East Narrows
Fl(2)G.10s
G

5

2_3

Saint Mawes
WC

St Mawes Castle

1_4
2.F.R(vert)
2.F.R
Town Quay
2.F.G
2.F.G

3_9
3_2
7_6
Eastern Breakwater

Western Breakwater
2Fl.Y.5s

West Narrows
Fl(2)R.10s
R

5_3
The Governor
VQ(3)5s
BYB

5_2

4_1

6_7

33

3_5

31

St Mawes Castle
Castle Pt

St Mawes
Q(6)+LFl.15s
YB

1_9 Polvarth Pt

Amsterdam Point

3_4

4_2
5_3

Port Pendennis Harbour Village

Pendennis Castle
Ro
Mast

0_3

0_5

5_8

Castle
Fl.G.2.5s
G

7_4

Carricknath Point

3_3

Cliffs

Black Rock
Fl(2)10s3M
(2_1)
BRB
R
Fl.R.2.5s

33

3_3

Pendennis Pt

5_4

Swanpool

Gyllyngvase Beach

2_9

3_1

6_8

6_8

8_9

6_5

0_4

4_1

Saint Anthony Head
Iso.WR.15s22m16/14M

11 8_1

Drake's Downs
WC

See plan p.163

Swanpool Beach

3_1

7_1

8_3

6_8

12

13

5_6

12

5

10

11

17

6_6

10

11

6_8

9_2

(Obscd)
Pennance Point

12

0 1000
Metres

0 1
Nautical Mile

11'

10'

50°
10'
N

09'

06' 04' 5°03'W 02' 01'

Cliffs

Penryn

Falmouth Yacht Marina

Visitors Yacht Haven

Port Pendennis

Flushing

N

Falmouth harbour

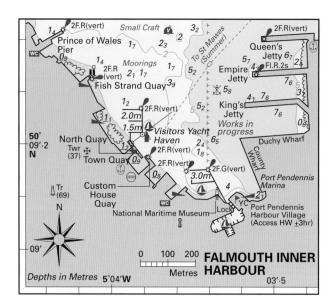

FALMOUTH INNER HARBOUR
Depths in Metres   5°04'W   03'·5

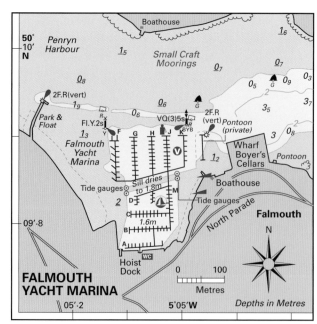

FALMOUTH YACHT MARINA
05'·2   5°05'W   Depths in Metres

Berthing & facilities

⚓ Port Pendennis Marina is located at the southern end of the inner harbour. It is relatively small but welcomes visitors and has water, electricity and showers. Check for space ahead. The inner harbour is accessed through a lock HW+/-3 but is for residents only.

⚓ Visitors' Yacht Haven is dedicated to visitors. Depths range from 1.6m to 2.0m. The route in to the inner area is over 1.2m off the end of the northern pontoon, so beware. Very busy in the summer with boats 2-3 abreast. Leaving in strong northeasterlies can be something of a challenge requiring lines ashore and some manhandling.

⚓ Anchoring is permitted up to 200m east of Visitors' Yacht Haven, away from the harbour jetties. Holding is good and exposure is only to northerlies.

Ⓥ Northwest of Visitors' Yacht Haven is Falmouth Harbour's swinging moorings (R101-R107, K1-K6, L1-L4, T5 with green pick buoys).

Ⓥ The Royal Cornwall Yacht Club has two swinging moorings marked 'RCYC Visitor'. The club has a quay where you can dry out by arrangement.

Challenger Marina in Flushing has a number of drying berths.

St Mawes Harbour

⚓ Falmouth Yacht Marina, further up the Penryn River, is accessed through a channel with 2m minimum depth. The marina has all facilities: fuel, good bar and restaurant, chandler and yacht services.

• Proceed slowly.

• Pass close of the outer pontoon 2FR(vert) and leave the east cardinal VQ(3)5s to starboard (ignore unlit red and green buoys north of the cardinal which lead along a channel beyond the marina).

• Park at the hammerhead of the second pontoon (J, also fuel berth) and await instruction.

There is a plan to build a new marina (Port Falmouth Marina) at the Western Breakwater quays but it had not been started when this book was published.

Penryn River

It is unlikely you will head far up the Penryn River unless going for repairs. The river is full of local moorings and dries to a muddy bottom. It is home to many marine service companies, including Challenger Marine who offer drying berths to visitors if required.

⚓ St Mawes

St Mawes harbour is across the water from Falmouth. When anchored east of Castle Point or attached to visitors' moorings further in, it offers shelter in all conditions except southwesterlies.

The village is a rather well-to-do sort of place, with attractive houses looking on to the harbour. Tourists flock here in great numbers as there are excellent views across the estuary.

Approach & berthing

The approach is straightforward but you must keep south of Lugo Rock south cardinal Q(6)+LFl.15s. The rock has minimum depth of 0.6m and is sited 250m south of Castle Point.

⚓ Anchor east of Castle Point. Shelter is very good except in southwesterlies (sadly the prevailing wind).

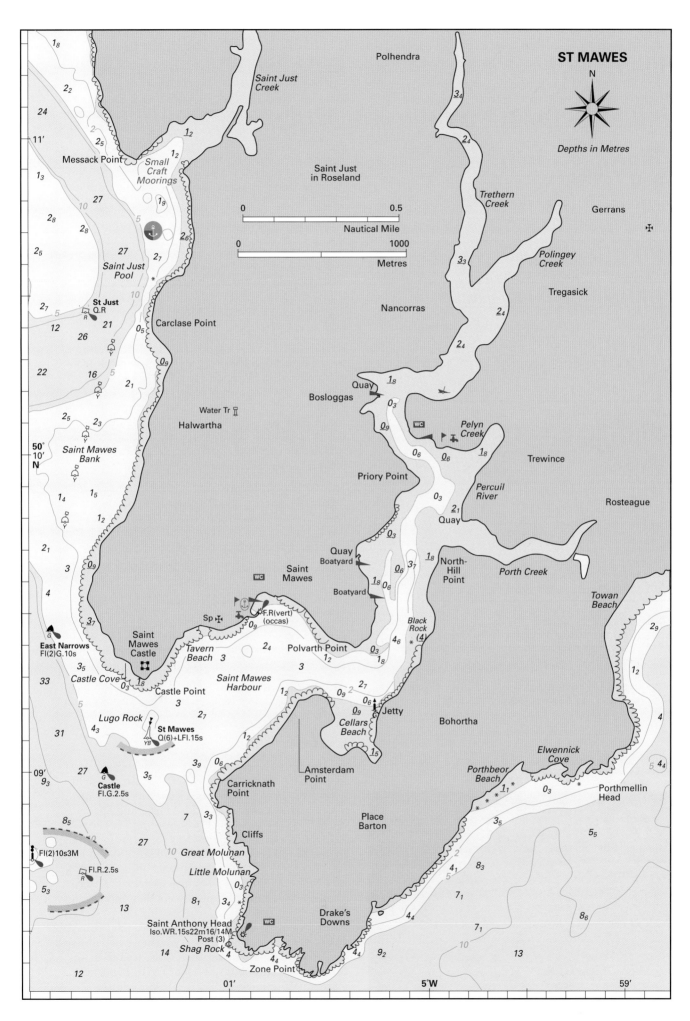

ST MAWES

N

Depths in Metres

Polhendra

Saint Just
Creek

Saint Just
in Roseland

Trethern
Creek

Gerrans

Polingey
Creek

Tregasick

Nancorras

Messack Point

Small Craft
Moorings

Saint Just
Pool

St Just
Q.R
R

Carclase Point

Water Tr

Halwartha

Saint Mawes
Bank

Bosloggas

Quay

WC

Pelyn
Creek

Trewince

Priory Point

Percuil
River

Rosteague

Quay

50°
10′
N

0   0.5
Nautical Mile

0   1000
Metres

Quay
Boatyard

Boatyard

WC

Saint
Mawes

F.R(vert)
(occas)

Sp

North-
Hill
Point

Porth Creek

Black
Rock
(4)

Towan
Beach

East Narrows
Fl(2)G.10s

Saint Mawes
Castle

Castle Cove

Castle Point

Tavern
Beach

Saint Mawes
Harbour

Polvarth Point

Lugo Rock

St Mawes
Q(6)+LFl.15s
YB

Castle
Fl.G.2.5s

Amsterdam
Point

Cellars
Beach

Jetty

Bohortha

Elwennick
Cove

Porthmellin
Head

Fl(2)10s3M

Fl.R.2.5s
R

Carricknath
Point

Cliffs

Great Molunan

Little Molunan

Place
Barton

Porthbeor
Beach

Drake's
Downs

Saint Anthony Head
Iso.WR.15s22m16/14M
Post (3)

Shag Rock

Zone Point

01′   5°W   59′

⚓ There are 13 green visitors' buoys southeast of the quay.

The Percuil river meanders upstream beyond St Mawes but mostly dries. It is a delightful trip in a dinghy and better still as a place to stay if you can dry out. The surrounding scenery is stunning.

🕐 ⚓ Mylor

Further upstream from Falmouth, Mylor Yacht Harbour marina and its associated large grid of swinging moorings can accommodate boats up to 15m (larger boats northern side of moorings). The area is open to the east and can get rolly in strong winds from that direction.

The channel into the marina, running east-west through the centre of the moorings, is dredged to 2m. The entrance to the channel is marked by buoys: red Fl.R.5s and green Fl.G.6s.

Liaise ahead and pick up a mooring or head for the outer side of the pontoons and await instruction.

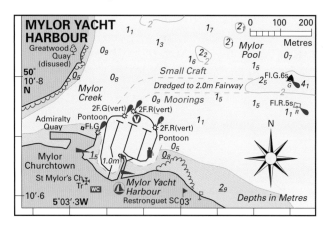

Diesel and petrol are available from the southern side of the outer pontoon.

The marina has space in the Mylor Valley for hard standing and winter storage. All facilities available including fuel, a chandlery and various marine services.

Mylor Marina and moorings

Food & Transport

Falmouth is well served by transport. Local and long distance buses and coaches leave from The Moor in the centre of the town. There is a ferry service from Prince Albert and Custom House Quays to Flushing, St Mawes, Mylor, Trelissick, Smugglers Cottage, Malpas and Truro. Falmouth has 3 railway stations: the docks, the Dell (Falmouth Town) and Penmere (west of the town). The nearest main line train is at Truro.

Falmouth is full of places to eat and drink. If you get up early you can watch pasties being made in the traditional way at Chokes, a 50-year-old family firm in Killigrew Street. They also provide the opportunity to make your own pasty, ingredients and tuition supplied (☎ 01326 312426). There is a small Tesco adjacent to the Maritime Museum and an M&S in the high street which sells food.

Indaba Fish on the Beach is an excellent restaurant by the beach in Swanpool, a 30-minute walk from Falmouth (☎ 01326 311886). In town Hunky-dory, 46 Arwenack St, serves good food in nice surroundings. Situated in a listed Georgian building, the interior has a contemporary beach house feel (☎ 01326 212997). Opposite the Maritime Museum is Fish and Chips, the first restaurant opened by Rick Stein outside of Padstow.

St Mawes is linked by bus to Truro and by ferry to Falmouth. There are many places to eat and drink looking onto the harbour. Hotel Tresanton has a lovely terrace and excellent food. The village has a Co-operative, wet fish shop, pharmacy and post office.

There is a water taxi (Shuttle ☎ 07970 242258) between Mylor Yacht Harbour and Custom House Quay, Falmouth. Mylor has a small store, café and restaurant.

An on-demand water taxi, the aquacab, services most destinations along the waterside and has a capacity of 12. It operates May to October (☎ 07970 242258)

At Restronguet the 13th-century Pandora Inn has good food and an extensive terrace overlooking the creek. It is possible to arrive by tender.

Interest

As you enter the Fal estuary Pendennis Castle and its twin opposite at St Mawes are a splendid sight. They were built in the 1540s by Henry VIII who was under threat of war from France and Spain, having just divorced his Catholic wife, Catherine of Aragon. Both have a clover-leaf footprint in a design by the King's German military architect Stefan von Haschenberg. They were improved and extended by Elizabeth I when the Spanish attacked Newlyn and Penzance but saw military conflict only during the English Civil War. An early surrender to General Fairfax's Parliamentary forces in 1646 left the castle at St Mawes immaculate. The carvings were praised by Pevsner and are better than those found on any other fortification built by Henry VIII. Pendennis Castle, a 30-minute walk from Falmouth town, is less architecturally special but its remote setting led to an historic siege that lasted 6 months and ended only after many of the King's supporters had died or were starving, having already eaten their dogs and horses. Both castles are well worth a visit. St Mawes has an excellent audio guide. Pendennis has a number of interactive displays, including an exhibit on Tudor battles, and medieval jousts take place periodically.

Falmouth developed as a port when local shipping merchant Sir John Killigrew built a harbour in 1613. Arwenack House, Killigrew's home, at the southern end of Arwenack Street is in part 14th-century and the oldest domestic building, though not open to the public. In 1689 Falmouth became a Royal Mail packet port and the harbour expanded further, as gold and silver bullion were sent in fast brigantines first to northern Spain and then, further afield, to the West Indies, South and North America. Passengers were also accepted but it was a precarious journey as the ships were often attacked by privateers, the French navy and even Algerian pirates. Smuggling provided additional income and the Custom House, built in 1670, stands next to a brick chimney that was known as The King's Pipe, because it was used to burn contraband tobacco. By 1830 over 40 packet ships worked out of Falmouth but 20 years later the service transferred to Southampton. By then boat building was well established and the town's importance secure. The Pendennis Shipyard is a small reminder of the once extensive docks and today the town is primarily dedicated to tourism and to a growing art scene. University College Falmouth is renowned for its courses in textile design, theatre, choreography, fine art, film, photography and popular music. Having merged with Dartington College of Arts in 2008, a £15m Performance Centre has been built on the Tremough Campus and the establishment of Arts University Cornwall is on the horizon.

The town itself has developed along a series of streets, like an interlocking chain, which run along the bank of the Penryn River. The Moor, once a muddy creek, is home to award-winning Falmouth Art Gallery (free entrance, paintings by Matisse and Picasso) and the start of Jacob's Ladder, 111 steps which take you to a bird's-eye view of the harbour and estuary. The Church of King Charles the Martyr, consecrated in 1665, is worth a visit to see some splendid Victorian stained and enamelled glass.

The National Maritime Museum Cornwall opened in 2002. Overlooking Falmouth harbour, its oak-clad exterior was designed to reflect wooden boat sheds in the area. Inside is Britain's national collection of historic and contemporary small craft. Spanning 150 years, there are about 140 boats and growing. Many are displayed in a central atrium with information alongside. Major exhibitions change every 2 years. 3 permanent galleries are dedicated to the maritime history of Cornwall and there is a replica packet ship cabin. For those with a scholarly interest, the Bartlett collection has over 10,000 marine reference books. The museum's Waterside Café is excellent.

Watching Falmouth's Working Boats race one another is an enjoyable spectacle during the summer. These small sailing boats were designed for dredging native oyster beds when, with exceptional foresight, ancient laws banned the use of engines which were thought to

'Retro' sweets in Falmouth. Aniseed balls, sherbet pips...

upset the natural ecology of the river. This restriction has helped preserve not just the fishery, whose stocks are still prone to pollution and disease, but also the boats. Today the Fal estuary has the only oyster fishery in Europe using traditional methods. Dredges are hand-pulled over the beds, or 'lays', from craft operated by one person who regulates towing speed by scandalising the mainsail and foresail of the gaff cutter rig. The sail area is minimal, usually no more than 300 sq ft, and the ideal boat is considered to be 24ft, with a draught of no more than 4ft 6ins. Some of the oldest oyster boats date back to 1860. For racing the sail area is dramatically increased and a brightly coloured topsail is added. With full racing rig even the most experienced sailor finds these craft a handful. With no engine, limited visibility and a long keel, they should be given a wide berth. Oysters can be gathered from October to March and in October there is the Falmouth Oyster Festival. Oysters are still gathered in large numbers around Carrick Roads and Truro River. In the past most were exported to France but today they grace the menus of local hotels and the dining rooms of London.

Racing takes place in the Fal estuary most days in the summer but those wanting a competitive feast attend Henri-Lloyd Falmouth Week in August. This is the largest regatta in the South West, rivalled only by Cowes Week. About 450 yachts and dinghies compete, including classic craft. The spectacle draws an additional 80,000 visitors and is complemented by some lively entertainment in the town, ending with

The castle at St Mawes

Falmouth working boat with racing rig

a Red Arrows fly-past and a magnificent firework display over the harbour.

The Falmouth International Sea Shanty Festival in June raises money for the RNLI. The word 'shanty', or 'chanty' is probably derived from the French word '*chanter*' meaning to sing. These songs were originally shouted out as sailors performed their various chores at sea, each rhythm commensurate with the task at hand. Thus there are capstan shanties, halyard shanties, even windlass and pumping shanties. Singers from Europe who performed in 2010 included Dutch Courage from the Netherlands, Emder Shanty-Gruppe from Germany and the Hooks and Crookes from Ireland.

National Maritime Museum Cornwall

The Roseland peninsula, across the estuary from Falmouth, is an idyllic backwater. St Mawes village has excellent views of the estuary and is pretty to wander around. A 20-minute walk uphill takes you to Lamorran House, whose gardens are in the UK's top 10 according to BBC Gardener's World. There are over 35 species of palm and an extensive collection of tree ferns and other plants associated with the southern hemisphere. The garden is laid out in the Mediterranean style with various water features and several ornate temples. Open Wed-Fri, April-Sept. A 3M walk north from St Mawes (signed paths) takes you to the pretty village of St Just-in-Roseland, though you can also anchor nearby. Here a 13th-century church stands so close to the bank of the creek that it is reflected in the water at high tide, and granite gravestones lie amidst palms and subtropical shrubs.

Cuauhtemoc made a visit to the West Country when Falmouth hosted the Funchal 500 Tall Ships Regatta in 2008. This three-masted barque was built in 1982 by the naval shipyards of Bilbao, Spain. Now used as a navy training ship by the Mexicans, it bears the name of the last Aztec emperor who was imprisoned and executed in 1525 by order of Hernán Cortés the conquistador. It has a steel hull and is 77.6m in length.

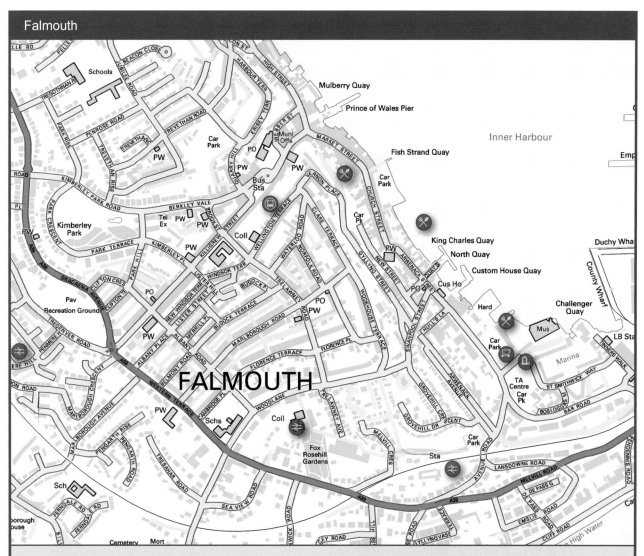

Bus station: Killigrew Street, The Moor
Buses to Truro, Gweek, Helston, Marazion,
Porthleven and Penzance

Falmouth branch line: three stops in Falmouth
(the Docks, the Dell/town centre and Penmere
/west of the town), Penryn

Main line from Truro

Europcar, Falmouth ① 01326 314850

From Truro: Avis ① 0844 5446109
Hertz ① 01872 270238 (from train station)

Tesco, Killigrew St
Tesco Express, Discovery Quay

Co-operative, St Mawes

Restaurants, pubs and cafés: Arwenack Street,
Church Street, Discovery Quay in Falmouth

By the quay in St Mawes

Tourist Information Centre: 28 Killigrew Street,
Falmouth ① 01326 312300

The Roseland Visitor Centre, The Square, St
Mawes ① 01326 270440

Chandlers:
Fal Chandlers, Falmouth Marina, North
Parade, Falmouth ① 01326 212411

Bosun's Locker Chandlery, Upton Slip,
Falmouth (near harbour) ① 01326 312212

Mylor Chandlery, Mylor Yacht Harbour, Mylor
① 01326 375482

Challenger Marine, Penryn ①01326 377222

Marine boatyards and services:

Falmouth Marina ① 01326 316620. Extensive
services at the boatyard

Challenger Marine, Penryn ①01326 377222.
Extensive services at the boatyard

SKB Sails, The Sail Loft, Commercial Road,
Penryn ① 01326 372107

Leach Boat Builders, St Mawes
① 01326 270004

Percuil Boat Yard, Porthscatho ① 01872
580564

Pendennis Shipyard, The Docks, Falmouth
①1326 211344. Superyachts + extensive
expertise

Mylor Yacht Harbour, Mylor ① 01326 372121.
Extensive services at the boatyard

Falmouth Hospital, Trescobeas Road,
Falmouth TR11 2JA ① 01326 434700

Rivers Fal and Truro

As you head upstream the character of the Fal estuary changes. There are still plenty of boats but the river bank is now likely to be wooded. The channel is deep until just south of Malpas. Options include anchorages, a number of swinging moorings and pontoons at Mylor Yacht Harbour.

Don't be surprised if you suddenly encounter some very large cargo ships. These are moored upriver until commercially viable work becomes available.

Navigation

There is no secret to navigating upstream other than judge the depth with care. As always the deepest water is on the outside of bends. The wide expanse of water nearer to the mouth can be deceiving. However, should you run aground the bottom is soft!

The King Harry chain ferry has priority at all times.

⚓ St Just

Opposite Mylor, on the east side of the river, St Just Creek provides a good anchorage, except in strong west/southwest conditions. You can sound in directly from the main channel, after passing St Just buoy Q.R. The anchorage is south of the local moorings. Further into the creek is idyllic if you can dry out.

St Just Creek

⚓ Restronguet

Just outside Restronguet Creek, in the main river, is an anchorage. Depth changes very gradually towards the shoreline and varies between 0.4m and 1.4m.

Approach from the Carick buoy Fl(2)G.10s. BEWARE of the Carick Rock, marked by north and south cardinal posts (unlit).

Restronguet Creek is full of local moorings (do not use) and anchoring in the pool is not possible.

Dinner at the Pandora Inn is a must. Dinghies can be attached to their pontoon and a shower and launderette are available.

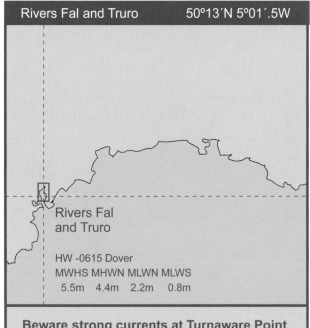

Rivers Fal and Truro   50°13′N 5°01′.5W

Rivers Fal and Truro

HW -0615 Dover

MWHS	MHWN	MLWN	MLWS
5.5m	4.4m	2.2m	0.8m

Beware strong currents at Turnaware Point

⚓ Anchorages off St Just Creek, Restronguet, Channal Creek, Tolcarne Creek, Lamouth Creek, Ruan Creek and Church Creek

Ⓥ Visitors' buoys at Smugglers Cottage and near Malpas

Ⓥ Four Truro Harbour Authority pontoons

• Water at pontoon near King Harry Ferry (short stay only)

• Truro harbourmaster VHF 12 ☎ 01872 225346

Restronguet and the Pandora Inn

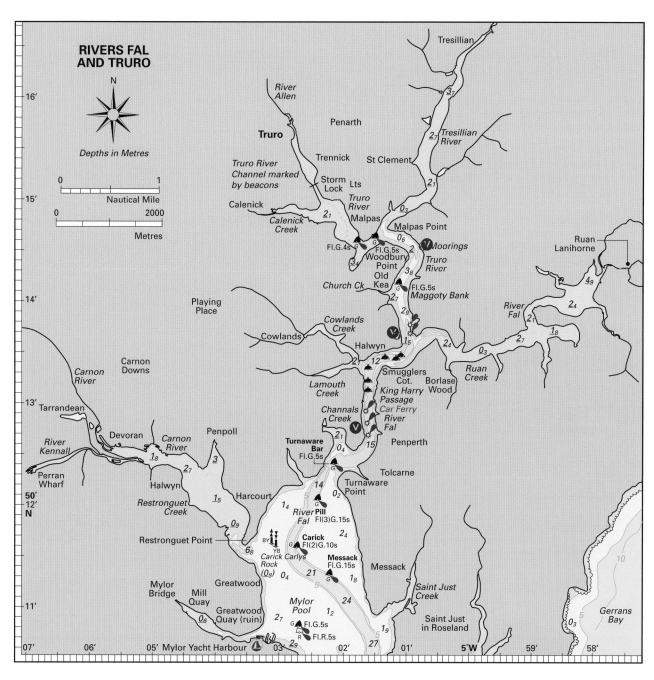

**RIVERS FAL
AND TRURO**

N

Depths in Metres

0   1
Nautical Mile

0   2000
Metres

Tresillian

River Allen

Penarth

Truro

Trennick

St Clement

Truro River Channel marked by beacons

Storm Lock   Lts

Calenick

Calenick Creek

Tresillian River

2_1

2_7

2_7

3_7

2_1

Truro River

0_3

Malpas   Malpas Point

2_1

0_6

Fl.G.4s   Fl.G.5s   Moorings

Woodbury Point   Truro River

3_4 Old Kea

3_8

Church Ck   Fl.G.5s

2_7 Maggoty Bank

Ruan Lanihorne

4_9

Playing Place

Cowlands Creek

2_9

River Fal

2_4

Cowlands

Halwyn

1_5

2_4

0_3

2_7

1_8

2_1 12

Smugglers Cot.

Borlase Wood

Ruan Creek

Carnon Downs

2_7

Carnon River

Lamouth Creek

King Harry Passage

Car Ferry

River Fal

Tarrandean

River Kennall

Devoran

Carnon River

Penpoll

Channals Creek

2_1

0_4

15

Penperth

Perran Wharf

1_8

2_7

3

Turnaware Bar
Fl.G.5s

Tolcarne

Turnaware Point

**50°
12'
N**

Halwyn

1_5

Harcourt

14

0_2

1_4 River Pill
Fal

5

Restronguet Creek

0_9

Fl(3)G.15s

Carrick
Fl(2)G.10s

2_4

Restronguet Point

6_8

YB
BY

Carrick Rock
(0_8)

0_4

Carlys

21

1_8

Messack
Fl.G.15s

Messack

Saint Just Creek

Mylor Bridge

Mill Quay

Greatwood

Mylor Pool

24

Saint Just in Roseland

Gerrans Bay

0_3

10

11'

Greatwood Quay (ruin)

0_6

2_7

Fl.G.5s

1_2

Fl.R.5s

5

1_9

5

27

0_3

05' Mylor Yacht Harbour   03 2_9

07'   06'   05'   04'   03'   02'   01'   **5°W**   59'   58'

Turnaware Point

Beware STRONG CURRENTS during tide ebb and flood at Turnaware Point where a narrow channel and river bend combine.

- En route do not stray from the main Carrick channel as both sides are shallow, in places down to 0m

- In order to clear the Turnaware Bar (NW of the Point, marked by a green Fl.G.5s) keep to the western side of the river as it bends.

Boats at anchor in front of Channals Creek

⚓♥ Anchorages and pontoons upstream

The wide expanse of water associated with the Carrick Roads changes dramatically at Turnaware Point. As you head upstream the river becomes quieter, a narrower channel with trees to the water's edge. Here there is peace to be had, except for some busy weekends in the summer.

Turnaware Point to Malpas (2M) has a number of sheltered anchorages and pontoons administered by the Truro harbourmaster. The pontoons do not have electricity or water. Expect to raft up in the summer. Water is available from the pontoon just before the King Harry ferry.

The anchorages, in shelves of silt and mud, change depth very gradually. Keel boats will generally swing with the stream, towards the centre of the river.

Temporary King Harry pontoon

Smugglers Cottage

In sequence from south to north:

⚓ North of Turnaware Point and the starboard hand buoy Fl.G.5s, Channals Creek and smaller Tolcarne Creek are good anchorages, both out of the main tidal stream. Channals Creek is exposed to southerlies.

♥ As the river turns northwards, east of Channals Creek, the first to port is 40m long.

• Beware of the mussel farm to port. This stretch was previously used as a large ship mooring.

♥ The pontoon just before King Harry Ferry is for short stay only. Fresh water is available and it is ideal for dropping people off so that they can visit Trelissick House. Dinghies may be left on the inside of the pontoon.

⚓ At the next bend of the river, opposite Smugglers Cottage, is an anchorage. There are moorings at the entrance but plenty of space between them and the deep channel. If you can dry out, Coombe village is a wonderful destination.

♥ After Lamouth the river turns east, the next stretch often populated with large ships moored fore-aft. The moorings belong to Smugglers Cottage and are free if you eat there (lunch, cream teas and ale). Deeper-draught boats may go aground in soft mud at low water. The pontoons may be used for dinghies.

⚓ Beyond Smugglers Cottage, at the next river bend, there is good anchorage off (River Fal). There are dry anchorages on the east side, leading to the start of the creek, and to the south of the creek. Entrance to the creek has 2m depth on the northern

Malpas

side. Beware large concrete blocks marked by a pole.

Ruan Creek, as far as Ruan Lanihorne (dries 4m), is another great expedition. Timings are essential: too long in the King's Head pub and you may find yourself aground.

Ⓥ Just after Ruan Creek as the river turns north there is a pontoon.

• After the pontoon the Truro River becomes shallow with the large Maggotty Bank (least depth 0.6m) to the east side. The channel is very narrow at the tip of the bank but is well marked by a green buoy Fl.G.5s to port.

⚓ Anchorage before Maggotty Bank Fl.G.5s.

Ⓥ At the next river bend (Woodbury Point) depth increases. Two further Truro Harbour Authority pontoons are to the west side.

Ⓥ Visitors' moorings in Malpas reach.

Ⓥ Pontoon nearby (up to 1m draught).

Malpas Marine has no facilities for visitors and charges for landing in the dinghy.

⚓ Truro

At Malpas the river forks. To the northeast the Tresellian dries. Truro River continues northwest and the city can be reached if you time your journey from HW-2.5h.

• The Truro River retains a trickle of water throughout but the mud banks shallow rapidly so stay in the centre of the channel.

• Beyond Malpas, the start of the channel is marked by buoys (2 green Fl.G.; Q.G.; 3 red Fl.R). Stay in the outside of the channel for the two bends after Malpas.

• The last red buoy is at Calenick Creek where the channel turns north towards the flood gate. Aim for Lighterage Quay on the western side.

• The flood gate is generally open but will be shut if a higher than normal tide surge is expected.

• Use the quay before the gate if you need to kill time.

• Go through the 12m wide gate (beware if tide in full flow). The channel to Truro swings N, then NW then NNW and finally N. It is marked by red and green posts.

• To reach the quay go past the old warehouses (now flats) to starboard. There are three short channels and berthing is to port, southwest of the harbourmaster's office. You will dry out in soft mud beyond HW+/-2.

Pontoon near Ruan Creek and large ships berthed in the River Fal

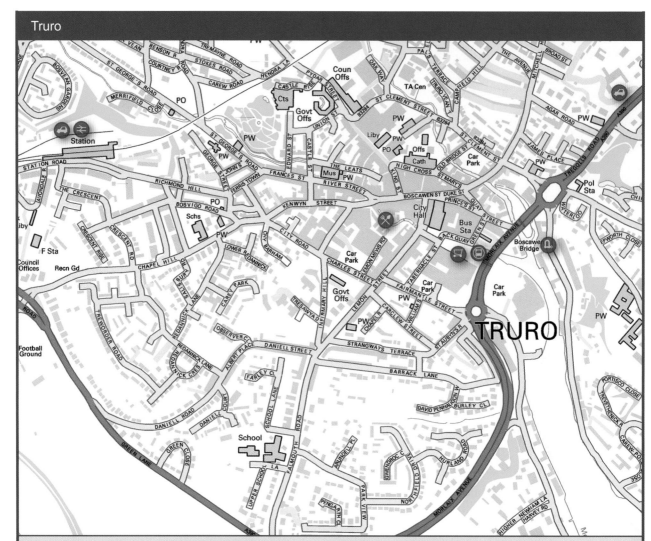

Truro

🚌 Buses from Prince's Street by the Quay to Falmouth, Malpas, Tressilian Garden, Mylor Bridge, Helford Passage, Penzance and Fowey

🚆 Main line to Penzance, Bristol and London
Branch line to Falmouth

🚗 Thrifty ① 01872 223638 (at Train Station)
Avis, Tregolls Road ① 0844 5810014
Europcar, Newham ① 01872 260610

🛒 Tesco, Princes St near the Quay

🍴 Restaurants, pubs and cafés: River St, Kenwyn St

ℹ Tourist Information Centre, City Hall, Boscawen Street ① 01872 274555

⚓ Langdon Marine Chandlers, New Bridge St, Truro TR1 2AA

✚ Royal Cornwall Hospital, Treliske, Truro, Cornwall, TR1 3LJ ① 01872 250000

Stained glass, Truro Cathedral.

CORNISH MINERS WORKING AT DOLCOATH

TO THE GLORY OF GOD AND IN MEMORY OF THEIR PARENTS
THIS WINDOW WAS GIVEN BY H. P. AND E. EDE   A.D. 1907

CORNISH FISHERMEN AT NEWLYN

The Town Quay has water and electricity. There are two chandleries next to the quay and the city centre is just a short walk away.

Food & Transport

Truro has a main line railway station and a branch line to Falmouth. Bus and coach services leave for local destinations and for long-distance travel.

A large Tesco supermarket is in walking distance of the Truro quay. The town has many coffee shops, pubs and restaurants. Indaba Fish in the City in Tabernacle Street is excellent (☎ 01872 274700).

Smugglers Cottage at Tolverne serves lunches, cream teas and local ale. The Pandora Inn at Restronguet Creek serves excellent food.

Interest

The idyllic journey all the way to Truro is a reward in itself but there are further attractions to be had. Gracious Georgian buildings reflect the town's prosperity during the 19th-century tin mining boom. It was once a stannary town (see 'The mining industry' on page 174) and the Royal Cornwall Museum in River Street is full of information about mining and also has an internationally important collection of minerals. The cathedral, built between 1880 and 1920, is Early English Gothic in style. The huge stained glass windows, created by Clayton & Bell, are amongst the finest in the world. Recitals are given on the Father Willis organ most Friday lunchtimes during the summer.

Trelissick (National Trust) is a very special place and can be reached on foot from the King Harry ferry pontoon. The house (not open to the public) was built around 1825 by the Daniells, whose wealth came from mining. Not everyone has been impressed: Pevsner called it 'The most severe neo-classical Greek Mansion in Cornwall' but the adjoining 500-acre park is exceptional. Paths originally laid out as carriage drives criss-cross the land to take advantage of panoramic views of the Fal estuary and there are delightful woodland walks beside the river. The garden as seen today was largely created by the Copelands who inherited Trelissick in 1937. In sheltered groves many unusual and exotic plants thrive, including some sub-tropical species. The gardens are particularly noted for over 100 species

Arriving at Truro: berth to port

King Harry Ferry
Visitors' pontoon at Woodbury Point

Truro Cathedral

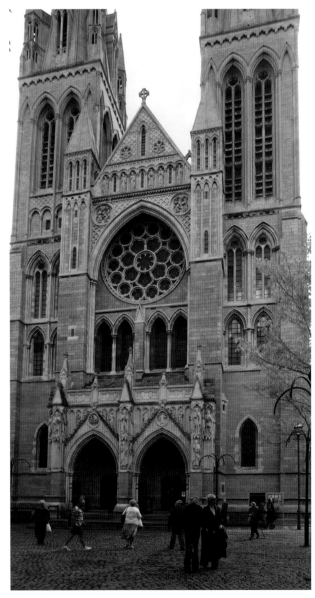

The mining industry

In July 2006 the Cornish and West Devon mining landscape was awarded World Heritage Status. Engine houses, mines, foundries, fuse works, industrial harbours and tramways, mining towns and chapels are the legacy of an industry that was at the forefront of the Industrial Revolution.

In 1862 the West Country had 340 mines employing 50,000 people. Luckily much of the landscape remains intact because, unlike coal for example, the minerals mined - tin, copper, zinc, lead, iron and arsenic - were found in deep vertical veins not conducive to opencast methods. Each lode was mined through a shaft that the men descended by ladder and some were hugely deep. Dolcoath, known as the 'Queen of Cornish mines', went down 3,500 feet and was, for many years, the deepest mine in the world. The derelict buildings we see today housed huge engines and pumps required for the removal of water once excavation dropped below the water table. Some shafts stretched out under the sea.

Tin is one of the earliest metals to have been exploited and the miners were considered so important that medieval kings enshrined their rights in law before written legal codes existed

Derelict engine house

elsewhere. In 1198 Henry II agreed that 'all the diggers and buyers of black tin, and all the smelters of tin, and traders of tin in the first smelting shall have the just and ancient customs and liberties established in Devon and Cornwall'. A charter granted by King John in 1201 confirmed that miners were beholden only to local Stannary Courts, 'stannary' coming from *stannum*, Late Latin for tin, from which we also get the symbol Sn. Stannery towns were visited twice a year by officials from London who would chip the corner of smelted tin if it was approved. This was referred to as 'coigning it', from the French for corner, and is the origin of the English word 'coin'.

The Cornish Stannary Parliament last assembled in Truro in 1752, but stannary law has never been abolished and Cornish nationalists recently claimed the right to veto British legislation, hotly disputed by the Ministry of Justice in a letter read to the House of Commons in March 2007.

Although land and mine owners became rich through tin, the miners themselves had a hard life. Usually whole families were involved and 7,000 children were employed in 1839. Boys as young as 12 would be working below ground while women and girls were shovelling, breaking up and sorting rock above ground. Many of the women wore cardboard hoods to protect their faces from the sun. Death and injury were everyday occurrences, as can be seen from tombstones in mining areas which read 'Aged 14 killed by a rockfall underground', 'Aged 19 killed by an explosion in a hole'. Few were fit to work beyond the age of 40.

By the end of the 19th century huge surface deposits of tin had been discovered abroad and many Cornish mines became uneconomic. In the first 6 months of 1875 over 10,000 miners emigrated to South Africa, Australia and the USA, becoming known as 'Cousin Jacks' and giving rise to the saying that 'down any mine, anywhere in the world, is a Cornishman'. South Crofty in Camborne, the last working tin mine in Europe, closed in 1998, although production may restart.

The National Trust (NT) has two huge beam engines on display in their original engine houses in Pool, near Redruth. The 1887 Michell Whim Engine can be seen in action, though rotated by electricity not steam. The only Cornish beam engine still in steam at a tin and copper mine can be found at Pendeen, near Penzance, where you can also take a short underground tour through the miners' dry tunnel (also NT). Geevor Tin

A.D. 1831 . . . . N° 6159.

Safety Fuze for Igniting Gunpowder used in
Blasting Rocks, &c.

BICKFORD'S SPECIFICATION.

TO ALL TO WHOM THESE PRESENTS SHALL COME, I,
WILLIAM BICKFORD, of Tuckingmill, in the County of Cornwall, Leather
Seller, send greeting.

  WHEREAS His present most Excellent Majesty King William the
5 Fourth, by His Letters Patent under the Great Seal of Great Britain,
bearing date at Westminster, the Sixth day of September, in the
second year of His said Majesty's reign, did, for Himself, His heirs
and successors, give and grant unto me, the said William Bickford,
my exors, adñiors, and assigns, His Majesty's special license, full
10 power, sole privilege and authority, that I, the said William Bickford,
my exors, adñiors, and assigns, and every of them, by myself and
themselves, or by my and their deputy or deputies, servants or agents,
or such others as I, the said William Bickford, my exors, adñiors, or
assigns, should at any time agree with, and no others, from time to
15 time and at all times thereafter during the term of years therein and
herein-after expressed, should and lawfully might make, use, exercise,
and vend, my Invention of "AN IMPROVEMENT FOR IGNITING GUNPOWDER
WHEN USED IN THE OPERATION OF BLASTING ROCKS AND IN MINING, (WHICH

Mine and Mining Museum nearby offers a more extensive experience. Underground mine workings from the 1700s can be seen at Poldark Mine near Helston.

The lives of miners became a lot safer once William Bickford (1774-1834) invented the 'safety fuze'. Born in Ashburton, Devon, Bickford was a leather merchant with no direct connection to the mining industry but knew of numerous accidents caused by fuses made from tubes of reed filled with gunpowder. Many exploded too early while others took so long to ignite they were approached by men assuming, wrongly, that they had gone out.

Watching a rope-maker friend spinning threads, Bickford realized that a strand of yarn impregnated with gunpowder would make a much more reliable fuse and took out a patent on his 'safety rods' in 1831. His factory in Camborne produced 45 miles of fuse in its first year but Bickford died soon after and the operation moved to America.

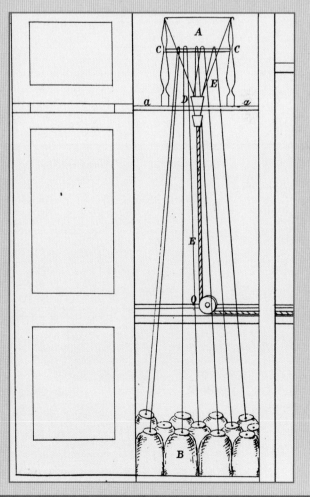

A.D. 1831 . SEPTEMBER 6 . N° 6159.
BICKFORD'S SPECIFICATION .

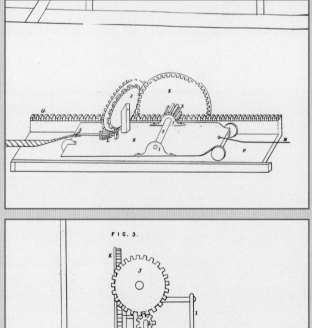

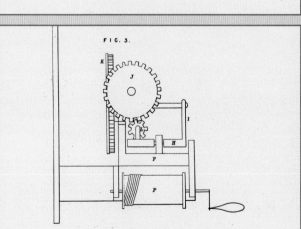

Helford River

Excellent shelter and straightforward approach except in easterly winds when a very uncomfortable swell reaches well into the river. Anchor only in permitted areas (eelgrass and oyster beds) or use one of the visitors' buoys.

The Helford River is a designated Site of Special Scientific Interest, Area of Outstanding Natural Beauty and Voluntary Marine Conservation Area. Upstream there are few facilities and little or no depth but away from the height of summer the reward is tranquillity in the most beautiful of settings. The estuary has seen little development and Frenchman's Creek remains 'still and soundless', as described by Daphne du Maurier in her eponymous novel. Forests of ancient oak fringe many of the creeks and there is easy access to some superb gardens.

Approach & entrance

Straightforward approach but only attempt in daylight as the entrance is not lit. AVOID in easterly conditions when significant swell builds up.

DANGERS:

- From the northeast: August Rock/Gedges Rocks (dries 1.4m) northeast of the entrance marked by Fl.G.5s (April to October).

- From the southeast:
Manacles 3M from entrance Q(3)10s.
Nare Point and Dennis Head either side of Gillan Creek.

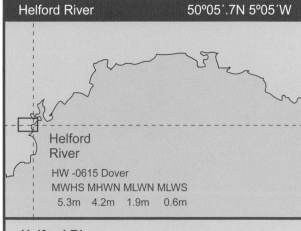

Helford River   50°05′.7N 5°05′W

Helford River

HW -0615 Dover

MWHS	MHWN	MLWN	MLWS
5.3m	4.2m	1.9m	0.6m

Helford River

- Daylight only approach - AVOID in easterly conditions
- Beware August Rock NE of entrance Car Croc /Men-Aver entrance to Gillan Creek, Manacles south
- Ⓥ 25 green visitors' berths, up to 14m LOA
- ⚓ Anchor only permitted areas - Oyster Beds
- Moorings Officer/Water Taxi VFH Channel M
  ℡ 01326 250770
- Helford River Sailing Club VFH80 Water, food, showers
- Sailaway St Anthony (Gillam)
  ℡ 01326 231357 info@stanthony.co.uk
- Porth Navas Sailing Club ℡ 01326 340065

Gweek Quay Boatyard

- 40ton hoist, water, showers & diesel
- ℡ 01326 221657

The River Helford

Gillam Creek

Car Croc
Unlit

→ N

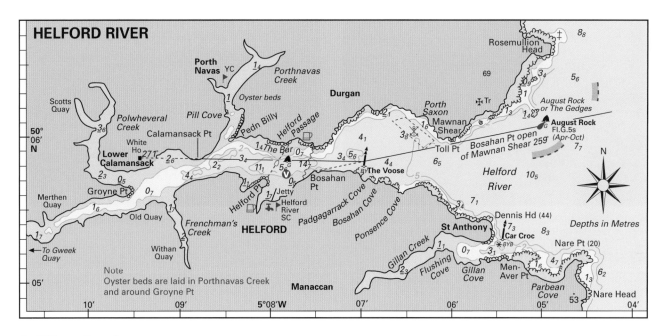

⚓ Gillan Creek

Gillan Creek dries beyond the local moorings.

DANGERS: Car Croc (marked by East Cardinal unlit) which extends S / SE. Men-Aver Point ledge extends N / NE.

- Pass halfway between Car Croc (East Cardinal, unlit) and the south shore.

Ⓥ Well into the creek, past St Anthony church, it is idyllic if you can dry out. Sailaway St Anthony has temporary small boat moorings that can be booked (☎ 01326 231357).

⚓ Durgan Bay

Durgan Bay, on the northern side as you enter the river, is a good anchorage in north to west winds.

There is a 200m anchoring restriction on the NE side, to protect eelgrass, with moorings adjacent so aim for the western side.

⚓ Bosahan Cove

Opposite Durgan Bay, Bosahan cove is good in winds with a southerly component. Beware of Voose rocks (marked by a north cardinal, unlit).

Narrows and the Bar

The course narrows towards Helford. Deep water is flanked by woodland up to Bosahan Point (fishermen's pots) on the south side and by The Bar on the northern side. The Bar extends, to the end of the visitors' moorings, 150m from the northern side.

Gillan Creek

Helford and The Pool with visitors' moorings

ⓥ The Pool at Helford

In front of Helford there are many local moorings. Visitors' moorings are located in The Pool (6m minimum depth). To stay: contact the Moorings Officer on VHF channel M. Dinghies can be left just upstream of the ferry pontoon on a private pontoon with honesty box. Do not anchor in the Pool or in the fairway channel as this is used by local traffic and fishing boats.

⚓ Porth Navas

Porth Navas creek opens to the north after Helford. The pool that retains water is full of moorings and beyond is an oyster bed, so no anchoring is permitted. Four hours either side of high water there is plenty of depth for shallow-draught boats to reach Porth Navas Yacht Club where there are showers, a bar and a restaurant. A few moorings and pontoon berths are available at the upper quay, built to ship granite from local quarries, where there is plenty of room for tenders if you are moored in the river.

⚓ Beyond Helford

It is possible to anchor as far as Calamansack Point/Helford Point in up to 2m. Anchoring beyond is not allowed due to oyster beds. The trip to Gweek, by boat or dinghy, passes spectacular scenery including Frenchman's Creek. Bilge keelers can dry out at Polwheveral Creek.

⚓ Gweek

Gweek can be reached on the tide by boats with a small draught. With reference to Penzance, high water at the quay is 3.05m less and 20 minutes later. Armed with a detailed chart (Admiralty 0147, Imray

2400.11) continue beyond Frenchman's Creek and Polwheveral Creek opposite.

The quay at Tremayne belongs to the National Trust, but you can land to access the woodland and some splendid walks. After Mawgan Creek the channel to Gweek is dredged and marked by buoys. Berth alongside Gweek Quay Boatyard (dries) which has a chandlery, 40ton hoist, water and diesel, plus engineering services.

Food & transport

Transport options are very limited: bus 35 from Falmouth to Helston passes through Mawnan Smith and Constantine on the north side of the river.

At Helford both the Shipwright Arms and the Riverside Café serve food. Across the river there is a post office and general stores which usually has pasties for sale. In the Helford Passage The Ferry Boat Inn has a restaurant with a daily menu and seafood specials. The Gweek Inn serves pub food and there are other restaurants nearby. Porth Navas Yacht Club has a bar and restaurant (☎ 01326 340065). The Helford River Sailing Club, housed in a beautiful wooden building, has a bar serving food, showers and a laundrette. New Yard Restaurant (☎ 01326 221595; closed Mon/Tues) at Trelowarren House, 4M from Tremayne Quay, is excellent. Just about everything, including the bread, is freshly made on site and most ingredients are sourced locally. There is usually fish and shellfish caught by local day boats, game from the estate and, in season, oysters from the Helford River. Although it is possible to walk there a journey by bike or taxi may be preferable.

Qweek Quay

Landing at Helford - honesty box end of the pontoon

Interest

The Helford estuary is a pristine marine environment in which there are over 80 species of fish living in a wide variety of habitats from sheltered muddy creeks to tide-swept, deep, rocky reefs. There are oyster beds and eel grass which act as a nursery for fish including bass. The shoreline is 30 miles in length, little of which has been developed. In places ancient oak forests still fringe the river and tawny owls are heard at night. Frenchmans' Creek was immortalised by Daphne du Maurier and can be reached via a delightful footpath from Helford.

Gweek Seal Sanctuary is well worth a visit. Started by Ken Jones in 1958, it moved to its current premises in 1975 and has continued to grow. Today there is a specially designed hospital and nursery pools, isolation pools, a pool for convalescence and for a resident population of seals that would not survive back in the wild. Most of the adults that are rescued have been entangled in fishing nets. The very young pups are likely to have been abandoned by their mother or separated from her in rough seas. All are usually exhausted and dehydrated and many have puncture wounds that require treatment. About 40 seals are rescued each year. The vast majority are nursed back to health and released.

From the Helford estuary there is easy access to three marvellous gardens. Trebah is a 20-minute walk uphill from the Helford Passage or, with prior permission (① 01326 252200), you can land your dinghy on their private beach. There are sub-tropical ferns and palms and century-old rhododendrons and magnolias. One tree fern, *Dicksonia antarctica*, came from Adelaide in 1890. A ravine garden ascends 200ft and there are two acres of blue, white and pink hydrangeas. Planters, an award-winning café, offers home-cooked seasonal food and in the summer a boathouse kiosk serves drinks on the beach. If you arrive by dinghy please remember to pay.

Glendurgan gardens are managed by the National Trust. Spread over three valleys, they contain exotic plants from all over the world and extensive woodland. Especially famous is a 176-year-old cherry laurel maze but there is also an outstanding display of magnolias and camellias in the spring. On foot from the Helford Passage Glendurgan is reached via the coastal path in 30 minutes and along the road in 10 minutes. If you seek permission ahead (① 01326 252020) you can arrive by tender at Durgan beach which is adjacent and also owned by the NT. The pay point is at the top of the garden where there is also a tea-room.

The Trelowarren estate has a very special garden which is in the process of being restored. 12 acres of 'Pleasure Grounds' were laid out in 1758 to a plan by Dionysus Williams which now resides in the County Record Office, Truro. The original garden embraced the ideals of the English Landscape Movement, eschewing obvious 'beauty' in order to free the mind for more lofty matters. Restoration is involving the removal of later species and hybrids including the rhododendrons, camellias and azaleas. The house is not open to the public but the grounds offer some superb walking (open April-September). After lofty contemplation and some exercise many head for Trelowarren's excellent New Yard Restaurant. From Tremayne Quay it is possible to walk to Trelowarren, though it involves 4M of hills. A taxi, or bike, if you have one on board, may be preferable.

Frenchman's Creek and Polwheveral Creek upriver

Helford River to Lizard Point

This stretch of the coast, though strikingly beautiful, is unforgiving and has claimed a large number of boats in the past. This is not to say that it cannot be enjoyed but great care must be taken in anything other than calm conditions.

The southern side is exposed to Atlantic swell and tides are very strong, in excess of 2kn in springs. The Lizard is a prominent headland standing in the way of the tidal stream and causing the sea to become confused. Further north the tide is less strong but difficult seas build up whenever there is wind against tide.

In the right conditions there are various coves and beaches to explore and close to the coast there is some protection from the west. Coverack is the only recommended anchorage but short stops at Cadgwith, Church Cove and House Bay near the Lizard are possible. Porthallow and Porthoustock, above the Manacles, are quarries.

From The Manacles to Lizard Point

- As you come south from Falmouth, or the Helford, it is worth establishing your distance from the shore. You can go close to the Manacles in calm conditions but move well towards the east in rough sea or strong easterlies.

- Follow a similar rule between the Manacles the Lizard. The coast offers some protection from the prevailing southwest but you are better off keeping clear of the area and seeking shelter elsewhere.

- Tides off Black Head are strong. Keep a wide berth.

- Aim at least 3M south of the Lizard where there is a tidal race, worst in west tidal streams against westerly winds. Shipping traffic and fishing vessels congregate below the headland so maintain a careful watch. As you round the headland the full force of any Atlantic storm or swell will make conditions more difficult so have fallback plans in place. Aim at least 3M south of the headland, more in difficult conditions.

- A course of 220° from the Manacles clears the dangers off the coast.

DANGERS, from north to south:

- Reef extending 400m from Nare Point.

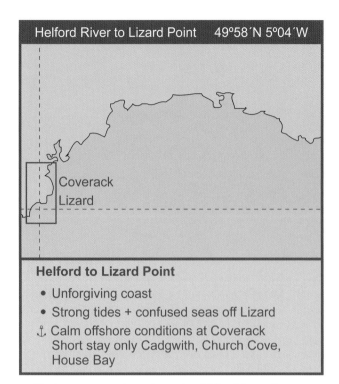

Helford River to Lizard Point   49°58′N 5°04′W

Helford to Lizard Point

- Unforgiving coast
- Strong tides + confused seas off Lizard
- ⚓ Calm offshore conditions at Coverack Short stay only Cadgwith, Church Cove, House Bay

- Entire area north and south of The Manacles, east cardinal Q(3)10s. Keep at least 1.5M off the coast. Under no circumstances take the passage between the cardinal buoy and the shoreline: the area is full of rocks.

- Isolated rock (dries 1.6m) east of Chynhallis Point, immediately south of Coverack.

- Boa Rock on the northern side of Cadgwith Cove.

- Craggan Rocks, SSE off Cadgwith, depth only 1.5m.

- Vrogue Rock, SE off Bass Point, depth 1.8m.

- Numerous rocks and shallows extending 0.5M south of The Lizard.

⚓ Coverack

Coverack Cove is a good anchorage in calm offshore conditions. Dinghy landing is possible on the beach or in the tiny harbour. Anchor anywhere in the wide bay but take care towards the south side where there are a number of private buoys.

The village is picturesque and a popular tourist destination. There are some cafés and The Lifeboat House Restaurant (☎ 01326 281212), housed in the old lifeboat station, is excellent. You can see the

Small drying harbour at Coverack

Coverack Cove

The beach at Cadgwith

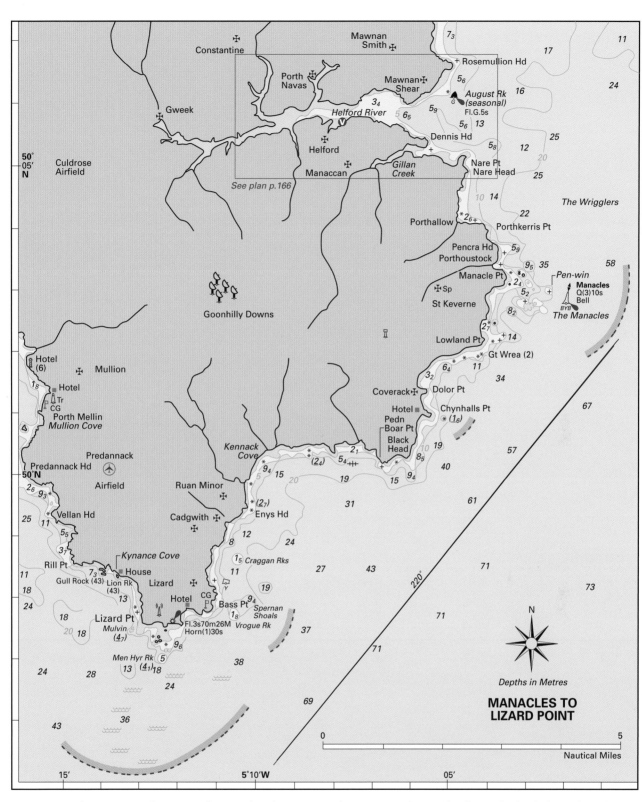

MANACLES TO
LIZARD POINT

Depths in Metres

0   5
Nautical Miles

precipitous descent into the water that used to be taken by the lifeboat. Its new location is at Kilcobben Cove further southwest.

A windsurfing school uses the cove. The beach is popular but rarely crowded.

⚓ Cadgwith

This diminutive harbour is used by fishing boats which are hauled up the shingle beach with a winch or tractor. The village, comprising a few cottages, is somewhat spoilt by a road passing through. A shop

facing onto the road sells cooked whole crab and crab sandwiches in the summer. There is a pub nearby.

Anchor a good 200m off and only in calm, offshore conditions. Suitable for just a few hours.

⚓ Church Cove, House Bay

Close to the Lizard, use only in completely calm conditions for a short stay in daylight. House Bay is slightly more sheltered in winds with a northerly component.

Mounts Bay

West Cornwall

Mounts Bay

St Michael's Mount, Penzance, Newlyn and Mousehole

The coast from Lizard Point to Land's End is varied with dramatic cliffs, pretty coves, workaday harbours and a fairytale castle looking out to sea atop St Michael's Mount. Sailing here, against the prevailing south-westerlies, can be a challenge but time it right and you can enjoy some of the most remote and treasured seascape the West Country has to offer. On shore, Cornish traditions are alive and well. You can attend the Golowan festival, dance the Furry Dance and tuck in to starry-gazey pie.

An overnight anchorage in Mullion Cove would be very special. Porth Mellin, administered by the National Trust, can be approached by dinghy. A short walk along part of the South West Coast Path takes you to the Mullion Cliffs National Nature Reserve where rare plants include land quillwort and fringed rupture-wort. Breeding colonies of kittiwakes, cormorants and guillemots can be seen on Mullion Island bird sanctuary and there are guided boat trips around the island for those with a special interest.

Porthleven is a popular holiday destination. Nearby a shingle bank, known as Loe Bar, separates the sea from the largest freshwater lake in Cornwall and prevents a passage up to Helston. The area is treacherous in bad weather and the scene of many a shipwreck. However, a five-mile walk around the lake in good weather is a delight. There are woods and creeks and rare flowers to be seen, including the yellow horned poppy. Helston, inland, is known for its folk museum and the famous furry dance which takes place in May and includes a portrayal of St Michael slaying the dragon.

Penzance is a bustling market town with many fine buildings. There are buoys to use but also a very safe wet dock that would allow you to berth up for several days if you wanted to explore inland. The Penlee House Gallery and Museum is a must for anyone interested in the Newlyn school of painting that flourished betwen 1882 and 1940. Stanhope and Elizabeth Forbes, Walter Langley and others became known for their realistic portrayal of local fishing and farming communities which they painted *en plein air*. Tate St Ives, which opened in 1993, is just eight miles from Penzance and can be reached on foot along St Michael's pilgrims' way or by a very scenic train journey. Newlyn can be reached on foot from Penzance along a wide promenade. Newlyn Art Gallery and The Exchange both display art.

Mousehole (pronounced Mowzle) is a very pretty drying harbour and a tourist magnet but suitable only for bilge keelers.

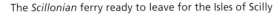

The *Scillonian* ferry ready to leave for the Isles of Scilly

St Michael's Mount

MOUNTS BAY

One of the real treats associated with sailing in the West Country is the sight of dolphins. If you are very lucky they will play in your bow wave, shooting like a torpedo into the swell, rotating and squeaking with delight. The sad occasion in June 2008 when 26 common dolphins died in Cornwall after beaching themselves is still a mystery. Various theories abound, including the ludicrous notion that the animals had wanted to commit suicide. A better explanation is that sonar imitating the sound of killer whales, their natural predator, brought about frantic and misguided attempts at escape. Thirty Royal Navy vessels were engaged in live firing exercises involving a submarine just before the beachings, which happened at four different sites. The MOD issued a statement saying that short-range sonar had been used twelve miles off Falmouth but 'an environmental impact assessment' had been carried out. They consider it 'extremely unlikely that this operation could have affected the mammals in any way' but a dolphin's hearing is very sensitive - it is their most important sense - so the jury is still out.

At least the Navy's sober concern is reassuring. The same cannot be said of the attitude expressed by the CEO of the National Federation of Fisherman's Organisations, Barrie Deas, when asked to comment on the death of dolphins as a result of fishing. 'It's a question of proportion', he said, adding, 'Why don't you stop motor cars because of the death of hedgehogs?' The death of dolphins, porpoises and whales (collectively known as cetaceans) is mostly due to entanglement in fishing nets and up to 250 are found dead around the Cornish coast and Scilly every year, a fivefold increase since 2000. Even this is likely to be an underestimate as tidal currents carry the majority of carcases onto French shores or out to sea. Theories about the increase in numbers include an expansion in fishing but also the possibility that more cetaceans now visit the West Country as a result of climate change. Although, they are all legally protected there is no prosecution if caught accidently through 'by-catch'. The reporting procedures are burdensome, however, and Greenpeace UK have found recently dead dolphins with their stomach slit in an attempt to sink them. The most lethal fishing method is pair-trawling where nets up to a mile long are strung between two boats. The seas around Cornwall are a magnet for French, Spanish and Irish trawlers especially during the seabass season, September to April, and Joana Doyle, Marine Conservation Officer for Cornwall Wildlife Trust, has expressed the need for Marine Conservation zones, by-catch mitigation measures and an EU-wide ban on pair-trawling. Of course as individuals we can still make an impact by eating fish such as seabass only if it has been line caught.

Bottled-nosed and common dolphins are those most often seen in West Country waters, though much excitement surrounds the population of white-beaked dolphins now found in Lyme Bay as these may be the most southerly resident population in the world. The most likely sighting, however, is of groups of harbour porpoises. These can be distinguished from dolphins by their smaller stubby bodies, lack of visible snout or beak and small triangular dorsal fin.

If you find a live porpoise, dolphin or whale that is stranded or injured, please act quickly by phoning the RSPCA on ☏ 0300 1234 999. Speed of response by a professional rescue team is crucial.

MOUNTS BAY

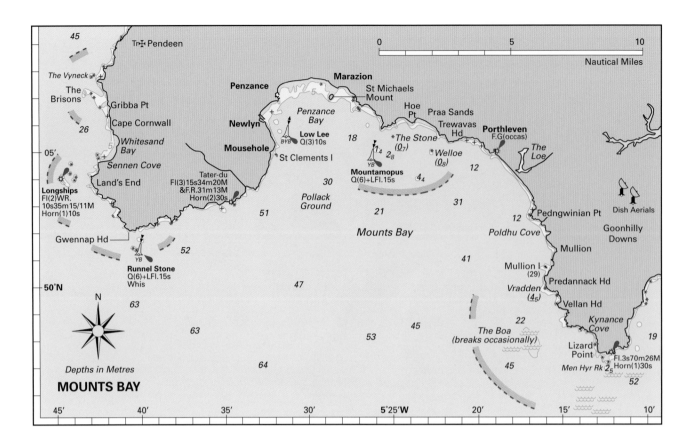

Sailing from the Lizard to Land's End

Open and set between two very significant headlands, Mounts Bay is the most westward part of the English coastline. The sea and prevailing winds can make the bay an unwelcoming place but two important harbours, Penzance and Newlyn, offer shelter. With good weather an investigation of the smaller harbours and rugged anchorages is most enjoyable.

The Lizard headland to the east creates races and overfalls. Remain 5M south, even more in adverse weather, to avoid disturbed water. A passage exists close to shore but it is never free of confused seas.

Once round the Lizard, Mullion Cove is a delightful anchorage and behind Mullion Island there is some protection from the southwest. Closer to the Lizard, Kynance Cove has a lovely beach and the adventurous sailor might anchor here for a short stay in good weather.

Porthleven is the first harbour when sailing in from the east. Visitors can berth alongside the quay in an inner harbour that dries. The entrance faces directly towards the southwest and the open sea, so should not be attempted if conditions are difficult.

The next practical stop is at St Michael's Mount, either at anchor on the west side or, by arrangement, alongside the quay in the drying harbour. The anchorage has little protection from southerlies so swell can build but on calm days this is a delightful place in sight of the castle.

Penzance and Newlyn are the main harbours and both lie on the western side. Penzance has a totally protected basin with a lock that opens at high water. Newlyn is a busy fishing harbour and although

visitors can use the pontoons priority is given to fishing vessels.

Mousehole is the final port heading west. A tiny bijou semicircular harbour, it is only suitable for boats that can dry and space is very tight. However, there is anchorage outside where land offers some protection from the west.

Off Land's End there are very dangerous reefs and rocks. Tides close to shore are strong and unpredictable. In adverse winds or bad weather stay well south of Runnel Stone Q(6)+LFl.15s, and west of Carn Base Q(9)15s and Longships Fl(2)WR.10s.

Initial shelter

Newlyn is the best option as it is always accessible, but there are dangers at the entrance so care is required. The inner basin at Penzance is excellent but subject to timing of the lock. In the summer there are buoys nearby for waiting.

Emergencies

The RNLI stations are at The Lizard, Penlee, Sennen Cove, St Mary's, St Ives, St Agnes, Newquay and Padstow. The main boats are at The Lizard, Penlee, St Ives and Padstow.

The Maritime Safety Co-Ordination Centre (MRCC) is based at Falmouth and monitors Channel 16, MF 2182kHz and DSC Channel 70.

Penzance and Newlyn have significant medical facilities.

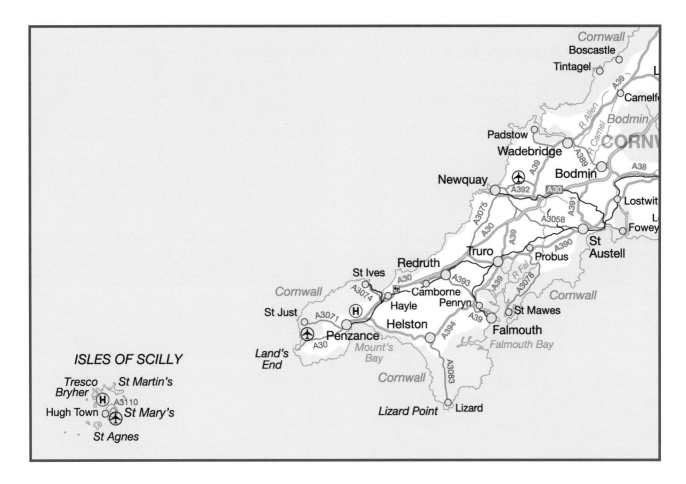

Provisioning

Penzance and Newlyn have supermarkets, shops, pubs and restaurants, which are easily accessible from their respective harbours.

Porthleven is small but there are shops and two well known pubs at the harbour. Marazion, reachable by a causeway from St Michael's Mount, has a pharmacy and bakery.

Repairs and chandleries

A slip in Newlyn can take boats up to 24m, although it is used mainly by commercial vessels. Penzance and Newlyn have a good number of engineering and marine specialists, primarily serving the fishing fleet.

Fuel

Fuel is dispensed in the inner basin at Penzance. At Newlyn there are fuelling points on the northern pier. At Porthleven fuel can be obtained in cans.

Transport

High speed trains from London and Bristol end their journey at Penzance. Newlyn is within walking distance of Penzance and can also be reached by bus and taxi. Porthleven is near Helston where there are connections to Falmouth and Penzance.

Buses are numerous, with routes and stops at all the seaside towns.

From Penzance it is possible to reach the Isles of Scilly by helicopter and by the *Scillonian* Ferry, but both are dependent on the weather.

Newquay airport handles domestic flights only.

Passages

From The Lizard to Porthleven is 8M. There are no significant dangers other than The Boa which breaks.

To St Michael's Mount it is another 7M but a detour is necessary to avoid Moutamopus which is marked by a south cardinal Q(6)+LFl. There are several other dangers within 1M of the shore.

Only 3M separate St Michael's Mount from Penzance and Newlyn. There are many offlying dangers along this part of the coast.

From The Lizard to Runnel Stone it is 20M, or 4 hours at 5 knots. Timing of passages is critical in order to have a fair tide for passing The Lizard, Runnel and Longships.

If arriving from the west a fair tide for Newlyn from Runnel Stone begins at HW Dover +5h.

If aiming to reach the Helford River or Falmouth, the 20M stretch between Runnel Stone and The Lizard has a fair tide between HW Dover +5h and HW Dover -3h (5 hours).

The sea between Cornwall and the Isles of Scilly has a traffic separation zone which is very busy. Maintain a good lookout and cross at 90°.

Eastern Mounts Bay

As you round the Lizard there are very impressive cliffs facing the Atlantic and the prevailing southwest. This is the setting for many maritime mishaps but if conditions are calm there are opportunities to explore some of the most remote spots in Cornwall. However, in winds with any westerly component or in swell from deeper in the Atlantic, this is not the place to be.

Approach

Coming from the east, keep at least 3M off Lizard Point. Staying south of 49°54′N and west of 5°19′W keeps you away from the race. Westerly winds against west-going tide creates extremely rough water so in these conditions the area is best avoided altogether.

The southeast coast of Mounts Bay is steep-to, with no off-lying dangers apart from around The Lizard. Further north beware of rocks Welloe (0.8m), Carn Mallows (2.8m), Mountamopus (1.4m) and The Stone (0.7m).

Immediately south of Porthleven is Loe Bar. This long, attractive sandbank shelves steeply so is not recommended for anchoring. Southwesterly gales have driven many a vessel aground here.

⚓ Kynance Cove

In flat, calm conditions it is possible to anchor between prominent Porth Mellin and Mullion Island. The space is just under 300m but it is possible to tuck right in. The cove is stunning and right by the beach.

Only approach with detailed charts and local knowledge on board. Time your stay to take account of the strong tidal streams and be prepared to leave promptly if a westerly picks up. It is best to plan a

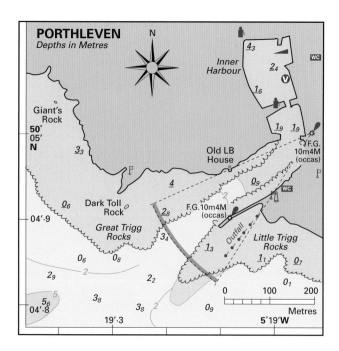

route out in advance as this involves passing between the Lizard race and the Boa shallows.

⚓ Mullion Cove

Mullion Cove is a delightful anchorage in calm conditions with Mullion Island providing some protection from the prevailing southwest. The tiny, drying Port Mellin harbour may be entered for short periods to load/unload but only by arrangement.

• Anchor in 5m between Mullion Island and the harbour. Keep a distance of at least 200m from the cliffs to avoid offlying rocks on the southern side.

• Beware of rocks by the harbour entrance.

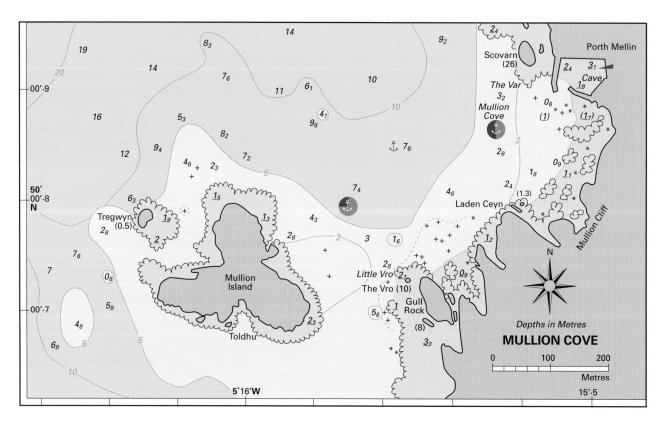

Porthleven harbour entrance

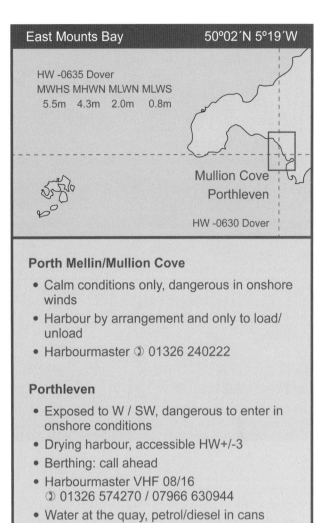

East Mounts Bay   50°02′N 5°19′W

HW -0635 Dover
MWHS MHWN MLWN MLWS
5.5m   4.3m   2.0m   0.8m

Mullion Cove
Porthleven

HW -0630 Dover

Porth Mellin/Mullion Cove

- Calm conditions only, dangerous in onshore winds
- Harbour by arrangement and only to load/ unload
- Harbourmaster ℃ 01326 240222

Porthleven

- Exposed to W / SW, dangerous to enter in onshore conditions
- Drying harbour, accessible HW+/-3
- Berthing: call ahead
- Harbourmaster VHF 08/16
  ℃ 01326 574270 / 07966 630944
- Water at the quay, petrol/diesel in cans

The island and harbour are managed by the National Trust. Two hotels provide wonderful views of the sea and there are plentiful opportunities for walking along the coast.

⚓ Porthleven

Porthleven harbour has sturdy walls but they face directly into the prevailing southwesterlies and distant Atlantic. The approach becomes dangerous in difficult weather. The harbour dries to within 100m of the end of the entrance wall.

Call ahead to arrange a berth and receive guidance from the harbourmaster.

- AVOID in strong S / SW.
- DANGERS: Great Trigg Rocks to port off the end of the pier wall and Little Trigg Rocks to starboard of the line of approach. There are no dangers inside the harbour once you have passed the old lifeboat building to port.
- In daylight, approach on a transit of 60° between the south pier wall (F.G.10m (occas)) and the prominent clock tower behind.
- Alternatively follow the transit on 45° between the pier wall F.G.10m(occas) and the inner light F.G.10m(occas) on the first wall spur inside the harbour.
- At 200m from the end of the pier wall aim for the centre of the channel (wall to starboard and shore to port).

- Continue into the inner harbour. Ⓥ Berth alongside the quay, east side immediately after the entrance.

The inner harbour is full of local boats on moorings. There is little space for manoeuvring.

Food & transport

From Porthleven you can get to Helston which has bus connections to Falmouth and Penzance. Porthleven has a number of restaurants and a pub on each side of the harbour (the Ship Inn and the Harbour Inn). There is a deli, a butchers, and the post office has a minimarket. Helston has a Somerfield supermarket.

Interest

If you are lucky enough to have an overnight anchorage in Mullion Cove a brief dinghy trip ashore would take you to Porth Mellin, also known as Mullion Harbour. Porth Mellin is Cornish for 'cove of the mills' and there were 3 mills nearby. The quay and two stone block breakwaters were built around 1895 at a cost of £9,300. Continual battering by heavy seas has taken its toll and in 1998 82 knots of wind (sea state phenomenal) was recorded. Since 1945 the harbour has been in the hands of the National Trust who are taking a long-term view with regard to preservation. The expectation is that by 2100 sea levels in the West Country will have risen by 0.5m and a corresponding 0.3m increase in the wave height will

Mullion Cove

give them even more battering potential! Ashore, a short walk along the South West Coast Path takes you to the Mullion Cliffs National Nature Reserve where rare plants include land quillwort and fringed rupture-wort. The clough, Cornwall's national bird, has recently been found nesting here. Mullion Island is a bird sanctuary with breeding colonies of kittiwakes, cormorants and guillemots. Landing is not permitted.

North of Mullion Cove an obelisk erected in 1937 stands as a monument to Guglielmo Marconi. In December 1901 the first ever wireless communication across the Atlantic was made from the new high-power transmitting station at Poldhu. The beaches of Poldhu and Polurrian, north of Mullion Cove, are popular destinations for surfing.

Porthleven is a tourist hotspot. The inner harbour is lined with shops, galleries, cafés, restaurants and pubs. Nearby a sand and shingle bank, known as Loe Bar, separates the sea from the largest freshwater lake in Cornwall. The lake was originally the estuary of the River Cober from which ships could reach Helston, 3M inland. The bar, or dam, began to form around 1300. Legend says it was created when a giant threw sand at an opponent, St Michael's Mount being the result of the stone that was thrown back. According to geologists many factors were involved, including rock eroded during the last Ice Age, a rise in sea level, longshore drift (whereby storms move vast quantities of shingle) and the effects of tin and copper mining inland. With the entrance to the Cober blocked, Helston is prone to flooding. For years gangs of diggers were employed to breach the bar when necessary but today use is made of a late 18th-century tunnel blasted though rocks at the northern end.

A well-signed five-mile walk around the lake's perimeter is a delight in good weather. There are woods and creeks and rare flowers, including the yellow horned poppy. In bad weather, however, it is best to keep well away, especially from the sea. Southwesterly gales have driven numerous ships onto the bar including, in 1807, HMS *Anson*, en route to the French blockade at Brest. Unable to make way, the lives of 120 sailors were lost, but there was a silver lining. Observing from the shore with a sense of helplessness was Helston man Henry Trengrouse. Sometime later while watching fireworks, he had the idea of sending a rocket-propelled line from shore to ship along which people could be winched back to safety in a suspended chair. Next to the lifeboat this is the most important means of saving lives from shipwrecks today. An example of Trengrouse's apparatus can be seen in the Folk Museum in Helston.

Helston is famous for its annual Flora Day celebrations involving the Furry Dance. This takes place on May 8th (unless this is a Sunday or Monday when the previous Saturday is used). It probably began as a spring fertility festival but now commemorates an apparition of St Michael, the town's patron saint. Men dressed in morning coats and top hats are joined by women in brightly coloured dresses and summer bonnets to act out various legends such as St Michael slaying the dragon. There are five dances in all (7am, 8.30am, 9.30am, noon and 5pm), each accompanied by the Helston Brass Band.

Penzance Bay

Penzance or Newlyn in the western part of Mounts Bay are the usual destination for yachts waiting to make a passage to or coming from the Isles of Scilly. Penzance offers total shelter in its wet dock but the entrance is dangerous in strong south to southeast winds.

Newlyn is a very busy fishing harbour, nowadays with pontoons in place. It is the port of refuge in Mounts Bay. The pontoon berths are only for overnight stay and priority is given to the fishing fleet.

Mousehole's small harbour in the south of the bay dries so is only practical for bilge keelers. The village is a popular tourist destination.

There are many rocks in the north of Mounts Bay, so it is not suitable for anchoring.

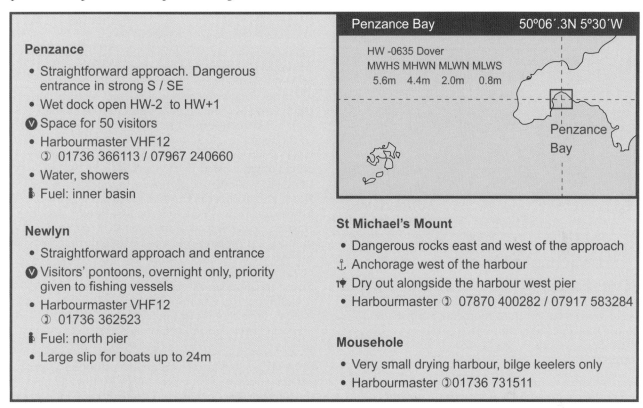

Penzance

- Straightforward approach. Dangerous entrance in strong S / SE
- Wet dock open HW-2 to HW+1
- Ⓥ Space for 50 visitors
- Harbourmaster VHF12
  ☎ 01736 366113 / 07967 240660
- Water, showers
- ⛽ Fuel: inner basin

Newlyn

- Straightforward approach and entrance
- Ⓥ Visitors' pontoons, overnight only, priority given to fishing vessels
- Harbourmaster VHF12
  ☎ 01736 362523
- ⛽ Fuel: north pier
- Large slip for boats up to 24m

Penzance Bay   50°06′.3N 5°30′W

HW -0635 Dover

MWHS	MHWN	MLWN	MLWS
5.6m	4.4m	2.0m	0.8m

Penzance Bay

St Michael's Mount

- Dangerous rocks east and west of the approach
- ⚓ Anchorage west of the harbour
- ⚓ Dry out alongside the harbour west pier
- Harbourmaster ☎ 07870 400282 / 07917 583284

Mousehole

- Very small drying harbour, bilge keelers only
- Harbourmaster ☎01736 731511

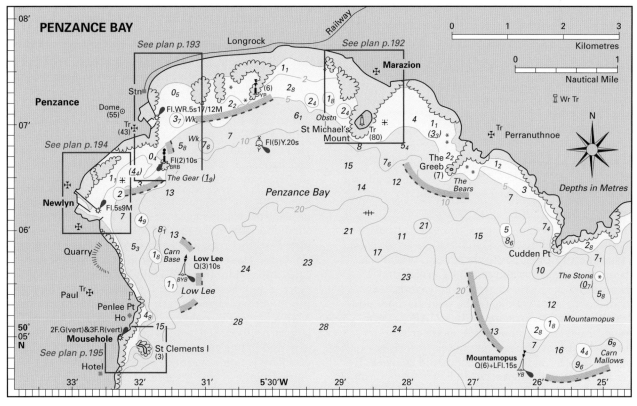

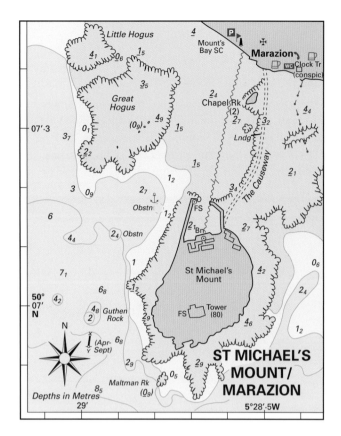

St Michael's Mount

⚓ St Michael's Mount

St Michael's Mount is a granite island with a fairytale castle and some magnificent gardens. The anchorage is sheltered from north to southeast but swell builds so use only in calm conditions.

Approach

Aim for the west of the harbour, where you can anchor in clean sand. Do not attempt at night.

- DANGERS:
- Great Hogus Rocks, a large patch of rocks with drying peaks (5.5m) northwest of the harbour.
- Outer Penzeath Rock (0.4m) 0.5M west of the harbour.
- Guthen Rock (2m) 0.1M west of the Mount. A yellow post is placed south of this rock from April to September.
- Maltman Rock (0.9m) 0.1M south/southwest of the Mount.

⚓ Anchor west of the harbour in 2-3m of clean sand.
⛵ You can dry out alongside the west pier inside the harbour but make arrangements ahead.

Interest

By the fourth century BC Greek traders are thought to have settled on St Michael's Mount, which was then known as the island of Ictis. Cornish tin, transported across the causeway in wagons, was loaded onto ships waiting in the small harbour and bound for the Mediterranean. In 495AD Cornish fishermen claimed to have seen an apparition of the Archangel St Michael on granite rock rising out of the sea and the fate of the island changed. It became a place of pilgrimage and a Celtic monastery is thought to have been at the centre of a thriving

religious community from the 8th-11th centuries. Around 1150 the island was given to the monks of Mont-St-Michel in Normandy by Robert, Earl of Cornwall after he acquired it from William the Conqueror, and the French Abbot Bernard le Bec built a Benedictine monastery modelled on its French counterpart. In 1425, during the Hundred Years War, it was appropriated by the Crown as alien property and finally dissolved by Henry VIII in 1539. The buildings were used as a fortress in the Wars of the Roses and during the Cornish Rebellion against Edward VI. It was here that the first beacon was lit warning of the arrival of the Spanish Armada. The mount's last military role was in 1646 during the English Civil War when Royalist supporters valiantly held out against the forces of Oliver Cromwell until forced to capitulate to the Parliamentarians. In 1660 it was bought as a family home by Colonel Sir John St Aubyn, the mount's last military commander. In 1964 it was transferred to the National Trust.

From Marazion you can walk across the causeway to St Michael's Mount or if the tide is in take a ferry, but it is much more fun arriving by dinghy. Around the harbour are the remains of a thriving 18th-century village with net lofts, stables and a pilchard press. There is a café and the Sail Loft Restaurant offers pre-booked meals to groups (☏ 01736 710748). The St Aubyn Arms still stands but it stopped serving in 1902. The castle, something of a jumble of styles, includes a Tudor doorway bearing the St Aubyn coat of arms, a 14th-century hall and a drawing room from the 18th century. In Sir John's room be sure not to miss Roger Wearne's historic tidal clock made around 1780. From the terraces there are magnificent views of Mounts Bay, Marazion, the Lizard Peninsula and Lamorna and of the gardens that thrive in the shelter of the mount's heat-retentive granite cliffs.

Marazion was the main trading port of Mounts Bay until surpassed by Penzance in the 16th century. A small museum in the market square describes the history of the town and has a display of agricultural artefacts. There are antique shops, craft shops, pubs, cafés and restaurants and Philip's Bakery is a good place to buy pasties. The beach offers safe bathing and is popular with windsurfers. Just inland is Marazion Marsh, an RSPB reserve which is home to Cornwall's largest reedbed. Sedge, reed and Cetti's warblers breed here and in late summer the spotted crake and aquatic warbler visit on migration. Bitterns are often seen during winter. There are guided walks and a hide for those wishing to linger out of sight.

ⓥ⚓ Penzance

Approach & entrance

The approach is straightforward but there are no leading marks and at night the entrance light can be confused with lights in the town.

- DO NOT attempt to enter the harbour in strong south to southeast winds.

- DANGERS northern approach:
- Western Cressar rocks (drying 2.3m) marked by a south cardinal unlit post 0.4M NE of the entrance.
- Cressar rocks (2.9m) east of Western Cressar.
- Ryeman Rocks (drying 2m south, 3.9m north), marked by south cardinal unlit post 0.9M NNE of the entrance.

- DANGERS southern approach:
- The Gear (drying 1.9m) south of the entrance, marked by an isolated danger mark Fl(2)10s.

- Approach in the white sector of the harbour entrance light Fl.WR.5s on a course between 270° and 345°. This clears the dangers north and south of the harbour.

Berthing & facilities

ⓥ There is space for 50 visitors in a totally protected wet dock. The dock gate is operated between HW-2 and HW+1. There is diesel available on a hose and access to showers. The town is a five-minute walk away.

Is is possible to dry alongside the northern Albert Pier by arrangement with the harbourmaster. ⓥ South of the entrance, in season, 12 visitor buoys are laid out (depth 2m). These are good if waiting for the dock gate to open or for an overnight stay in good weather. ⚓ In swell anchoring northeast of the entrance may be preferable but beware of the shallow rocky area along Albert Pier.

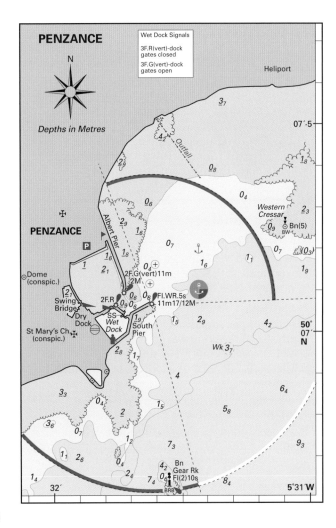

Penzance wet dock and gate which opens HW-2

Newlyn harbour looking towards the entrance

Food & transport

Penzance has a mainline train station and buses to Newlyn and to the rest of Cornwall. The *Scillonian* ferry links Penzance to the Isles of Scilly every day March to November except Sunday, weather permitting. There is also a helicopter to the Isles of Scilly from Penzance.

The town has many places to eat and there are supermarkets for victualling. The Bay at Hotel Penzance exhibits the work of local artists and has a good restaurant. Weather permitting, food can be eaten on a terrace overlooking the bay (☎ 01736 366890). Harris's (46 New Street ☎ 01736 364408) has good food which includes fish landed in the town. The Turks Head in Chapel Street is a popular pub serving bar food.

Ⓥ ⚓ Newlyn

Approach & entrance

The approach to Newlyn is straightforward but there are dangers and the southern entrance light Fl.5s is often confused with the white sector of the Penzance entrance light Fl.WR.5s.

- DANGERS:
- Mountamopus shallows Q(6)+LFl.15s 4.4M south southeast of the entrance.
- Low Lee shallows Q(3)10s south of the entrance.
- St Clements Isle, east of Mousehole, 2M south of the entrance.
- Numerous fishing pots and extensive fishing activity at night.

- From the east: pass south of Mountamopus shallows 4.4M from Newlyn entrance, marked by a south cardinal Q(6)+LFl.15s.

- From the south: keep to the east of Low Lee shallows marked by an easterly cardinal Q(3)10s. This is cleared if you are in the white sector of the Penzance entrance sectored light Fl.WR.5s (which does not clear Montamopus).

- Closer in, approach the entrance on a course between 245° and 300°, towards lights Fl.5s (southern pier) and F.WG (northern pier.)

- If you are north of the entrance stay in the green sector of northern pier light F.WG.

Berthing & facilities

Head for one of the Newlyn harbour pontoons (dredged 2m) which allow visitors to stay overnight. Check with the harbourmaster ahead of arrival. Priority is given to fishing vessels and you may be asked to move at short notice.

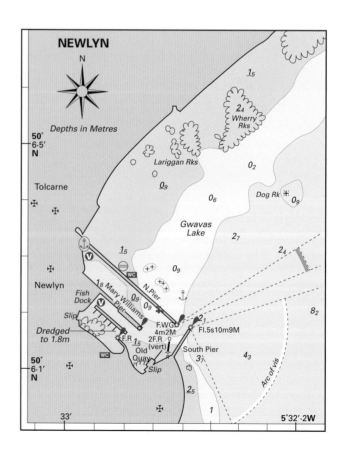

⚓ Anchorage in offshore conditions 300m southeast of the entrance in 4-6m. Anchorage is also feasible in Gwavas Lake in 2-4m. Beware isolated rocks close to the north pier. At all times keep clear away from the harbour entrance.

Food & transport

Newlyn is a working port with pubs and restaurants serving catch of the day.

Penzance, 1.5 miles from Newlyn, has a mainline train station and good transport links including to the Isles of Scilly.

⛵⚓ Mousehole

Mousehole (pronounced 'Mowzle') has a tiny harbour (dries 1.9m near the wall and rocks outside). Space is tight and drying so this is a destination for bilge keelers. The entrance may be closed in strong east or southeasterlies.

Approach & entrance

Approach the harbour from the south, between St Clement's Isle and the shore. The island, which has an obelisk, can be difficult to identify visually because it is low-lying. Do not attempt at night without local knowledge.

- DANGERS:
 - The northern passage between the island and the shore is narrow and between rocks. Do not attempt.
 - Tom Kneebone rock (0.9m) about 100m south of the obelisk.
 - Chimney Rock (dries 2.3m) 120m south of the harbour entrance.
 - Numerous pots along the shore and round the island.

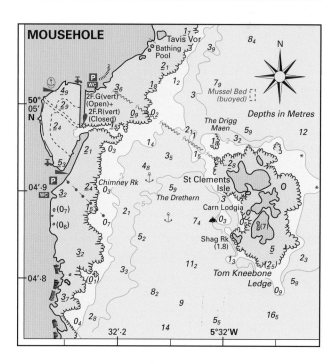

- Start your approach from well south of the island.

- Follow a course midway between the island and the shore, roughly in a northwesterly direction, until level with the harbour entrance. Turn towards the entrance as it opens.

- Visitors should go to the south pier.

Contact the harbourmaster ahead of arrival to make arrangements.

⚓ The anchorage between St Clement's Isle and the shore is good in westerly conditions (3-5m). Stay south of the cable. As this is the approach channel a cabin light as well as an anchor light is recommended.

MOUSEHOLE

MOUNTS BAY

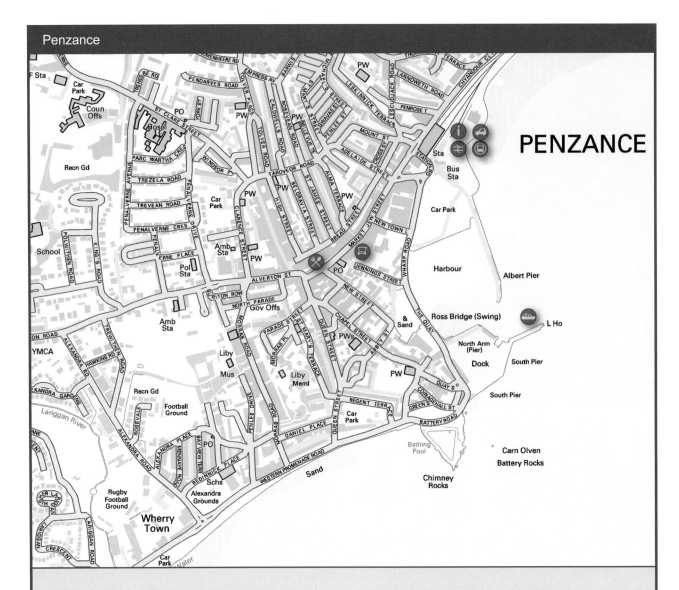

⊟ Bus Station: adjacent to train station

Buses to Newlyn, Helston, Marazion, Porthleven, Mousehole, St Ives and Truro

⇄ Train station: Wharf Road, Penzance TR18 2LT Main line to Exeter, Bristol and London

⛴ *Scillonian* III, Isles of Scilly Steamship Company ℗ 01720 422357 www.ios-travel.co.uk

🚗 Europcar at the Train Station ℗ 01736 360356

🛒 Co-operative, Market Jew St, Penzance ℗ 01736 363759 Tesco, Branwell Lane, Penzance TR18 3DU

🛒 Co-operative, The Strand, Newly TR18 5HN

✗ Restaurants, pubs and cafés: Market Jew Street, Chapel Street near wet dock in Penzance

Fore Street, The Strand and New Road in Newlyn

❶ Tourist Information Centre, Station Road, Penzance ℗ 01736 362207

⚓ Chandlers & marine services Penzance: Albert Pier Engineering, Albert Pier ℗ 01736 363566 WM Hosking Engineering, Wharf Road ℗ 01736 361081 A.Mathews Sail Loft, New Street ℗ 01736 364004 Penzance Chandlers, Wharf Road ℗ 01736 333139 Penzance Dry Dock & Engineering, Wharf Road ℗ 01736 363838

⚓ Chandlers & marine services Newlyn: Cosalt, Harbour Road ℗ 01736 363094 Kernow Marine Electronics, The Strand ℗ 01736 368606 Mounts Bay Engineering, North Pier ℗ 01736 363095 Dudley Penrose, The Strand ℗ 01736 331166 Sea Com Electronics, The Strand ℗ 01736 369695

✚ West Cornwall Hospital (Penzance), St Clare Street, Penzance TR18 2PF ℗ 01736 874000

The small harbour at Mousehole

Interest

Penzance was a port of some prominence by the 16th century but was burned by the Spanish in 1595. The present town dates predominantly from the 1800s. There are some splendid Georgian and Regency buildings, most especially along Chapel Street. The Union Hotel was a coaching inn but had originally housed the town's assembly room which has been restored. It can be visited if you eat at the hotel. It is said that from the minstrels' gallery, in 1805, Nelson's victory and death at Trafalgar were first announced. Opposite is the remarkably decorated, Grade I listed, Egyptian House from about 1835. The architect is thought to be John Foulton of Plymouth. Brightly painted with lotus bud capitals, it originally housed a small collection of natural curiosities. It is now owned by the Landmark Trust. There are two shops downstairs and some rentable apartments above.

Market Jew Street derives its name from the Cornish 'Marghas Jew' meaning 'Thursday Market'. Market House, with its distinctive white dome, was built in 1837 and is now a bank. In front is a statue of Humphry Davy, an outstanding chemist born in Penzance in 1778. Davy pioneered the process of electrolysis and is credited with the discovery of calcium, magnesium, potassium, barium and boron. His most famous invention was the miners' safety lamp in which an ingenious wire gauze prevented the flame from igniting gases in the air. With remarkable generosity he refused to take out a patent in order not to restrict its use.

Penlee House Gallery and Museum holds the largest collection of art from the Newlyn School (1882-1940). Newlyn offered sparkling seas, granite cliffs and scenes from everyday life similar to those in Brittany where many of the artists had worked after training in Paris or Antwerp. In the first 20 years the resident 'colony' grew to nearly 30 and at least 100 others joined in from time to time. They were united by a desire to paint '*en plein air*' and capture the real lives of the local fishing and farming community in a naturalist style. There was no attempt to romanticise and the hazards and tragedy of everyday life were depicted, including the distressed faces of young women as their menfolk leave to go fishing and tears at the news of boats lost at sea. Stanhope Forbes is often called 'the father of the Newlyn School' and it was his painting *A Fish Sale on a Cornish Beach* from 1885 that brought the colony national recognition.

Market Jew Street, Penzance

Walter Langley was one of the first artists to settle in Newlyn and his self-portrait, painted in 1885, hangs alongside those of Raphael, Rubens and Rembrandt in the Uffizi in Florence. Penlee House Gallery exhibits the work of Stanhope and Elizabeth Forbes, Walter Langley, Harold Harvey, Laura Knight and others from the Newlyn school, but there is no permanent collection on display. The museum covers West Cornwall's archaeology and social history. Penlee House, a creamy Victorian villa built in the Italian style in 1865, has a delightful orangery café and garden. In New Street the old telephone exchange has been made into an art gallery and education centre. The Exchange has a nice café, open during the day, Tues-Sat. For those particularly interested in art, Tate St Ives, which opened in 1993, is only 8 miles away. It can be reached on foot along the St Michael's Way pilgrims' route (details from Penzance Tourist Information Centre) or by a very scenic train journey which involves changing at St Erth onto a branch line.

A wide promenade along the seafront makes a pleasant walk from Penzance to Newlyn, 1.5 miles away. It was built in 1861 for a tourist trade that thrived once a rail link to the west of the country had been established. The open-air art deco swimming pool that juts out into Mount's Bay is tidal and the largest lido in the UK. It was built to mark the Silver Jubilee of George V in 1935 and is now Grade II listed.

In the middle of June Penzance celebrates Golowan which is Cornish for 'The Feast of John' (Gol-Jowan). St John The Baptist is the town's patron saint and the name Penzance is a corruption of 'Pen Sans' meaning 'Holy Head'. Images of the head of St John can be spotted throughout the town. Golowan was celebrated for many years until outlawed in the 1890s when blazing tar barrels paraded around the streets were such a fire hazard that the business community could no longer afford their insurance premiums. It was revived in 1991 by a group of local artists, performers and school children on the Saturday nearest to the church Feast of St John which they have called Mazey Day. Celebrations before and after make for a 10-day event with street entertainers, dancing, mock elections for the mayor and a firework display.

Just outside Penzance is Trengwainton Garden, now in the hands of the National Trust and open Feb-Oct. Nine magnificent walled gardens display species not seen anywhere else on mainland Britain. Many are hybrids created from plant-hunting expeditions to Assam and Burma in the 1930s. The garden covers 25 acres and has stunning views across Mount's Bay to The Lizard.

Newlyn is Cornwall's largest fishing port. Pilchards are still caught in large numbers and exported to Spain, France and Italy (see www.pilchardworks. co.uk). Brittany still processes the fish *à l'ancienne*, 'as in the old days', which involves selecting fish individually and flash-frying before canning. In Italy *salacche inglesi* are traditionally eaten at Easter as well as being the key ingredient in *spaghetti alla putanesca*. In this country pilchards landed in Newlyn can be found in most supermarkets. The tins are often decorated with art from the Newlyn school.

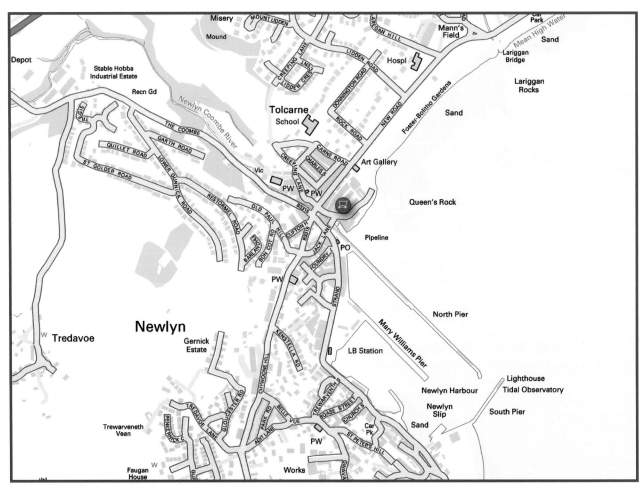

The Newlyn Fish Fair takes place over August bank holiday. Newlyn Art gallery is on the seafront.

'The loveliest village in England' was how Dylan Thomas described Mousehole when visiting on his honeymoon in 1938, There are records of a lively fishing community here as early as 1266 and part of the south quay, built from finely-grained Lamorna granite, originates from 1390. Just one building, Keigwin House (private residence), survived the Spanish raid in 1595, but centuries-old yellow-lichened houses line the inner edge of the harbour and a maze of narrow cobbled lanes make for a pretty scene. It was here that starry-gazey pie originated in the 16th century, when Tom Bowcock saved the village from famine by going to sea during a lull in prolonged bad weather. He returned laden with fish and the town folk feasted on pies in which the fish heads gazed skywards from a crisp golden pastry crust. Within the pie were cleaned whole fish, chopped leeks and hard-boiled eggs. Mousehole is a very popular tourist destination. There are numerous art galleries, potteries, pubs, restaurants and a village shop.

Further west Porthcurno Bay is home to the Minack Theatre. Minack is Cornish for 'rocky place'. Seats hewn out of the cliff face the bay and are accessed by a flight of 90 steps up from the beach. This unique venue was created by Rowena Cade when open-air theatre productions in her garden required more space. It took 6 months to build and was done on a shoestring, cement being used more often than granite. The first performance was lit mainly from the headlights of parked cars. Rowena worked physically on the project until her mid-80s and was planning

A short stop at the Penzance harbour wall

improvements until her death at 89. Her plan to offer some protection from the elements has not been forthcoming so rain clothes may be required! The season runs for about 16 weeks and booking is essential. Although originally a venue for Shakespeare, there is now a varied programme including Gilbert and Sullivan. *The Pirates of Penzance* is a favourite.

'The Greeting' by Walter Langley

Newlyn 1901 by Walter Langley

Isles of Scilly

The semi-tropical outpost

Isles of Scilly

The Scilly archipelago, just twenty-eight miles southwest of Land's End, is a superb sailing destination. There are five inhabited islands, St Mary's, Tresco, St Martin's, Bryher and St Agnes, and fifty-one named uninhabited islands. Hugh Town on St Mary's is the commercial centre and home to eighty per cent of the resident population. Its harbour is host to over 2,000 visiting yachts and about 25 cruise ships each year.

With fierce currents and hundreds of jagged islets lying in wait for the unwary, this is not a good destination for novices - over 700 wrecks have been recorded - but for experienced sailors with time on their hands the islands have much to offer. There is the satisfaction of successfully navigating difficult channels to anchor alone in crystal clear water, while the land has prehistoric remains to investigate, gardens to visit, birds to watch and, with over 60 miles of footpaths and trails, superb walking opportunities. Of late, even foodies have been well catered for!

The islands are part of a granite mass that stretches from Dartmoor in the east to the undersea outcrop of Haig Fras forty miles northwest. Legend has it that there were once 'handsome maids and strong men' living in the land of Lyonnesse, which stretched all the way to the mainland. It was said that from a turreted castle standing on what is now the Sevenstones reef, halfway between Scilly and Land's End, you could

count the steeples of one hundred and forty graceful churches before all was lost to the sea. Whatever the truth, submerged roundhouses and boundary walls from the Bronze Age can be seen between the islands and on the foreshore of Bryher and Tresco. These were built three thousand five hundred years ago when St Mary's, St Martin's, Tresco and Bryher were still attached to each other. Extra care should be taken on low spring tides in August when it is still possible to wade between some of the islands on banks of sand.

The Isles of Scilly were granted to the first Duke of Cornwall, the Black Prince, in 1337 but only came out of obscurity in Tudor times when they became a base for privateers heading home from the New World laden with booty (see 'Drake he was a Devon man' on page 125). Elizabeth I, having seen off the Spanish Armada but aware of possible future risks and of the islands' strategic position, ordered fortifications. The Star Castle (now a hotel) on St Mary's was begun in 1593 and nearby you can climb Garrison Hill and walk the ramparts. The islands then gradually fell into destitution until Augustus Smith turned their fortunes around. Leasing land from the Duchy of Cornwall in 1831, he established a hugely successful flower industry that is still important, albeit now secondary to tourism.

New Grimsby Sound

The islands were designated an Area of Outstanding Natural Beauty in 1975 and over half the land is of Special Scientific Interest. With no industrial pollution the air is pure and the Milky Way crystal clear. Around the coast there are over 150 dive sites with numerous species of sponge: slime sponge, chimney sponge, hedgehog sponge and the rare finger sponge. Seventy-four species of algae have been recorded together with fan and sunset corals, dead man's fingers and jewel anemones. Sixty per cent of the land is managed by the Isles of Scilly Wildlife Trust, who take conservation very seriously. Many of the uninhabited islands are permanently or seasonally closed to protect wildlife. This includes the Western Rocks and Annet, both of which have breeding colonies of Atlantic grey seals, puffins, lesser black-backed gulls and storm petrels. English Nature has identified thirteen wildlife habitats, two of which, tidal sediment and eelgrass beds, are of international importance. The islands' remoteness has given a number of species protection not afforded by the mainland. There are still hedges of elm, unaffected by Dutch elm disease, and the breeding population of song thrush is twelve times higher than anywhere else in the UK. Western ramping-fumitory, a globally rare arable weed, is found here in profusion and if you are very lucky you might even get a brief glimpse of the Scilly shrew. On most days in the summer resident naturalists offer guided walks, as do local archaeologists. Occasional visitors you may be lucky enough to see in the water include dolphins, porpoises, fin, minke and pilot whales, basking sharks, sunfish and leatherback turtles.

Figurehead from the Valhalla collection, Tresco Abbey

Cromwell's Castle in Tresco

Sailing in the Isles of Scilly

Scilly is not a sailing destination for novices. It is off shore, with low-lying islands and hundreds of jagged islets that protrude only when the tide is low. Facing into the Atlantic, the dominant southwesterlies can create considerable swell along the south, west and northern side and between the islands there are often tidal races as 2 billion tons of water are on the move. Hell Bay got its name for good reason! However, if you have experience do not be daunted. The Isles of Scilly are a superb destination, well worth all the effort and planning involved.

Important considerations

The weather, the state of the tide, the standard of your boat and the experience of your crew are all important considerations. Preparation is crucial but should conditions not be right then the best decision will be NOT to go. There is always another year.

- Weather: consider not just your arrival but your stay and return trip. While in the islands you may need to keep moving to find shelter.

- Arrival: enter Scilly only through St Mary's Sound or Crow Sound unless you are familiar with the area. Do not go exploring if you are tired or unsure of the weather.

- Initial shelter: arrive in daylight with plenty of time to find a suitable mooring or anchorage. There are no guarantees. Even the buoys at St Mary's, an obvious first choice, may be unsuitable (for example in strong NW) or already taken.

- Anchorages: the anchorages around Scilly are often in fine sand with dubious holding. Expect to set a second anchor or keep the boat attended.

- No place of refuge: Scilly does not have a single all-weather, all tide location that will provide safety in bad conditions. The closest ports of refuge are Penzance and Newlyn in Mounts Bay. St Ives can provide some shelter at anchor. Coming from Ireland it may be best to return to Cork. Coming from France there are a number of choices along the northern coast of Brittany. All of these ports of refuge are almost a day's sail away from the Isles of Scilly, reinforcing the point that this is only a good destination when conditions are right.

- Dangerous approaches: approaching Scilly in bad weather is dangerous. There are numerous rocks and shallows that are not marked and can be difficult to locate. Landmarks and transits are difficult to identify even in good visibility.

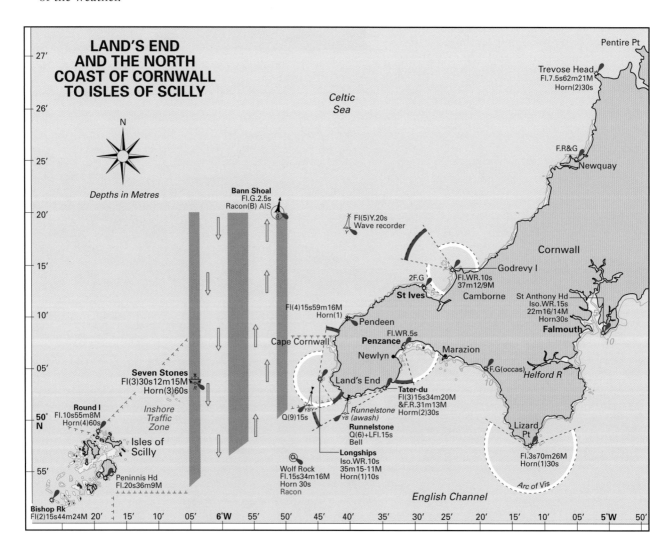

ISLES OF SCILLY

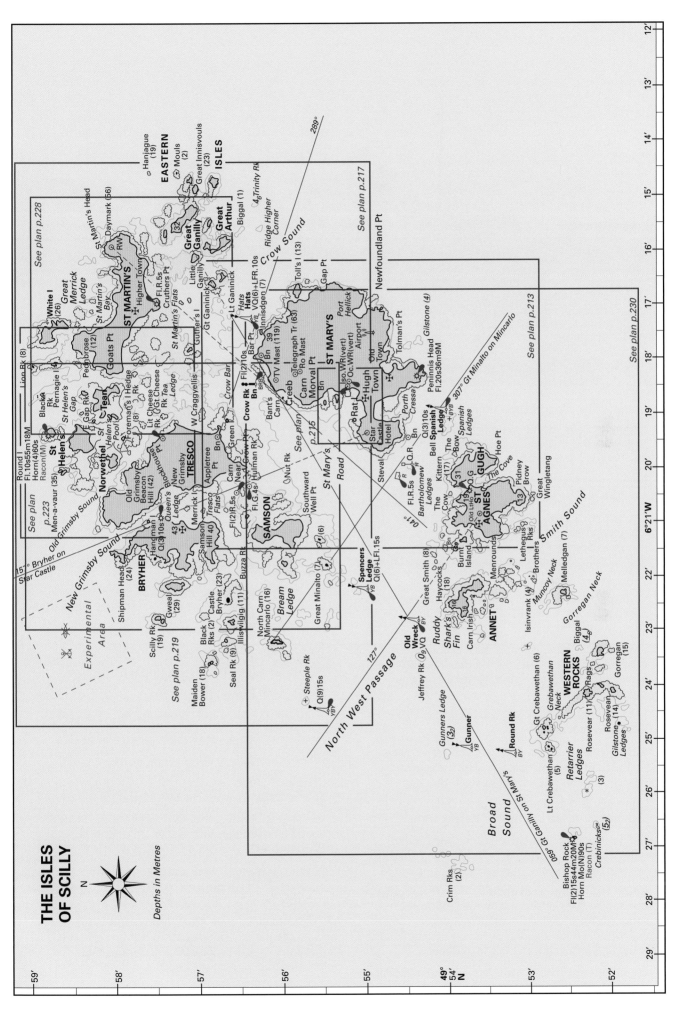

THE ISLES OF SCILLY

N

Depths in Metres

EASTERN ISLES

Hanjague (19)
Mouls (2)
Great Innisvouls (23)
Biggal (1)
Trinity Rk
Ridge Higher Corner
Great Arthur
Great Ganilly
32

See plan p.228
St Martin's Head
Daymark (56)
Great Merrick Ledge
St Martin's Bay
White I
Higher Town
Fl.R.5s
Cruthers Pt
ST MARTIN'S
Little Ganilly
Lt Ganinick
Gt Ganinick
Guther's I
Crow Bar
St Martin's Flats
Goats Pt
Pernagie I
Pednbrose (12)
Crow Sound
Newfoundland Pt
Lion Rk (8)

Round I
Fl.10s55m18M
Horn(4)60s
Racon(M)
St Helen's
Men-a-vaur (35)
See plan p.223
Black Rk
Pernagie I
St Helen's Gap
E Gap Rk
Foreman's Hedge
Lit Cheese Rk
Gt Cheese Rk
Tea Ledge
W Craggyellis
Norwethel
Tean
Helen's Pool
Rk
Bn
St Helen's
Green I
Hats
VQ(6)+LFl.10s
Innisidgen (7)
Toll's I (13)
Port Hellick
Gap Pt
Gilstone (4)

Old Grimsby Sound
Old Grimsby
Blockhouse Pt
New Grimsby
Appletree Pt
Carn Near
Crow Pt
Hulman Rk
Crow Rk
Fl(2)10s
Bar Pt
Bn
Bn 39
TV Mast (119)
Telegraph Tr (63)
Ro Mast
ST MARY'S
Bant's Carn
Morval Pt
Tolman's Pt

15° Bryher on Star Castle
Hangman I
Qk Fl 10s
43 Queen's Ledge
Merrick I
Tresco Flats
Fl(2)R.5s
Fl.G.4s
Nut Rk
Carn Creeb
Bn
Iso.WR(vert)
Oc.WR(vert)
Airport
Peninnis Head
Fl.20s36m9M

New Grimsby Sound
TRESCO
Buzza Rk
Samson Hill 40
SAMSON
Southward Well Pt
St Mary's Road
Rat I
Bn
Porth Cressa
Old Town
Hugh Town
Star Castle
Hotel
307° Gt Minalto on Mincarlo

Experimental Area
Scilly Rk (19)
Gweal (29)
Castle Bryher (23)
Illiswilgig (11)
BRYHER
Shipman Head (24)
Hangman I
Samson Hill 40
Great Minalto
Steval
047°
Q(3)10s
Bn
Old Lt Ho
Old Lt Ho
BYB
Spanish Ledges
The Bow
Hoe Pt
ST AGNES
ST. G.
31
Great Wingletang
Pidney Brow
Smith Sound

See plan p.219
Maiden Bower (18)
Black Rks (2)
Seal Rk (9)
North Carn Mincarlo (16)
Bream Ledge
Spencers Ledge
Q(6)+LFl.15s
YB
Great Smith (8)
Bartholomew Ledges
Fl.R.5s
Q.R
Q.R
R
R
The Cow (17)
The Kittern
Bn
Burnt Island
Menrounds
Lethegus Rks
The Brothers
Muncoy Neck
Melledgan (7)
Gorregan Neck

North West Passage
127°
Old Wreck
Jeffrey Rk
Q.9
VQ
Ruddy
Shark's Fin
Haycocks
Carn Irish
Shark's (18)
ANNET
Isinvrank (4)
Gorregan Neck
Biggal (4)

See plan p.213
See plan p.215
See plan p.217
See plan p.230

Gunners Ledge (3)
Gunner
YB
Round Rk
BY
WESTERN ROCKS
Gt Crebawethan (6)
Grebawethan Neck
Lt Crebawethan (5)
Retarrier Ledges (3)
Rosevear (11)
Rags
Rosevean (14)
Biggal
Gilstone (14)
Gorregan (15)
Gorregan

Broad Sound
Steeple Rk
Q(9)15s
YBY
059° Gt Ganilly on St Mary's
Crim Rks (2)
Bishop Rock
Fl(2)15s44m20M
Horn Mo(N)90s
Racon (T)
Crebinicks (5)
Crebinicks

289°

THE WEST COUNTRY **205**

- Shipping: a significant amount of shipping uses the traffic separation zone between Scilly and Land's End.

- Experience: long passages and piloting in a complex environment are not for the inexperienced.

- Equipment: a bearing compass, a depth gauge and a good pair of binoculars are essential. GPS is a great addition but not to be relied on. The numerous rocks and shallows are best negotiated by keeping a watchful eye.

- Charts: up-to-date large-scale charts are essential. Admiralty charts 34 and 883 are the best source of all soundings.

- Swell: expect some Atlantic swell. Though not dangerous at sea it can create difficult conditions, particularly along the south, west and northern sides of the islands.

- Low-lying: the islands are low-lying, thus difficult to spot from a distance.

- Currents: tidal streams and wind create currents that are not easily predictable. Use transits and reference points to guide your steering.

- Contours: it is generally safe beyond the 50m contour but depth can reduce sharply within.

- Tidal range: although the tidal range is similar to other locations in the Channel (2.3 - 5m), shallow water options increase significantly during neaps.

- Races and eddies: wind and tide can create rough water, especially in the northwest. Conditions sufficient to overwhelm a yacht can occur anywhere around the islands in very strong winds, when an approach should be abandoned.

- Popularity: the Isles of Scilly are a popular sailing destination in July and August when visitors come from France, Holland, Ireland, Germany and Belgium. French boats are almost as common as British, not least because the passage from France abeam the prevailing southwesterlies is easier than a beat from the Solent, where many UK boats are based.

Sailing to the Isles of Scilly

Tides near the islands

The tidal streams around the Isles of Scilly rotate. The general directions are:

- West from HW Plymouth +5h to -6h

- North from HW Plymouth -5h to -4h

- Northeast from HW Plymouth -3h to -1h

- East at HW Plymouth

- South/southeast from HW Plymouth +1h to +2h

- Southwest/west from HW Plymouth +3h to -6h.

Significant overfalls develop south, northwest and northeast of the islands as follows:

- South: at all times except HW Plymouth -4h to +2h

- Northwest (approach to Old and New Grimsby Sounds): HW Plymouth -4h to -3h and HW Plymouth +1h

- Northeast (Eastern Isles and approach to Crow's Sound): HW Plymouth -4h to -1h, HW Plymouth +1h to +3h.

It is recommended that a first approach is made through the main east entrance to St Mary's Road, to the south of St Mary's Island. If coming from the north, aim to arrive on the north side of the islands

ISLES OF SCILLY

From St Mary's Quay to the Garrison

with a fair tide to approach St Mary's Sound, between HW Plymouth +2h and -6h.

Traffic Separation Zone

There is a traffic separation zone between Land's End and the Isles of Scilly. The lanes are used by south and north-bound shipping. Traffic is less intensive than along the English Channel but is nevertherless significant. Cross the lanes on a heading of 90°.

Coming from South Cornwall

The distances to the Isles of Scilly from The Lizard and Land's End are 43M and 23M respectively (just over 8 and 4 hours at 5 knots). The best tide to cross from the Runnel Stone, south of Land's End, is between HW Dover -2h to +1h (southwest to west direction). The tide will be across the passage for most of the way, so heading is important.

Significant races and overfalls develop off The Lizard, which can be avoided by remaining 5M south. A passage exists close to shore but it is never free of confused seas.

There are very dangerous reefs and rocks off Land's End, and tides close to shore are strong and unpredictable. In adverse winds or bad weather stay well south of Runnel Stone Q(6)+LFl.15s, and west of Carn Base Q(9)15s and Longships Fl(2)WR.10s.

Coming from North Cornwall

From North Cornwall or the Bristol Channel the tide runs largely in line with the passage. Except when crossing the traffic separation zone it will therefore be with or against you.

From the northern coast of Cornwall, Scilly involves a long passage without many options for refuge. St Ives

Bay offers protection from the southwest at anchor. Padstow is a locked harbour, totally protected but only accessible with the right height of tide.

Location	Distance	Total distance	Hours at 5 kn
Padstow	0	0	0
Newquay	12M	12M	2.4
St Ives	17M	29M	5.8
TSS start	15M	44M	8.8
TSS end	11M	55M	11
Scilly	17M	72M	14.4

Coming from Ireland

The passage from Cork to the Isles of Scilly or Land's End is 140M, or 28 hours at 5 knots. Tide is not a strong consideration until close to the English coast as it is largely across the passage heading. Given that just over one day is required to cross the Celtic Sea it is advisable to set off in the very early morning so as to arrive at Scilly or starting to round Land's End with plenty of daylight ahead.

Coming from France

The passage from France or the Channel Islands varies significantly in length depending on the departure point. A passage between Brest and Scilly is 120M or 24 hours at 5 knots, that is one whole day and night.

The prevailing conditions with southwesterly winds are on the beam and thus favourable on average, but given the variability of weather this cannot be relied on and a good forecast, as always, is necessary. Swell in the English Channel is not of oceanic size, but there tends to be a mixture of comfortable and confused sea depending on the particular combination of tide and wind during the passage.

There are traffic separation zones between the Channel Islands and mainland England and around Ushant (Isle d'Ouessant) off Brest. You must maintain a good lookout and cross on a heading of 90°. You are certain to cross shipping at some point, whether in the TSS or in other areas, as the English Channel is a very busy commercial route.

Initial approach

For the initial approach into Scilly it is best to use St Mary's Sound or Crow Sound. You can approach from other directions but the challenge and risks are significant in any difficult sea.

St Mary's Sound is easier but Crow Sound offers protection from the south and west. Crow Sound requires clearing Crow Bar but Watermill Cove may be used to wait for sufficient water.

St Mary's Sound to St Mary's Pool

The entrance Sound is broad and not too difficult to identify. The lighthouse at Bishop Rock and Peninnis Head provide good guidance at night.

To reach a point on the main entrance transit:

- Remain southeast below the latitude of Bishop Rock Lighthouse Fl(2).15s44m24M (49°52′.5N) and east of 6°15′.5N. Alternatively sail on a course of 318° towards Peninnis Lighthouse Fl.20s36m9M.

- When Bishop Rock Lighthouse is due west and Peninnis Lighthouse is on a bearing of 318° alter course to 307°. Peninnis Lighthouse is then 2M away.

- This 307° bearing is the entrance transit between the western extremity of Great Minalto and North Carn of Mincarlo (Great Minalto is the smaller of the two). These two islets are 2M and 3M respectively away from the entrance to the Sound so you may not be able to distinguish them, even in good visibility.

Once on the 307° entrance transit:

- St Mary's Sound has three lit marks almost in line and close by, just west of the transit. A further unlit cardinal beacon contribute to mark the following DANGERS IN THE SOUND:
  - Spanish Ledges marked by Spanish Ledge East cardinal buoy Q(3)10s at the southeastern end of the Sound.
  - Woolfpack South Cardinal YB post (unlit) marking drying (dries 0.6m) isolated beacon south of Garrison Hill.
  - Bartholomew Ledges beacon marked by Q.R towards the northwest end of the Sound.

North Bartholomew buoy Fl.R.5s is soon after Bartholomew Ledges.

- Remain on the 307° course, towards the first lit East Cardinal Spanish Ledge Q(3)10s, which you leave to port.

- Leave Bartholomew Ledges Q.R and North Bartholomew Fl.R.5s to port.

Once past the last lit entrance mark Fl.R.5s:

- St Mary's Road opens. This is a wide expanse of water with a bottom mostly of sand and average depth of 15m. In good visibility it is very easy to distinguish St Mary's Harbour (most boats' initial destination).

- Continue on 307° until you have passed Garrison Hill by 0.3M. Alternatively turn on to the 40°30′ transit between Creeb (small rock islet NW of St Mary's) and the day mark on St Martin's. This clears Woodcock Ledge, a 2.7m shallow on the approach to the harbour.

- Turn towards the harbour on the 97° leading lights Iso.RW(vert)2s and Oc.WR(vert)10s. The transit clears Bacon Ledge (0.3m) to port and the rocks in front of the harbour wall.

- Pass the harbour Fl(4)R.5s to port and find a visitor buoy in St Mary's pool. Anchorage is possible beyond the buoys (dries 0.9m) towards Porth Mellon or in front of Porth Loo (0.9m) between Newford and Taylors islands.

Crow Sound to St Mary's Pool

Crow Sound is located on the northeastern side of the islands, between St Mary's and the Eastern Isles/ St Martin's. It is a wide entrance that is not difficult to identify but you will need to clear Crow Bar, a sand bank which dries 0.7m. DO NOT ATTEMPT in strong east or southeast winds. The Round Island lighthouse is visible between Tean and St Helen's.

If waiting for sufficient water to clear the bar, in south or west winds anchor northeast of St Mary's. Watermill Cove is a nice spot in 3-8m but keep 300m from the shore to avoid several rocks drying or awash at chart datum.

- DANGERS:
  - Trinity Rock (4.6m) and the Ridge (9.7m), south of the Eastern Isles, create breaking seas in bad weather.
  - Hats shallows (0.4m) and uncovering boiler structure from a wreck in the Sound, marked by south cardinal Hats VQ(6)+LFl.10s.
  - Isolated rocks off Innisidgen near the Hats cardinal buoy.
  - Crow Bar, a sand bank (drying 0.7m) stretching north-south across most of the sound, north of St Mary's Island.
  - Crow Rock, steep, close to NW St Mary's, marked by isolated danger mark Fl(2)10s.

Buzza Hill Tower in transit with white mark on shelter 151°

97° leading lights transit into St Mary's Pool

- TIDES:
  - There is a tidal race along the entrance to Crow Sound and up to 2M out to sea during the northeast-going tide for two hours (Plymouth HW -2h30 to -0h30, St Mary's HW -1h30 to +0h30). This can be dangerous in strong northeasterlies (wind-over-tide), particularly over an Atlantic swell.
  - The tidal stream past Crow Sound can reach 2.9knots during springs (Portsmouth HW+2h).

- Crow Bar dries, 0.7m on the southern side. Time your entrance to provide enough tide to clear the bar.

- The entrance transit for Crow Sound is on a 284° bearing from the northeast extremity of Innisidgen (roughly NE edge of St Mary's) and the summit of Samson Hill on Bryher. The transit clears the Ridge and dangers close to St Mary's, but it is difficult to see!

- Alternatively (in poor visibility) follow the coast of St Mary's going north and northwest keeping a distance of 500m from the shore until you can identify the Hats south cardinal. This clears the Ridge and dangers close to St Mary's. You can distinguish St Mary's by the conspicuous TV and telegraph towers.

- Pass south of Hats cardinal buoy VQ(6)+LFl.10s, leaving it to starboard. Keep close as there are isolated rocks (drying 1.6m) near Innisidgen, 100m west of Hats.

- Turn to 322° onto a transit between the centre of Landing Carn on St Helen's and Men-a-vaur beyond St Helen's (northwest Scilly). Alternatively continue on a course parallel to St Mary's keeping a distance of 200m (later you need to navigate around Crow Rock).

- Turn towards Crow Rock (isolated danger mark Fl(2)10s) when it is seen below the southern end of Samson.

- Cross Crow Bar which dries 0.7m. A gap of 150m remains wet 0.8m between the southern end of the bar and St Mary's.

- Leave Crow Rock to port. The rock is steep and dries 4.6m. You may pass between the rock and the shore but this is best avoided on a first arrival.

- A course of 220° from Crow Rock (40° towards Crow Rock) leads to the centre of St Mary's Road. This clears The Pots (dries 1.8m) and Round Rock (dries 1.5m) to starboard 300-400m after Crow Rock, and the Creeb islets to port.

- Alternatively follow the 207° transit between the old lighthouse on St Agnes and Steval (most western point of St Mary's). This passes close to Creeb.

- Continue until St Mary's pool opens out to port.

- The easiest route into the harbour is by rounding the entrance red buoy Fl(4)R.5s and then following the western transit.

- Western approach: turn towards the harbour on the 97° transit between leading lights Iso.RW(vert)2s and Oc.WR(vert)10s. This transit clears Bacon Ledge (0.3m) to port and the rocks in front of the harbour wall.

- Northwestern approach: 151° transit between Buzza Hill Tower and the white mark on shelter. This clears The Cow (dries 0.6m) and Bacon Ledge (0.3m) though it passes quite close to both of them.

Initial shelter

St Mary's Pool in front of Hugh Town on St Mary's is the simplest initial destination, with buoys and the wide expanse of St Mary's Road providing smoother water than outside the islands in strong weather. The Pool is exposed to the west and can be uncomfortable.

New Grimsby Sound offers good shelter at anchor or on swinging moorings. Watermill Cove on the northeast side of St Mary's can be good in southwest winds and when waiting for the tide in order to cross the bar at Crow Sound.

All anchorages are exposed and have approaches that are difficult, sometimes dangerous, in strong weather. If uncertain turn back.

Emergencies

There are RNLI stations at The Lizard, Penlee, Sennen Cove, St Mary's, St Ives, St Agnes, Newquay and Padstow. The main boats are at The Lizard, Penlee, St Ives and Padstow.

The Maritime Safety Co-ordination Centre (MRCC) is based at Falmouth and monitors Channel 16, MF 2182kHz and DSC Channel 70.

St Mary's has a small hospital and there is a medical boat that can reach anywhere in the islands.

Provisioning

Hugh Town on St Mary's has the largest number of stores, pubs, cafés and restaurants. Tresco has a good minimarket, a hotel and a pub. Bryher and St Martin's both have hotels and pubs serving food.

Repairs and chandleries

St Mary's is where boat services are based, at or near the quay.

Fuel

On a hose at the quay in St Mary's Pool.

Transport

British International Helicopters offer a regular service from Penzance to St Mary's and Tresco. A ferry, *Scillonian* III, sails between St Mary's and Penzance every day except Sunday March to November, weather permitting. Skybus operates scheduled flights to St Mary's from Southampton, Bristol, Exeter, Newquay and Land's End. St Mary's has a bus service and bicycles to rent, as does Tresco. All the islands are small and conducive to walking.

Reference marks in the Isles of Scilly

Peninnis Head lighthouse on St Mary's

Buzza Tower and chimney - Porth Cressa, St Mary's

St Martin's daymark

Men-a-vaur islands northwest of St Helen's

Crow Rock and St Mary's TV tower

Round Island lighthouse

Old lighthouse at St Agnes

St Mary's

St Mary's is the largest of the islands and the hub of island life. Hugh Town, the capital, is home to about eighty per cent of the resident population. It has a post office and a cluster of shops, restaurants, banks and art/craft galleries.

This is the only place to get fuel and assistance for any problems with a boat.

St Mary's Pool has buoys and anchorage space. St Mary's Road has a large area for anchoring. Porth Cressa in the south and Watermill Cove in the north can also be used as anchorages in the right conditions.

Ⓥ⚓ St Mary's Pool

Approach & entrance

The initial approach to St Mary's is described previously (see 'Initial approach' on page 208). From St Mary's Road the easiest route into the harbour is by rounding the entrance red buoy Fl(4)R.5s and then following the western transit.

- Western approach: turn towards the harbour on the 97° transit between leading lights Iso. RW(vert)2s and Oc.WR(vert)10s. The transit clears Bacon Ledge (0.3m) to port and rocks in front of the harbour wall.

- Northwestern approach: 151° transit between Buzza Hill Tower and the white mark on the shelter. This clears The Cow (dries 0.6m) and Bacon Ledge (0.3m) though it passes quite close.

Berthing & facilities

The pool is exposed to the NW and in strong winds being at anchor is very uncomfortable.

Ⓥ Visitors' buoys are located in the square marked on the plan, minimum depth 1.5m. All other buoys are for local boats. Given the amount of moorings, it is not possible to anchor in the harbour.

28 visitors' moorings (4 trots nearest the shore) are for boats up to 12m, 11 are for boats up to 18m (2 outer trots) and 1 is for a boat up to 30m. These moorings have very little space between them. Mostly, boats will swing in the same direction but it may be advisable to set fenders astern in case of collision. During the summer and in bad weather boats may need to raft up.

Anchoring is not permitted to seaward of the lifeboat mooring and near the large ship buoys. This area is used by the *Scillonian* ferry for turning.

⚓ You may anchor in the harbour beyond the visitors' buoys towards Porth Mellon and Porth Thomas, in decreasing depth. Beware of fishermen's keep pots.

⚓ Anchoring is also feasible in Porth Loo, between Taylor's Island and Newford Island immediately the north of the harbour. Beware of ledges extending from both islands.

It is possible to dry against the quay (near the dinghy pontoon) if repairs are required.

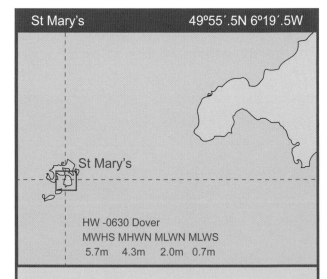

St Mary's	49°55′.5N 6°19′.5W

HW -0630 Dover
MWHS MHWN MLWN MLWS
5.7m 4.3m 2.0m 0.7m

St Mary's Pool
- Follow entrance transit to avoid shallows
- Exposed to NW
- Ⓥ 40 visitors' berths: 12m(28) 18m(11) 30m(1) 1.5m minimum depth
- Harbourmaster VHF 14/16
  ☎ 01720 422678 / 07789 273626
  hm@stmarys-harbour.co.uk
- Fuel (Sibleys Marine), water at the quay
- Temporary drying berth at the quay near dinghy pontoons for repairs, by arrangement
- Showers at the harbour office

Porth Cressa
- ⚓ Anchorage protected W to N to E
- Toilet, laundry

Watermill Cove
- ⚓ Anchorage protected SW to W

Diesel, petrol and water are available from the quay. The area dries (0.9m) so a favourable tide is required for refuelling.

There are showers and toilets in the harbour office and laundry facilities at Porth Cressa.

St Mary's Pool and Hugh Town

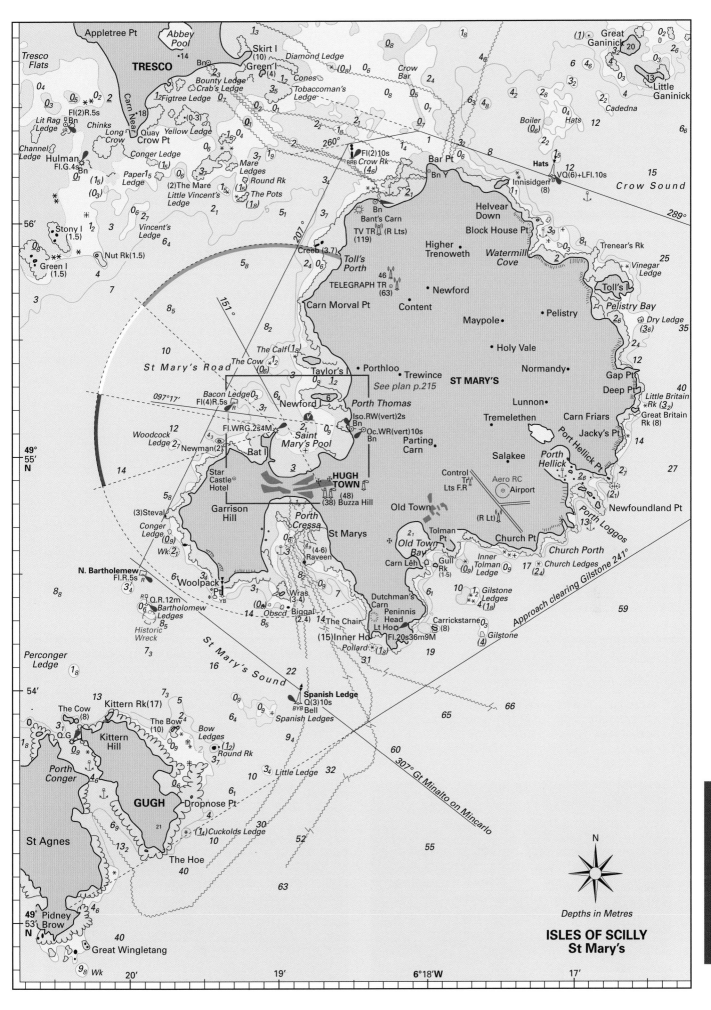

**ISLES OF SCILLY
St Mary's**

Depths in Metres

The Quay at St Mary's with the *Scillonian* at its berth

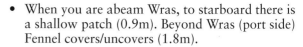

⚓ St Mary's Road

The wide expanse of water in front of St Mary's can be used for anchoring, up to Nut Rock east of Samson, where holding ceases to be good. The area is open on all sides and is used by large boats seeking protection in bad weather. Only use in northwest to north to east and avoid the historic wreck area to the south of Green Island off Samson.

St Mary's Road

⚓ Porth Cressa

This is an alternative to St Mary's Pool as it is protected from west to north to east.

- Approach on 340° leaving Biggal (2.4m) and Wras rock islands (3.4m) to port. Ensure clearance of at least 150m.

- When you are abeam Wras, to starboard there is a shallow patch (0.9m). Beyond Wras (port side) Fennel covers/uncovers (1.8m).

⚓ Anchor between Raveen and Morning Point in 2-8m. Sound in to find a suitable depth.

The anchorage must be abandoned if the wind turns to S-SE as holding is not very good and swell will build up quickly.

Cables run from the shore. Their position is theoretically indicated by two beacons with large yellow topmarks on the shore. In practice the cables run all over but they are well buried under sand and not a problem.

There is public toilet and laundry ashore. A dinghy can be landed on the beach.

⚓ Watermill Cove

This delightful anchorage in the northeast of St Mary's is protected from southwest to west, and also provides a convenient place to wait until there is enough water to cross Crow Bar. The swell builds quickly in winds from the north and south.

There is more protection closer to the shore, but beware of isolated rocks. A course of 45° towards the furthest point of the beach clears the rocks but consult a detailed chart. In good visibility the sandy bottom closer in can be seen and serve as a guide.

Food & transport

Connections to and from the mainland are from St Mary's. The *Scillonian* ferry makes a return trip from Penzance (March-November everyday except Sunday). Skybus runs flights to/from Land's End and Newquay. British International helicopters connect to Penzance.

Small ferries service the off islands and there are boat trips to see seals and bird colonies. All run from the quay.

The shops in Hugh Town are easily accessed from St Mary's Pool and Porth Cressa. There is a Cooperative supermarket, cafés, pubs and restaurants.

A tourist bus, departing from outside the Town Hall, does a circuit of the island.

Hugh Town

Porth Cressa on St Mary's

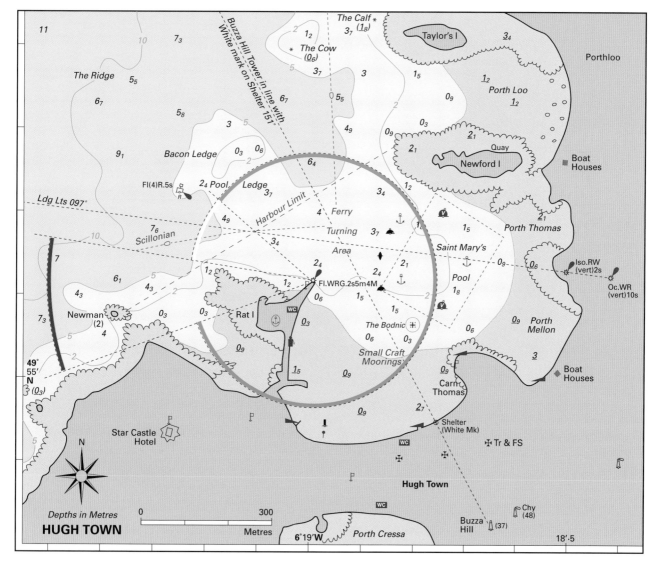

HUGH TOWN

Depths in Metres

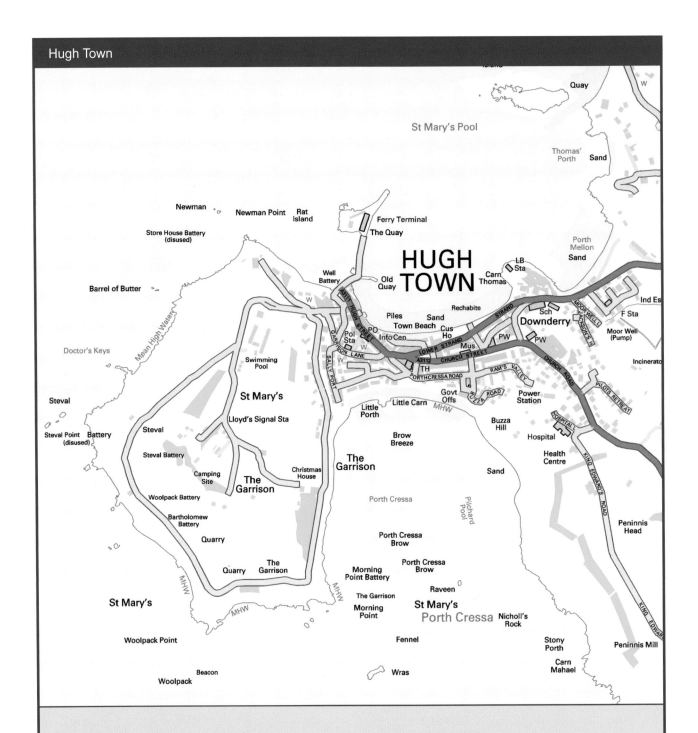

Island Circular bus from The Parade

Skybus, flights to Newquay and Land's End
℧ 0845 710 5555

• British International Helicopters service to
Penzance ℧ 01736 363871

Scillonian III, Isles of Scilly Steamship
Company ℧ 01720 422357
www.ios-travel.co.uk

Post Office, Hugh St, Hugh Town

Restaurants, pubs and cafés in the centre
Star Castle Hotel, Garrison Hill

Tourist Information Centre, Porth Cressa
www.simplyscilly.co.uk
℧ 01720 424031

• Gas from Sibleys or Islands Home Hardware,
Garrison Lane ℧ 01720 422388

Chandlers and marine services:

Southard Engineering, Thorofare, Hugh Town
℧ 01720 422539

Nike Engineering, Porth Mellon
℧ 01720 422991

Rat Island Sail Locker, Rat Island/Quay
℧ 01720 422037

Health Clinic and Hospital, Hospital Lane off
Church Street ℧ 01720 422392
Doctor ℧ 01720 422628

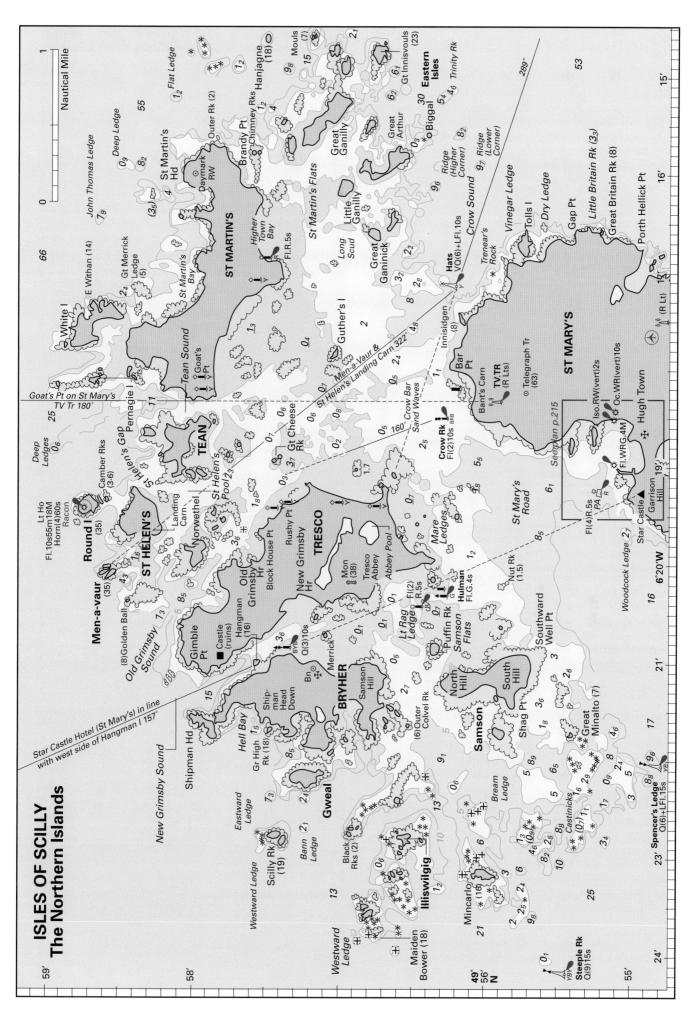

ISLES OF SCILLY
The Northern Islands

Star Castle Hotel (St Mary's) in line
with west side of Hangman I 157°

Goat's Pt on St Mary's
TV Tr 180°

Men-a-Vaur & St Helen's Landing Carn 322°

The northern islands

Samson, Bryher, Tresco, St Helen's, Tean and St Martin's lie across the northern side of Scilly. There are anchorages and moorings, each offering protection in specific conditions. Approach in daylight only. Tidal streams are considerable in the northwest, as fast as 2 knots in springs, creating confused seas and overfalls in wind against tide.

Tresco, St Martin's and Bryher are inhabited but have limited facilities in comparison to St Mary's.

Tresco has a hotel, pub, café and a general store which is well-stocked with gourmet food, including local beef, lobster and crabs, and a large selection of Cornish cheeses. The Abbey Gardens offer an agricultural world tour. Started by Augustus Smith in the 1830s, there are plants from over 80 countries including many subtropical species.

St Martin's has an exceptional bakery, selling sweet and savoury pastries and even pasties made with locally raised island beef. There is a wholefood café which doubles as an award winning evening fish and chip shop and the Seven Stones pub serves food. St Martins on the Isle Hotel is open to non-residents. In Higher Town there is a post office.

Bryher has the smallest resident community on Scilly. There is a post office, grocery store, café, hotel (open to non-residents) and a pub.

Approach & entrance - general

The easiest way to approach the pools and sounds of the northern islands is from the sea but this can be dangerous in bad weather. During springs the tidal stream is strong (2 knots).

The passage from St Mary's Road is much more protected but considerable piloting skills are required. There are numerous rocks to negotiate but the water is often clear enough to see the bottom. The route is not well marked. It is best attempted on a rising tide, after half flood.

⚓ New Grismby Sound

Approach during DAYLIGHT ONLY as there are several off-lying dangers and no lit marks. The tide runs up to 2 knots through the Sound in springs.

New Grimsby Sound from seaward

- DANGERS:
 - Kettle Bottom ledge and rocks, spreading 500m northwest from Tresco,
 - Little Kettle rocks 200m from Tresco at the entrance to the Sound.

- Consult tide tables and tidal atlas diagrams. Awareness of the timing of tidal streams is required to avoid overfalls and rough water in wind-over-tide.

- Keep to the 50m contour line or further out until you can see the Sound and identify the entrance transit.

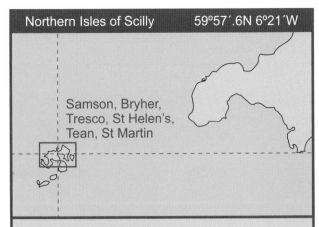

Samson, Bryher, Tresco, St Helen's, Tean, St Martin

New Grismby Sound

- Possible overfalls at the entrance
- Protected, uncomfortable in strong NW or S
- Tidal stream through Sound up to 2kn
- Ⓥ 22 Tresco Estate visitors' moorings
- ⚓ Anchorage before Hangman Island/Tower (7-12m), on Bryher side (2-5m) or beyond moorings (0.5m)
- Harbourmaster
  ☎ 01720 422792 / 07778 601237
- Water and toilets at Tresco Quay
- 🛢 Fuel in cans from Tresco Estate

Old Grismby Sound

- Possible overfalls at the entrance
- Tidal stream through Sound up to 2kn
- More exposed than New Grimsby Sound
- Ⓥ 6 Tresco Estate visitors' moorings
- ⚓ Anchorage 3m clear of moorings Forbidden beyond Long Point to Blockhouse Point

St Helen's Pool

- Tidal stream through the pool is up to 2kn
- ⚓ Good anchorage in 1-7m
- Swell can be significant at high water

Tean Sound

- Rock dangers from seaward
- Tidal stream through Sound is up to 2kn
- Ⓥ 6 Hotel visitors' moorings ☎ 01720 422092
- ⚓ Porth Seal protected E to S
- In Sound before/after moorings, exposed depending on wind

Other anchorages

- NE Samson (0.4m), between Bar Point and Puffin Island
- East of Crow Point, south Tresco (0.6m), rocks and ledges
- Martin's Bay (N St Martin's) for short stop

NORTHERN ISLES

ISLES OF SCILLY

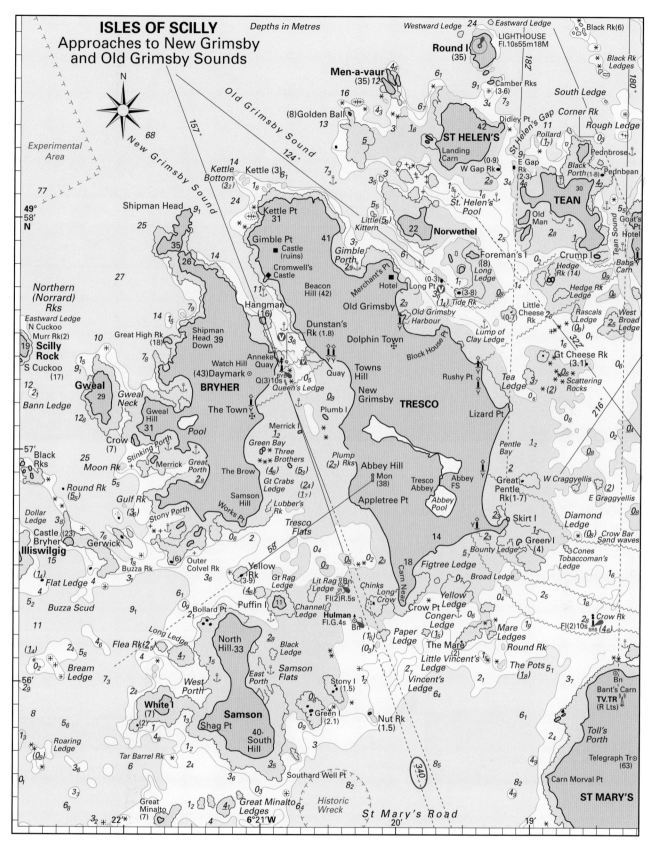

ISLES OF SCILLY
Approaches to New Grimsby and Old Grimsby Sounds

Depths in Metres

- Approach the Sound from seaward on a 157° transit between the west side of Hangman Island in the Sound and the Star Castle Hotel on Garrison Hill, St Mary's.

- Once you enter the Sound steer slightly towards starboard, the steep-sided shore of Bryher. This gives you more clearance of Little Kettle than if you stay on the 157° transit.

- Depth decreases but remains above 2m until the end of the moorings.

- ⚓ Anchor before Hangman Island in 5 to 15m of sand or anywhere to the west of the moorings (the east side has a ledge of rock all the way along).

- Ⓥ Tresco Estate moorings: book ahead with the harbourmaster or take and empty buoy when you arrive. Rafting up is not permitted.

New Grimsby Sound

Visitors' moorings

Tresco quay

Green Bay

⚓ Alternatively anchor beyond the moorings, but be aware depth decreases rapidly (to drying 0.3m). There is a 'pool' (0.4m) alongside Plumb Island. You must remain clear of the cables that run between Tresco and Bryher, clearly marked by beacons with large yellow top marks.

If your boat has legs or can dry you can anchor in sand in Green Bay (dries 1.2m) west of Merrick Island. Stay well above 49°57′ to avoid Brow Ledge and the Three Brothers rocks.

New Grimsby Sound from St Mary's Road

A large part of this passage dries. There are numerous rocks to avoid but in good light they can be seen in the clear water. Time your passage to half flood and do not attempt at night.

- In St Mary's Road get to a position where you can identify Nut Rock and the Hulman beacon Fl.G.4s. The beacon is small and flimsy, and has a green triangle top mark.

Gig training in New Grimsby Sound

- Head for Hulman and leave the beacon 50m to starboard in order to clear the rock ledge (dries 3.7m).

- Round Hulman and turn N-NE. Little Rag Ledge to port and Chinks to starboard dry 1.3m level with Little Rag beacon Fl(2)R.5s. The beacon is small with a red square top mark.

There are two options from Little Rag:

1 From the Little Rag beacon there is a transit between Merrick Island and Hangman Island that clears the isolated rocks but passes over a sand bar (drying 1.7m) and near to rocks (drying 1.1m) which extend from Appletree Point.

    or

2 Alternatively, round the Little Rag beacon and turn towards Samson Hill on a bearing of 302°.

- The next line is difficult to judge. You are going to head towards Plumb Hill on Tresco when it is on 45°. You may be able to rely on two white posts in transit (placed there by the harbourmaster) which clear rocks from Appletree Point. In addition a line to Mincarlo clear of Works Point (southern point of Samson Hill) clears Lubbers Rock to port.

- Pass between Lubbers Rock (dries 1.7m) and the sand bank (dries 1.7m) which extends SW from Plumb Hill/Abbey Hill on Tresco.

- Aim towards Merrick Island to clear Plump Rocks (dries 2.2m) to starboard.

- When passing between Merrick Island and Plumb Island, stay towards Merrick Island to avoid two isolated rocks (drying, depth uncharted) to starboard.

- Depth begins to increase. Head for the Sound and anchor or pick up a buoy as described in the approach from seaward.

New Grimsby Sound from the southwest

From the soutwestern side of Scilly the passage to the Sound is straightforward as far as the Tresco Flats. However, do not attempt it in strong southwest winds, in poor visibility or if there is significant swell.

- Staying south of the Steeple Rock west cardinal Q(9)15s, identify Mincarlo island to port and Samson further ahead to starboard.

- In the distance you should be able to make out Yellow Rock island, roughly half way between Bryher and Samson.

- The transit on 58° between Yellow Rock and the monument on Tresco (above Appletree Point) is a good guide. 500m before Yellow Rock beware 0.9m, almost on the transit.

- Round Yellow Rock, leaving 50m to starboard. When you are abeam the Little Rag red beacon proceed with the approach from St Mary's Road.

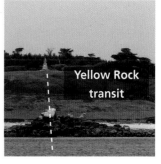

Yellow Rock transit

⚓ Old Grismby Sound

Access to Old Grimsby Sound is less easy than to New Grimsby Sound, as there are dangerous rocks and no transit that clears them all. In addition, the only light is from the lighthouse at Round Island.

Approach during DAYLIGHT ONLY and in calm conditions. From seaward it may be helpful to approach at low water when the dangers are easily seen.

Before a first approach we recommend a reconnaissance trip on foot from Tresco at low water to gain familiarity.

The tidal stream is strong (2 knots) along the northwest during springs, and overfalls appear between Kettle Bottom and Golden Ball (rock formations on either side as you enter from the sea). In springs the tide runs up to 2 knots through the Sound.

The passage from Crow's Sound will exercise your piloting skills in full. Time your route to a rising tide, best after mid-tide. In good weather the bottom is visible most of the time.

Old Grimsby Sound from seaward

- DANGERS AT THE ENTRANCE:
- Kettle Bottom ledge and rocks, spreading 500m northwest from Tresco (W of entrance)
- Golden Ball, Golden Ball Brow and ledge extending 0.7M from Saint Helen and Men-a-vaur.

- DANGERS IN THE SOUND:
- Little Kittern (dries 1.9m) in the centre of the channel, NE of Gimble Porth

- Tide Rock (dries 1.4m) in the channel between Block House Point (Tresco) and rock islands Peashopper, Crow's and Foreman's NE of the point
- Ensure you know the location of Kettle Bottom and Golden Ball.

- Get into a position where you can clearly identify Norwethel Island on the east of the Sound and the gap between this island and Tresco. Aim for the centre of the gap, on a bearing of 124° (close to NE Tresco).

- Once the northern shore of Tresco is on your starboard quarter you are in the start of the Sound. Remain 100m from the Tresco shore.

- Little Kittern (dries 1.9m) is NE of Gimble Porth cove, on a line between the centre of the cove and the lighthouse at Round Island. It is also on a line between the highest point on Norwethel and the NE tip of Tresco. At low water it can be seen. If it is covered take great care to ensure you leave it to port.

- Once past Little Kittern aim east of the moorings, NE of the quay. Beware of a ledge (0.3m) in the channel beyond the moorings and Tide Rock (on a line between Block House Point and Peashopper).

Ⓥ Pick up one of the Tresco Estate buoys. ⚓ There is room to anchor either side in 2.5m, but anchoring is not permitted inside the harbour.

Old Grimsby Sound

NORTHERN ISLES

ISLES OF SCILLY

Old Grimsby Sound from Crow's Sound

The route to Old Grimsby Sound from Crow's Sound or St Mary's Road needs to be timed to have sufficient water, ideally from a flood tide.

Start from near the Crow Rock isolated danger mark Fl(2)10s, on the northern side of St Mary's Road. Keep on a course of 160°, transiting the danger mark and the TV tower on St Mary's:

• DANGERS to port, from the transit bearing:
- Diamond Ledge (5.4m to drying 0.6m), east of the southern side of Tresco (sand dunes).
- Pentle Rocks (2.8m to 1.7m), east of the centre of Pentle Bay.

• After Pentle Rocks aim to pass 100m away from Lizard Point, to avoid an isolated rock (dries 2m NE of Lizard Point), Tea Ledge (dries 3.7m, 200m NNE of Lizard Point) and a scattering of rocks to the east below Great Cheese Rock (always visible 3.1m).

• Pass the two-yellow-diamond post at Rushy Point and aim for the line of mooring buoys.

• DANGERS before the buoys:
- Tide Rock (dries 1.4m) in the channel between Block House Point (Tresco) and the rock islets: Peashopper, Crow's and Foreman NE of the point.
- Cook's Rock (dries 4.3m) off Block House Point.

Alternatively follow the transit on 322° between the centre of Men-a-vaur, beyond St Helen's, and the prominent hillock Landing Carn on SW St Helen's.

• When you are abeam Great Cheese Rock (always visible 3.1m) at 49°57′.4N bear to port to avoid the Chinks and Hunter's Lump which are close, either side of the transit. The yellow cable indicator beacon on Rushy Point is a useful reference.

• Once you are 200m from Rushy Point, head for the line of mooring buoys. Take care to avoid Tide Rock and Cook's Rock.

Pick up a Tresco Estate buoy or anchor.

Men-a-vaur

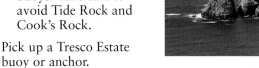

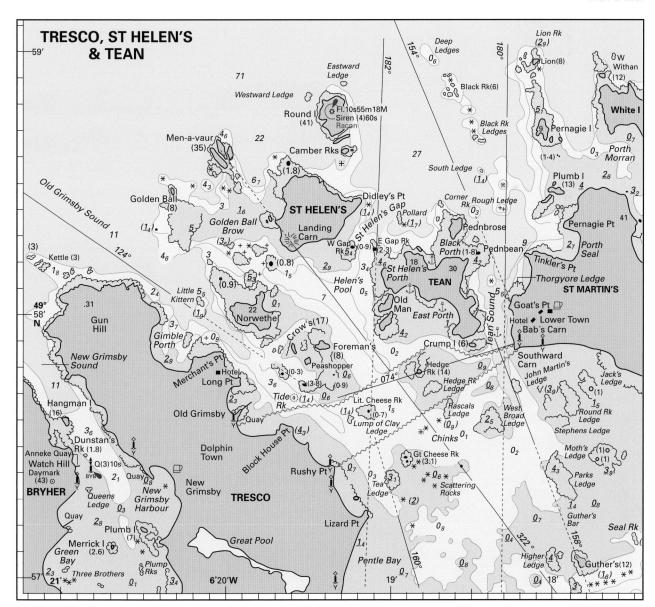

⚓ St Helen's Pool

St Helen's Pool, on the opposite side of Norwethel Island from Old Grimsby, is a quiet anchorage which is protected most of the time. The rocks of Golden Brow, west of St Helen's, block the swell from the west during low water, and this makes the pool a very useful bolthole.

⚓ At high water there is swell but some areas are protected. The anchorage, in sand, holds well with depths between 1 and 7 metres and plenty of space to swing.

The Porths, east of St Helen's Pool and to the south of Tean, is a pristine and protected anchorage in sand if you can dry out.

From Old Grimsby

With sufficient tide it is possible to cross south of Peashopper and Foreman's, and in good visibility the various rocks and shallow patches can be easily distinguished.

- Take care with Tide Rock (dries 1.4m) in the main Grimsby channel, between Block House Point and Peashopper.

- Pass in a NNE direction 200m south of Little Cheese Rock (roughly half way between Little Cheese Rock and Great Cheese Rock, which is always visible).

- Bear round towards the Pool. The transit between Men-a-vaur and Landing Carn on St Helen is a useful guide but there is plenty of space.

From Crow's Sound

Follow the transit on 322° between the centre of Men-a-vaur, beyond St Helen's, and the prominent hillock Landing Carn at the southwestern end of St Helen's.

- When you are just past Great Cheese Rock steer to port (away from the transit) to avoid Chinks rocks and Hunter's Lump which narrowly enclose the transit. The south of Chinks rocks is at the latitude of the ruin on Block House Point, Tresco.

- Use Great Cheese Rock (always visible 3.1m) and Little Cheese Rock (always visible 0.7m) as a guide.

- Keep 100m from Great Cheese Rock, then when it is to the south aim for St Helen's Pool.

From seaward, St Helen's Gap

The gap NE of the Pool, between West Gap rock and East Gap rock, is deep but narrow and runs between two reefs. Beyond the reefs a sand spit extends south from St Helen's and dries 2.9m. Do not attempt this passage until you have gained some familiarity, and never in poor visibility, strong winds or swell.

The Pool from St Helen's Gap, Tresco beyond

St Helens' Pool, an isolated and protected anchorage

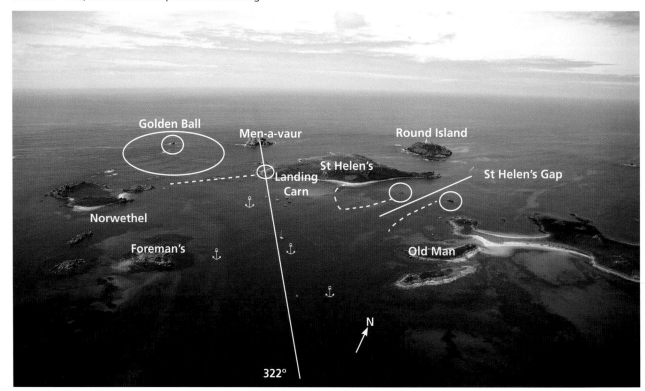

⚓⚓ Tean Sound

Tean (pronounced Tee-an) Sound lies between St Martin's and uninhabited Tean. It is deep, picturesque and generally quiet but needs to be approached with great care as there are dangerous isolated rocks throughout. Do not attempt in strong winds or swell.

⚓ Porth Seal is very exposed to the W / NW and any swell. ⚓ Shelter is better in the Sound, where you can pick up one of the visitors' moorings that belong to St Martin's on the Isle, a posh hotel owned by the Prince of Wales which opened in 1989. The hotel is right by the quay and there is no mooring fee if you eat there. The narrow pool where the buoys are located is protected but can get choppy in wind-over-tide, a tide that can be 2 knots in springs. ⚓ South of the buoys there is an anchorage.

Tean Sound from seaward

This approach is tricky at the best of times. DO NOT ATTEMPT IN STRONG WIND OR SWELL. There are two rock ledges that stretch from the Sound and reach beyond the level of Round Island, plus several isolated rocks close to the entrance. The sea may break as far as Porth Seal.

The approach is easier at low water when many of the rocks are exposed. At high water there are few visual clues to establish your position.

Keep to a depth of 50m or beyond until you have planned your entrance.

- DANGERS FROM SEA: rock ledges extending east and west of the north-south approach.
- East: Lion Island and Rock (always visible) mark the northern end on the east side, with a dangerous wreck 50m beyond. Lion's position is 400m beyond the northern edge of White Island.
- West: Black Rock and ledges.

There are two options for entering the Sound: on a 180° course towards St Mary's TV Tower or coming from Round Island.

Option 1: 180° course towards St Mary's TV Tower

- Approach on the 180° transit between St Mary's TV Tower and Goat's Point, St Martin's (where the Hotel is located).

- Turn to starboard on the 30m contour line to avoid rocks west of Lion. You need to be 250m away from Lion, but too far west takes you to the Black rocks. Stay in at least 20m when passing Lion.

- Once you are past Lion return to the TV Tower/Goat's Point transit. To starboard, the western ledges Black Rock is always visible and the southern end of Black Rock Ledges uncovers (dries 1.9m).

- Depth decreases rapidly. Abreast of Pernagie Island you cross the 10m contour line.

Tean Sound

Tean Sound looking towards Tean from St Martin's

- DANGERS west of the TV Tower/Goat's Point transit:
- Rock awash at chart datum, north side of Plum Island.
- Rough Ledge (1.4m), south side of the exposed rock extending SW from Plumb Island.

- Before you come level with the north of Plumb Island steer to port to avoid the rock awash danger followed by Rough Ledge.

- After passing the southern end of exposed rocks SW of Plum Island, return to the transit and head for the hotel's buoys.

  ⚓ Anchor in Porth Seal, just beyond Plumb Island. Sound in to 2-4m in sand.

- Ⓥ If you are proceeding to pick a hotel buoy you need to be careful of two further DANGERS: isolated rock (dries 1.4m), east of the transit just south of Tinklers Point, and Thongyore Ledge (dries 1.4m), east of the transit. Depth decreases to 2.7-3.7m at the level of Thongyore. Once close to Goat's Point head for the buoys, which are in 5-8m depth. ⚓ Anchoring is also possible south of the buoys in 5-7m.

Option 2: coming from Round Island

The second option provides more space to seaward but it is less easy to judge position and there are several isolated dangers difficult to locate close to the Sound.

- From a position north of Round Island, sail to the 50m contour line. The island is steep-to but take care with Eastward Ledge (dries 2.9m) which lies between the 10m and 20m contour lines to the north.

- Proceed southeast around the island keeping a distance of 200m from the shore. Aim for Pednbrose, north of Tean. Alternatively follow a 154° course towards Goat's Point on St Martin's.

- Staying in at least 20m get into a position where you are due west of Plumb Island and due north of Pednbrose. DANGERS, NE to SE, facing Plumb Island are:
  - South Ledge (dries 1.4m)
  - Rock awash at chart datum
  - Rough Ledge (dries 1.4m)
  - Corner Rock (0.3m)

- Heading for Plumb Island you can clear the rock awash at chart datum with sufficient tide. Better still, aim to sail around Rough Ledge at low water when all but Corner Rock is exposed.

- Ⓥ⚓ Once you are on the St Mary's TV Tower/ Goat's Point 180° transit, follow the instructions above to a hotel buoy or anchorage beyond.

Tean Sound from Crow's Sound

The route to Tean Sound from Crow's Sound or St Mary's Road is straightforward but requires sufficient water, ideally from a flood tide.

The hotel plus landing quay at St Martin's

Porth Seal

On the transit between Men-a-vaur and St Helen's Landing Carn, follow a course of 322° (or keep on a bearing of 135° from the Hats south cardinal VQ(6)+LFl.10s):

- Pass Guther's Island, keeping sufficiently to the west to avoid Higher Ledge (dries 4m).

- When the St Mary's TV Tower is due south turn onto a northerly course, keeping the tower on a back-bearing of 180°.

- The TV tower transit is then clear of dangers to Tean Sound, except for West Broad Ledge (dries dries 2.5m) which is a broad expanse of rock right on the transit. The ledge begins when the ruin on Block House Point is due west. You are clear when Hedge Rock is due west (always visible).

Bulb collection on St Martin's

⚓ St Martin's & the Eastern Isles

St Martin's is surrounded by dangerous rocks but the careful navigator is rewarded with beautiful anchorages which are often deserted. These are best considered for daytime visits only, unless the weather is very calm.

St Martin's has some stunning beaches of golden sand and the crystal-clear turquoise sea gives a tropical feel. Ashore is a vineyard, bakery, farm shop and superb walking on the downs, which are often covered in purple heather and golden gorse.

The Eastern Isles require extremely careful navigation and should be attempted only in settled weather. The approach from seaward needs to take into account dangerous rocks and tidal races. This is a favourite place of grey seals who haul out to bask in the sun. Ragged Island is one of their breeding grounds and is seasonally closed.

⚓ St Martin's anchorages

Higher Town Bay in St Martin's Flats is an anchorage for boats that can dry (dries 0.2m). The bay is open but St Martin's provides protection from west to north to northeast.

Perpitch, a little drying cove to the east of the flats, is less inviting due to a rock ledge protruding from Chimney Rocks.

On the northern side, Bread and Cheese Cove (and Stony Porth) has a sand, rock and weed bottom (3-5m) and is protected from east to south to west. Approach on the western side to avoid Tearing Ledge, north of the cove.

St Martin's Bay is a large area. It has a mixture of sand, rock and weed in 2-5m and is protected from east to south to west. From east to west, consideration must be given to Murr Rock (visible island 12m), Santamana Ledges (dries 4.9m), Mackerel Rocks

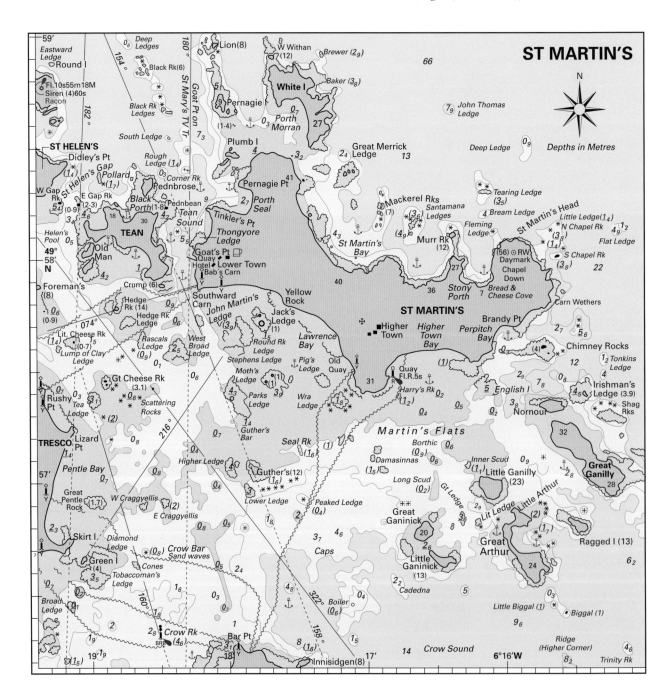

(visible islands 4.1m and 7m), Little Ledge of Mackerel Rocks (dries 3.6m) and Great Merrick Ledge (visible islets 1-5m plus expanse of rock drying 3.9m). Blocking your way on the northwestern side is White Island and surrounding ledges. This may seem a daunting list but there is a fair bit of space. On the eastern side Bull's Porth is backed by cliffs, while to the west there is a beautiful white sandy beach to enjoy.

Around White Island, Porth Morran is quite exposed and has a bottom of sand and rock. The setting is stunning, but only good in calm conditions.

⚓ The Eastern Isles

This area should be considered for temporary daytime anchorages only, and not attempted until you have graduated to advanced level Scilly navigation! There are many rocks and not much room for error, although the gap between Great Ganilly and Little Ganilly/ Little Arthur/Ragged Island and between Great Arthur and Little Ganinick is feasible. Remember that the tidal stream can make the sea treacherous to the east.

Use a trip line in case of rocks and TAKE GREAT CARE.

St Martin's

The southern islands

St Agnes, Gugh, Annet and the Western Rocks are the most southerly of the Isles of Scilly, beyond which is the Bishop Rock Lighthouse. Annet and the Western Rocks are permanently closed to protect populations of seals and breeding birds. The Atlantic swell, overfalls and granite outcrops make the Western Rocks notoriously dangerous, even on a calm day, and they are witness to hundreds of wrecks. In 1707 over 2,000 lives were lost in a single night when the British Fleet, under the command of Sir Cloudsley Shovell, foundered here on their return from the Mediterranean and it was this disaster that spurred the Admiralty on to find a reliable method of establishing longitude (see 'Longitude' on page 237).

St Agnes and Gugh are joined by a sand bar, which is covered except towards HW springs. Either side of the bar are anchorages that are protected in some conditions. When the bar is uncovered the current between the islands is strong.

St Agnes is inhabited. There are two cafés, a fish restaurant, post office and grocery store and a pub, the Turk's Head, that serves food.

⚓ Porth Conger

The approach to Porth Conger is straightforward from St Mary's Road. In sequence, be aware of Perconger (1.9m), Littler Perconger (2.4m) and the visible Cow islet. It is best to start due west of the Bartholomew Ledges beacon Q.R rather than cut the corner.

- Approach on a southeasterly course toward the cove, leaving The Cow rock islet (visible 8m) to port.

⚓ Anchor in 1-4m before the jetty, or beyond if you can dry out. Ensure you are sufficiently away from the private moorings. **Ⓥ** The Turk's Head has a couple of buoys that can be used by visitors ☎ 01720 422434.

St Agnes and Gugh

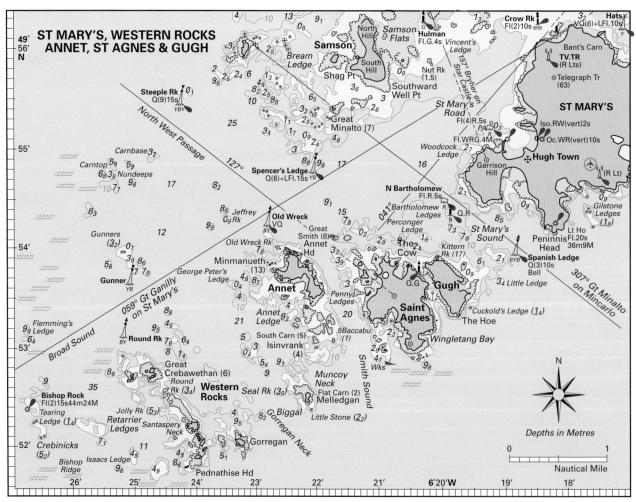

Porth Conger between St Agnes and Gugh

The Cove with the bar between St Agnes and Gugh clearly visible

The anchorage is protected from northeast to south to southwest but holding is reputedly not very good. There is protection from the southeast but not if the bar uncovers, when there is a strong stream and swell.

⚓ The Cove

The approach to the Cove is straightforward on a NNW heading. Stay in the centre to avoid a couple of isolated rocks close to shore. Cables that are marked on the charts are well buried.

The Cove is protected from southwest to north to east. If the bar uncovers the stream runs hard and you are exposed to NW.

Transit: Old Lighthouse and Tins Walbert beacon 127°

St Agnes and Gugh

Interest

The Isles of Scilly are made of granite formed when two continental landmasses, Gondwana and Laurussia, collided about 300 million years ago. Lying initially under the Variscan Mountains, erosion and changing sea levels eventually exposed a chain of dome-like intrusions that stretched from Dartmoor in the east to the undersea outcrop of Haig Fras forty miles northwest. Archaeological finds, such as flint arrowheads, suggest that the first humans to reach Scilly were Mesolithic peoples who moved north from the Mediterranean about 10,000 years ago. Neolithic people (4000BC-2500BC) then left their mark but the majority of archaeological remains date from the Bronze Age (2500BC-700BC) when Scilly was detached from the mainland but St Mary's, Tresco, St Martin's and Bryher formed one large island, known as the isle of Ennor. By this time, there were settled communities living in small round huts whose stone foundations can be seen today on land and, at low tide, covered with seaweed between the islands. Each house would have been conical, with timbers supporting a roof made from turf or straw. Cooking would have taken place in the centre over an open fire. During the Bronze Age the dead were disposed of by cremation and interment. On Scilly there are the remains of burial cists, stone chests sunk into the ground, and over seventy entrance graves, large underground repositories that exist only here and in West Cornwall.

The courtyard house was a feature of the Iron Age (700BC-400AD) and an example can be seen on St Mary's. Frequent contact with trading ships came later, when Britain was ruled by Rome, and then around 1,000AD the low-lying central plain of Ennor was breached and the islands of today emerged. Land was granted to those favoured by the king, to Richard de Wika and the Benedictine monks of Tavistock Abbey by Henry I and to the Black Prince, the first Duke of Cornwall, by Edward III, but as more and more agricultural land was lost to the sea and the islands became a target for Viking and Irish raiders they sank into obscurity for about 400 years. It was the Godolphin family, a Cornish dynasty, who turned their fortune around. Taking a lease from the Duchy of Cornwall in 1570 they set about creating some order by, for example, dividing the land into manageable plots and building defences, though it was Elizabeth I who, having been spooked by the Spanish Armada, ordered the construction of the Star Castle on St Mary's in 1593. The future King Charles II stayed in the Star Castle in 1646 while fleeing from Parliamentary forces during the English Civil War and Royalist attacks on Dutch Ships led to Holland declaring war on the Isles of Scilly in 1651, the Dutch Government declaring peace formally only in 1986!

Pilotage fees provided a small income by the end of the 18th century, but the islanders' fortunes were again at a low ebb. Many were farming at barely subsistence level when Augustus Smith (1804-1872) bought the lease for £20,000 in 1834. Although not universally popular, he turned the islands' fortune around for a second time by developing a cut flower industry. Smith recognised that frost-free winters made it possible to produce flowers earlier than anywhere on the mainland and the development of the railway meant that they could be taken to Penzance by boat and on to London by train within a day. Smith also planted trees to provide shelter for agriculture, established proper schooling and built a new quay at Hugh Town.

New coastal batteries were built on St Mary's at the beginning of the 20th century in response to political instability, and during the first world war flying boats were stationed at Tresco. A squadron of Hurricanes were based on the islands during the second world war to provide cover for the convoys coming across the Atlantic.

While sailing around the Scilly islands it is likely that you will come across the Cornish pilot gig, a six-oared rowing boat. There are races for women every Wednesday and for men every Friday, April to September, and in between the teams are out practising. Gigs were originally a general-purpose work boat and there are records of them being used in rescue attempts from the 17th century. They were also used to take pilots out to ships arriving from across the Atlantic and a lot of competition ensued because the first gig to get their pilot on board got the job. All modern racing gigs are based on the *Treffry*, which was built in 1838 by William Peters of St Mawes. The Standard's Officer of the Cornish Pilot Gig Association, the sport's governing body, inspects each gig three times during construction. It must be 32ft long with a beam of 4´10˝ and built of Cornish narrow leaf elm. Although most pilot gigs are in the West Country they are also found as far away as France, the Faroe Islands, Australia and the USA. Since 1990 the annual World Pilot Gig Championships have taken place on the Isles of Scilly during the first May bank holiday weekend. More than 2,000 rowers and spectators usually attend, thus doubling the resident population.

The Bishop Rock lighthouse is a marvel of engineering. The rock itself, rising almost vertically from 50m below sea level, is only about 15 by 30 metres wide and completely covered in high spring tides. An early lighthouse, built on St Agnes 5 miles away, had a coal-burning crescent that was barely visible, but for many years the construction of a lighthouse on The Bishop seemed impossible. A first attempt was made in the late 1840s. During the summer months of three consecutive years a cast iron structure was put together and then attached to the rock with huge bolts. All seemed well but it was washed away by a huge storm just before it was commissioned. Work restarted in 1858 on a design involving a solid tower of dovetailed blocks of Cornish granite but neither did this stand the test of time. A huge storm in April 1874 generated waves over 40 metres high which engulfed the tower and washed away the lantern. Seven years later, in 1881, a outer stone skin was built around the remaining structure and extra height was added. This third attempt was successful and since then the structure has been without problems. The lighthouse became fully automated in 1992.

The old lifeboat station on St Mary's

St Mary's

St Mary's is the largest of the Isles of Scilly and home to about 80% of the resident population. Hugh Town, situated on the sandbar that separates the Garrison from the rest of the island, is the 'capital', but don't be fooled into thinking big. Less than 2,000 people live on St Mary's and it is just 2½ by 1¾ miles in size.

St Mary's is where most of the visitors to the Scillies arrive and stay. There is a small airport and the *Scillonian* ferry, crossing from Penzance, arrives at Hugh Town quay. From the Old Pier nearby, colourful inter-island launches ferry people to the off-islands, as all inhabited islands other than St Mary's are collectively known.

Hugh Town has a hospital-cum-health centre, various banks and some shops. Tourists are well catered for with numerous pubs, restaurants, cafés and art galleries. The Tourist Information Centre is situated on Main Street. Cars are common and a circular bus (Easter to October from The Parade) links most of the island's communities. Vintage car and bus tours run during the summer and there are bicycles for hire. Taxis are normally available throughout the year.

The 9-mile coastal footpath can be walked in a single day but you may prefer to take a bus from Hugh Town to the north of the island and walk back. The Higher and Lower Moor Nature Trails are a delight. Their flora and fauna are described in some leaflets produced by the IOS Environment Trust, available from the Tourist Information Centre. The highest point on the island, and the setting for the telegraph

mast, is only 46m, so walking is not a serious challenge!

About a mile from Hugh Town is Carreg Dhu. This community garden, started by Richard and June Lethbridge in 1986, has 1.5 acres of sub-tropical plants, lying within a disused ram-pit quarry. There is an area dedicated to the preservation of narcissi that were grown on the island in the 1840s when the flower industry began.

Those interested in archaeology should not miss Halangy Down Ancient Settlement and Bant's Carn Entrance Grave. The settlement dates from the Iron Age and includes some roundhouses and one courtyard house. The grave is one of the best examples on the Isles of Scilly and dates from late Stone Age/early Bronze Age. A booklet, available at the site, gives details. The largest entrance grave on Scilly is at Porth Hellick Down and is known as the Giant's Tomb.

Pelistry Bay has a fantastic beach and Toll's Island, accessible at some states of tide, has a number of kelp pits, once used to burn seaweed to make soda and potash for the glass and soap industry.

Old Town is built on the site of an early medieval settlement, called Porthennor. This ancient administrative centre was serving the community before the landscape of today had emerged from the single island of Ennor. A medieval granite trough once used for salting and preserving fish can still be seen, as can a curve of jumbled rocks, visible at

low tide, which are the remains of a medieval pier. There is little left of a 13th-century castle as it was demolished to provide stone for the Star Castle within the Garrison.

Fortifications around the Garrison headland, west of Hugh Town, are worth exploring and the ramparts make an enjoyable stroll. The eight-pointed Star Castle built in 1593 by Elizabeth I is now a hotel. It is open to non-residents and has an exceptional restaurant. It is part of a chain of castles that stretch along the south coast of England, including Pendennis castle in Falmouth.

Hugh Town has a small museum where the displays include a fully rigged pilot gig from 1877. Gig racing takes place twice a week on Wednesdays and Fridays

Tresco Abbey Gardens

during the summer. Races begin from Nut Rock, east of Samson, and finish at St Mary's quay.

Tresco

When Augustus Smith leased the Isles of Scilly from the Duchy of Cornwall in 1834 he settled on Tresco and the island is still in the hands of his descendants, the Dorrien-Smiths. It is the only island that is leased privately by one family. Augustus built his home, Tresco Abbey, in 1841 and, amidst the adjacent ruins of the 12th-century Benedictine Priory of St Nicholas, set about establishing a garden in a series of walled enclosures that offered protection from winter gales. Windbreaks of Monterey pine and Monterey cypress from California enabled the south-facing hillside to be incorporated and exotic plants from around the world gradually became established. Five generations have now made a contribution and today the gardens, dubbed 'Kew with the roof off', contain over 20,000 plants from more than 80 countries. There is Burmese honeysuckle, Australian scarlet bottle-brush, echeiums from the Canary Isles, the South African bird of paradise and a New Zealand flame tree that is over 40ft tall. Towering eucalyptus and date palms, gigantic ice plants and cacti, together with rarities such as lobster claw, make this a world-class garden. Many of these plants would stand no chance just a few miles away on the mainland, yet here, even at the winter equinox, more than 30 are likely to be in flower. Within the garden there are still some architectural remains from the priory, which was abandoned in the 16th century, and also a splendid Roman shrine with relief carvings of a dagger and axe, indicating that it was probably a sacrificial altar. Thirty figureheads from ships lost around the Isles of Scilly's rocky coast make up the Valhalla collection, which was begun by Augustus Smith and dates mainly from the middle to the end of the 19th century.

Tresco is the second-largest of the islands. The north, wild and wind-swept, contrasts with the gentle south, where there are some splendid sandy beaches. Most of the accommodation and facilities are run by Tresco Estate. New Grimsby is the location for the Island Hotel, the New Inn (which serves food), a café and Tresco Stores (℡ 01720 422806). The stores are exceptionally well-stocked with food from Scilly and the West Country. There is usually local beef, lobsters and crabs and up to 20 different types of Cornish cheese. Bikes can be rented from the Estate Office nearby.

A walk around the whole island is about 5 miles. There are prehistoric hut circles and boundary walls on the foreshore at Pentle Bay and Bathinghouse Porth. Although submerged, they can sometimes be seen at low tide. In the north of the island the remains of Cromwell's Castle, constructed to guard the main approach to the island in 1651, can be seen. Nearby are the ruins of its predecessor, King Charles's Castle, built in 1550. Piper's Hole is an underground cave with a freshwater pool that goes back 50 metres into the cliffs. It can be reached from the cliff edge but with some difficulty. Remember to take a torch! Tregarthen Hill has wonderful views across to St Martin's and on the southern side of the summit there is a fine entrance grave. East of Green Porth is a block house built in 1554 to protect the anchorage of St Helen's Pool.

There are occasional bird-watching walks guided by RSPB wardens. The Great Pool and Abbey Pool are good places to see wading birds and on the heathland there are linnets and stonechats. Details from the Tourist Information Centre on St Mary's.

St Martin's

St Martin's is the third-largest island and many people think it is the most picturesque. Anchored, in vivid aquamarine water and looking onto golden sandy beaches fringed with marram grass, you have to remind yourself that this is not the Caribbean! There are palm trees and hedgerows full of wild agapanthus, lily and Hottentot fig. The downs are covered in purple heather and golden gorse and flowers and vegetables are cultivated in tiny sheltered fields.

St Martin's has just over one hundred residents and there are three main settlements: Higher Town, Middle Town and Lower Town. Just 2 miles in length and approximately half a mile wide, this island caters exceptionally well for foodies. St Martins' Bakery (℡ 01720 423444) in Higher Town is victualling heaven. There are cakes, quiches, a wide selection of English and continental breads, and pasties containing beef from cows raised on the island. Often there is Atlantic salmon and grey mullet which has been smoked on the premises. Toby Tobin-Dougan and Paul Websdale's experience of setting up the bakery and merging with the Seven Stones Pub (Lower Town) is told in *The Island Ingredient*, which also contains photos and some delicious recipes. Little Arthur Wholefood Café, which at night becomes Adam's Fish and Chips (℡ 01720 422457), is also in Higher

Lobsters for sale

Town. The café uses ingredients from the owner's adjacent organic farm and there are some delicious surprises, such as nettle and onion soup. The fish, anything from lobster, ling, pollack or monkfish, is likely to have been caught earlier in the day. Glenmore shop sells produce from the farm, including eggs and vegetables. Top quality lobster, crab and crawfish can be bought to eat on board, cooked or alive, from Mark and Suzanne Pender who run Isles of Scilly Shellfish (℡ 01720 423898). Mark comes from a Scillonian seafaring family that stretches back over 400 years. He works alone and is mindful of conservation, for example returning females carrying eggs to the sea. St Martin's Vineyard (℡ 01720 423418) is open for tours and for wine tasting from Easter to October. The grapes, chosen to suit a cool damp northern climate, include Madeleine Angevine, Orion, Seyval Blanc, Rondo and Regent. Wines from the Camel Valley, Cornwall, and from the Sharpham estate in Devon are also for sale here. If you prefer to eat out there is a hotel, St Martin's on the Isle (℡ 01720 422092), which is open to non-residents. Higher Town also has a post office.

A walk around St Martin's (6 miles) would help work up an appetite. The south-facing coast path is easy but the north is wilder and harder going. St Martin's Head daymark was erected in the 17th century. Nearby are the remains of a Napoleonic signal station where semaphore messages were relayed to ships off shore. If the vegetation is not too high you may be able to see the foundations of an early Christian chapel that probably operated an early lighthouse. They were usually run by religious orders, the reason why so many English headlands are named after saints.

Those with an interest in geology should cross over to White Island, which is just off St Martin's most northerly tip and accessible only at low water. In the north is the only remnant of sediment, slate, from the Variscan Mountain that was once up to 5 miles above the granite of the Scilly Islands we see today. In the south of White Island is the remains of a kelp pit. The Nance family from Falmouth established a cottage industry here in the 17th century providing ash for soap and glass making. Seaweed would be dried on the shore, set alight, covered with stones and turf and left to smoulder for up to eight hours. Twenty tons of seaweed produced just one ton of kelp, so it was labour intensive, and the noxious smoke was very unpopular. Burnt vegetable matter such as kelp is what gives old glass its green tinge.

Knackyboy Carn, between Higher and Middle Town, is an entrance grave where seventy pottery urns filled with cremated human remains were found in the 1950s. Cruther's Hill, south of Higher Town, has a number of entrance graves and there are splendid views towards Tresco and St Mary's over Crow Bar.

Bryher

Bryher has less than a hundred residents and is the smallest community on Scilly. The rugged west coast is open to the full force of the Atlantic and the prevailing southwesterlies, and Hell Bay lashed by gales is an awesome sight. In contrast, the east coast looks out across a sheltered channel to Tresco and in spring and early summer the hedgerows are full of delicate wild flowers, including daffodils and narcissi. The roads are little more than tracks and there are very few vehicles. Three quarters of the island is open heathland.

Archaeological sites include a line of large seaweed-covered boulders disappearing into the water at Green Bay that were once the boundary of a Bronze Age field. On Samson Hill there are a number of Bronze Age entrance graves and a large concentration of burial mounds are to be found on Shipman Head Down.

Rushy Bay has the best beach on Bryher and from the east coast of the island it is possible to wade across to Tresco when the tide is especially low. Facilities include the splendid Hell Bay hotel (open to non-residents) a couple of cafés, a post office and grocery store and England's most Westerly pub, The Fraggle Rock.

Landing is at Church Quay (high water) and at Anneka's Quay (low water). The latter was built during one of Anneka's Rice's television challenges and is known affectionately as 'Annequay'.

St Agnes and The Gugh

St Agnes is the most southerly of the Scilly Islands. It is just over a mile wide and is inhabited by less than a hundred people.

St Agnus is the first land that vessels meet on a prevailing westerly and there are numerous wrecks around its rugged coast. From 1890-1920 there was a lifeboat stationed here, the crew making up ten per cent of the island's population! The lighthouse, the second oldest in Britain, is now holiday accommodation. It was built in 1680 and stands 74ft above the ground, 138ft above mean high water. It was superseded in 1910 by Peninnis Head Lighthouse on St Mary's.

St Agnes can be walked in a few hours. Wind-sculpted granite rocks around the coast and on the heathland have taken on animalistic shapes and have names such as 'The Nags Head' and 'The Beast'. On the west side of Wingletang Down is St Warna's Well, which is thought to have been dedicated to a Celtic deity, possibly a savage water goddess. Additional income from wrecks was welcomed in hard times and when the well was excavated it was found to contain some gold pins and other votive offerings. Beady Pool gets its name from ceramic beads that are sometimes washed up onto the beach from the wreck of a Venetian ship. Examples are to be found in the Museum on St Mary's. Periglis and Cove Vean are excellent beaches, as is The Bar, which at low water links St Agnes to The Gugh. The Gugh is rich in archaeological remains including entrance graves and hut circles. The Old Man of Gugh is a Bronze Age menhir, a monumental stone that is thought to have been standing for about 3,500 years.

St Agnes has a post office and stores that sells pasties. There are a couple of cafés and the Turk's Head pub serves food. However, no trip to the island would be complete without a visit to Troytown farm shop. About 30 varieties of the most delicious ice cream are made on the farm, including banana, baileys and cinnamon, St Agnes rose geranium and vanilla Madagascar. This is also an excellent place to replenish supplies of milk, yogurt and butter, and to stock up with clotted cream (see 'Cream teas' on page 97).

Fine sailing off St Agnes

Longitude

In the evening of the 22nd of October 1707 Admiral Sir Cloudesley Shovell's ship HMS *Association* struck the rocks near the Isles of Scilly, followed shortly afterwards by HMS *Eagle*, HMS *Romney* and HMS *Firebrand* in one of the greatest disasters of the British Navy. Returning from a campaign in the Mediterranean as Commander-in-chief of the fleets, the admiral had earlier in the day requested a position from his navigators. Out of sight of land, and with only dead reckoning records for the calculations, the consensus of the navigators had placed the ships further towards the Channel than their true location. The consequences of this navigational error resulted in the loss of the four ships, the Admiral and nearly 2,000 sailors, but it would trigger a search for a method that could provide accurate longitude at sea.

Seamen could already establish latitude reliably, by measuring the altitude of the north star or the sun at midday. The north star had a fixed position in the sky and the altitude of the sun was also known for each day of the year. Longitude, on the other hand, had eluded astronomers and sailors, and no scientific basis existed nor had a method been devised at the time of the Scilly tragedy. As sea trade by the maritime powers increased the need for accurate position fixes was paramount. Philip II of Spain had offered a significant prize to anyone who could come up with a satisfactory system that would spare his captains the risks of not knowing where they were. France, Portugal and Holland also offered prizes and glory in return for safety, but it was the events of that night that finally led to a solution, through the British Act of Longitude.

Parliament enacted the requirements and prize money in 1714, starting a process that would last sixty years before its final conclusion and establishing the Board of Longitude that would continue its functions up until 1828, such was the importance of this matter to the nation. £20,000 would be awarded for a system that could establish longitude within $1/_2°$, £15,000 for $2/_3°$ and £10,000 for 1°.

The lure of the money led to a continuous flow of proposals to the Board. Most were fanciful or impractical, such as using the difference between magnetic and true north. It was two competing approaches that would dominate the headlines as well as the corridors of intrigue and vested interest. The moon calculation method was favoured by the establishment, senior chiefs of the Navy and the astronomers at the Greenwich Observatory. The idea was to measure at sea the angular distance between the moon and another celestial object. Given such an angle and a suitable reference table the time at Greenwich during the measurement could be established. In parallel, local time could be calculated by standard methods (for example noon is the time when the sun peaks in altitude). The difference between the two times gives longitude, at the rate of 15° per hour of difference (given 360°

John Harrison, the winnner of the Longitude prize

full rotation of the Earth every 24h). The method is sound and reliant on celestial objects, which are always there, but the challenge was significant as at the time there were no celestial maps or tables that could be used to support the calculations. It would take Astronomer Royal John Flamsteed 40 years of work at the Greenwich Observatory to compile a comprehensive celestial map.

The second, and ultimate winning method, was invented by John Harrison, a man of great genius and persistent character but without titles or connections amongst the elite in London. His approach was based on having a reliable clock with which the time at Greenwich could always be known on a ship, thus removing the need for complex celestial measurements. No such clock existed that could maintain the time accurately, indeed even the best could lose or gain several minutes a day due to friction, temperature or humidity. Harrison dealt with these problems, first creating the H1 clock in 1735, a frictionless mechanism with counterbalances that not only worked consistently independently of temperature or humidity changes, but would also continue functioning reliably even if subject to the motions of a ship at sea. His meticulous attention to detail and an uncompromising attitude to quality would in time lead to better versions of the clock, H2 in 1739, H3 in 1740 and H4, the ultimate winner, in 1759. All of them kept the time with errors of only seconds over sea voyages, amply beating even the $1/_2°$ stricter requirement of the Act.

Harrison's method was simple and his clocks magnificent, but they provided an answer that had not been invented by the learned astronomers or members of the illustrious official bodies, and they employed questionable tactics to ensure their proposal would be the winner. In the end the praise of Captain Cook on his return in 1772 and the sheer difficulty of the lunar method settled the matter, and King George III sidestepped the board and Astronomer Royal Maskelyne, directing Parliament to award the prize to Harrison. London became a world centre for clock-making and Harrison's inventions, frictionless movement, bimetal strips and double balances, are still in use today. Visit the Greenwich Observatory where Harrison's clocks are kept and where they still keep the time accurately, more than 200 years after they were made.

Appendix

Weather – sources and times

All transmissions in English unless specified.

English Channel, west of Isle of Wight

All times are UT except shaded areas, which are in British Local Time.

Time	Source	Frequency	Information
0000	Navtex, Corsen, Ushant	518 kHz	Shipping forecast
0040	Navtex, Niton, Isle of Wight	518 kHz	Extended, 5 day, outlook
0048	BBC Radio 4	198 kHz FM	Shipping & Inshore Forecast
0110	Brixham Coastguard	Working Channel but announced on VHF Channel 16, MF 2182 kHz	Inshore forecast + outlook
0110	Falmouth Coastguard	Working Channel but announced on VHF Channel 16, MF 2182 kHz	Inshore forecast + outlook
0120	Navtex, Niton, Isle of Wight	490 kHz	Inshore & 3 day outlook
0130	Solent Coastguard	Working Channel but announced on VHF Channel 16, MF 2182 kHz	Inshore forecast + outlook
0130	Portland Coastguard	Working Channel but announced on VHF Channel 16, MF 2182 kHz	Inshore forecast + outlook
0410	Brixham Coastguard	Working Channel but announced on VHF Channel 16, MF 2182 kHz	Inshore forecast
0410	Falmouth Coastguard	Working Channel but announced on VHF Channel 16, MF 2182 kHz	Inshore forecast
0430	Solent Coastguard	Working Channel but announced on VHF Channel 16, MF 2182 kHz	Inshore forecast
0430	Portland Coastguard	Working Channel but announced on VHF Channel 16, MF 2182 kHz	Inshore forecast
0440	Navtex, Niton, Isle of Wight	518 kHz	Extended, 5 day, outlook
0520	BBC Radio 4	198 kHz FM	Shipping & Inshore Forecast
0520	Navtex, Niton, Isle of Wight	490 kHz	Inshore & 3 day outlook
0710	Brixham Coastguard	Working Channel but announced on VHF Channel 16, MF 2182 kHz	Shipping forecast + inshore forecast + outlook
0710	Falmouth Coastguard	Working Channel but announced on VHF Channel 16, MF 2182 kHz	Shipping forecast + inshore forecast + outlook
0730	Solent Coastguard	Working Channel but announced on VHF Channel 16, MF 2182 kHz	Shipping forecast + inshore forecast + outlook
0730	Portland Coastguard	Working Channel but announced on VHF Channel 16, MF 2182 kHz	Shipping forecast + inshore forecast + outlook
0840	Navtex, Niton, Isle of Wight	518 kHz	Shipping forecast
0920	Navtex, Niton, Isle of Wight	490 kHz	Inshore & 3 day outlook
1010	Brixham Coastguard	Working Channel but announced on VHF Channel 16, MF 2182 kHz	Inshore forecast

1010	Falmouth Coastguard	Working Channel but announced on VHF Channel 16, MF 2182 kHz	Inshore forecast
1030	Solent Coastguard	Working Channel but announced on VHF Channel 16, MF 2182 kHz	Inshore forecast
1030	Portland Coastguard	Working Channel but announced on VHF Channel 16, MF 2182 kHz	Inshore forecast
1200	Navtex, Corsen, Ushant	518 kHz	Shipping Forecast
1201	BBC Radio 4	198 kHz	Shipping & Inshore Forecast
1240	Navtex, Niton, Isle of Wight	518 kHz	Extended, 5 day, outlook
1310	Brixham Coastguard	Working Channel but announced on VHF Channel 16, MF 2182 kHz	Inshore forecast + outlook
1310	Falmouth Coastguard	Working Channel but announced on VHF Channel 16, MF 2182 kHz	Inshore forecast + outlook
1320	Navtex, Niton, Isle of Wight	490 kHz	Inshore & 3 day outlook
1330	Solent Coastguard	Working Channel but announced on VHF Channel 16, MF 2182 kHz	Inshore forecast + outlook
1330	Portland Coastguard	Working Channel but announced on VHF Channel 16, MF 2182 kHz	Inshore forecast + outlook
1610	Brixham Coastguard	Working Channel but announced on VHF Channel 16, MF 2182 kHz	Inshore forecast
1610	Falmouth Coastguard	Working Channel but announced on VHF Channel 16, MF 2182 kHz	Inshore forecast
1630	Solent Coastguard	Working Channel but announced on VHF Channel 16, MF 2182 kHz	Inshore forecast
1630	Portland Coastguard	Working Channel but announced on VHF Channel 16, MF 2182 kHz	Inshore forecast
1640	Navtex, Niton, Isle of Wight	518 kHz	Extended, 5 day, outlook
1720	Navtex, Niton, Isle of Wight	490 kHz	Inshore & 3 day outlook
1754	BBC Radio 4	198 kHz FM	Shipping & Inshore Forecast
1910	Brixham Coastguard	Working Channel but announced on VHF Channel 16, MF 2182 kHz	Shipping forecast + inshore forecast + outlook
1910	Falmouth Coastguard	Working Channel but announced on VHF Channel 16, MF 2182 kHz	Shipping forecast + inshore forecast + outlook
1930	Solent Coastguard	Working Channel but announced on VHF Channel 16, MF 2182 kHz	Shipping forecast + inshore forecast + outlook
1930	Portland Coastguard	Working Channel but announced on VHF Channel 16, MF 2182 kHz	Shipping forecast + inshore forecast + outlook
2040	Navtex, Niton, Isle of Wight	518 kHz	Shipping forecast
2120	Navtex, Niton, Isle of Wight	490 kHz	Inshore & 3 day outlook
2210	Brixham Coastguard	Working Channel but announced on VHF Channel 16, MF 2182 kHz	Inshore forecast
2210	Falmouth Coastguard	Working Channel but announced on VHF Channel 16, MF 2182 kHz	Inshore forecast
2230	Solent Coastguard	Working Channel but announced on VHF Channel 16, MF 2182 kHz	Inshore forecast
2230	Portland Coastguard	Working Channel but announced on VHF Channel 16, MF 2182 kHz	Inshore forecast

BBC Radio 4: LW 198kHz FM 92.4-94.6MHz

- 0048 LT: shipping, inshore waters, coastal station reports.
- 0520 LT: shipping, inshore waters, coastal station reports.
- 1201 LT- LW only: shipping.
- 1754 LT: shipping.

Navtex: coverage up to 270M around the coast, on 490kHz (UK inshore forecast in English, foreign forecast in national languages) and 518kHz (forecast in English). Niton Navtex broacasts in UT:

- 518kHz at 0040, 0440, 0840, 1240, 1640, 2040
  490kHz at 0120, 0520, 0920, 1320, 1720, 2120

Brixham and Falmouth Coastguard VHF transmit on VFH 16 announcing MSI will be broadcast on channel 10, 23, 73, 84 or 86.

Brixham and Falmouth Coastguard VHF 10,23,73,84,86

UT	Shipping	Inshore	Wind warnings	Outlook
0110		√	√	√
0410		√	√	
0710	√	√	√	√
1010		√	√	
1310		√	√	√
1610		√	√	
1910	√	√	√	√
2210		√	√	

Portland Coastguard VHF transmit on VFH 16 announcing MSI will be broadcast on channel 10, 23, 73, 84 or 86.

Portland Coastguard VHF 10,23,73,84,86

UT	Shipping	Inshore	Wind warnings	Outlook
0130		√	√	√
0430		√	√	
0730	√	√	√	√
1030		√	√	
1330		√	√	√
1630		√	√	
1930	√	√	√	√
2230		√	√	

- Marinecall: Met Office weather forecasts on demand. Dial 09068 96 96 + area number for a voice message, 09065 2223 + area number for a faxed message.
  Area numbers:
  47 Selsey Bill to Lyme Regis
  48 Lyme Regis to Hartland Point.

HF Radio Facsimile Broadcasts

With a suitable receiver and equipment (usually a PC and some software) these useful broadcasts can be received at sea. Northwood transmits the following on 2618.5, 4610, 8040, 11086.5 kHz. All times are UT.

0000 / 1200	Surface analysis
0012 / 1212	24hr surface prognosis
0100 / 1300	Schedule
0300 / 1500	Surface analysis
0336 / 1536	Sea surface temperature
0348 / 1548	Gale warning summary
0400 / 1600	Surface analysis
0412 / 1612	24hr surface prognosis
0500 / 1700	Surface analysis
0512 / 1712	24hr surface prognosis
0524 / 1724	48hr surface prognosis
0548 / 1748	96hr surface prognosis
0600 / 1800	Surface analysis
0612 / 1812	24hr surface prognosis
0724 / 1924	48hr surface prognosis
0748 / 1948	96hr surface prognosis
0800 / 2000	120hr surface prognosis
0824 / 2024	48hr significant wind contour
0836 / 2036	72hr significant wind contour
0848 / 2048	96hr significant wind contour
0900 / 2100	Surface analysis
1000 / 2200	Surface analysis
1024 / 2224	24hr reduced visibility prognosis
1100 / 2300	Surface analysis
1124 / 2324	24hr sea and swell prognosis
1148 / 2348	Gale warning summary

Internet weather

The following are useful links:

- UK Met Office:
  http://www.met-office.gov.uk/
  http://www.met-office.gov.uk/weather/charts/index.html - synoptic charts (3.5 days)

- Wetter Zentrale: the Bracknell black and white fax synoptic charts (5.5 days).
  http://www.wetterzentrale.de/topkarten/fsfaxbra.html - Index
  http://www.wetterzentrale.de/pics/bracka.html - midnight
  Change letter 'a' to get other times: 0 24hr, 0a 36hr, 1 48hr, 2 96hr, 4 120hr, 4a 132hr

- Windguru, the Czech forecasts for windsurfers and flyers
  http://www.windguru.cz - general index
  http://www.windguru.cz/int/index.php?sc=48738 - La Lanzada beach

- Meteo France
  http://www.meteofrance.com/FR/index.jsp

- Frank Singleton's extensive web site for everything you may want to know about weather information sources and connections
  http://weather.mailasail.com/

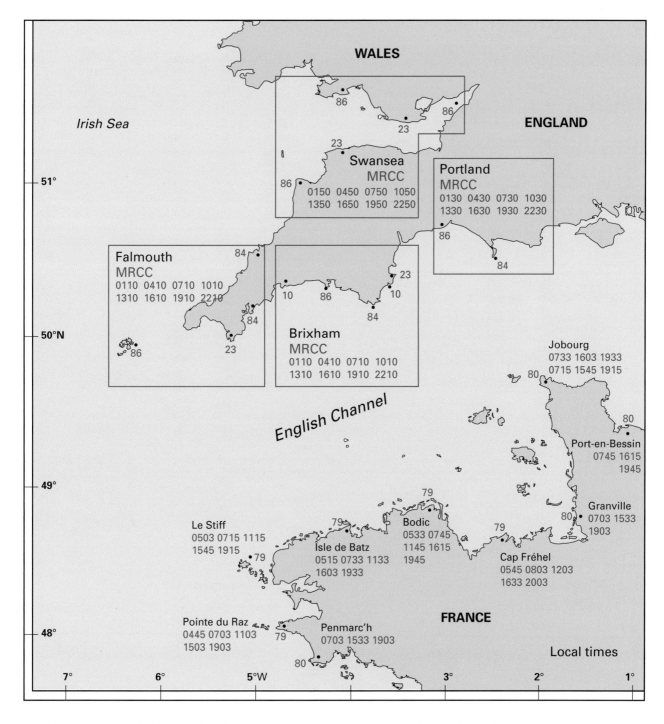

WALES

Irish Sea

ENGLAND

86

86

23

23

51°

**Swansea
MRCC**
0150 0450 0750 1050
1350 1650 1950 2250

86

**Portland
MRCC**
0130 0430 0730 1030
1330 1630 1930 2230

86

**Falmouth
MRCC**
0110 0410 0710 1010
1310 1610 1910 2210

84

84

50°N

86

84

23

**Brixham
MRCC**
0110 0410 0710 1010
1310 1610 1910 2210

10

86

23

10

84

English Channel

Jobourg
0733 1603 1933
0715 1545 1915

80

80

Port-en-Bessin
0745 1615
1945

49°

79

Le Stiff
0503 0715 1115
1545 1915

79

79

Bodic
0533 0745
1145 1615
1945

79

80

Granville
0703 1533
1903

Isle de Batz
0515 0733 1133
1603 1933

Cap Fréhel
0545 0803 1203
1633 2003

80

FRANCE

48°

Pointe du Raz
0445 0703 1103
1503 1903

79

Penmarc'h
0703 1533 1903

Local times

80

7°   6°   5°W   3°   2°   1°

- GRIB US - free NOAA grib files (7 day pressure, wind) and Windows display software http://www.grib.us/

If possible raise an alarm through DSC, as this conveys position accurately and is preferred for rescue coordination.

Safety

There are three Maritime Rescue Coordination Centres (MRCC): Portland (Portland to Topsham), Brixham (Topsham to Dodman Point) and Falmouth (Dodman Point to Cape Cornwall).

HM Coastguard monitor VHF Channel 16 on speaker and DSC Channel 70 H24, in addition to broadcasting Maritime Safety Information every 4 hours. There are Maritime Rescue Coordination Centres at Portland, Brixham and Falmouth. Only Falmouth monitors DSC on MF 2182kHz.

Tide predictions

The source of all UK tide data is the UK Hydrographic Office (UKHO), based in Taunton. Their information can be accessed at www.easytide. com. Tidal predictions beyond seven days requires payment HW/LW predictions are printed in the Almanacs and in local tide tables. The authors' own Tides Planner app for the iphone is a handy and extensively used tide tool, based on UKHO data. All UK ports are covered. Tides Planner also displays currents for the entire British coast.

Wind speed conversions

Beaufort	Knots	m/s	km/h
0	<1	0- 0.2	0-1.8
1	1-3	0.3- 1.5	1.9-5.5
2	4-6	1.6- 3.3	5.6-11.1
3	7-10	3.4- 5.4	11.2-18.5
4	10-16	5.5- 7.9	18.6-29.6
5	17-21	8.0-10.7	29.7-38.9
6	22-27	10.8-13.8	39.0-50.0
7	28-33	13.9-17.1	50.1-61.0
8	34-40	17.2-20.7	61.1-74.0
9	41-47	20.8-24.4	74.1-86.9
10	48-55	24.5-28.4	87.0-101.8
11	56-63	28.5-32.6	101.9-116.6

Symbols

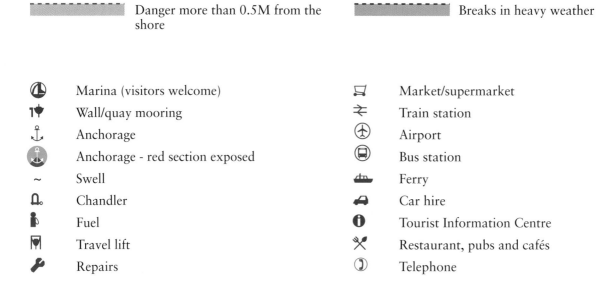

━━━━━	Danger more than 0.5M from the shore	┄┄┄┄	Breaks in heavy weather

Marina (visitors welcome)

Wall/quay mooring

Anchorage

Anchorage - red section exposed

~ Swell

Chandler

Fuel

Travel lift

Repairs

Market/supermarket

Train station

Airport

Bus station

Ferry

Car hire

Tourist Information Centre

Restaurant, pubs and cafés

Telephone

Distances

Nautical Miles

	Bill of Portland	West Bay	Lyme Regis	Beer	River Exe	River Teign	Torquay	Brixham	River Dart	Totnes	Start Point	Salcombe	Bigbury Bay	River Yealm	Plymouth Sound	Devonport	River Lynher	Looe	Polperro	Fowey	Mevagissey	Falmouth	River Helford	Lizard	Porthleven	St Michael's Mount	Penzance	Newlyn	Land's End	St Marys
Bill of Portland	-	17	22	27	37	39	40	41	43		49	53		70	72			82		89		104		112			127		132	155
West Bay	17	-																												
Lyme Regis	22	7	-																											
Beer	27	13	6	-																										
River Exe	37	25	19	14	-																									
River Teign	39	29	24	18	5	-																								
Torquay	40	32	27	22	11	7	-																							
Brixham	41	33	29	24	13	9	3	-																						
River Dart	43	38	34	29	19	15	12	9	-																					
Totnes									8	-																				
Start Point	49	46	43	38	28	25	22	21	11		-	3	9	16	18			31	33	38	42	52	53	60					80	101
Salcombe	53										3	-										49								
Bigbury Bay											9	7	-									44								
River Yealm	70										16	14	7	-								38								
Plymouth Sound	72										18	16	10	3	-							36		48					69	92
Devonport															4	-														
River Lynher															6	2	-													
Looe	82										31	28	22	16	12			-				27								
Polperro											33				15			5	-			24								
Fowey	89										38	35	29	22	20			10	5	-		21								
Mevagissey	94										42									7	-	16								
Falmouth	104										52	49	44	38	36			27	24	21	16	-		19					38	60
River Helford	105										53											5	-							
Lizard	112										60	57	54	50	48			39	38	34	29	19	14	-	12	19	18	18	21	44
Porthleven																								12	-					
St Michael's Mount																								19	7	-				
Penzance	127																							18	9	3	-			
Newlyn																								18	9	4	2	-		
Land's End	132										80				69							38		21	17	14	13	11	-	24
St Mary's	155										101				92					76		60		44					24	-

Charts

Charts for the West Country

Imray Charts

C10   **Western English Channel Passage Chart**
1:400,000 WGS 84
Radiobeacons, Lights, Tides

C18   **Western Approaches to the English Channel and Biscay**
1:1,000,000 WGS 84

C5   **Bill of Portland to Salcombe Harbour**
1:100,000 WGS 84
Plans Bridport, Lyme Regis, Exmouth, Tor Bay, Torquay, Brixham, Dartmouth, Teignmouth

C6   **Salcombe to Lizard Point**
1:100,000 WGS 84
Plans Fowey Approaches, Looe, Mevagissey, Charlestown, Polperro, Plymouth Sound, Falmouth, Salcombe

C7   **Falmouth to Isles of Scilly and Trevose Head**
1:120,000 WGS 84
Plans St Mary's Road, Mousehole, Newlyn, St Ives, St Michael's Mount, Porthleven, Penzance, Newquay Bay, Hugh Town, Mullion Cove

C58   **Trevose Head to Bull Point**
1:130,000 WGS 84
Plans Barnstaple and Bideford, River Camel, Ilfracombe, Bude Haven, Port Isaac and Port Gaverne, Lundy, Padstow Yacht Harbour, Birdham Pool & Chichester Marina

Y58   **River Fal**
Falmouth to Truro
1:20,000 WGS 84
Plans Falmouth Yacht Marina, Falmouth Inner Harbour, Mylor Yacht Harbour

C14   **Plymouth Harbour and Rivers**
1:20,000 WGS 84
Plans River Tamar to Gunnislake, St German's River, Sutton Harbour and Queen Anne's Battery Marinas, Mayflower Marina, Plymouth, River Yealm

Imray chart packs are A2 size in plastic wallets but are also available as individual sheets.

Imray and British Admiralty charts are available from
Imray, Laurie, Norie & Wilson Ltd
Wych House, The Broadway,
St Ives,
Cambs PE27 5BT
www.imray.com

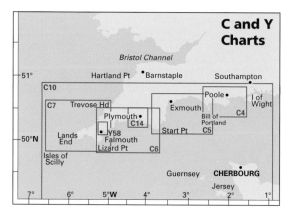

Imray Digital Charts

Imray charts can be accessed through the iPhone/iPad Chart Navigator app which also displays tides (from Tides Planner) and aerial photographs.

Also available for PC users is Imray Digital Chart ID20 The English Channel which provides coverage of the West Country with integrated GPS plotter.

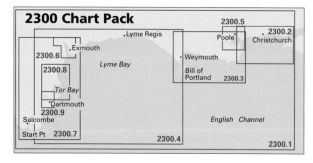

2300 The Devon And Dorset Coasts

2300.1   **Needles to Start Point** 1: 400,000

2300.2   **Western Approaches to the Solent** 1: 60,000

2300.3   **Poole Harbour to Bill of Portland** 1: 75,000
Plans Weymouth, Lulworth Cove

2300.4   **Lyme Bay – Portland to Start Point** 1: 175,000
Plans Lyme Regis, Bridport Harbour

2300.5   **Poole Harbour** 1: 20,000
Plans Salterns Marina, Moriconium Quay and Lake Yard Marina, Continuation of Studland Bay, Continuation to Wareham

2300.6   **River Exe** 1:21,500
Plans Continuation of River Exe to Exeter, Exmouth Dock

2300.7   **Exmouth to Salcombe** 1:100,000

2300.8   **Teignmouth and Tor Bay** 1:55,000

2300.9   **River Dart** 1:15,000
Plans Continuation to Totnes, Kingswear

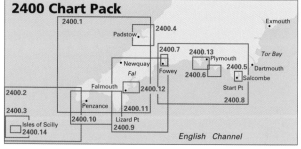

2400 The West Country

2400.1   **Land's End to Trevose Head** 1:180,000
Plans Newquay Bay, Saint Ives

2400.2   **Approaches to the Isles of Scilly** 1:120,000

2400.3   **Isles of Scilly** 1:40,000
Plans St Mary's Road

2400.4   **River Camel** 1:30,000
Plans Padstow Harbour

2400.5   **Salcombe** 1:15,000

2400.6   **River Yealm** 1:12,500
Inset Continuation of River Yealm

2400.7   **River Fowey to Lostwithiel** 1:9,000
Inset Continuation to Lostwithiel

2400.8   **Start Point to Fowey** 1:150,000

2400.9   **Fowey to Lizard Point** 1:110,000
Plan Mevagissey Harbour

2400.10   **Lizard Point to Land's End** 1:75,000

2400.11   **Helford River** 1:17,000
Inset Continuation of Helford River to Gweek

2400.12   **Falmouth Harbour** 1:20,000
Plans Mylor Yacht Harbour, Falmouth Yacht Marina, Falmouth Inner Harbour

2400.13   **Plymouth Harbour** 1:20,000
Plans Plymouth Yacht Haven, Mayflower International Marina, Sutton Harbour and Queen Anne's Battery Marina

2400.14   **Saint Mary's, Tresco and surrounding islands** 1:20,000

British Admiralty Charts

Admiralty Chart coverage is either as standard
Admiralty charts or as Admiralty Leisure Folios.
Both are available from Imray as above.
www.ukho.gov.uk

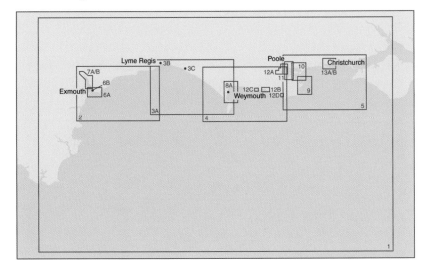

SC5601 East Devon and Dorset

SC5602 West Country

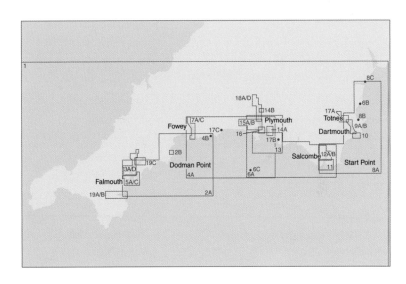

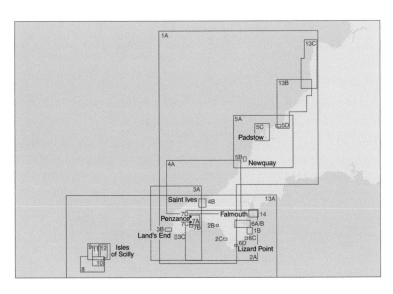

SC5603 Falmouth to Hartland Point

Index

LYME BAY

West Bay
Lyme Regis
River Exe
Teignmouth
Torquay
Brixham
River Dart
Salcombe

WEST DEVON

Bigbury Bay
River Avon
River Yealm
Plymouth
River Tamar

EAST CONRWALL

Looe
Polperro
Fowey
St Austell Bay
Mevagissey
Falmouth
River Helford

MOUNTS BAY

Mullion Cove
Porthleven
St Michael's Mount
Penzance
Newlyn

ISLES OF SCILLY

St Mary's
St Agnes
Grimsby Sounds
Bryher
Tresco
St Martin's

Weather

BBC Radio 4: LW 198kHz FM 92.4-94.6MHz

- 0048 LT: shipping, inshore waters, coastal station reports.
- 0520 LT: shipping, inshore waters, coastal station reports.
- 1201 LT- LW only: shipping.
- 1754 LT: shipping.

Brixham and Falmouth Coastguard VHF 10,23,73,84,86

UT	Shipping	Inshore	Wind warnings	Outlook
0110		√	√	√
0410		√	√	
0710	√	√	√	√
1010		√	√	
1310		√	√	√
1610		√	√	
1910	√	√	√	√
2210		√	√	

Portland Coastguard VHF 10,23,73,84,86

UT	Shipping	Inshore	Wind warnings	Outlook
0130		√	√	√
0430		√	√	
0730	√	√	√	√
1030		√	√	
1330		√	√	√
1630		√	√	
1930	√	√	√	√
2230		√	√	

✚ Health emergencies:

Bridport ☎ 01308 422371
Teignmouth ☎ 01626 772161
Exmouth ☎ 01395 279684
Exeter ☎ 01392 411611
Torquay ☎ 01803 614567
Dartmouth ☎ 01803 832255
Salcombe ☎ 01548 852349
Devon's out of hours GP service (including unregistered patients) ☎ 08456 710270

Plymouth Mount Gould ☎ 0845 1558085
Plymouth Derriford ☎ 01752 777111
Looe ☎ 01503 756956
Fowey ☎ 01726 832241
Falmouth ☎ 01326 434700
Truro ☎ 01872 250000
Penzance ☎ 01736 874000
St Mary's ☎ 01720 422392